DEEP WATER

Southern Literary Studies

SCOTT ROMINE, SERIES EDITOR

DEEP WATER

The Mississippi River in the Age of Mark Twain

THOMAS RUYS SMITH

LOUISIANA STATE UNIVERSITY PRESS

BATON ROUGE

Published by Louisiana State University Press
Copyright © 2019 by Louisiana State University Press
All rights reserved
Manufactured in the United States of America
First printing

DESIGNER: Michelle A. Neustrom
TYPEFACE: Whitman
PRINTER AND BINDER: Sheridan Books, Inc.

Portions of chapter 1 first appeared in "'The Mississippi Was a Virgin Field': Reconstructing the River before Mark Twain, 1865–1875," *Mark Twain Journal*, 53 (Fall 2015). Portions of chapter 4 and the epilogue first appeared in "Roustabouts, Steamboats, and the Old Way to Dixie: The Mississippi River and the Southern Imaginary in the Early Twentieth Century," *Southern Quarterly* 52, no. 3 (Spring 2015): 10–29.

LIBRARY OF CONGRESS CATALOGING-IN-PUBLICATION DATA

Names: Smith, Thomas Ruys, 1979– author.
Title: Deep water / Thomas Ruys Smith.
Description: Baton Rouge : Louisiana State University Press, [2020] | Includes
  bibliographical references and index.
Identifiers: LCCN 2019029979 (print) | LCCN 2019029980 (ebook) | ISBN 978-0-
  8071-7109-7 (cloth) | ISBN 978-0-8071-7286-5 (pdf) | ISBN 978-0-8071-7287-2
  (epub)
Subjects: LCSH: Twain, Mark, 1835–1910—Homes and haunts—Mississippi River.
  | Twain, Mark, 1835–1910—Criticism and interpretation. | River life—Mississippi River. | Mississippi River—In literature. | Mississippi River Valley—Social
  life and customs. | Mississippi River—Description and travel.
Classification: LCC PS1334 .S65 2020 (print) | LCC PS1334 (ebook) | DDC
  813/.4—dc23
LC record available at https://lccn.loc.gov/2019029979
LC ebook record available at https://lccn.loc.gov/2019029980

For Tabitha and Delilah

Mark Twain and the Mississippi River are inseparable in my mind. When I told him that *Life on the Mississippi* was my favourite story of adventure [. . .] Mr. Clemens's manner changed. A sadness came into his voice. "Those were glorious days, the days on the Mississippi. They will come back no more, life has swallowed them up, and youth will come no more. They were days when the tide of life was high, when the heart was full of the sparkling wine of romance. There have been no other days like them." . . .

There he stood—our Mark Twain, our American, our humorist, the embodiment of our country. He seemed to have absorbed all America into himself. The great Mississippi River seemed forever flowing, flowing through his speech, through the shadowless white sands of thought. His voice seemed to say like the river, "Why hurry? Eternity is long; the ocean can wait."

—HELEN KELLER, *Midstream,* 1929

CONTENTS

ILLUSTRATIONS

DEEP WATER

Introduction

"THE MISSISSIPPI WAS A VIRGIN FIELD"

The deep places in the river are not so obvious as the shallow ones
and can only be found by carefully probing it.
So perhaps it is with human nature.
—HENRY DAVID THOREAU, *Journal,* 1859

The stream of our thought is like a river.
—WILLIAM JAMES, *The Principles of Psychology,* 1890

No river of the world, great or small, is so wayward in its ways
as this wonderful stream. [. . .] He is never satisfied; always changing.
Ever breaking away old boundaries, old landmarks, and making for himself new. In fact it seems that no landmark of his ever reaches the dignity
of age. So soon as it has been sufficiently long established as to be called
"old," this grand old river of ours remorselessly demolishes it, and creates
for himself new idols, in their turn to be broken and destroyed.
—"MAD FREAKS OF THE MISSISSIPPI,"
Memphis Old Folks' Record, 1875

In July 1895, near the start of his post-bankruptcy lecture tour around the world, Twain was holed up in a hotel room in Winnipeg, Manitoba, nursing a carbuncle. Already one of the most traveled Americans of his moment, he had a long journey ahead of him—to Australia, New Zealand, India, South Africa. Still, as always for Twain, the Mississippi River was never very far away. A journalist for the *Winnipeg Tribune* was admitted to his room, and after some reminiscences about his early adventures, the reporter prompted the American writer to talk about the river: "However excellent these European incidents may be [. . .] you doubtless consider the Mississippi your real field of work? You are, so to speak, the prophet of the Mississippi." Twain's response was unequivocal: "Yes, and the reason is plain. By a series of events—accidents—I was the only one who wrote about old times on the Mississippi. Wherever else I have been some better have been there before and will come after, but the Mississippi was a virgin field [. . .]. Here then was my chance, and I used it." Twain was, he felt, uniquely qualified to take the river as his "real field of work." After all, he had been a steamboat pilot in his youth, more than thirty years ago now, and as far as Twain was concerned, "no one could write that life but a pilot entered into the spirit of it." Yet most pilots "did not run naturally to literature." They would have "no connected style, no power of describing anything"—just an endless stream of details.[1] Twain, though, was different. He, and only he, could tame the Mississippi in words.

Throughout his career, Mark Twain claimed the Mississippi River as his own. There were good reasons for that sense of ownership. By 1895 he had already completed a profoundly important sequence of river writings; though the Mississippi would never leave his imagination, he had made the enduring statements on the river that would stand as central pillars in his literary legacy. In very different moods, to very different ends, the Mississippi flowed through the heart of "Old Times on the Mississippi" (1875), *The Adventures of Tom Sawyer* (1876), *Life on the Mississippi* (1883), *Adventures of Huckleberry Finn* (1884/5), and *Pudd'nhead Wilson* (1894). The two decades at the heart of his life and writing career were dominated by shaping these interpretations of the river. Certainly for his contemporaries, to borrow Edwin Cady's words, "Clemens owned the river."[2] As Helen Keller put it, "Mark Twain and the Mississippi River are inseparable in my mind." Even though she couldn't hear Twain's voice, she still caught the echo of the river in it and understood the way that the "Mississippi River seemed forever flowing, flowing through his speech."[3] In Philo and Leslie Read's assertion, "The whole age of the charming, intriguing, villainous, romantic, old-time Mississippi River is summarised in one name: Mark Twain."[4] For us still, the relationship between Twain and the Mississippi remains proverbial. As American literary icons go, the symbol of Huck Finn and Jim on a raft on the Mississippi remains indelible and essential. As Janice McIntire Strasburg has noted, because of Twain's writings, "the Mississippi River and its small town environs resonate in the memory of many an American who has never seen the banks of the Big Muddy."[5]

Yet at the same time, the river was never his alone. While Twain wrote the defining portraits of the Mississippi in the nineteenth century, he was not, as he claimed in 1895, "the only one who wrote about old times on the Mississippi." The Mississippi, to borrow Twain's phrase ripe with images of conquest and desire, was not a "virgin field." Walter Blair recognized many years ago that when Twain finally turned to the river in earnest, "he had gravitated toward a popular subject," not pioneered a new one.[6] Nor should we take Twain at his word when he claims that it was only a steamboat pilot "entered into the spirit of it" who could write about the river. Twain might have always privileged the view from the pilothouse, figuring it as a kind of panopticon, but the steamboat and the riverbank afford many vantage points from which to view the Mississippi, not all of them known to a pilot. Just as the river had already proved a fertile cultural symbol in the early decades of the nineteenth century, so, in the age of Mark Twain, did a wide variety of writers, artists, travelers, musicians, river workers, and engineers leave their mark on the Mississippi in manifold ways. At the same time that Twain was shaping and reshaping his imagined Mississippi, he was surrounded by others who were putting forward competing visions of the river and its ongoing significance for American life and identity—in ways that chime with and challenge Twain's narratives in equal measure. Long overshadowed by the image of Twain's Mississippi, another river runs through this defining period in American culture. This river was a polyphonic place, not a monologue, composed of diverse voices each telling their own story of the Mississippi. For too long, Twain's river has been read in a vacuum, not as part of a continuing conversation about the place of the Mississippi in America's life and imagination. Framing his river books in this light gives us new landmarks by which to navigate them. In such company, Twain's multivalent Mississippi begins to look rather different: no less distinctive or dominant and perhaps more singular than ever, but also part of a much wider miscellaneous and ambiguous chorus discussing the meaning of the river in American life—and the meaning of American life on the river—at this crucible moment.

The purpose of this book, then, is twofold. First, it foregrounds Twain's lifelong relationship with the river and traces its twisting course throughout his writings. Whereas previous books have looked intensely at Twain's river books in isolation, this is a unique attempt to take readers on a voyage down the entirety of Twain's Mississippi, from source to sea. It seeks to explore the question: what does it mean for this river to flow through the heart of the life and work of one of the world's most significant literary voices? The other intention of this book is to tell the larger story of the Mississippi in the age of Mark Twain—to illuminate those other lost stories of river life from this vital and fertile period long swamped by Twain's sprawling floodplain. Not least, this book also serves to provide a rich context for Twain's river writings, putting them up against a panoply of contemporary accounts of the Mississippi to see what they look like in new company.

In both respects, this book ventures into largely uncharted waters. For all that the Mississippi remains central to both our idea of Mark Twain, his most beloved books, and even America itself, there have been surprisingly few attempts to think at length about this vital relationship. Still the most complete examination of his river years, for example, is Allan Bates's unpublished thesis from 1968.[7] In some sense, there has been resistance to this approach to thinking about Twain and the river. Andrew Dix, while stressing the "insistent, many-stranded discourse of the Mississippi in his writing," has warned that "we should be cautious about centering Twain's work on the Mississippi, since this risks producing static, nostalgic, merely regionalist versions of the author and takes him out of those complex national, even international geographies that have been the focus of some of the most exciting criticism in recent years."[8] Yet the Mississippi itself was never a static or merely regional symbol, least of all in Twain's own work. As Brander Matthews recognized in 1907: "With all his exactness in reproducing the Mississippi Valley, Mark Twain is not sectional in his outlook; he is national always. He is not narrow; he is not Western or Eastern; he is American."[9] The Mississippi was certainly an American river—a potent symbol of national identity—but it was also an international one, central to ideas of America outside its borders during this period and beyond. And its streams, in a whole host of ways, mingled with international waters in an era that was defined by rivers, real and imagined, from the Congo to the Thames, the Amazon to the Rhine. Still, a resilient patina of exceptionalism surrounds our understanding of Twain's relationship to the Mississippi. This is despite a significant trend in the field of Mark Twain studies, exemplified by Leland Krauth's *Mark Twain and Company* (2003), for reading Twain in closer proximity to his contemporaries and contexts. When it comes to the river, though, Twain still stands in splendid isolation, alone at the wheel in the pilothouse, ossified into certain fixed poses.

The lack of a sustained account of the river's social and cultural history from the years of Reconstruction to the early decades of the twentieth century is equally surprising, an absence made all the more startling by a recent renaissance in river writing. Alongside my own books on the cultural history of the Mississippi—particularly *River of Dreams: Imagining the Mississippi before Mark Twain* (2007) and *Blacklegs, Card Sharps, and Confidence Men: Nineteenth-Century Mississippi River Gambling Stories* (2010)—a number of recent works have helped to build on the groundbreaking work of scholars such as John Francis McDermott and Horst Kruse to develop a small but significant field of twenty-first-century writing around the river.[10] Thomas Buchanan's essential *Black Life on the Mississippi: Slaves, Free Blacks, and the Western Steamboat World* (2004) profoundly reshaped our understanding of the significance of the river to African Americans in the antebellum years. Both Christopher Morris's *The Big Muddy: An Environmental History of the Mississippi and Its Peoples, from Hernando de Soto to Hurricane Katrina* (2012) and Christine A. Klein and Sandra B. Zellmer's *Mississippi River Tragedies: A Century of Unnatural Disaster* (2014) explored the Mississippi's troubled environmental history in the wake of Hurricane Katrina. Walter Johnson examined the tangled connections of slavery, capitalism, and imperialism in the widely acclaimed *River of Dark Dreams: Slavery and Empire in the Cotton Kingdom* (2013). Michael Pasquier's collection *Gods of the Mississippi* (2013) focused attention on the vibrant religious history of the river. Another sign of the renewed interest in the meaning of the Mississippi can be found in *Open Rivers: Rethinking Water, Place & Community*, an interdisciplinary journal established in fall 2015 by the River Life program at the University of Minnesota. Yet for all that and more, this extraordinary moment in the river's rich cultural life remains neglected. The Mississippi, as Twain himself put it, remains "the crookedest stream." By taking the long view of the river in this period, we can better see the wider significance of the twists and turns of the Mississippi in Twain's writing and its sinuous shape in American culture more broadly.

There are, of course, good reasons why Twain's contrary visions of the Mississippi dominate our sense of this time and place; no other artist, literary or otherwise, had such a sustained and intense relationship with the river. And like the river, Twain's Mississippi grew from innumerable tributaries of experience, imagination, and imitation. His river books ebb and flow in their sense of what this waterway means. While the Mississippi was a permanent wellspring for Twain, it held a wealth of meanings for him that inevitably shifted over time. It meant memory—the nostalgia for childhood mingled with a sense of its loss. It meant experience—his years as a pilot and the crucial knowledge and identity that those years had given him. But it also meant imagination and reading and cultural consumption, not just empiricism and observation. After all, Twain's Mississippi took shape in a variety of locations: in Elmira, New York, gazing out from Quarry Farm at the Chemung River; in Hartford, Connecticut, at home with his family and on walks with Joseph Twichell; in Florence, in the Villa di Quarto, punctuated by strolls near the Arno. And, too, it was an abstract river shaped by comparison with Twain's interactions with other international rivers through these years—not just the Arno but the Thames, the Rhine, the Rhône; rivers that he read about, too, from the Congo to the Amazon. Throughout those encounters, the Mississippi remained an American measuring stick that Twain carried with him around the globe.

It was also, as rivers always are, an endlessly malleable metaphor. As T. S. McMillin has described, "Metaphorically, at least, water is everywhere, figuring prominently in life's flow."[11] Unlike other monumental geographical landmarks, rivers are more human in scale, more entwined with human lives, a simultaneous symbol of consistency and flux, and therefore a powerful image of mortality. After Twain's acquaintance William James coined the idea of the "stream of thought, of consciousness" in 1890, it was also a way to understand the mysteries of the human mind: "Consciousness, then," James explained, and Twain read, "does not appear to itself chopped up in bits. [. . .] It flows. A 'river' or a 'stream' are the metaphors by which it is most naturally described."[12] As such, what Henry Nash Smith has described as "the matter of the river" in Twain's work was far more than just a useful backdrop for adventure and incident, a piece of stage machinery that could be wheeled out when invention failed.[13] It was a space to play with big questions, to explore irreconcilable binaries—home and exile, borders and connections, individualism and society, autonomy and inexorable destiny, freedom and slavery, dream and nightmare, life and death, heaven and hell. While it was somewhere very specific, locatable on a map, loaded with meanings, it could be everywhere and nowhere too. As John Bird has noted, in Twain's work "the river is literal, yet it is metaphorical at the same time, so much so that it transcends metaphor to become symbol."[14]

Not least, it was a fitting metaphor for Twain himself. In 1875, when the *Memphis Old Folks' Record* described the "Mad Freaks of the Mississippi"— "never satisfied; always changing. Ever breaking away old boundaries, old landmarks, and making for himself new"—it might have been describing Mark Twain.[15] Mercurial, unpredictable, capable of great creation and great destruction, always changing: little wonder that Twain came back, time and again, to the image of the river, that his sense of the river changed throughout his work, or that the Mississippi was the place where he worked out the most personally resonant and deeply rooted of his creations. Little wonder, too, that his vision of the river developed such a tenuous hold on the idea of America. Across his river writings, the Mississippi became a shifting emblem of the hope that America offered, but it was also a symbol of the despair that America so routinely engendered. It was rarely a simple idyll or easy escape. And as it was for him, so was it for countless others who rode the river, real and imagined, that twisted through the heart of the nation in these testing times in American life.

The account of the Mississippi River in the age of Mark Twain that follows, then, is shaped chronologically by the publication of Twain's major river writings. Following the development of Twain's river in this way, in the company of his contemporaries and their distinctive visions of the river, allows us to trace the contours of his relationship with the Mississippi across his life and career. At the same time, those contemporaries present their own Mississippi to us; from their accounts, complementing and contradictory, a new river bubbles up. As Heraclitus put it roughly twenty-five hundred years ago (here rendered in an 1889 translation), "Into the same river we both step and do not step."[16] The Mississippi is the most consistent site and symbol in Twain's writings, but it is never the same river twice. Chapter 1 explores Twain's first significant writings about the river in *The Gilded Age* (1873) and "Old Times on the Mississippi," a series of articles published, with the encouragement of William Dean Howells, in the *Atlantic* in 1875—texts that established a burnished, nostalgic sense of the antebellum steamboat world at the moment that the river encapsulated the contradictory tensions and trends running through the nation, fostering a nascent sense of reunion in the wake of the Civil War. Fresh from those experiments, Twain turned from his piloting years to mine his boyhood on the river in Hannibal, Missouri, for inspiration. Chapter 2 places *The Adventures of Tom Sawyer* (1876) in the company of other popular adventure books for boys from this moment that also put their young protagonists in communion with symbolically charged waterways. Chapter 3 sees Twain back at the physical river in 1882 for a long-anticipated return to his roots that became the hybrid travel account *Life on the Mississippi* (1883), a patchwork and intertextual vision of the river that was explicitly in conversation with both European travelers, new and old, and with contemporary southern voices, like George Washington Cable, who were implicating the river in their accounts of the postwar South.

The complex of emotions stirred up by this return home also helped Twain to complete his defining account of the river: *Adventures of Huckleberry Finn* (1884). The image of Huck and Jim alone on their raft on the Mississippi might stand peerless as an icon of the Mississippi, but it is also an image that speaks to multiple contemporary ideas of the river. Chapter 4 therefore explores Huck and Jim's raft in the light of various images of black life on the Mississippi that were circulating at this moment. At the same time, their journey chimed with a new passion for outdoors culture that saw a variety of (largely white, male, and middle-class) would-be adventurers heading to the river for their own forms of recreative escape. Chapter 5 explores the author's life and writing a turbulent decade later, when Twain took his leave of the Mississippi with his last major statement on the river, *Pudd'nhead Wilson* (1894), a bleak account of race in America and the river's place in its merciless machinations that echoed a wider vogue for stories and songs of corruption, crime, punishment, and death on the Mississippi. Yet Twain never really left the river behind, and the epilogue explores his last engagements with the Mississippi in the light of a popular culture that, now indelibly shaped by the legacy of Twain's river writings, rediscovered the river in myriad ways at the dawn of the twentieth century and cultural modernity.

This book, then, was born out of my abiding fascination with the Mississippi and its place in Twain's life and career; my surprise that this crucial space and symbol in his work, and in American history and culture, had not yet received its own study; and my ongoing astonishment at the richness of the cultural material that the river generated in the years between the Civil War and the early decades of the twentieth century. It was also driven by a belief that understanding the Mississippi in the age of Mark Twain still matters—precisely because that enigmatic river still flows through our idea of what America was, is, and could be; because, too, it remains so central to a broad understanding of the development of American culture. We need, therefore, to plumb its depths to come to a truer reckoning of its contrary currents; we need to leave the shallows and head for the deep water. But first, before we journey along that river and turn to both the works that defined the Mississippi for generations to come and a host of forgotten voices from the river, it is necessary to think about the legacies that this teeming waterway gave Mark Twain when he was still Sam Clemens, a boy growing up on the river in Hannibal, Missouri, who achieved his dream of becoming a steamboat pilot on the Lower Mississippi.

"Yours Is a Watery Planet"

Samuel Clemens, the boy who would be Mark Twain, grew up in a world defined by water. When his family moved to Hannibal in 1839, he was four. From that point onward, the Mississippi flowed through his life and imagination; when he left, the imprint of the river went with him. But what did it mean to grow up in a small town on the Upper Mississippi in the decades before the Civil War? In a profile of Mark Twain written for the *Atlantic Monthly* in 1897, Charles Miner Thompson waxed lyrical about the "piece of singular good fortune" of his youth: "Amid these surroundings, which were curiously American, if not especially apt to nourish literary genius [. . .] flowed the mighty Mississippi. The river was the one thing which he knew in all his early days that could appeal to his imagination and uplift it. Its fascination was upon all the boys in the village. [. . .] Their young thoughts were always of the river, which, huge and sombre, flowed out of the land of mystery, by their commonplace doors, in the land of promise, and how they envied the river-men to whom both lands were as familiar as the streets of Hannibal. [. . .] Nor is it difficult to comprehend how it is that through whichever of his books the Mississippi flows, it fills them with a certain portion of its power and beauty. To it is owing all that in his work which is large and fine and eloquent."[17] But young life on the Mississippi was more complicated than Thompson suggests. The "huge and sombre" river might have fascinated, but its currents threatened to drag the youth of Hannibal down to its depths as much as it buoyed them up.

Thompson's vision was at least right in its focus on the river as the hub of childhood experience and imagination. Certainly, life on the Mississippi enlivened the small town. It made Hannibal part of a river network that extended for thousands of miles at all points of the compass. The daily arrival of steamboats brought evidence of a wider world to a small community. Mark Twain would feature the river in this role across a variety of his works. Allan Bates, though, cautions how much we should position the Mississippi of Sam Clemens's youth as a busy, cosmopolitan thoroughfare. While the river was an omnipresent determinant of town life, "it is possible to exaggerate the rush of the world toward Hannibal and the incipient author being reared there. [. . .] In Sam's early years, only a few relatively small boats went up past St. Louis; the world tended to remain on the Ohio River and the lower Mississippi."[18]

If Hannibal was a backwater for much of his youth, it was still part of the mainstream of river life in a variety of ways. For one, it was a slaveholding town, and slavery's complicated relationship to the river was part and parcel of town life. For all that Mark Twain would make the inequities of race in America one of his defining subjects, he never really came to a full reckoning with the slavery he witnessed in his youth. In a sketch of his mother, and his childhood in Hannibal more generally, that he wrote immediately after her death in 1890, Twain defined the slavery that surrounded him in his youth as "the mild domestic" kind, "not the brutal plantation article." Even in 1890, he was drawing distinctions that in some ways justified the institution he had known as a child. Though he knew that slavery was "a bald, grotesque and unwarrantable usurpation," he still felt that the slaves of Hannibal were "content." Yet at the same time, he also remembered—"vividly"—"seeing a dozen black men and women chained to each other, once, and lying in a group on the pavement, awaiting shipment to the southern slave market." They bore, he also remembered, "the saddest faces I ever saw." As Twain understood it, being sold "down the river" in this way was akin to being sent to "hell."[19] While this was another lesson in the ethics of the river, it was also part of a rationalization of the slavery of his youth. Hell was elsewhere, somewhere far along the Mississippi, not in Hannibal.

But Samuel Clemens was also well aware what terrible things could happen to slaves in his hometown. Many important threads coalesce in the fate of one nameless fugitive slave in 1847. According to Albert Bigelow Paine's biography of Twain, Benson Blankenship, older brother of Clemens's friend Tom (one of the models for Huckleberry Finn), discovered a runaway hiding on the Illinois shore of the Mississippi. Handbills had circulated, reported the *Hannibal Journal*, describing the man as "a runaway from Neriam Todd, of Howard Country," offering a reward for his return.[20] Blankenship, however, defied the law, ignored the chance of remuneration, and, according to Paine, "kept the runaway over there in the marshes all summer. The negro would fish and Ben would carry him scraps of other food." But then, Paine reported, "it leaked out. Some woodchoppers went on a hunt for the fugitive, and chased him to what was called 'Bird Slough.' There trying to cross a drift he was drowned."[21] The *Hannibal Journal* gave more revealing details about his fate: "While some of our citizens were fishing a few days since on the Sny Island, they discovered in what is called Bird Slough the body of a negro man. [. . .] The body when discovered was much mutilated."[22] According to Paine, eleven-year-old Clemens was one of the "citizens," along with his friends John Briggs and the Bowen brothers, who found the maimed corpse when it suddenly rose up "straight and terrible" out of the water. The boys "thought he was after them and flew in wild terror."[23] Presumably, at such a moment, confronted with a gothic vision of the horrors of slavery, the hell of down the river didn't seem quite so far away. It was an event, too, that contained within it much that would echo throughout Twain's writing career—at one and the same time, the Mississippi could be a treacherous path to freedom, a space for moral action that challenged legal and social norms, and a place where the terrible cruelties of society found their full expression.

Primarily, though, it was as a space of play and freedom that Sam Clemens and his friends experienced the Mississippi—though as their terrible discovery in the summer of 1847 suggested, it was play and freedom frequently freighted by disturbing terrors. The prospect of fun was always attended by the possibility of disaster. In later life, Twain bragged about his multiple brushes with death in the water. As a boy, playing in Bear Creek, he slipped from "a loose log which I supposed was attached to a raft." Just before his "third and fatal descent" beneath the surface, a "slave woman" pulled him out. A week later, "I was in again." Thereafter, he was "drowned seven times [. . .] before I learned to swim—once in Bear Creek and six times in the Mississippi."[24] To Will Bowen, in 1870, he reminisced about another act of braggadocio that almost ended in disaster: "Heavens what eternities have swung their hoary cycles about us [. . .] since I jumped overboard from the ferry boat in the middle of the river that stormy day to get my hat, & swam two or three miles after it (& *got* it,) while all the town collected on the wharf & for an hour or so looked out across the angry waste of 'white-caps' toward where people said Sam. Clemens was last seen before he went down."[25] Others were less lucky, though, and the drowning of his companions seems to have been profoundly more disturbing than his own brushes with mortality. In *Life on the Mississippi*, he remembered Lem Hackett, "who fell out of an empty flat-boat, where he was playing. Being loaded with sin, he went to the bottom like an anvil. He was the only boy in the village who slept that night. We others all lay awake, repenting." Dutchy, a German boy who was "exasperatingly good," met the same fate while Clemens and his friends had a diving competition. Dutchy got trapped underwater; Sam, he remembered, was the one chosen to dive down and confirm his fate, grasping his "limp wrist" in the black water.[26] The boys fled in terror again.

What the river also represented was a chance to head out for a new life in parts unknown. His friends Will and Bart Bowen soon took to the Mississippi as steamboat pilots, but Clemens himself took a suitably circuitous route onto the crooked river that wound its way through his life and imagination. After years of working in printing, he toyed with becoming a steamboat pilot in 1855, but a lack of funds got in the way. Then he made plans to seek out another river. He was, he told younger brother Henry in August 1856, headed to South America, inspired by William Lewis Herndon and Lardner Gibbon's rousing *Exploration of the Valley of the Amazon, Made under Direction of the Navy Department* (1854). Throughout that account, Herndon made constant comparisons to the river that Clemens already knew intimately. "I was reminded of our Mississippi," Herndon mused in one description of the Amazon, "but this stream lacked the charm and the fascination which the plantation upon the bank, the city upon the bluff, and the steamboat upon its waters, lends to its fellow of the North." Nevertheless, Herndon was equally adamant that the economic destinies of these emblematic rivers were linked. "The trade of this region *must* pass by *our* doors," Herndon exhorted, "and mingle and exchange with the products of *our* Mississippi valley." The two rivers, he felt sure, would be "commercial complements of each other."[27] So inspired, after a few more months setting type in Orion's print shop in Keokuk, Iowa, Clemens set off to make his fortune on the Amazon—except he didn't. In February 1857, he boarded the steamboat *Paul Jones*, the first step in a journey that was supposed to take him to New Orleans, where he would find a boat to take him to Brazil. Instead, he never got beyond the Mississippi. When he arrived in New Orleans, there was a snag: there was no passenger service to Brazil. So he changed tack. After some negotiations, he came to an arrangement with the man who had piloted the *Paul Jones* to New Orleans. Horace Bixby would teach him the river as a steamboat pilot had to know it—for a fee. After borrowing some money from his brother-in-law William Moffett for a down payment to Bixby, Clemens began his new career. It was one of many professions and poses that he would adopt across the course of his miscellaneous life, but its effect on all that followed was indelible.

Over the next four years, Clemens spent time on as many as nineteen boats and undertook over one hundred trips up and down the Lower Mississippi before the Civil War closed the river.[28] As a pilot, as part of the steamboat trade that was still (despite the looming railroads) an essential part of life and culture in the region, he certainly felt himself to be something of a minor celebrity. That there was a glamorous cachet to steamboating was undeniable. When steamboats had first plied the Mississippi, they had revolutionized life on the river frontiers, opening up the region to settlement and agricultural exploitation in radically new ways. More than just their economic effects, steamboat life seemed to bestow upon the marginal inhabitants of the Mississippi Valley, whether directly or vicariously, a sense of sophistication that left a lasting regional pride. As early as 1827, Timothy Flint provided a description of steamboat life that defined its deep and lasting appeal: "An Atlantic cit[izen], who talks of us under the name of backwoodsmen, would not believe, that such fairy structures of oriental gorgeousness and splendor [. . .] had ever existed in the imaginative brain of a romancer, much less, that they were actually in existence, rushing down the Mississippi, as on the wings of the wind [. . .] bearing speculators, merchants, dandies, fine ladies, every thing real, and every thing affected in the form of humanity, with pianos and stocks of novels, and cards, and dice, and flirting, and love-making, and drinking, and champagne." "A steam boat coming from New Orleans," he declared, "brings to the remotest villages of our streams, and the very doors of the cabins, a little Paris, a section of Broadway, or a slice of Philadelphia, to ferment in the minds of our young people."[29] Thirty years later, and it still, just about, held a spell. That Samuel Clemens relished being part of this world—and always loved its memory—is abundantly clear.

It took him two years (he was licensed on April 9, 1859), and he never ceased to be amazed at what he had achieved while learning to pilot a steamboat; for the rest of his life, he would position it as one of the most remarkable human achievements. In time, he would write the defining book on this lost science. But in 1856, the prospect that faced a Mississippi initiate was an intimidating one. Piloting a steamboat on the Mississippi required a cub to learn the river, by day and by night, from St. Louis to New Orleans and back again—a distance of more than a thousand miles. Theoretically, if a pilot was dropped into the pilothouse of any boat on the river on an overcast night, he was meant to be able to immediately pinpoint his position with reference to whatever landmarks he could discern—landmarks that themselves often changed from one journey to the next. Then, too, he had to constantly read the river itself, looking out for the hints of hazards—snags, sawyers, planters—that could rip the bottom out of a boat, all while making sure there was enough water to keep afloat. To help with this formidable task, Bixby recommended he should get hold of a notebook and start writing things down. And so Samuel Clemens began his first book on the river, written in a technical language that has a poetry of its own. Here is the necessary detail that a pilot had to internalize and continually refresh to deal with just one moment of a journey of over a thousand miles: "*Outside of Montezuma.*—6 or 8 feet more water. Shape bar till high timber on towhead gets nearly even with low willows do. do., then hold a little open on right of low willows—run 'em close if you want to, but come out 100 yards, when you get nearly to head of T. H."[30]

To keep abreast of changes in the river, pilots had to do what, after piloting, pilots did best: talk. A formal and informal network of information circulated along the river both by word of mouth and through the columns of local newspapers. The pilothouse was a talking shop; pilots were, according to Mark Twain in later life, "tireless talkers"; they shared information, gossiped, and spun yarns during the long hours at the wheel.[31] Fellow trainee pilot George Byron Merrick noted, "It was proverbial that river men 'talked shop' more than any others [. . .]. The doings of all the river men were pretty thoroughly discussed sooner or later."[32] Across his career, Twain would frame sketches and stories by placing them in the mouths of steamboat pilots of one stripe or another. Albert Bigelow Paine quotes an unnamed "associate of those days" who remembered the young Clemens amusing his colleagues in the pilot-house: "He was much given to spinning yarns so funny that his hearers were convulsed."[33] Whether or not he really was a notable wit on the river, Clemens's evident desire to amuse the steamboat fraternity found expression on the printed page. Learning the river had necessitated a break in the fitful writing career he had developed while setting type. In March 1858, he had written to older brother Orion and sister-in-law Mollie, "I cannot correspond with a paper, because when one is learning the river, he is not allowed to do or think about anything else."[34] But in May 1859, perhaps flush with the liberation of gaining his pilot's license six weeks earlier, perhaps keen to blow off some steam by burlesquing the kind of river knowledge that he had spent years acquiring, he turned his hand to satire. Isaiah Sellers was a veteran steamboat pilot, having begun his career close to the dawn of the steamboat era in 1825. It's possible that Clemens and Sellers had spent time on the same steamboat, the *William M. Morrison*, in 1857, and that neither had enjoyed the experience much; either way, Sellers's apparent pomposity became Clemens's target in his first foray into print since taking to the river.

On May 7, 1859, as was his wont, Sellers sent in a report of the condition of the Mississippi that was published in the "Steamboat and River Intelligence" column of the *New Orleans True Delta*; an editorial preface described him as "one of the oldest pilots on the river [. . .] a man of experience."[35] This item became a springboard for Clemens's parody. To make his attack, he took on the mantle of "Sergeant Fathom," described as "one of the oldest cub pilots on the river," currently employed on the steamboat *Trombone*. In a preface filled with in-jokes for the river crowd—"It is related of the Sergeant that upon one occasion he actually ran the chute of Glasscock's Island, down stream, *in the night*"—Clemens turned the knife in an ironic description of Fathom's attributes: "He hath a winning way about him, an air of docility and sweetness, if you will, and a smoothness of speech, together with an exhaustless fund of funny sayings; and lastly, an ever-flowing stream, without beginning, or middle, or end, of astonishing reminiscences of the ancient Mississippi [. . .]. His remarks are entitled to extraordinary consideration, and are always read with deepest interest by high and low, rich and poor [. . .] for be it known that his fame extends to the uttermost parts of the earth." In Fathom's report of the river, Clemens has him talk of steaming down the river, in 1763, in "a singular sort of a single-engine boat with a Chinese captain and a Choctaw crew." At the sketch's crescendo, Fathom even reminisces about the time that "me and DeSoto discovered the Mississippi."[36]

According to Gary Scharnhorst, this parodic attack on a renowned river personality was an instant hit: "It became something of a legend on the lower Mississippi and was occasionally copied by papers across the country [. . .] for the next twenty years."[37] It was also an instructive moment in the trajectory of Clemens's thoughts about what it meant to write about the river. Sellers became a model of the limitations of authority and experience—the point at which those attributes tipped over into pomposity and monotony. Yet this creation of Sergeant Fathom also opened up further possibilities—the possibilities offered by an imagined river, a comedic river, a river that could be a stage for invention that transcended the rigid practicality of the pilot's memory. It even, however ludicrously, introduced the idea that writing about the river could bring you fame that extended "to the uttermost parts of the earth." At least as he told the story in later years, it wasn't just dignity that Samuel Clemens took from Isaiah Sellers. He also took his pen name. Though scholars have found no evidence for it, Twain repeatedly insisted that he had claimed the mantle of "Mark Twain"—itself a familiar leadsman's call on the river—from Sellers. He wrote to an old river colleague in 1888: "Capt. Sellers used the signature, 'Mark Twain,' himself, when he used to write up the antiquities in the way of river reminiscences [. . .]. When he died, I robbed the corpse—that is I confiscated the nom de plume." As was Twain's wont, perhaps especially for unreliable reminiscences, he insisted that this was "about the only fact that I can tell the same way every time."[38]

Once Samuel Clemens began to work as a licensed pilot—and to earn the very good wages that a pilot commanded—he took some time to boast to his brother Orion about his new position in life, demonstrating the same competitive spirit that would often flare up in his literary career. He had just secured a covetable position on a prestigious steamboat:

> This is the luckiest circumstance that ever befell me. Not on account of the wages—for that is a secondary consideration—but from the fact that the

City of Memphis is the largest boat in the trade and the hardest to pilot, *and* consequently I can get a *reputation* on her, which is a thing I never could accomplish on a transient boat. I can "bank" in the neighborhood of $100 a month on her, and that will satisfy me for the present [. . .]. Bless me! what a pleasure there is in revenge! [. . .] The young pilots, who used to tell me, patronizingly, that I could never learn the river, cannot keep from showing a little of their chagrin at seeing me so far ahead of them. Permit me to "blow my horn," for I derive a *living* pleasure from these things.

As he would for the rest of his life, he liked spending the money that he earned too (and more besides). He reveled in the companionship of fellow steamboat-men and the conspicuous consumption that came with his position on the river. In another note to Orion, he described some fun in New Orleans: "Yes-terday I had many things to do, but Bixby and I got with the pilots of two other boats and went off dissipating on a ten dollar dinner at a French restaurant—breathe it not unto Ma!—where we [. . .] ate, drank & smoked, from 1 P.M. until 5 o'clock, and then—then—the day was too far gone to do anything."[39]

Yet to be part of the steamboating brotherhood was also to know different, darker aspects of the river—parts of the trade that also helped to pay for long New Orleans lunches. If the steamboat was a world unto itself, then it was a society that had a hierarchy. As a pilot, Sam Clemens was at the top; there were many layers beneath him. Flint's loving description of steamboat life in 1827 only touched on the experiences of wealthy passengers who could afford cabin passage. No mention was made of the poverty, disease, and danger of life for those who had to travel on the decks. Flint mentioned "cards, and dice," but he didn't mention the destructiveness and dishonesty of the gambling that often took place on board steamboats (often with the full knowledge of, and a portion of the profits to, the boat's crew). Prostitution, certainly endemic in river towns, must have been present on board steamboats for all that it is invisible in the public record. Moreover, as Bernard DeVoto vociferously claimed long ago, the steamboat industry was marked out by corruption: "It was an American commerce, without conscience, responsibility, or control [. . .] a competition ruthless and inconceivably corrupt. [. . .] Everything that chicanery, sabotage, bribery, and malfeasance could devise was a part of the commonplace mechanism of the trade."[40]

At its heart—absolutely inescapable on the Lower Mississippi, as it had been in Hannibal—was slavery, a fundamental aspect of antebellum steamboat life that many biographers fail to mention in their accounts of Sam Clemens's steamboating years (perhaps because he himself mentioned it so little). The Mississippi was crucial to the African American experience in the antebellum years. Steamboats transported the enslaved along the Mississippi in extraordinary numbers. As Walter Johnson specifies, "Between 1820 and 1860 as many as a million people were sold 'down the river' through an internal slave trade."[41] One of the reasons for this mass movement of the enslaved was to supply labor for the cotton plantations that boomed in the Lower Mississippi valley in the antebellum decades, revivifying American slavery in terrifying ways. In turn, steamboats transported that cotton to market. As Thomas Buchanan elucidates, "Fifty-five percent of the South's cotton crop, 1,915,852 bales in all, came down the Mississippi in 1860, bound for the textile mills of Liverpool and New York."[42] The enslaved were hired out to work on steamboats too. Slavery, then, was a vital aspect of steamboat life, and steamboats were utterly complicit in the slave system—including their glamorous pilots, like the young Clemens. Little wonder that Herman Melville would set *The Confidence Man* (1857), his apocalyptic satire of antebellum American life, on a steamboat heading down the Mississippi to New Orleans.

Steamboat life could be dangerous too. Explosions on the Mississippi were ubiquitous and proverbial in reports of the river. So popular were voyeuristic newspaper accounts of steamboat conflagrations that in 1856 James Lloyd of Cincinnati published a directory of steamboats running on the Mississippi and the Ohio that also included graphic descriptions of "disasters on the western waters." Lloyd masked his sensation with a campaign for reform: "We have introduced a copious detail of the awful and heart-rending accidents which have been of too frequent occurrence [. . .]. There are *many* Boats on the Ohio and Mississippi Rivers *unsafe* and *dangerous*."[43] Clemens himself was involved in a handful of relatively minor accidents during his time on the river (a couple of which might have been his fault). Perhaps the most significant was a collision, while racing, between the *Pennsylvania*, the boat on which Clemens was then cubbing, and the *Vicksburg* on November 26, 1857. No one was injured, but the *Pennsylvania* needed significant repairs, and Clemens later had to give a deposition about the accident when the owners of his boat attempted to sue the *Vicksburg* for damages. "I am learning the river," he detailed in his statement. "I was not at the wheel at the time."[44]

It was, though, an accident that Clemens narrowly avoided that left the worst scars. When the *Pennsylvania* had been put back in operation in February 1858, Clemens went back to the boat to continue learning the river. During his time on the *Pennsylvania,* he was under the tutelage of new mentors. Horace Bixby, off piloting on the Missouri, had temporarily transferred his cub to the care of George Ealer, who read him Shakespeare in the pilothouse, and William Brown, whose manner was rather less solicitous. In *Life on the Mississippi,* a monster magnified by memory, Twain would describe Brown as an "ignorant, stingy, malicious, fault-hunting, mote-magnifying tyrant."[45] But he also had another new colleague on the river: his younger brother, Henry Clemens. Encouraged by Sam, the unemployed Henry took up the lowly position of "mud clerk" on the boat—"measuring woodpiles, counting coal boxes, and other clerkly duties," Sam described to Orion and Mollie.[46] It was a start: Horace Bixby had risen to the rank of pilot from the same position. From February to June, the brothers steamed up and down the river together. Then one day, Henry fell foul of William Brown. Sam explained to Mollie that Brown had "quarreled with Henry without cause, while I was steering—Henry started out of the pilothouse—Brown jumped up and collared him—turned him half way around and *struck him in the face!*" Outraged at this treatment of his brother, Sam was "wild from that moment. I left the boat to steer herself, and avenged the insult." In the wake of this unseemly fracas, he insisted that "the Captain said I was right" to avenge Brown's abuse of Henry. Nevertheless, he still asked Sam to leave the boat. The captain sent him to "the A. T. Lacey"—a boat piloted by Sam's Hannibal acquaintance Bart Bowen—"with orders to her Captain to bring me to Saint Louis." All of this meant that when the *Pennsylvania* exploded a few days later, Samuel Clemens was not on board. Henry was, though. As he sorrowfully explained to Mollie, to the best of his knowledge, "Henry was asleep—was blown up—then fell back on the hot boilers, and I suppose that rubbish fell on him, for he is injured internally." Along with the other wounded survivors, Henry was taken to Memphis. The *Alfred T. Lacey* arrived there in time for Sam to be with him as he died. "O, God!" he lamented to his family, "this is hard to bear. [. . .] Men take me by the hand and congratulate me, and call me 'lucky' because I was not on the Pennsylvania when she blew up! My God forgive them, for they know not what they say." It was a trauma that always stayed close to the center of his river memories.

Looking back on his river years in *Life on the Mississippi,* Twain remembered, "I supposed—and hoped—that I was going to follow the river the rest of my days, and die at the wheel when my mission was ended." Yet the world had other plans. To borrow Twain's famously passive construction, "by and by the war came, commerce was suspended, my occupation was gone."[47] When the Civil War began, the economic and strategic importance of the Mississippi was understood immediately; many of Clemens's former friends and colleagues would stick to the river in wartime, some of them—like Horace Bixby—seeing active duty in the thick of battle; steamboats were pressed into service by Union and Confederate forces alike. Sam was keen not to join them. At least according to his niece Annie, he "was obsessed with the fear that he might be arrested by government agents and forced to act as a pilot on a government gunboat while a man stood by with a pistol ready to shoot him if he showed the least sign of a false move."[48] Before long, aged twenty-five, he was gone from the river, heading west to find new occupations—to begin the transformation of steamboat pilot Samuel Clemens into Mark Twain. Of course, all of this had been foretold. In February 1861, not long before the war would force him from the Mississippi, Clemens had time to kill in New Orleans. As "novelties begun to grow alarmingly scarce," he paid a visit to famous fortune-teller Madame Caprell for some insight into what an uncertain future held for him. "Yours is a watery planet," she told him; "you gain your livelihood on the water." But Madame Caprell knew that the man in front of her had other strings to his bow: "You have written a great deal; you write well— but you are rather out of practice." But "no matter—you will be *in* practice some day." Still, she concluded, "you will continue upon the water for some time yet."[49] She was wrong, of course—but she was also more right than even she knew. The man in front of her would stay on the Mississippi for the rest of his life, even after he had left it far behind.

"River of Dreams and Wild Romance"

What Samuel Clemens learned from the river as he navigated its treacherous currents as a child and relearned how to tackle them as a steamboat pilot were only a portion of his Mississippi inheritance. Throughout those years, he could hardly have avoided the ubiquitous images of the river that circulated internationally across a wide variety of media. What the representative river meant in a rich and complex blend of poetry, art, travel accounts, and a wealth of other sources was deeply connected to what America itself meant in the wider imagination. Before Samuel Clemens attempted to take imaginative ownership of the Mississippi, he was part of a culture saturated by conflicting visions of the river, echoes of which made their way into his own work. A telling example can be found in his first published piece of writing about the Mississippi—his debut foray into print. The river was there from the start. In 1852, in his late teens, Clemens composed "The Dandy Frightening the Squatter," a sketch of a humorous altercation on the banks of the river—set, tellingly for his future work, "about thirteen years ago, when the now flourishing young city of Hannibal, on the Mississippi River, was but a 'wood-yard.'" The Dandy attempts to play a trick on the Squatter to kill time and impress his fellow passengers while their steamboat takes on wood. In the end, though, the Squatter has the last laugh, dunking the Dandy in the "turbid waters of the Mississippi."[50] It was published in the *Boston Carpet-Bag* on May 1, 1852. Even at the beginning of his literary career, Clemens was shaping visions of the river that reached for a national appeal.

However, he already had some debts to pay; from the start, his river was an intertextual creation. As Bernard DeVoto wrote of this seminal sketch, "When young Sam Clemens took to writing, he had to look for a model no farther than the nearest newspapers and for material no farther than the boiler deck"—implying that this youthful example of southwestern humor was inspired by an equal combination of literary inspiration and direct observation of life on the Mississippi.[51] He took what he learned from other humorous writers and applied it to his own environment. Yet that even-handed account of Clemens's methodology here does not quite cover the genesis of this sketch. As Fred Lorch demonstrated many years ago, the essential ingredients of "The Dandy Frightening the Squatter" were not original. A sketch entitled "A Scene on the Ohio," which contained all the elements of Sam's sketch, had been published in 1849. That dandy ends up "floundering in the Ohio."[52] However the tale had reached Clemens, it is clear that his debut account of life on the Mississippi did not originate from his own experience of the river; instead, it was a reworked account of someone else's imaginative sense of the western rivers. And yet that awareness clearly does not rob this journeyman sketch of interest. Instead, it serves to highlight more particularly what Sam Clemens brought to the tale—most significantly, a historical frame, a vernacular richness, and a very particular geographical setting. It established immediately that his view of the river would often be couched in a backwards glance—and that Hannibal itself would prove a vital model throughout his life and career.

It was not only in such fugitive sketches that the Mississippi enchanted readers (and writers) like Sam Clemens. The river starred in some of the most widespread texts of the antebellum years. Henry Wadsworth Longfellow's popular sensation *Evangeline* (1847) painted a rich and largely idyllic vision of "the golden stream of the broad and swift Mississippi":

> Day after day they glided adown the turbulent river;
> Night after night, by their blazing fires, encamped on its borders.
> Now through rushing chutes, among green islands, where plumelike
> Cotton-trees nodded their shadowy crests, they swept with the current,
> Then emerged into broad lagoons, where silvery sand-bars
> Lay in the stream, and along the wimpling waves of their margin,
> Shining with snow-white plumes, large flocks of pelicans waded.
> Level the landscape grew, and along the shores of the river,
> Shaded by china-trees, in the midst of luxuriant gardens,
> Stood the houses of planters, with negro-cabins and dove-cots.[53]

Longfellow himself, for all that his visions of the river were deeply influential on conceptions of the Mississippi in the antebellum years, never visited the river. He found another popular source to inform his description. In December 1846, Longfellow noted in his diary: "I see a diorama of the Mississippi advertised. This comes very à propos. The river comes to me instead of my going to the river; and as it is to flow through the pages of the poem, I look upon this as a special benediction." After he had visited this extravaganza, he enthusiastically described the new cultural phenomenon that he had witnessed: "One seems to be sailing down the great stream, and sees the boats and the sandbanks crested with cottonwood, and the bayous by moonlight. Three miles of canvas, and a great deal of merit."[54]

What Longfellow had experienced would have been familiar to thousands—perhaps millions—around the world. Moving panoramas drew huge international audiences in the antebellum years. Their invention is credited to artist and entrepreneur John Banvard. In 1846, he created his first enormous moving panorama of the Mississippi River—a painting on a long roll of canvas (advertised as three miles though in reality much shorter) that was stretched between two rollers that turned slowly, simulating movement for a paying audience who could imagine themselves on board a steamboat. Both implicitly and explicitly, the panorama provided a patriotic vision of America that centered the river in national life. In a booklet written to accompany the panorama, Banvard lauded the river's "grandeur." He described his motivation in creating the panorama as "a patriotic and honorable ambition, that America should produce the *largest painting* in the world."[55] Only a river like the Mississippi could be commensurate with such a determination or such a nation. Not only did Banvard soon achieve enormous popularity with his panorama in America and Europe (including a command performance for Queen Victoria), but he sparked a craze for moving panoramas of the Mississippi from a variety of creators which lasted throughout the antebellum years. For many Americans—and far beyond—the moving panorama provided a defining experience of the river. According to Curtis Dahl, Samuel Clemens was one of them: he "must surely have seen panoramas either in his boyhood [. . .] or later when he was a printer in St. Louis or a pilot on the river" and "unconsciously absorbed much of their technique into his writing."[56] He incorporated a panoramist into *Life on the Mississippi* too.

Famously, Charles Dickens went to see Banvard's panorama when it was on display in London in December 1848. Declaring the enterprise "a truly American idea," Dickens concluded that the panorama was a "true and faithful representation [. . .] of one of the greatest streams of the world" and realized its representative significance in the portrait of America—and Americans— that it provided: "slaves and free republicans, French and Southerners; immigrants from abroad, and restless Yankees and Down-Easters ever steaming somewhere; alligators, store-boats, show-boats, theatre-boats, Indians, buffaloes." The river, in Banvard's depictions, was a vivid, cosmopolitan, intensely American space, redolent of progress. Indeed, Dickens concluded his review with a hope to see a panorama of England that was similarly "*moving*" rather than one "that stood still, or had a disposition to go backward."[57] But while Dickens could appreciate the river as an optimistic symbol of America in Banvard's portrait, at other times he used the Mississippi as an image of all that troubled him about life across the Atlantic. He incorporated the river into the narrative of *Martin Chuzzlewit* (1842–44) as a dismal symbol of his hero's, and his own, disillusionment with the New World. The river and the ironically named town of Eden become desolate, nightmarish counterpoints of

Banvard's sanguinity: "On they toiled through great solitudes, where the trees upon the banks grew thick and close; and floated in the stream; and held up shrivelled arms from out the river's depths; and slid down from the margin of the land, half growing, half decaying, in the miry water. [. . .] Fatal maladies, seeking whom they might infect, came forth at night in misty shapes, and creeping out upon the water, hunted them like spectres until day."[58] Twain was well aware of this. In 1860, while he was still on the river, he read *Martin Chuzzlewit*, referring to it in multiple letters to his family.[59]

Dickens's vituperative attack on the river in *Martin Chuzzlewit* was itself based on his own experiences of the Mississippi. Accounts of the river by high-profile European travelers like Dickens were a crucial part of the river's cultural life in the antebellum years—a constant source of irritation to Americans who bristled at the bruising critiques these travelers frequently produced. In *American Notes* (1842), Dickens himself notoriously labeled the Mississippi "a foul stream," "an enormous ditch, sometimes two or three miles wide, running liquid mud [. . .] alive with monsters [. . .] filthy [. . .] intolerable."[60] In *Domestic Manners of the Americans* (1832), Frances Trollope also despaired about the river that she found "utterly desolate," a "murky stream." She concluded: "Let no one who wishes to receive agreeable impressions of American manners, commence their travels in a Mississippi steam boat; for myself, it is with all sincerity I declare, that I would infinitely prefer sharing the apartment of a party of well conditioned pigs."[61] In his *Diary in America with Remarks on Its Institutions* (1839), Frederick Marryat expressed regret that "life was so short, and the Mississippi so long." He became morbid: "I cannot help feeling a disgust at the idea of perishing in such a vile sewer, to be buried in mud, and perhaps to be rooted out again by some pig-nosed alligator." His conclusion: "I hate the Mississippi."[62] If the members of this disparate, influential triumvirate were the harshest critics of the river—each seeing something representative in the waters of the river that matched their disappointment and distaste for America as a whole—they were only the leading edge of a European vein of rhetoric throughout the antebellum decades that positioned life on the Mississippi as the most troubling and extreme example of American democracy. Twain enthusiastically reached for their accounts when composing *Life on the Mississippi*.

At least for Dickens, some of the reason for his despair on the river related to what he described in *American Notes* as America's "most hideous blot and foul disgrace": slavery.[63] By far the greatest association that the river carried in the antebellum decades was related to its role in the internal slave trade. One of those who knew the system all too intimately was William Wells Brown. Born enslaved, Brown spent most of his adolescent life in slavery somewhere along the Western River network. Indeed, Brown spent almost twice as long working on the river as Sam Clemens—roughly seven years, all told—and his accounts of life on the Mississippi certainly stand in powerful complement to the perspective from the pilothouse. After his escape from slavery, Brown explored his conflicted responses to the Mississippi in the first of a number of accounts he would give of his life: "I was hired to Capt. Otis Reynolds, as a waiter on board the steamboat Enterprize [. . .]. My employment on board was to wait on gentlemen, and the captain being a good man, the situation was a pleasant one to me;—but in passing from place to place, and seeing new faces every day, and knowing that they could go where they pleased, I soon became unhappy." The full horror of slavery's intimate relationship to both the river and the steamboat trade became apparent to Brown in a telling location: "On our downward passage, the boat took on board, at Hannibal, a drove of slaves, bound for the New Orleans market [. . .] an occurrence so common, that no one, not even the passengers, appear to notice it, though they clank their chains at every step." Yet the river would also prove to be Brown's salvation. After a failed attempt to cross the Ohio with his mother in a small skiff, Brown finally used his knowledge of the steamboat world to achieve an audacious escape: "When the boat was discharging her cargo, and the passengers engaged carrying their baggage on and off shore, I improved the opportunity to convey myself with my little effects on land. Taking up a trunk, I went up the wharf, and was soon out of the crowd. I made directly for the woods."[64]

One particular account of the river's relationship to slavery was utterly inescapable in the antebellum decades. Undoubtedly the most widely circulated description of the Mississippi River in the nineteenth century was found in Harriet Beecher Stowe's *Uncle Tom's Cabin* (1852), begun in the same year as Clemens's first sketch of river life. Leland Krauth has described the dynamic between Twain and Stowe, "Whatever genre Twain turned to as a writer, Stowe had already written in."[65] This was true of writing the river too. In Stowe's epochal book, Tom's descent of the Western Rivers away from his old Kentucky home—including his iconic rescue of Eva from the Mississippi itself—forms the central narrative of the book. Like Longfellow, Stowe's picture of the Mississippi was an imagined one, a composite of popular images of the river circulating in popular culture. She, like John Banvard, positioned the river at the heart of national life—and positioned slavery squarely at the center of the Mississippi's antebellum identity: "This river of dreams and wild romance [. . .]. What other river of the world bears on its bosom to the ocean the wealth and enterprise of such another country?—a country whose products embrace all between the tropics and the poles! Those turbid waters, hurrying, foaming, tearing along, an apt resemblance of that headlong tide of business which is poured along its wave by a race more vehement and energetic than any the old world ever saw. Ah! would that they did not also bear along a more fearful freight,—the tears of the oppressed, the sighs of the helpless, the bitter prayers of poor, ignorant hearts to an unknown God."[66] Clemens certainly paid attention to one aspect of *Uncle Tom's Cabin:* its enormous success. Writing to mentor Horace Bixby in 1870 about his recent literary triumphs, there was only one competitor in which he was interested: "Thirty tons of paper have been used in publishing my book Innocents Abroad. It has met with a greater sale than any book ever published except Uncle Tom's Cabin."[67] From 1871 onward, he and Stowe would be neighbors at Nook Farm, another measure of success.

Clemens also took in a stage performance of *Uncle Tom's Cabin* in 1853 in New York—one of many enormously popular adaptations of Stowe's novels that circulated throughout the final decades of the nineteenth century.[68] These adaptations were intimately connected to another American art form that drew heavily from the river. The development of American minstrelsy as both medium and message was closely bound up with the Western River system. Alexander Saxton has rightly noted that the most important pioneers of minstrelsy in its three distinct phases in the antebellum years—Thomas Rice, Dan Emmett, and Stephen Foster—all "had direct contact through their wanderings in the lower Mississippi Valley with [. . .] the music and dance of slaves and [. . .] the half-horse, half-alligator braggadocio of the river."[69] And as Ken Emerson has argued, "Early blackface music owed as much to the backwoods and rivers of the Midwest as it did to the plantations of the South or to the urban North."[70] As much as the personal contacts of these men with the wider Western River system was vital for the development of minstrelsy, no less important was the degree to which the Mississippi and its tributaries sat at the center of the imagined American geography of the minstrel stage. The black river worker became an archetypical minstrel figure who persisted long past the Civil War and whose image indelibly colored descriptions of black Americans living and working on the river well into the twentieth century. As James V. Hatch has lamented, "Who knows the slave musicians, street performers, church singers, and riverboat roustabouts whose songs and jokes and dances were stolen by the white minstrel men?"[71]

If there is a mythical birthplace for minstrelsy in America, then it is somewhere on the banks of the Western River system. As Noah Ludlow—the famous impresario who managed theaters and traveled widely throughout the Mississippi Valley in the antebellum years—told it in his entertaining autobiography in 1880, it all began on a "clear, bright morning" in Louisville (though others placed this story in Pittsburgh or Cincinnati). Either way, Thomas Dartmouth Rice was a struggling actor killing time at the stage door during rehearsals for a play in which he "had but little to do." Looking out onto some stables, Rice watched—in Ludlow's words—a "very black, clumsy negro" at work, "attracted by the clearness and melody" of his voice. The song the man was singing was "the negro version of 'Jump, Jim Crow.'" Rice listened to this song "with delight [. . .] for several days, and finally went to him and paid him to sing the song over to him until he had learned it." When Rice was cast as "a Kentucky corn-field negro" in an upcoming production, he successfully lobbied to incorporate "his newly acquired negro song" into his performance: "The result was that 'Jim Crow' ran the piece to full houses for many nights."[72] Rice took "Jim Crow" around the country and across the globe before becoming one of the most popular fixtures of the New York stage. Even aside from the layers of folk river culture that must have flowed into whatever nascent version of Jim Crow that Rice encountered by the stage door, the Western Rivers weren't just an incidental birthplace for the character—they remained intimately wrapped up with the character's depiction and the development of minstrelsy thereafter. Twenty years later, Rice would neatly square the circle when he took the role of Tom in an 1854 adaptation of *Uncle Tom's Cabin*.[73]

Jim Crow was, in multiple ways, a creature of the river. In one retelling of the genesis of the character from the *Atlantic Monthly* in 1867, for his first performance of Jim Crow, Rice borrowed the clothes of Cuff, who earned a living "carrying the trunks of passengers from the steamboats to the hotels." The line between performance and life on the river was blurred when Cuff, desperate for the return of his clothes, burst onto the stage in the middle of Rice's performance: "Massa Rice, Massa Rice, gi' me nigga's hat,—nigga's coat,—nigga's shoes,—gi'me nigga's t'ings! Massa Griff wants 'im,—STEAMBOAT'S COMIN'!!"[74]As Dale Cockrell has argued, "No version of the song known to me fails to base Jim Crow in the Southwest at some point, often by reference to the Mississippi River."[75] At least one version of the song describes Jim Crow's birth and development on, along, and in the Mississippi in terms that echoed along the river throughout the antebellum years:

> I was born in a cane break, and cradled in a trough,
> Swam de Mississippi, whar I cotch'd de hoopen coff.
> To whip my weight in wild cats, eat an alligator,
> And drink de Mississippi dry, I'm de very critter.[76]

As minstrelsy developed, the river remained a vital location for its imaginative development. According to William John Mahar, "Minstrelsy focused on relatively few occupations, the most typical being involved with the riverboat transportation and shipping characteristic of the prerail era in southern labor history."[77]

Another very early minstrel song—predating "Jim Crow," by some estimates—was perhaps most influential in forging that association.[78] "Gumbo Chaff" (sometimes called "Gombo Chaff") was a profoundly popular song that was widely performed and reprinted early in the life of minstrelsy as a medium—Thomas Rice himself famously took on the role. More centrally than "Jim Crow," this was a song that explored the possibilities of river life for black Americans—its inequities but also its possibilities for self-definition and resistance on the river in the heart of the space of slavery, as demonstrated by the illustration of Rice in the role from the cover of a sheet music version of the song published in 1838 (fig. 1).

The song itself tells the story of Gumbo Chaff's varied experiences along the Western Rivers. The beginning of the song finds him enslaved and set to work on the Ohio:

> On de Ohio bluff in de state of Indiana,
> Dere's where I live, chock up to de Habbanna.
> Eb'ry mornin early Massa gib me licker,
> I take my net and paddle and I put out de quicker,

I jump into my kiff. And I down de river driff,
And I cotch as many cat fish as ever nigger liff.

But the river intervenes: a flood destroys his master's fortune. In short order, the master dies (and is sent "to de debil [. . .] to tote de firewood way down below"), Gumbo's mistress embarks on a disastrous marriage to "Big Bill de weaver," who turns out to be a "gay deceiver" (a snippet of the song that would make its way into "Dixie"), and Gumbo himself lights out:

FIGURE 1. "Gumbo Chaff" (also "Gombo Chaff"), sheet music
(Baltimore: John Cole & Son, 1838).

Now one day de sun gone down an' de days work over,
Old Gumbo Chaff he tink he'd live in Clover;
He jump into a boat wid his old Tamobrine,
While schoonerhead Sambo play'd de Violin;
De way we sail'd to New Orleans never be forgotten,
Dey put me on de Levy dock to roll a bale of Cotton.

Tiring of life in New Orleans and surfeited with "fun and frolick," he sneaks on board a steamboat to make his way back home—where he amuses "de white folks at home" with tales of his travels and surprises "de Niggers" when he introduces them to "Mrs. Gumbo Chaff," a wife that he has apparently brought back as a souvenir from his travels.[79] While "Gumbo Chaff" might be a white fantasy of black agency along the river, it still hints at the possibilities of river life for black Americans. As Louis S. Gerteis explicates: "Freed of an abusive master, Gumbo Chaff is footloose and fancy free for a time, traveling the river highways [. . .]. A masterless man, Gumbo Chaff enjoyed physical mobility and could play with his identity, albeit within the theatrical confines of blackface racial representation."[80] Moreover, its popularity suggests the appeal of this vision of slavery and freedom along the Western Rivers. For Robert Nowatzki, Gumbo Chaff was a model of "transracial, mobile masculinity."[81]

Throughout the permutations of minstrelsy as it developed in the antebellum years, the Western Rivers remained at its heart. Daniel Decatur Emmett spent plenty of time along the Western Rivers. Born in Mount Vernon, Ohio, Emmett made his way to Cincinnati by the late 1830s, working in a circus. One of Emmett's most famous compositions—what Mahar has termed "the best-known festive minstrel song"—was titled "De Boatman's Dance."[82] The Western Rivers were equally important—physically and imaginatively—in the life and work of Stephen Foster. Born in Pittsburgh in 1826, Foster and his family had close connections to life along the Western Rivers. His father and brothers were deeply involved in the flatboat and steamboat trades, and during a particularly formative moment in his life and career, Stephen himself worked as a clerk at the firm of Irwin & Foster in Cincinnati. As Ken Emerson explains: "When Stephen Foster looked out the front windows of Irwin & Foster he could see the steamboats his firm represented [. . .] bound downriver to St. Louis, Memphis, and New Orleans. [. . .] Foster had more opportunities to hear genuine black music in Cincinnati, both because of the greater number of African Americans there and because his new job brought him further down the river and closer to its edge."

Images of the river can be found in a number of Foster's songs. Indeed, hidden away from contemporary listeners, a casually violent image of black life on the Mississippi sits at the center of one of his—indeed, one of America's—most famous compositions. "Oh! Susanna," probably composed at some point in 1847, narrates a journey to New Orleans. Though the second stanza is mostly elided these days, it details a steamboat explosion—"the telegraph" mentioned in the first line is probably a reference, as Emerson annotates, to "either of two brand-new steamboats, *Telegraph No. 1* and *No. 2* [. . .] familiar sights from the windows of Irwin & Foster":

> I jump'd aboard the telegraph
> And trabbled down de riber,
> De lectrick fluid magnified,
> And kill'd five hundred Nigga.
> De bulgine bust and de hoss ran off,
> I really thought I'd die;
> I shut my eyes to hold my bref
> Susanna, don't you cry.[83]

Young Sam Clemens and old Mark Twain unabashedly loved the minstrel show as he experienced it in his youth on the river. Looking backward, in 1906, while dictating his autobiography, Twain fondly reminisced about "the first negro-minstrel show I ever saw. It must have been in the early '40s. It was a new institution. In our village of Hannibal, on the banks of the Mississippi, we had not heard of it before, and it burst upon us as a glad and stunning surprise." The minstrel show—"the real nigger show—the genuine nigger show, the extravagant nigger show—was the show which to me had no peer and whose peer has not yet arrived, in my experience."[84] Its echoes can be found at various points along his Mississippi journey.

In the antebellum decades, then, the Mississippi was a rich and multiple symbol that generated a wealth of commentary and an extraordinary range of representations. In tangled and ambiguous ways, it was particularly a space to explore issues of race and national identity. It was, indeed, an intensely representative symbol of America. From panoramas to poetry, travel accounts to minstrelsy and a multiplicity of Uncle Toms, the Mississippi was an intensely intertextual space, contested and ambiguous. When Mark Twain finally turned to write about the river, then, he was fully aware that he was not approaching a tabula rasa. Instead, he was entering into a conversation—with the Mississippi and with those who had already found meaning in its waters. And Twain himself was deeply aware of this fact, actively seeking out other accounts of the river as he shaped his own defining Mississippi. Some he would push against; some he would burlesque; some he would echo. All of them helped shaped his own vision of the Mississippi as a river that, as the nation reconstituted itself after the Civil War and forged onward toward the twentieth century, was still deeply representative of America's essential identity. Ultimately, Twain's accounts of the river were no less contested, ambiguous, or multivalent than these antebellum accounts, nor were they produced in a vacuum. Twain continued to explore meaning in the Mississippi along with a plethora of others who were attempting to define America with reference to its waters.

Just as Samuel Clemens was leaving the river, at the same moment that Madam Caprell was prophesying his future as a writer, he composed a story that drew on the folklore of the Mississippi—a turn to fiction that was itself prescient. As if to mark the finality of the moment, it was a story freighted with death and departures, trauma and terror, spectral returns. It was, in short, a ghost story—repeated, Clemens narrated, "from the lips of a dying man [. . .] an old Saint Louis and New Orleans pilot." The story begins in the pilothouse of the *Boreas* as steamboat pilot William Jones attempts a dangerous run on the river in adverse conditions. He makes a reckless assertion: "I'll take her through, if the Devil seizes me for it in five minutes afterwards!" Sure enough, Jones makes the run, declares himself the "king of pilots!" and promptly disappears from the boat in mysterious circumstances. On the boat's next run, at the same dangerous point in the river, disorientated by a blizzard, Joe Millard, the dying narrator of the story, becomes conscious that "some one was in the pilot house with him." He was confronted by "a horrid vision": "A sudden gleam of light from a crack in the stove pipe revealed the ghastly features of William Jones, with a great piece of skin, ragged and bloody, torn loose from his forehead and dangling and flapping over his left eye—the other eye dead and fixed and lustreless—hair wet and disordered, and the whole body bent and shapeless, like that of a drowned man." The spectral Jones takes the wheel, steers the boat safely through the crossing, and promptly disappears—leaving only his watch behind, as proof of his presence. Millard swears his copilot to secrecy, fearing that he would become "the laughing stock of the whole river."[85] Clemens's niece Annie Moffett remembered being "transfixed with horror, and yet fascinated" as he read the story to his family.[86] It was another lesson that his words, and the river, could move an audience. And with that farewell to his piloting identity, he left the Mississippi behind for two decades, forever to be haunted by its ghost.

1

"There Is a World of River Stuff to Write About"

RECONSTRUCTING THE MISSISSIPPI

Within a year the Mississippi will be at the mercy of her conquerors.
She may grind her sands in rage, and lash her sides in wrath,
but never again can she be called, in the old sense,
the autocrat of western prosperity.
—A. S. TWOMBLY, *Scribner's Monthly*, 1871

And this was all the religion he had—
To treat his engine well;
Never be passed on the river;
To mind the Pilot's bell.
—JOHN HAY, "Jim Bludso," 1871

The genial "Mark Twain" served his apprenticeship as pilot [. . .].
One sees, on a journey down the Mississippi, where Mark found many
of his queerest and seemingly impossible types.
—EDWARD KING, *The Great South*, 1874

S amuel Clemens might have left the river, but the river never left him. He set out for Nevada with brother Orion in the summer of 1861, skipping out on the war that would consume the Mississippi and involve many of his old colleagues (not to mention his future friend Ulysses S. Grant). He wouldn't return to the river, except for brief lecture stops in 1867 and 1869, for just over two decades. These were the years that would transform Samuel Clemens into a writer, a lecturer, a celebrity, a husband, a father—all of the things that went into the phenomenon that was Mark Twain. The enormous success of *Innocents Abroad* in 1869, an account of his travels in Europe and the Holy Land in the summer of 1867, established his fame. His marriage to Olivia Langdon in February 1870, the sister of one of his fellow passengers on his European journey, secured his fortune—at least for a while. Their move to Hartford in 1871 and the birth of their children raised the kind of respectable domestic edifice that would provide the backdrop to Twain's public career. The decade after the Civil War made Mark Twain. In turn, as he moved farther and farther away from the river, temporally and geographically, it would mark the beginning of his most profound literary engagements with the Mississippi.

Indeed, the river remained insistently on his mind during these extraordinary transformations. Throughout his writing in this period—whether his correspondence or the books that would establish his name, tracking his peregrinations across the globe and America—the Mississippi was a steady topic, always floating back to the surface of his thoughts. In a letter home in May 1862, for example, he commented on the wartime experiences of his colleagues still on the river. Noting that Bixby was "on the flag-ship," he proudly judged, "He always was the best pilot on the Mississippi." His old river friends the Bowen brothers, from whom he was currently estranged after arguments about politics or money or both, fared less well: "They have done a reckless thing, though, in putting Sam. Bowen on the 'Swon' for if a bombshell happens to come his way, he will infallibly jump overboard. It would be refreshing if they would catch Will Bowen and hang him." In August that year, he declared peremptorily, "I never have *once* thought of returning home to go on the river again, and I never expect to do any more piloting at any price." But that was hardly his final thought on the matter, and at other moments, he clearly missed life on the Mississippi. In January 1866, writing from San Francisco, he lamented to his mother and sister: "I wish I was back there piloting up & down the river again. Verily, all is vanity and little worth—save piloting."[1]

At the same time, something else was brewing. In the same letter to his family in which he lamented the loss of his old profession, Twain included a clipping of a report by the *San Francisco Examiner* that declared: "That rare humourist [. . .] informs us that he has commenced the work of writing a book. He says that it will treat on an entirely new subject, one that has not been written about heretofore." To his family, he offered a little more enigmatic detail: "The book referred to in that paragraph is a pet notion of mine—nobody knows what it is going to be about but just myself. [. . .] I expect to make about three hundred pages, and the last hundred will have to be written in St. Louis, because the materials for them can only be got there." Who knows, he concluded, "I may be an old man before I finish it." These were, perhaps, the first hints that Twain was thinking of turning to the river in earnest as a subject. If so, it was indeed the beginning of a process that would take the self-proclaimed "Genius of Indolence" half a lifetime to complete. In March 1866, another western newspaper reported that Twain planned a trip "down the Missouri river in a Mackinac boat—he's an old Mississippi pilot—to New Orleans; where he intends writing a book." If nothing came of those plans in 1866—"I am slow & lazy, you know," as he told his family—they did not evaporate.[2]

When he briefly returned to the Mississippi in May 1867, during a lecture tour, he made no mention of any imminent literary plans. But writing a letter to *Alta California* about his return to his "old home" of St. Louis, Twain naturally took stock of the river: "I find the long levee bordered with steamboats its entire length, as formerly, and now that the Mobile and Ohio Railroad is mostly under water, they are doing a heavy business South. The other river trades are good also."[3] By November 1871, though, writing at length about the river was clearly back on his agenda. Twain wrote to Livy, contemplating the imminent publication of *Roughing It* (1872) with a promise: "But when I come to write the Mississippi book"—as if this was a subject already familiar to both of them—"*then* look out! I will spend 2 months on the river & take notes, & I bet you I will make a standard work."[4] Again that plan was apparently deferred. The river was rising, but it hadn't yet crested.

In the meantime, though, the Mississippi insistently made itself felt in the books—particularly *Innocents Abroad* (1869)—that built his international audience. Throughout Twain's satirical travel account, mocking the mores of the Old World and the New, the Mississippi stood as his favorite, all-American measuring stick—a symbol of patriotic magnitude to place up against the marvels of Europe. Lake Como ("I did not like it") is "as crooked as any brook, and only from one-quarter to two-thirds as wide as the Mississippi." The Tiber "is not so long, nor yet so wide, as the American Mississippi." In the Holy Land, at "the fountain they call Ain-et-Tin, a hundred yards from ruined Capernaum," Twain mocked the way that "every rivulet that gurgles out of the rocks and sands of this part of the world is dubbed with the title of 'fountain,' and people familiar with the Hudson, the great lakes and the Mississippi fall into transports of admiration over them, and exhaust their powers of composition in writing their praises." The Nile "is muddy, swift and turbid, and does not lack a great deal of being as wide as the Mississippi." Only the pyramids measured up, as Twain dug into memories of childhood and the river to find something commensurate to the sense of awe that ancient Egypt generated: "The first time I ever went down the Mississippi, I thought the highest bluff on the river between St. Louis and New Orleans—it was near Selma, Missouri—was probably the highest mountain in the world. It is four hundred and thirteen feet high. It still looms in my memory with undiminished grandeur. [. . .] In still earlier years than those I have been recalling, Holliday's Hill, in our town, was to me the noblest work of God. It appeared to pierce the skies. It was nearly three hundred feet high. [. . .] Still, that mountain, prodigious as it was, was nothing to the Pyramid of Cheops."[5] In *Roughing It,* too, the Mississippi remained his benchmark for waterways: "People accustomed to the monster mile-wide Mississippi, grow accustomed to associating the term 'river' with a high degree of watery grandeur. Consequently, such people feel rather disappointed when they stand on the shores of the Humboldt or the Carson and find that a 'river' in Nevada is a sickly rivulet." *Roughing It* also announced another dimension of Twain's river life to his readers—his steamboating past: "I was a good average St. Louis and New Orleans pilot and by no means ashamed of my abilities in that line; wages were two hundred and fifty dollars a month and no board to pay, and I did long to stand behind a wheel again and never roam any more."[6] Writing to Horace Bixby in 1870, he concluded the letter with a reaffirmation of his first love: "I would rather be a pilot than anything I ever tried."[7]

As Twain moved closer to a sustained engagement with his essential subject, trying out various poses as a writer, his correspondence also rehearsed some of the descriptions of the Mississippi that would soon make their way into his river writings. To Will Bowen, rifts healed, he delivered an encomium to the steamboat pilot that would echo throughout his career: "I hold those old river friends above all others, & I know that in genuine *manliness* they assay away above the common multitude. You know, yourself, Bill—or you *ought* to know it—that *all* men—kings & serfs alike—are *slaves* to other men & to circumstances—save, alone, the pilot—who comes at no man's beck or call, obeys no man's orders & scorns all men's suggestions. [. . .] It is a strange study,—a singular phenomenon, if you please, that the only real, independent & genuine gentlemen in the world go quietly up & down the Mississippi river, asking no homage of any one, seeking no popularity, no notoriety, & not caring a damn whether school keeps or not."[8] In a letter to Livy while on tour in January 1872, a note of nostalgia crept in as he described the riverfront in Steubenville, Ohio, and began the process of imaginatively condemning the steamboat world of his youth to a gilded past: "These windows overlook the Ohio—once alive with steamboats & crowded with all manner of traffic; but now a deserted stream, victim of the railroads. Where be the pilots. They were starchy boys, in my time, & greatly envied by the youth of the West. The same with the Mississippi pilots—though the Mobile & Ohio Railroad had already walked suddenly off with the passenger business in my day, & so it was the beginning of the end." That his memory was tending backwards to the river years is also confirmed by an account of Twain's conversation at a dinner after a lecture he gave at Amherst College in February 1872: "He kept the company in the best of humor by narrating some of his experiences in piloting on the Mississippi."[9]

By the end of the year, Twain would begin work on his first novel, *The Gilded Age* (1873), a collaboration with Charles Dudley Warner that would see Twain's initial extended imaginative use of the Mississippi. In the autumn of 1874, Twain would turn to his memories of piloting to produce his first Mississippi masterpiece, "Old Times on the Mississippi," serialized in the *Atlantic Monthly* by his new friend William Dean Howells. He wouldn't return to the physical river in those years—nor for almost a decade to come. Instead, he would finally come to understand the full imaginative potential of the Mississippi in Hartford, Connecticut, as he became a part of the Nook Farm community, neighbors with the likes of Warner and Harriet Beecher Stowe, and built the lavish, eccentric house that would become his most iconic, and happiest, dwelling. The house itself, at least to some observers, smacked a little of the river too. In Michael Egan's words, some of the design notes seemed to echo the aesthetics of the river craft of the Mississippi and thus "revealed the paradox at the centre of his personality and marriage: the awkwardly reconciled elements of steamboat and middle class establishment."[10]

At least for some witnesses, the fragrance of the river that still clung to Twain had other meanings. In the early 1870s, at the same time that Twain met Thomas Bailey Aldrich, he also met his wife, Lilian. They swiftly developed a mutually enjoyable distaste for each other ("a strange and vanity-devoured, detestable woman!" Twain concluded in 1908).[11] Lilian had the last word, though, in her description of Twain in her 1920 memoir, *Crowding Memories:* "The years which Mr. Clemens had passed on the Mississippi, and the rough life in California, lacked greatly the refining influence of a different civilization. With that sharp schooling he had become too well acquainted with all the coarser types of human nature." Twain himself was sometimes provoked to play up to this image, revealing knowledge of a cultural history, alien to his new friends and neighbors, in which the river was closely concerned. In respectable Hartford, surrounded by the lights of literary Boston, Twain would put on his own one-man minstrel shows. Once, when the Howellses and Aldriches were visiting, he launched into a particularly memorable performance, though whether he was drawing from childhood memories, his years on the river, minstrel shows, or an amalgam of all of those worlds is unclear. Lilian Aldrich described the way that Twain "with most sober and smileless face [. . .] twisted his angular body into all the strange contortions known to the dancing darkies of the South."[12] In Howells's recollection of the event, Twain performed the role of "a crippled colored uncle to the joy of all beholders."[13] Both remembered his cowskin slippers.

As a rich seam of material, as nostalgia, as eccentricity, as cultural heritage (his own and others), even as social stigma as he sought an ambiguous respectability, Twain's years on the Mississippi took on a variety of personal meanings for him at this moment, just as his literary river began to flow through the floodplains of his imagination. Yet although he would soon become its most famous avatar, Twain was not the only one rediscovering the river in these years of national recovery and reconstruction. It was a time of flux in the fortunes of the Mississippi—the encroachment of the railroads on passenger and freight traffic was already underway—and a time when the meaning of the river was being debated by a variety of voices. At the moment that Americans turned to their country and its landscape with fresh interest, in the wake of the Civil War, the Mississippi frequently encapsulated the often contradictory tensions and trends running through the nation. Representations of the river across a variety of media—from travel accounts to popular prints—multiplied during Reconstruction and helped to foster a nascent sense of reunion. Recently a major battlefield, the postwar river became an important route to the defeated South and a conspicuous location in the pioneering internal travel accounts that proliferated during this decade. Frequently, its waters were freighted with a spirit of nostalgia for life—particularly southern life—before the war. The memory of slavery, which had once been synonymous with a trip down the Mississippi, was increasingly elided from these melancholic visions of river life.

At the same moment, the Mississippi became a fertile environment for an array of pioneering writers who, at a literary crossroads, profoundly implicated the river in the early development of a realist aesthetic. Many of them, like John Hay and William Dean Howells, were intimately involved with Twain during this period. Throughout, bolstered by national interest in steamboat races and other important events in the life of the river, the Mississippi also became characterized as a space of white male power and play and by a style of rugged and capable masculinity best encapsulated by the figure that Twain embodied and would soon frequently evoke: the Mississippi steamboat pilot. In short, just before Twain made his major interventions in its imaginative life, the river performed a great deal of cultural work as the nation reordered itself in the wake of the war. As Twain made his way back to the river, the Mississippi had a vital role to play in the cultural reconstruction of America. Walter Blair recognized many years ago that when Twain finally turned to the river in earnest, "he had gravitated toward a popular subject," not broached a new one.[14] Yet the implications of that statement still require significant elaboration. What did the Mississippi mean to Americans when they finally began their journey on Twain's river in *The Gilded Age* and his *Atlantic* articles?

"Even the Mississippi Seems to Realize Her Rule Is Over"

The Civil War changed life on the Mississippi profoundly. The Mississippi's value as a symbol of American wealth and enterprise was already diminishing. Even before the war suspended the river's commercial activities, the steamboat trade was under pressure from the burgeoning force of the railroads—

what Louis C. Hunter described as "the beginning of the trend which within a few years was to relegate steamboats to a minor role in the economic life of the West."[15] Postwar, that transfer of power intensified quickly: the total mileage of America's railroad network more than doubled from 1865 to 1873. Symbolically and commercially, America was now riding on rails to the West. In Richard White's terms, "Railroads defined the age," just as the rise of the steamboat had helped to characterize the antebellum years.[16]

A vital moment in this process, widely trumpeted throughout American culture, was James Buchanan Eads's construction of a bridge over the Mississippi at St. Louis. Eads—visionary engineer, entrepreneur, and one of the most celebrated river characters of the postwar period—had established his reputation on the Mississippi in the prewar decades. Starting as a steamboat's mud clerk in the late 1830s, he moved to the construction and operation of salvage boats and diving bells on the river, hauling up cargoes from sunken steamboats. During the war, he gained a national profile building ironclad gunboats that helped to secure the river for the Union. Then, from 1867 to its official opening on the Fourth of July 1874, Eads was the mastermind behind the construction of a brick and steel bridge—pioneering in its methods and materials—over the Mississippi River at St. Louis. As Christopher Morris explains, the triumphant symbolic value of this achievement was profound: "He accomplished this feat five years *after* the completion of the first transcontinental railroad. For five years, West and East remained divided not by mountains or deserts or plains, but by a mile-wide ribbon of water."[17] It was, unreservedly, a marvel of the age: an awestruck correspondent for the *New York Times* described the structure as "without doubt, the eighth wonder of the world."[18] Walt Whitman, in St. Louis in 1879, was equally entranced, noting in *Specimen Days & Collect* (1882): "I have haunted the river every night lately, where I could get a look at the bridge by moonlight. It is indeed a structure of perfection and beauty unsurpassable, and I never tire of it."[19]

When A. S. Twombly went to visit the bridge for *Scribner's Monthly* in 1871, however, he struck a different note. He immediately discerned "a certain poetic sadness [. . .] a sentiment excited by the contrast between the present and the past" accompanying the "admiration" that the construction inspired. As Twombly saw it, he was witness to a profound shift in power from the river—"the mistress of the West"—to the railroad "that to-day flings chains about the captive queen of rivers, and, like Augustus, hopes to lead the Cleopatra of the

West in triumph." Part of the reason for the river's subjugation was the reorientation of national life itself: "Westward flows the stream of human life on this continent. No highways leading north or south can possibly compete in the race for fortune with those tending towards the setting sun." For Twombly, therefore, "even the Mississippi seems to realize her rule is over [. . .]. Within a year the Mississippi will be at the mercy of her conquerors. She may grind her sands in rage, and lash her sides in wrath, but never again can she be called, in the old sense, the autocrat of western prosperity."[20]

Yet the river was also gaining a new symbolic value, specifically linked to its role connecting North and South. The nostalgia inherent in Twombly's lament for the river would be a vital aspect of its new place in the national imagination. This shift in the Mississippi's meaning was vividly discernible in a series of images of the river released by the popular New York printmaking firm of Currier & Ives in the late 1860s and early 1870s. Indeed, the company even released a print to commemorate the opening of Eads's bridge. The most iconic of its numerous river pictures, though, were the work of one artist, Frances "Fanny" Palmer, a British immigrant. Her name may never have been as famous as Stowe's, but her work was almost as ubiquitous: "It is likely that during the latter half of the nineteenth century more pictures by Mrs. Fanny Palmer decorated the homes of ordinary Americans than those of any other artist, dead or alive."[21] Like Stowe, Palmer had never seen the Mississippi itself, but her imagined depictions of life on and along its waters must be counted as some of the most influential renderings of the river at this pivotal moment. Palmer's stock-in-trade, before and after the war, were iconic steamboat prints—images like A Midnight Race on the Mississippi (1860), "Wooding Up" on the Mississippi (1863), The Champions of the Mississippi (1866), and "Rounding a Bend" on the Mississippi (1866). These are dramatic and exhilarating imaginings of American industrial might: the sublime craft fill the frame, dwarfing even the giant river (apparently rendered to a scale commensurate with Palmer's knowledge of Old World rivers), reinvigorating the steamboat as a powerful symbol of national confidence while simultaneously projecting a deep nostalgia for a golden age that fast seemed to be slipping away.

At the end of the war, Palmer moved away from that formula, producing two diptychs that used the river to tell a more complicated version of the story. A month before Lee's surrender at Appomattox, in 1865, Currier & Ives released Palmer's The Mississippi in Time of Peace and The Mississippi in Time *of War.* In the first image, the viewer was presented with a vibrant scene of (apparently) antebellum river life: as the setting sun bathes the landscape in golden light, the river is crowded with steamboats, flatboats, and other craft; plantation houses are visible on the bank. Then the war comes. Palmer's second image is an extraordinary evocation of conflict, devastation, and death. Night has fallen, and a fearsome Union ironclad now commands the middle of the river. It is in the process of systematically destroying everything from the former scene—steamboats burn, flatboats sink, plantation houses crumble. The Mississippi has become a river of fire. But if the image lays the blame for the war at the door—or the river—of the South, it also arguably contains within it a nostalgic glance backward to the antebellum plantation.

From fire to flood—the same nostalgia can be read in the second pair of Palmer's prints, *"Low Water" in the Mississippi* and *"High Water" in the Mississippi,* both released in 1868. While this time the destruction on display is ostensibly natural, it is difficult not to see the river's floodwaters as an allegory for the destruction of war. In *Low Water,* Palmer sketches another plantation idyll: the viewer is drawn to the slave cabins in the foreground, evidently inspired by both Stowe and, in its benign rendition of slavery, the minstrel stage. After the deluge—or, we might say, after the war—the destruction of the plantation landscape means that the same slave family from the first image has been cast out of its former happy home, drifting into an uncertain future. The imagined Mississippi of Frances Palmer, displayed in homes throughout the nation, was prescient in its sympathies and its symbolism. Others would soon turn to the river as an escape into an imagined and idealized prewar South.

In 1870, the famous steamboat race between the *Robert E. Lee,* built in 1866 for John W. Cannon, and the *Natchez,* built for Thomas P. Leathers in 1869, crystallized many of the issues nascent in both the interpretation of Eads's bridge and Palmer's prints. The race provided a potent spectacle that was followed throughout America. Cannon and Leathers were both famous figures on the river and had a notoriously fraught personal history. The legends of Leathers and the steamboat dynasty that he sired, particularly, would echo down the years. In November 1868, for example, the *Cincinnati Daily Gazette* reported a "personal encounter" between the pair in New Orleans about a business matter.[22] Almost as soon as the *Natchez* was ready to work the river, newspapers began to stoke the rivalry between the two men. Asked by a reporter what he thought about the "great deal of talk" suggesting that Leathers's new boat would break the *Lee's* speed records, Cannon replied "sarcastically," "I suppose she will beat us." Pushed for more, Cannon became "somewhat spirited": "She may pass the Lee, but they will think she is ten miles long before they go by her."[23]

Such provocation finally brought about a contest: the *Natchez* and the *Lee* both set out from New Orleans, bound for St. Louis, on June 30. America was watching. The race was front-page news in New Orleans, where the *Picayune*, with correspondents on both boats and pundits providing commentary, eagerly declared: "Never before in New Orleans has there been such excitement regarding a steamboat race [. . .]. Every whisper is caught up, iterated and reiterated until the wildest rumors as to the positions of the two steamers are circulated and received as truth. Enormous sums of money have been staked."[24] Spectators came out in the thousands along the river, and many more followed along at home. The event was "reported throughout the country in one of the most extensive telegraphic accounts of any nonpolitical event prior to that time."[25] The *New York Times*, one prominent example of many, provided regular updates about the progress of the "Mississippi steamers testing their powers" from points all along the river.[26]

The men at the center of the competition received as much attention as their boats, as exemplified by the vignette captured by the admiring correspondent for the *Memphis Avalanche* on board the *Lee:* "The engineer, of course, was at his post with corrugated brow and compressed lip, a flat eye sharply set and a hand oily and bony, but steady as if its nerves were made of steel [. . .]. Then the pilot was away aloft looking ahead with practiced and steady vision, and guiding the rapid course of the boat with confident and artistic touch. Capt. Cannon [. . .] spares not his oaths, but his voice is not loud nor his talk voluble. He wants to win the race."[27] And he did. The *Robert E. Lee* was victorious, arriving in St. Louis on the morning of July 4, roughly three days and eighteen hours after its departure. In the middle of its report on the celebrations following Cannon's triumph, the *Cincinnati Daily Gazette* reported the presence of one prominent individual: "J. B. Eads, the well known bridge man [. . .] was very glad to be acquainted with the man who had the honour to command such a boat as the Lee."[28] At the banquet thrown for Cannon and Leathers at the Southern Hotel in St. Louis, complete with "sugar representations of the Natchez and the Lee" and with Robert E. Lee's daughter in attendance, one speaker offered up a plea for "never ending harmony between the North and South"—as if the excitement generated by a race between two southern steamboats pointedly named for people and places of the Confederacy could, like the Mississippi itself, act as a bond between old enemies.[29]

On some level, it clearly did. The race generated sufficient widespread appeal for Currier & Ives to release a number of prints commemorating the event, the most famous of which, *The Great Mississippi Steamboat Race* (fig. 2), was a reworking of Frances Palmer's 1860 image, *A Midnight Race on the Mississippi*. The Stars and Stripes now flew conspicuously from the *Robert E. Lee*. A contemporary gloss for these machines in the Mississippi's garden might be found in a breathless meditation on the race and the river published in the *St. Louis Republican*, a telling blend of the pastoral and the industrial: "The Mississippi [. . .] yellow as liquid gold, sweeps through the heart of a rare garden such as earth can not match [. . .]. Along the borders of this paradise [. . .] the Lee and the Natchez fly onward like uncaged eagles [. . .]. Night and day, day and night, the tireless muscles of steel and steam toil on, struggling for final victory [. . .]. If song and story, marble and canvas have given deathless fame to the Olympic games of Greece and the gladiatorial shows of Rome, some small meed of praise may surely be awarded to these marine athletes racing on the Mississippi for the laurel crown."[30] Even those who were less enamored with the event provided other clues to its appeal. The *New York Times*, though following the race closely, took time to criticize what it described as "a revival of the criminal practice of steam-boat racing, once so prevalent upon Western rivers."[31] The hint of nostalgia embedded even within this lament highlights the degree to which—as with Eads's bridge and Palmer's pictorial river—a retrospective quality underpinned this moment. These icons of industrial power, burning brightly for one last time, were inevitably fading into history, increasingly valuable as symbols of myth rather than modernity. In turn, the river was becoming a place of imaginative escape and adventure, of masculine endeavor, and a gateway to burnished memories of flush times before the Civil War—all of which had implications for Twain's first steps back to the river.

"Countless Rhines and Many Danubes"

The river's numerous appearances in postbellum travel writing added their own nuances to these tropes. The Mississippi had, of course, been a prominent location in antebellum travel accounts of America—particularly those

FIGURE 2. [After Frances Palmer], *The Great Mississippi Steamboat Race*
(New York: Currier & Ives, 1870).

written by European travelers who often found little to love in its waters and
who used the river as an unflattering looking glass for American mores and
manners. The postwar decade, however, saw a distinct shift in the nature of
internal tourism and in the reputation of the Mississippi. In deeply influential
publications like *Picturesque America* (1872, 1874) and Edward King's account
of *The Great South* (1875), the river would be aesthetically rehabilitated, im-
bued with a new romance, and entangled in the reconciliatory motivations
that underpinned such projects.

In the immediate aftermath of the war, the Mississippi featured prominently in the pioneering journeys of northern journalist-travelers touring the
defeated South in 1865 and 1866. Inevitably, the recent conflict indelibly colored their accounts of the river. "Descending the Mississippi," declared John
Trowbridge (later a friend of Twain's), "the first point of interest you pass
is Davis's Bend, the former home of the President of the Confederacy [. . .]
now used as a Home Farm for colored paupers." Since the primary concerns
of these travelers were political and sociological, the cabin of a Mississippi

steamboat provided them with a crucial contact zone in which to study the defeated enemy. "I made the acquaintance of all sorts of Southern people," Trowbridge declared about his time on the river. What he and his colleagues heard was not always edifying. Trowbridge's description of his unreconstructed fellow travelers was particularly condemnatory: "The majority were Mississippi and Arkansas planters going down the river to their estates: a strongly marked, unrefined, rather picturesque class,—hard swearers, hard drinkers, inveterate smokers and chewers [. . .]. How shall I describe the conversation of these men? Never a word did I hear fall from the lips of one of them concerning literature or the higher interests of life; but their talk was of mules, cotton, niggers, money, Yankees, politics, and the Freedmen's Bureau."[32] While Whitelaw Reid (another future friend of Twain) echoed such judgments during his account of the South, the social space provided by a journey on the river afforded him moments that were more reconciliatory. "On a Mississippi steamboat, one evening," he described, "I encountered an intelligent, substantial-looking Arkansas planter, hirsute, and clad in Confederate gray. [. . .] I soon discovered that the companion, with whom I was passing an idle evening in talk about planting and politics, was the Rebel General, E. C. Cahell. [. . .] He was giving the free-labor experiment a fair trial; and risking upon it pretty nearly all he was worth."[33]

It would, once again, be the spirit of reunion, embryonic in Reid's text, that would frequently come to dominate travel accounts of the river. As Nina Silber has described, the postwar decade was the moment during which tourism became "a mass industry," and "tourism and reconciliation often went hand in hand."[34] These journeys were accompanied by a new proliferation of travel accounts: as Richard Brodhead has highlighted, the "great staple" of postwar journals, "the virtually mandatory item in their program of offerings," was "the short piece of touristic or vacationistic prose, the piece that undertakes to locate some little known place far away and makes it visitable in print."[35] The South featured heavily in both developments: for Sue Rainey, such accounts "anticipated the return of a recovering South to national life," since American readers "wanted information about a region that had been largely off limits for more than a decade, but which held special attractions."[36]

The Mississippi was deeply involved in these trends too. Evidently, the river could and did incarnate the idea of reunion. A contributor to the *Ladies' Repository* in March 1873 caught this mood. "The Mississippi River," she explained, "is not, to a reasoning mind, merely a stream of water [. . .]. It may be regarded as a sign, given by the Creator, that the people inhabiting this country should always be one nation. It is a symbol stamped into the surface of the earth, and its import to the American people is UNION and PEACE."[37] A journey from North to South along the Mississippi—whether real or textual— could provide a similarly unifying panorama of American life and landscape at this pivotal moment. At the same time, it was one that still recognized and enshrined regional differences.

One of the most influential postbellum publications in this regard was the *Picturesque America* project—first a series of articles in *Appletons' Journal* in 1870, later collected in two richly illustrated volumes in 1872 and 1874. An enormously popular set of publications—Rainey suggests that as many as one million copies were sold through subscription—they did much to precipitate the postbellum vogue for American scenes.[38] *Picturesque America*, significantly, featured two separate chapters on the Mississippi. They were both illustrated by Alfred Waud, an artist who had achieved renown with his illustrations of the Civil War for *Harper's Weekly* and who happened to be another British émigré whose work would prove highly influential on the visual life of the river at this moment. In his essay on the Upper Mississippi above St. Louis, Rodolphe E. Garczynski—after a nod to Eads's bridge, "magnificent [. . .] one of the largest and handsomest in the world"—waxed highly romantic about the river's place in the national imagination. "In the description of American scenery," he declared, "the Mississippi River, as of royal right, claims a leading place. It is our Nile, our mythic stream." Sounding a nationalistic note in opposition to both lingering European visions of the river and the contemporary vogue for European travel, Garczynski staked a claim for American scenery along the Upper Mississippi: "This [. . .] place ought to be visited by every painter and poet in America, and should become the headquarters of everyone who loves the scenery of his country, during the summer months. It is a grief that Americans should wander off to the Rhine and the Danube when, in the Mississippi, they have countless Rhines and many Danubes."[39] His exhortations had been anticipated by the first tourist guide to the river above St. Louis, published in 1866, which rhapsodized about the Upper Mississippi's "varied beauties of the most romantic and picturesque character."[40]

The Lower Mississippi, described in an essay by southwestern humorist Thomas Bangs Thorpe, was a different story. Thorpe's vision was firmly regional in its focus. He asserted that the apparent "sameness and monotony" of much of the Lower Mississippi actually belied a profound and "mysterious interest [. . .] a sort of awe which it is difficult to define or account for."[41] In elucidating and shaping that enigmatic appeal, Thorpe's text exemplified much travel writing about the South at this moment. To borrow Silber's terms, the Lower Mississippi of *Picturesque America* becomes a typically southern space of "leisure, relaxation and romance," a place marked out by "distinctive" scenery and landscape and the "familiar features of the antebellum legend" of the South.[42] The exotic and the romantic are privileged. "The magnolia-tree, in full blossom," he writes, in a typically lush passage, "with the Spanish moss enshrouding it in a gray, neutral haze, makes a superb picture." The residences visible from the Mississippi, until recently the landscape of slavery, become intoxicating Edenic spaces: "Hedges of jasmine lead up the door-ways of the planters' residences, and vie in fragrance with the flowing pomegranate and night-blooming cereus [. . .]. At nightfall [. . .] the atmosphere predisposes to lassitude and dreamy repose."[43] For Thorpe, as for others, the Mississippi was already understood to be a gateway to a deeply nostalgic and romanticized South loaded with Lost Cause associations.

Appletons' pioneering *Hand-Book of American Travel: Southern Tour*—one of a series of travel guides evidently released to complement the publication of *Picturesque America*—succinctly described the river's revivified reputation and its multifaceted place in the American landscape, simultaneously representing both reunion and regionalism: "There is no river scenery of the world more picturesque and beautiful than that of the upper section of the Mississippi, from St. Paul to the mouth of the Missouri. Travellers have truly said, however, that the scenery of the Lower Mississippi lacks both grandeur and beauty; but there is no scenery on earth more striking."[44] It was, in short, "the grandest river-trip the world affords"—or, as another commentator put it in 1872, speaking for many more, "one of the mighty curiosities of the Western Continent [. . .] one of the wonders of the Universe."[45]

However, the renewed appeal of a journey along the Mississippi was not simply located in the diverse sights and scenes along its banks. Life on board a western steamboat, particularly life among the men who worked on those boats, was a topic of fascination in the early 1870s. It was a theme that provided travelers with a unifying figure that, at least ostensibly, transcended some of the dichotomies and regional differences that were attached to the river itself. When George Ward Nichols headed "down the Mississippi" for *Harper's New Monthly Magazine* in 1870, he felt so confident in his readers' knowledge of life on the river that he began his description of steamboat design with an acknowledgment that he was "at the risk of telling many [. . .] readers what they will know as well as I." But he made no apologies for devoting space to another topic. "The mention of the officers who control the movements of the boat is necessary to our narrative," Nichols asserted, before outlining the complex racial and gendered hierarchies of a steamboat: "They are the captain [. . .] then there are the two pilots; the clerk, to whom we all go for everything we wish; two mates, of whose harsh voices and terrible looks we have more fear, probably, than the forty or fifty dark-skinned deck-hands, toward whom they are usually directed; there are the engine-drivers, coal-heavers, cooks, waiters, barbers, porters, laundresses, and last, but not least, Spencer, our good-natured, handy, irrepressible cabin-boy, who is blacker than darkest night." Though "all the incidents which go to make up human life and society are represented on this steamboat of ours," the real point of interest for Nichols was clear. "Of all that belongs to life on our great Western rivers," he outlined, "the business and experiences of the pilots interest me most. Truly, must he be a man of rare and natural gifts of memory of localities, quick observing comprehension, a sure hand, rapid judgement, determination of will, iron nerve, even temper, and good habits."

In particular, Nichols was deeply impressed with the art of steamboat navigation (in ways that prefigure Twain's approach to the subject in "Old Times on the Mississippi"): "I stand by the side of our pilot, and watch with curious interest the movement of the boat. To my eye the surface of the water is all the same, and there appears no reason why a course should not be pursued straight down the stream [. . .] but suddenly the large wheel whirls swiftly around [. . .]. First one side, and then the other, until your wits are fairly puzzled, and you are almost willing to believe that the pilot is a sham, or that he has some insight beyond that of human ken, which permits him to pursue his dangerous way among snags and shoals and sand-bars with perfect certainty and safety." Nichols boggled at the "prodigious effort of the memory" that the process required. By way of explanation of the mysteries of his profession, the pilot informed him: "Well, it's sort of instinct [. . .] I can tell something by the color of the water, something by its motion, and something in the habits of the beast; and between 'em all I manage to find my way."[46] Thomas Cooper de Leon, in his account of "A Western River-Race" for *Appletons'* in 1872, was equally fascinated with his boat's pilot, "a rough old river-dog, weather-beaten, battered, and grim—a man with a huge thirst carefully controlled, and an amazing aptitude for destroying [. . .] tobacco"—and with his distinctive turns of profane phrase: "D—nation! I'll overstep her yit, or *bust!*"[47]

Not all portraits of river men were encomiums. A vivid counterpoint can be found in the work of John Morris (writing as John O'Connor)—an itinerant gambler who published a memoir–cum–travel account, *Wanderings of a Vagabond*, in 1873. Morris flatly declares the Mississippi "a disappointment," a journey on its waters "dreary monotony." But far more trenchant criticisms were directed at steamboat life: in Morris's blistering critique, the heroic monarchs of the Mississippi were characterized as brutal tyrants: "In those palmy days, steamboat officers did what seemed good in their own sight, with none to molest or make them afraid. [. . .] The mate or engineer who could wield a billet of wood or a bar of iron the most scientifically on the heads of deck-hands, firemen and deck-passengers, was considered 'a regular screamer,' and received the highest wages. [. . .] To those of wealth and influence the most slavish attention was shown [. . .]. Deck passengers were stowed like hogs on the lower deck of the steamer, where they were made to feel all the degradation of poverty [. . .]. High old times were these on the Mississippi River."[48] Morris's voice was aberrant, though. The work that best exemplified the Mississippi's role in postwar travel narratives—the most influential travel account published in the immediate postbellum period—contained no such ambiguities. What's more, it drew a clear line of connection between the river and Mark Twain, just before Twain explored and exploited that apparently "virgin subject" himself. Edward King's *The Great South* began life as a series of sketches for *Scribner's Magazine* in July 1873, before being collected in a single volume in 1875 by Elisha Bliss's American Publishing Company, Mark Twain's publisher at that moment. The Mississippi—both as conduit and subject—was given significant space in King's text, organizing much of his time in the South. Throughout, it provided King with "a perpetual succession of novel episodes." Deep in Louisiana, for example, the river transported him to a southern reverie that outstripped even Thorpe: "Some evening, just as sunset is upon the green land and the broad stream, you stand high up in the pilot-house [. . .]. You may almost believe yourself removed out of the sphere of worldly care, and sailing to some haven of profoundest peace."[49] Like Nichols, what King also implicitly underscored, characteristically adopting what Silber terms "the picturesque formula" when writing about black Americans, were the racial hierarchies that underpinned the privileged view from the pilothouse:[50] "Down below, the firemen labor at the seven great furnaces, and throw into them cords on cords of wood, tons on tons of coal; the negroes on the watch scrub the decks, or trundle cotton bales from one side of the boat to the other, or they lie listlessly by the low rails of the prow, blinking and shuffling and laughing with their own rude grace. Above, the magic perfume from the thickets filled with blossoms is always drifting, and the long lines of green islets bathed by the giant stream, pass by in rapid panorama."[51] King's portrait of the pleasures of river travel, particularly his sense of the river as a magical passage to a lost South, was undeniably influential, at home and abroad.

Up near St. Louis, after a mandatory visit to Eads's bridge ("He knows the Mississippi as well as any one can know that most capricious and uncertain of streams"), it was the men in the pilothouse that captured King's attention. Traveling on the *Great Republic*—"a floating palace"—he ascended to the steamboat's sanctum sanctorum, a potent viewpoint also vividly depicted by King's illustrator, James Wells Champney (fig. 3). "The pilots," King described, "perched in their cosy cage, twisted the wheel, and told us strange stories. [. . .] They are men of great energy, of quaint, dry humor, and fond of spinning yarns." One particular former pilot was singled out by King for pointed comment: "The genial 'Mark Twain' served his apprenticeship as pilot, and one of his old companions and tutors, now on the 'Great Republic,' gave us reminiscences of the humorist. One sees, on a journey down the Mississippi, where Mark found many of his queerest and seemingly impossible types."[52] This prominent allusion to Twain's life on the river was originally published in *Scribner's* in October 1874, the very same month that Twain wrote to Howells pitching "Old Times on the Mississippi" for publication in the *Atlantic*.[53] Walter Blair judged that "it was barely possible that this very passage started the author reminiscing"; it certainly seems implausible that Twain would not have been aware of this reference to his steamboating past.[54] But whether or not King directly inspired Twain, it still helped to establish his authority in relation to the river in the literary marketplace. Moreover, King's account also helped to enshrine the steamboat pilot as a rugged, garrulous, capable icon of

FIGURE 3. James Wells Champney, "The Pilot-House of the 'Great Republic,'" in Edward King, *The Great South* (Hartford, Conn.: American Publishing Co., 1875), 261.

white Gilded Age masculinity, pointedly perched at the top of a racial hierarchy. When Twain came to the river as a subject, he also moved to enshrine himself as an embodiment of these tropes.

Nor was King the only one publicizing Twain's steamboat career around this moment. In early December 1874, apparently unaware of Twain's forthcoming series for the *Atlantic*, Twain's old California friend William Wright (better known as Dan De Quille) wrote "Pilot Wylie," what he described as "a Mississippi river sketch," which also mentioned Mark Twain by name as a steamboat pilot.[55] It was reprinted in the *Hartford Daily Courant* on February 8, 1875, and may well have inspired Twain's own memories of Pilot Wylie in "Old Times on the Mississippi."[56]

"Natives of the Same Vast Mississippi Valley"

For Twain in 1875, the Mississippi provided a point of connection to the members of an informal and influential coterie of literary men—men who had also grown up around the steamboat trade—who were pushing toward a new concern for literary verisimilitude. The Mississippi featured frequently in their work as both setting and subject. Indeed, the river arguably became a space that telegraphed in and of itself a certain set of literary values. At the heart of this group, as both editor and author, was William Dean Howells. In ways that have seldom been acknowledged, the Western Rivers were at the heart of Howells's own life and work. As he himself pointed out in *My Mark Twain* (1910), "We were natives of the same vast Mississippi Valley; and Missouri was not so far from Ohio but that we were akin in our first knowledges."[57] Edwin Cady, in the only sustained consideration of this aspect of Howells's life, work, and context, asserted that "Howells knew steamboating [. . .]. River experience played a role in the drama of his inner life. He wrote, early and late, a definite if small corpus of river literature."[58] As editor, he would encourage a variety of writers—Twain included—to push toward a new realist aesthetic using the Mississippi itself as both backdrop and theme.

The Western Rivers bookended Howells's own literary career. In 1858, recovering from one of the periodic nervous episodes that afflicted his younger years, he took passage on one of his uncle's steamboats. He traveled down the Ohio to St. Louis, publishing nine letters describing the journey in the *Ashtabula (Ohio) Sentinel*. On the Mississippi, he evinced a distinct preference for the river of his youth: "None of the lovely hills that make the upper Ohio so gloriously picturesque, are to be seen; and for miles and miles, the eye rests only on broad expanses of river, terminating in thick, unwholesome looking forests." What captured his attention, though, was slavery. "The first thing for which I looked about me with interest," he wrote, upon his arrival in St. Louis, "was some indication that I was in the metropolis of a slave state." Elsewhere on the river, looking toward the Kentucky shore, he described "many cabins of Uncle Tom."[59] This journey and these observations undoubtedly fed into the poem that provided Howells with his debut in the *Atlantic* in 1860: "The Pilot's Story" was a melodramatic and romantic tale, consciously echoing Longfellow's *Evangeline* (1847), narrated by a steamboat pilot on the Mississippi. A planter gambles away his slave mistress, who is also mother to his children. Confronted with her fate, she leaps to her death in the river, leaving both the pilot and the Mississippi haunted by her memory and their complicity in her death:

"This is the place where it happened," brokenly whispered the pilot.
"Somehow, I never like to go by here alone in the night-time."
Darkly the Mississippi flowed by the town that lay in the starlight [. . .].
All was serene and calm, but the odorous breath of the willows
Smote like the subtile breath of an infinite sorrow upon us.[60]

Though the river shifted from the center of Howells's creative vision, the Mississippi was still a presence in his first novel, *Their Wedding Journey* (1871). Involved in a steamboat accident on the Hudson River during the course of his honeymoon, Basil March comments flippantly, "They manage better on the Mississippi and both boats often go down without waking the lightest sleeper on board."[61] Before receiving Twain's pitch for "Old Times on the Mississippi" in October 1874, therefore, Howells was well primed by both deep life experience and his own writing career to understand the potential value of the Mississippi as an imaginative space. He was certainly not alone.

Of the other "natives of the same vast Mississippi Valley" turning to the river at this moment, the work of John Hay—writer, journalist, statesman, diplomat—arguably did the most to establish the place of the Mississippi in postbellum literature, particularly its role in the development of an early realist aesthetic. Hay had grown up along the river in Indiana and Illinois, and the Mississippi took a central role in his pioneering work in the postwar decade. It provided him, for example, with the antebellum setting for a melodramatic short story dealing with the unfinished business of slavery. "The Foster-Brothers," published in *Harper's New Monthly Magazine* in 1869, saw an escaped slave and his erstwhile master encounter each other unexpectedly in a river town, before meeting their end in the Mississippi itself: "The foster-brothers went to the bottom locked in each other's arms."[62]

It was Hay's poetry, though, that had the most profound effect on postwar literature. The pioneering vernacular verses in Hay's *Pike County Ballads* (1871) were extremely popular and deeply influential. As editor and writer George Cary Eggleston remembered decades later, they "were under discussion everywhere. Phrases from them were the current coin of conversation. Critics were curiously studying them as a new and effective form of literature."[63] Of all Hay's ballads, none was more famous than his portrait of a steamboat man, "Jim Bludso (of the Prairie Belle)," first published in the *New York Tri-*

bune on January 5, 1871, and reprinted widely thereafter. The poem tells the sentimental-realist story of a steamboat engineer who "weren't no saint":

> And this was all the religion he had,—
>> To treat his engine well;
> Never be passed on the river,
>> To mind the Pilot's bell.

As the narrator explains, "All boats has their day on the Mississip," and when the *Prairie Belle* explodes while racing on the river (a subject that Twain would turn to in *The Gilded Age*), Jim acts with immediate heroism, sacrificing himself to save others: "I'll hold her nozzle agin the bank / Till the last galoot's ashore." "He weren't no saint," the narrator concludes in the poem's most famous stanza:

> but at jedgement
>> I'd run my chance with Jim,
> 'Longside of some pious gentlemen
>> That wouldn't shook hands with him.
> He seen his duty, a dead-sure thing,—
>> And went for it thar and then:
> And Christ aint a goin' to be too hard
>> On a man that died for men.[64]

The fame of "Jim Bludso" traveled far and wide. The poem was clearly influential in its depiction of life—and particularly men—on the Mississippi. In his account of "A Western River-Race," for example, de Leon noted that the "rough old river-dog" piloting the boat "was cast rather in the Jim Bludso mould."[65] One prominent fan was George Eliot who, at a literary gathering in London, apparently declared "Jim Bludso" to be "one of the finest gems in the English language," before reciting it from memory, "the tears flowing from her eyes as she spoke the closing lines."[66]

Mark Twain, too, was paying attention. He wrote to Hay immediately after the poem's publication with, in Hay's words, "generous commendations"— but also to let him know, as Hay put it, "that I was all wrong making him an engineer,—that only a pilot could have done what I represented him as do-ing." Hay replied agreeably and enthusiastically to Twain, "I think the pilot is a much more appropriate and picturesque personage and should certainly have used him except for the fact that I knew Jim Bludso and he was an engi-neer and did just what I said."[67] The quibble evidently lingered, however. In correspondence with George Cary Eggleston—himself an Indianan—after the turn of the twentieth century, Hay was still defending his decision to make Jim Bludso an engineer. Eggleston responded by telling Hay a story about a similarly heroic pilot that he had heard from the lips of one particularly nota-ble figure from the river's history, closing the circle between life and art: "The details of the story were related to me by Captain John Cannon, of the steamer 'Robert E. Lee,' and the weather-beaten old navigator was not ashamed of the tears that trickled down his cheeks as he told the tale."[68]

Another Eggleston—Edward, brother of George Cary—also turned to life on the river for subject matter in the postwar decade. Edward Eggleston is now best remembered for *The Hoosier Schoolmaster* (1871)—an enormously popular and influential novel dealing with antebellum life in Indiana. As Mark Storey describes, it is also a text that, deeply expressive of its moment (and like Hay's poetry), "sits uneasily between the sentimentality of popular fiction and the emerging self-consciousness of literary realism."[69] Eggleston's next book, *The End of the World* (1872), devoted significant attention to the na-ture of antebellum life on the Western Rivers. The book's noble German hero, August Wehle—disappointed in love, racially abused, and falsely accused of robbery—decides, as one character puts it, "to take to steamboat life in hopes of havin' your sperrits raised by bein' blowed up." In many ways, August's luck does not improve on the river. Employed as a "'striker,' as the engineer's ap-prentice was called," he first makes good progress, allowing Eggleston, echoing the ethos of Jim Bludso, to meditate on his new position: "The alarm-bell rang in the engine-room, and Wehle stood by his engine. [. . .] There is something fine in the faith with which an engineer obeys the bell of the pilot, not know-ing what may be ahead, not inquiring what may be the effect of the order, but only doing exactly what he is bid when he is bid." But Eggleston's picture of life on the river was ultimately a bleak one: gamblers operate on August's steamboat. He tries to break up their dishonest game and ultimately saves one of them from a lynching. His reward is to be unjustly fired, not know-ing that one of his captain's "perquisites" was "a percentage of the gamblers' gains [. . .] and he was not the only steamboat captain who profited by nice little games in the cabin upon which he closed both eyes."[70] Reviewing *The End of the World* for the *Atlantic,* Howells particularly approved of the "great reality in the characters," singling out "the gamblers on the river-steamboat" and the boat's "mud-clerk."[71] Twain, again, was paying attention too, at least to Eggleston's success. While trying to drum up some favorable reviews for *The Gilded Age* in 1873, Twain bristled at the praise being lavished on Eggleston. He clipped one notice that referred to Eggleston's books as "literary events" and "the success of genuineness" and sent it to Whitelaw Reid, then editor of the *New York Tribune,* with certain passages scornfully underlined, noting that Eggleston's latest novel was "an absolutely worthless book."[72]

Howells, Hay, and Eggleston might have known the river as informed laymen, but writers who had actually worked on the Mississippi were also proliferating. John Henton Carter was a St. Louis journalist better known as Commodore Rollingpin because of his time as a cook on a Mississippi steamboat. He, too, was a friend of Twain who would also spend decades writing about the river. In 1872, and for many years afterward, he produced *Commodore Rollingpin's Almanac,* what Lee Ann Sandweiss describes as "an annual of river folklore, humorous sketches, and stories" that sold fifty thousand copies a year at its peak.[73] In 1874, just before Twain's own turn to the river, Carter published *Commodore Rollingpin's Log,* a collection of comic sketches and poems that dealt with a variety of aspects of life on the Mississippi. Carter's renditions of the river—evidently indebted to the world of southwestern humor and the poetry of John Hay—were more anarchic than Twain's "Old Times on the Mississippi" would be: his steamboatmen fight, gamble, and generally like to "go on a spree." He was capable of flights of fancy too: in "Rollingpin's Travels," for example, he embarked on a tour of the "Mississippi River in the year 2000" and dreamed of a time when the river's influence and power would be renewed: when "trans-continental packets [. . .] eight hundred feet in length" would leave St. Paul bound for Liverpool, when the river would have a "uniform depth of twenty feet of water," and when the "days of bridges" would be long gone, the railways banished to tunnels underneath the river—a very different kind of river paradise compared to that of his contemporaries.[74]

Another writer who knew the Mississippi intimately—forgotten now but very significant to Twain and his circle in the early 1870s—was also developing a particular vision of the river at this moment. Ralph Keeler lived a life almost unrivaled for its unlikely twists and turns. Born in Ohio, orphaned at the age of eight, and passed between relatives "very much as wood is loaded upon Mississippi steamboats," Keeler ran away from home at the age of eleven. Thereafter, he scraped together a meager existence as a cabin boy on Lake Erie steamboats before discovering a modicum of fame, if not much fortune, as a "juvenile prodigy of jig-dancing and negro-minstrelsy," traveling the Mississippi on a showboat.[75] Giving up the stage to pursue his education and travel in Europe, he then spent time in San Francisco, where he first met Twain, and started writing. Then, before Twain made the move, he went east, working and writing for a variety of literary publications. Twain remembered in his autobiography that their friendship grew greatly at this moment: "Ralph Keeler was pleasant company on my lecture flights out of Boston, and we had plenty of good talks and smokes in our rooms."[76]

In the late 1860s, encouraged and mentored by William Dean Howells, Keeler's autobiographical accounts of his many and varied adventures started to appear in the pages of the *Atlantic*, before being collected in a single volume, *Vagabond Adventures*, in 1870. It was a work suffused with his experiences of both steamboat life and life on the Mississippi—experiences that differed, in many ways, from other visions of the river circulating at this moment. Keeler enthused about his "early love of" and "boundless affection for [. . .] steamboats," though his time as a cabin boy was largely marked by hardship, seasickness, and exploitation. More agreeable was his time on the famous *Floating Palace* showboat. As Keeler put it, "Some unexpected thing was always happening [. . .]. We saw, indeed, a great deal of wild life [. . .] for we steamed thousands of miles on the Western and Southern rivers." In marked contrast to the developing sense of the Mississippi as a gendered and exclusionary space of masculine mastery, Keeler introduced his readers to an eccentric and anarchic cast of men, women, and children. The showboat's makeshift family—"strange contrasts in human nature," as Keeler put it—was marked out by "a spirit of bohemianism [. . .] a touch of hearty, reckless good-nature" kin to, but ultimately at odds with, other venerations of pilots and engineers at this moment.[77]

Reviewing the book warmly for the *Atlantic*, Howells noted, "That company on the Floating Palace is one that is charming to know through him." Soon Keeler was poised to paint the river again. On May 6, 1871, Thomas Bailey Aldrich's illustrated journal, *Every Saturday*, announced the beginning of a major new series: "Special Artist and Correspondent Mr. A. R. Waud and

Mr. Ralph Keeler [. . .] shall begin a series of Sketches [. . .] entitled ON THE MISSISSIPPI, which will give, in a more graphic manner than has ever been attempted before, the various features of scenery, life, and character along this great national highway."[78] Over the next six months, Keeler and Waud fulfilled that brief, relating their experiences along the river up to St. Louis in lushly illustrated articles. If the journey was likely to have been inspired by *Appletons' Picturesque America* series (Waud, after all, supplied illustrations of the river for both projects), it was itself a clear and unacknowledged precursor to King's voyages through "the Great South" two years later. (Aldrich's editorial interest in this project might also have spoken to his own experiences: he had spent a number of years in New Orleans as a child, and he, too, knew the river, as his early biographer Ferris Greenslet made clear: "In the spring and fall the boy would be taken on trading-trips up and down the Mississippi, and to the end of his life he could vividly recall the weird-flaring torches of the negroes who came down to light their landings.")[79]

Compared to other accounts of the river at this moment, Keeler's description of the Mississippi was far more concerned with the tensions, racial and political, that ran along its length. As in Reid and Trowbridge's earlier accounts of the river, Keeler highlights its recent status as a battlefield. The "monotony" of the Lower Mississippi, he avers, is only alleviated by the "interest [. . .] lent [. . .] by the late war."[80] Though there are moments of picturesque description ("the beautiful Spanish moss, of whose exquisite grace there is no danger of saying too much"), his tone throughout is ironic rather than romantic. Unlike many of his contemporaries, Keeler certainly does little to valorize the various steamboatmen they encounter. A day trip to report on a break in the levee near New Orleans during a flood, for example, ends in farce: "We had not been long under way on our return down the river when we learned that the crew of our little stern-wheeler had [. . .] so far succeeded as to get hopelessly drunk."[81]

The same lightly sardonic approach to life on the river is discernible in an article from the middle of the series entirely devoted to "a day on a Mississippi steamboat." An amalgam of Keeler and Waud's experiences on a variety of different boats, including both the *Natchez* and *Robert E. Lee*, the sketch takes the reader on a tour of steamboat life that candidly acknowledges the discomforts as well as the pleasures of a trip on the river. In Keeler's hands, it is a veritable Vanity Fair—"Perhaps two out of the two or three hundred will be reading; the rest gossip and smoke and flirt"—from breakfast until nightfall. Keeler, though, seems most fascinated by the boat's "stalwart" black roustabouts, their distinctive culture, and their river allegiances (presciently so, since roustabouts would become increasingly central to descriptions of life on the Mississippi in the coming decades): "They love, worship, nothing so much as the fastest boat [. . .]. If they fight it is nine times in ten in support of the opinion that the Lee is faster than the Natchez, or that the Natchez is faster than the Lee." He is no less charmed by a begging "ex-Confederate soldier, who won my sympathy and my dollar by displaying to me the havoc made upon his person by Northern arms." Even after it emerges that his wounds had nothing to do with the war, Keeler admires "the generosity and impudence of the man."[82] It is, perhaps, the closest that he comes to the spirit of reunion. When Keeler mysteriously disappeared in Cuba in December 1873, his distinctive vision of the Mississippi was lost with him.

The peak of Keeler's friendship with Twain came just after his return from the river, while "On the Mississippi" was still being serialized in *Every Saturday*. It can, at the very least, be assumed that the river featured prominently in the "plenty of good talks" the men shared late in 1871. A decade later, Twain would seek out Keeler's *Every Saturday* articles when writing *Life on the Mississippi* (1883).[83] Yet at this moment in the early 1870s, Keeler had another vital role to play for Twain. His old San Francisco acquaintance was also Twain's entry point into much closer communion with Howells and others near the center of the new literary establishment. On November 2, 1871, Keeler hosted a lunch at Louis Ober's restaurant to which Twain was invited. Howells vividly remembered the occasion. Having previously met Twain only briefly in 1869, when he visited the offices of the *Atlantic,* Howells recalled: "The next thing I remember of him is meeting him at a lunch in Boston given us by that genius of hospitality, the tragically destined Ralph Keeler [. . .]. There was T. B. Aldrich, there was J. T. Fields [. . .]; there was Bret Harte, who had lately come East in his princely progress from California." The event was, according to Howells at least, marked by exemplary "good fellowship": "Nothing remains to me of the happy time but a sense of idle and aimless and joyful talk-play, beginning and ending nowhere, of eager laughter, of countless good stories from Fields, of a heat-lightning shimmer of wit from Aldrich, of an occasional concentration of our joint mockeries upon our host, who took it gladly." Keeler was not the only one to be singled out for fun: Twain's sometime-friend and permanent rival Harte was clearly keen to note the disparity in their status at this gathering: "'Why, fellows,' he spluttered, 'this is the dream of Mark's life.'"[84]

"When the Sun Went Down It Turned All the Broad River to a National Banner"

Surrounded by a culture and new comrades that were turning to the river afresh, apparently already set on writing about the Mississippi, it was inevitable that Twain would soon mine his years of experience on the revivified national stream for literary gold. Both of his first significant attempts at writing about the river were also connected to his new social and literary connections—and the quest for new audiences. First came *The Gilded Age,* a collaboration with his Hartford neighbor, the popular essayist and travel writer (not to mention editor and co-owner of the *Hartford Courant*) Charles Dudley Warner. The genesis of their timely novel came about in the heart of Hartford domesticity, at a yuletide gathering in 1872. Albert Bigelow Paine narrates: "At the dinner-table one night, with the Warners present, criticisms of recent novels were offered, with the usual freedom and severity of dinner-table talk. The husbands were inclined to treat rather lightly the novels in which their wives were finding entertainment. The wives naturally retorted that the proper thing for the husbands to do was to furnish the American people with better ones. This was regarded in the nature of a challenge, and as such was accepted—mutually accepted: that is to say, in partnership. On the spur of the moment Clemens and Warner agreed that they would do a novel together, that they would begin it immediately."[85] The result—Twain's first experiment in long-form fiction—was a curious portmanteau of a book. The two writers took turns composing their panoramic exploration of political and financial corruption in postbellum America—a new Vanity Fair, at turns broadly comic, bitingly satirical, sensational and sentimental. Initially, it sold well and spiraled out into Twain's first experiments with the stage. It still gives the name to the era it described. It started Twain on a new fictional path, too, one with more cachet than his previous work. In Andrew Hoffman's words, "The literary Brahmins of Boston respected fiction much more than Mark Twain's sort of popular personal narratives."[86] Above all, of course, *The Gilded Age* marked Twain's literary turn to the river.

Twain's opening chapters demonstrate an indebtedness both to his youth on the river and to the image of the Mississippi in wider antebellum popular culture. In his inaugural use of the river as an extended subject for fiction, it was appropriate that he began with a child's sense of wonder. The reader learns about the Mississippi at the same time as his youthful characters moving west to Missouri, experiencing the river for the first time. Indeed, this vision of the Mississippi is perhaps the most sublime in Twain's entire bibliography. John E. Bassett might have rightly noted this is "Mark Twain's most Dickensian work," yet his first descriptions of the river feel directly opposed to Dickens's vision of the Mississippi.[87] Here the river is a "silver sea." The Hawkins children, as they "contemplated the marvelous river and discussed it," see only wonder, possibility, and magic—a brave new world: "The river astonished the children beyond measure. Its mile-breadth of water seemed an ocean to them, in the shadowy twilight, and the vague riband of trees on the further shore, the verge of a continent which surely none but they had ever seen before [. . .] so awed were they by the grandeur and the solemnity of the scene before them, and by their belief that the air was filled with invisible spirits and that the faint zephyrs were caused by their passing wings, that all their talk took to itself a tinge of the supernatural, and their voices were subdued to a low and reverent tone." Their first journey on a steamboat is equally splendid: "a glorious adventure, a royal progress through the very heart and home of romance, a realization of their rosiest wonder-dreams." In one extraordinary run-on sentence that climaxes in "an ecstasy of enjoyment," Twain hymns the glories of steamboating, apparently taken with the sheer pleasure of writing about the river and the rhythms of steamboat life. The children make the boat their own as they "revel [. . .] in their new realm of enchantment": "They ran races up and down the deck; climbed about the bell; made friends with the passenger-dogs chained under the lifeboat." When they are invited in to the pilothouse, that holy of holies, "their happiness was complete. This cozy little house, built entirely of glass and commanding a marvelous prospect in every direction was a magician's throne to them and their enjoyment of the place was simply boundless." In such a florid vision, the Mississippi becomes a "national banner laid in gleaming bars of gold and purple and crimson"—a reinstated symbol of reunion and national unification after the disruptions of the Civil War, genuine "gold" in a gilded age.[88]

Yet already, dangerous currents were discernible in Twain's vision of the river. Shifting from bucolic delight, Twain revisited one of the most traumatic moments of his life on the river—the death of his brother Henry—as well as one of the most popular tropes of Mississippi writing by describing a disastrous steamboat race in sensational detail. At first, excitement prevails: "The Amaranth drew steadily up till her jack-staff breasted the Boreas's wheelhouse—climbed along inch by inch till her chimneys breasted it—crept along, further and further, till the boats were wheel to wheel—and then they closed up with a heavy jolt and locked together tight and fast in the middle of the big river under the flooding moonlight! A roar and a hurrah went up from the crowded decks of both steamers." Then tragedy strikes: "There was a booming roar, a thundering crash, and the riddled Amaranth dropped loose from her hold and drifted helplessly away!" Death and destruction are everywhere. A steamboat worker, reminiscent of "Jim Bludso," stoically burns alive. Clearly drawing from painful memory, Twain describes the way that the wounded survivors were covered "with bulging masses of raw cotton that gave to every face and form a dreadful and unhuman aspect." In a particularly visceral moment that would seem to poke the bruise of Twain's own guilt about Henry's death, one dying brother blames another for his imminent death: "'You were on watch. You were boss. You would not listen to me when I begged you to reduce your steam. Take that!—take it to my wife and tell her it comes from me by the hand of my murderer! Take it—and take my curse with it to blister your heart a hundred years—and may you live so long!' And he tore a ring from his finger, stripping flesh and skin with it, threw it down and fell dead!" In keeping with the rest of the novel's crusading remit, however, Twain turned this distressing scene into political comment: "A jury of inquest was impaneled, and after due deliberation and inquiry they returned the inevitable American verdict which has been so familiar to our ears all the days of our lives—'NOBODY TO BLAME.'"[89]

The Gilded Age was Twain's first sustained fictional exploration of the river; the beginning of an arc that would end two decades later with the dour vision of *Pudd'nhead Wilson* (1894). For now, though, Twain was largely playing things for laughs. For along with owing a debt to the perennially popular subject of steamboat racing, Twain also apparently took some of his inspiration from the minstrel stage. When the migrating children first encounter a steamboat, it is the slave "Uncle Dan'l" who notices its approach: "Chil'en, dah's sum fin a comin'!" Terrified by the "fierce eye of fire," the "dense volumes of

smoke," the "coughing" that grew "louder and louder," the children are terrified by the approaching river "monster." Equally appalled, Uncle Dan'l declares
that the approaching creature is none other than "de Almighty! Git down on
yo' knees!" He leads the children in prayer, offering himself up to the "Lord
of heaven and earth" to ensure their safety: "Good Lord, good deah Lord, we
don't know whah you's a gwyne to, we don't know who you's got yo' eye on, but
[. . .] we knows by de way you's a tiltin' along in yo' charyot o' fiah dat some po'
sinner's a gwyne to ketch it [. . .] Let 'em off jes' dis once, and take it out'n de
ole niggah."[90] For all that Uncle Dan'l was a stock character, a racist caricature,
the image of an enslaved black man caring for the welfare of white children
on a journey along the Mississippi was an image that both echoed (and perhaps faintly parodied) Uncle Tom's Cabin while also pointing the way forward
to Twain's river books yet to come. Where Twain also chimed with John Hay
was in his willingness to find humor in the rhetorical disposability of black
life on the Mississippi. In Hay's depiction of a steamboat race in "Jim Bludso,"
he pictures "a nigger squat on her safety-valve, / And her furnace crammed,
rosin and pine."[91] In Twain's, in The Gilded Age, the engineer gleefully declares,
"Every time a nigger heaves a stick of wood into the furnace he goes out the
chimney with it."[92]

Perhaps owing to the novelty of its collaborative composition and the notoriety of both authors, the book reviewed widely on both sides of the Atlantic.
The river featured in a number of the reviews—not always positively. Old and
New praised the fact that "many of the scenes in the book are described with
great force" and singled out "the steamboat race on the Mississippi."[93] The Saturday Review noted that the "desperate race between two river steamers" was
"an incident essentially American" and described the section in some detail,
but it ultimately judged that the "effect produced upon the reader's mind by
the history of the explosion is simply one of disgust."[94] The Athenaeum sniffily
noted, "The negro's prayer at the sight of a steamboat verges on the profane."[95]
Still, it was a beginning.

"There Never Was So Wonderful a Book Written by Man"

In the wake of the success of The Gilded Age, Charles Dudley Warner set out
for Egypt to experience a different kind of river: "Do you think our voyage is
merely a thousand miles on the Nile?" he asked his readers. "We have com-

mitted ourselves to a stream that will lead us thousands of years backwards in the ages, into the depths of history."[96] Twain, on the other hand, stuck to a river he knew better—and the depths of his own history. But not straightaway. Even though Twain had finally tested the literary potential of the Mississippi in earnest, in *The Gilded Age,* and despite the plentiful prompts surrounding him, returning to the river again apparently took another nudge or two. That the Mississippi was already becoming closely associated with him is evident in a long and largely glowing profile of Twain published in *Appletons' Journal* on July 4, 1874, which devoted a significant number of column inches to his river years and their import for his writing: "After a few years, most of which were spent in itinerating from one country newspaper to another, young Clemens became a pilot on a Mississippi steamboat running between St. Louis and New Orleans. The picturesque life which he saw in this new business seems to have stimulated his literary faculties, for we soon find him writing for the newspapers. One day while he was pondering as to what *nom de plume* he should attach to his articles, he heard a sailor who was taking soundings of the river, call out, 'Mark twain!' The phrase tickled the fancy of our young literary pilot, and he adopted it for his own." Throughout his river years, *Appletons'* declared, "Mark Twain sedulously cultivated the art of writing."[97]

Yet despite the growing public connection of his literary identity to his Mississippi years and the experiment of *The Gilded Age,* Twain apparently still needed encouragement to write about the Mississippi, particularly for the new audiences that he was cultivating. On September 30, 1874, William Dean Howells sent Twain a request. After Keeler's introductory lunch, their camaraderie had blossomed. Howells had just accepted his friend's inaugural piece for the *Atlantic,* "A True Story, Repeated Word for Word as I Heard It," and was after more of the same: "Couldn't you send me some such story as that colored one, for our Jan'y number—that is, within a month?" At first, Twain demurred. His new house was full of carpenters, he told Howells on October 3, and he couldn't concentrate on work. "I kill them when I get opportunities," he wrote, by way of apology, "but the builder goes & gets more." It wasn't long before he had a very significant change of heart, writing to Howells on October 24: "I take back the remark that I can't write for the Jan. number. For Twichell & I have had a long walk in the woods & I got to telling him about old Mississippi days of steamboating glory & grandeur as I saw them (during 5 years) *from the pilot house.* He said 'What a virgin subject to hurl into a magazine!' I hadn't thought of that before." Howells's response, now missing, must have been enthusiastic. The subject, evidently, was one close to his heart—and to the trends of the literary marketplace. On October 29, Twain wrote to him, clearly having gained approval, "I think likely I will write the first No. tomorrow."

"Old Times on the Mississippi," Twain's claim to the imaginative copyright of the river, was underway. Somewhere around the middle of November, the first installment was ready: "Cut it, scarify it, reject it—handle it with entire freedom," he exhorted Howells. A week later, the editor was effusive in his praise: "The piece about the Mississippi is capital—it almost made the water in our ice-pitcher muddy as I read it [. . .]. I don't think I shall meddle much with it even in the way of suggestion. The sketch of the low-lived little town was so good, that I could have wished ever so much more of it [. . .]. I want the sketches, if you can make them, *every month*." On December 3, Howells offered more encouragement: "*All* that belongs with old river life is novel and now mostly historical. Don't write *at* any supposed Atlantic audience, but yarn it off as if into my sympathetic ear." "You're doing the science of piloting splendidly," read another letter on January 24. "Every word's interesting. And don't you drop the series till you've got every bit of anecdote and reminiscence into it." He passed on Elinor's compliments too: "I've just been reading it aloud to Mrs. Howells, who could rival Mrs. Clemens in her ignorance of Western steamboating, and she has enjoyed it every word—but the profane words."[98]

Howells was arguably aware of the value of this material before Twain himself. Writing to Howells on December 3, Twain showed concern about what to call the series, hinting at some anxieties that this writing task was clearly provoking. "Old Times on the Mississippi" suddenly seemed an uncomfortable fit as a working title:

Let us change the heading to "*Piloting* on the Miss in the Old Times"—or to "*Steamboating* on the M. in the Old Times"—or to "*Personal* Old Times on the Missi." We could change it for Feb. if now too late for Jan. I suggest it because the present heading is too pretentious, too broad & general. It seems to command me to deliver a Second Book of Revelation to the world, & cover all the Old Times the Mississippi (dang that word, it is worse than type or Egypt) ever saw [. . .]. Any muggins can write about Old Times on the Miss of 500 different kinds, but I am the only man alive that can scribble about the piloting of that day—& no man ever has tried to scribble about it yet. Its newness pleases me all the time—& it is about the only new subject I know of.

Whether or not that claim was strictly true, and regardless of the fact that the series still bore the title "Old Times on the Mississippi" throughout its run in the *Atlantic,* focusing his attention on piloting in this way seems to have unlocked something within Twain. The enthusiasm was palpable in his correspondence. A week after his title crisis, Twain wrote to Howells that "there are some things more, which I am powerfully moved to write." Couching his excitement in familiar terms, he continued, "Which is natural enough, since I am a person who would quit authorizing in a minute to go to piloting, if the madam would stand it. I would rather sink a steamboat than eat, any time."

By January 26, Twain's understanding of his material had shifted again. Now he felt he was really writing a book:

The piloting material has been uncovering itself by degrees, until it has exposed such a huge hoard to my view that a whole book will be required to contain it if I use it. So I have agreed to write the book for Bliss. I won't be able to run the articles in the Atlantic later than the September number, for the reason that a subscription book issued in the fall has a much larger sale than if issued at any other season of the year. It is funny when I reflect that when I originally wrote you & proposed to do from 6 to 9 articles for the magazine, the vague thought in my mind was that 6 might exhaust the material [. . .]. But in truth 9 chapters don't now seem to more than open up the subject fairly & start the yarn to wagging.[99]

If that time frame was optimistic, Twain's enthusiasm for the river was prescient: on and off, he would spend much of the next decade imaginatively on the Mississippi, shaping and reshaping his vision of the river across some of his most significant books.

In all, Twain would produce seven articles about piloting on the Mississippi for the *Atlantic.* Rooted in his own memories of learning the river as a cub pilot, the series inducted its readers into the fraternity of steamboat life. Alongside the mysteries of piloting, Twain held forth on a wealth of river lore, shifting course as the mood took him: "I find it won't cut up into chapters, worth a cent," he told Howells. "It needs to run right along, with no breaks but imaginary ones"—like the river or pilot's talk. As soon as the first installment appeared in the January 1875 issue of the *Atlantic,* the imaginative life of the river was changed forever. Compared to the relatively generic treatment of the Mississippi in *The Gilded Age,* Twain piloted his readers into new waters. For those who knew both Twain and the Mississippi, it was an electric performance. They lined up to congratulate him. John Hay's response, on December 18, was immediate, unequivocal, and typical: "It is perfect—no more nor less. I don't see how you do it. I knew all that, every word of it—passed as much time on the levee as you ever did, knew the same crowd & saw the same scenes,—but I could not have remembered one word of it all. You have the two greatest gifts of the writer, memory & imagination. I congratulate you." "Now isn't that outspoken & hearty, & just like that splendid John Hay?" Twain asked Howells. Howells, in return, teased his friend (with, perhaps, a little undercurrent): "What business has *Hay,* I should like to know, to be praising a favorite of mine?" Will Bowen was also enthusiastic: "Those river articles are delightful." And he encouraged Twain to do more with his material: "Sam I fear you are losing Capital by not making a 'Roughing It' of your river life—it would sell well [. . .] and be a splendid field for your fancy, to spread out over." Howells's uncle, Alec Dean, another former steamboat pilot, read Twain's articles "with a keen appreciation. It vividly recalls an experience in his life about which he is never tired of talking."[100] The only problem for Howells was that the series was almost too popular: meeting with "instant appreciation," it was swiftly reprinted around the nation, from coast to coast, which meant the *Atlantic's* "subscription list was not enlarged in the slightest measure."[101]

Of course, it is unsurprising that the series elicited such a reaction: it met a postbellum reading public that had been well conditioned to appreciate such tales of life on the Mississippi by an intertwined matrix of sources: by accounts and interpretations of steamboat races and bridges, by a multitude of influential travel sketches and popular prints, and by pioneering works of regional literature. Consciously or not, "Old Times on the Mississippi" echoed and amplified some of the most important tropes that those diverse texts helped to establish. It also elided some of their uncomfortable ambiguities. Many years ago, Bernard DeVoto recognized that "Old Times on the Mississippi" was more of an exercise in seductive "idyll-making" than it was a complete and accurate "description of the steamboat age."[102]

From the very title of the series, nostalgia was central to Twain's vision. "After all these years," he described early in the first installment, in one of the most celebrated moments of his entire career, "I can picture that old time to myself now, just as it was then: the white town drowsing in the sunshine of a summer's morning." If Twain had stopped "Old Times on the Mississippi" after its first installment, his wistful re-creation of antebellum river town life would still have marked a new moment in the cultural life of the river. Little wonder that Twain's fellow steamboatmen were so taken with what they read. The valorization of steamboat life was immediate and potent: "When I was a boy, there was but one permanent ambition among my comrades in our village on the west bank of the Mississippi River. That was, to be a steamboatman."[103] To emphasize the nostalgia of his re-creation of an apparently lost world, Twain rhetorically kills off the steamboat trade, unambiguously consigning its "glory" to the "dead and pathetic past," blaming the war and "the railroads intruding everywhere."[104] Even when he dwells on the reliably popular subject of steamboat racing—"royal fun"—and explicitly references the recent competition between the *Natchez* and the *Robert E. Lee,* it is only to denigrate it in comparison to antebellum achievements: "This last is called the fastest trip on record. I will try to show that it was not."[105] All told, it was a beguiling image of prewar life that centered the Mississippi as an image of America that transcended sectionalism while also performing a vivid regional identity. As Twain learned the Mississippi in his memories, so his readers learned to navigate on Twain's literary river.

"Old Times on the Mississippi" was not just a journey into a burnished past, though. As the series developed, Twain's memories meandered like the river, encompassing a variety of ways of understanding the river. At moments, Twain's prose has the quality of a contemporary travel account, offering its readers a voyage along the river that is, on occasion, more picturesque than it would be again in his work: "The great Mississippi, the majestic, the magnificent Mississippi, rolling its mile-wide tide along, shining in the sun."[106] As such, the series is also implicitly reconciliatory in tone, since it offers readers a journey into an imaginary South stripped of political anxieties, old and new: slavery and the steamboat's complicity in the domestic slave trade is all but invisible in these sketches. Such uncomfortable realities were apparently consciously elided from these articles. Blackness is almost entirely absent from Twain's account of "Old Times on the Mississippi" (especially compared, for example, to Howells's own debut in the *Atlantic* back in 1861 or even to the steamboat scenes in *The Gilded Age*). Twain's black steamboat colleagues appear marginally in vanishing and undifferentiated glimpses of "half-naked crews of perspiring negroes."[107] Only in snapshots—roustabouts "roaring such songs as De Las' Sack! De Las' Sack!" or a "stalwart darkey" evincing pride at his position in the engine room of the steamboat *Aleck Scott*—do the vibrant subcultures of steamboat life peek through.

In common with other river works produced at this moment by Twain's acquaintances, "Old Times on the Mississippi" was also ambiguous in its generic qualities. While striving for an apparent verisimilitude in his account of certain aspects of the trade and, in particular, the vernacular possibilities offered by the river—"I wished I could talk like that," his narrator declares after a typically rich outburst from one of his river colleagues—Twain dwells heavily on the idea that piloting "was a romantic sort of occupation."[108] Howells, of course, pushed for the former—"stick to actual fact and character in the thing, and give things in *detail*"—but ultimately, Twain's attempt to imbue the profession with rugged romance seems more vital to its immediate and prolonged appeal.[109]

Above and beyond these other important thematic concerns, what "Old Times on the Mississippi" took as its central theme, in common with much other commentary on the river in the postwar decade, was the men who worked on it—at least, those in the pilothouse. Twain's encomium to the steamboat pilot picks up the postbellum fascination with the steamboat worker as an icon of American masculinity and enlarges that idea to extraordinary dimensions. Twain's pilot—exemplified by his mentor, Horace Bixby—is a powerful and multiple figure. In his description of the steamboat hierarchy, he is adamant that the "pilot was the grandest position of all."[110] A pilot's ability to memorize the river, we are told, "is about the most wonderful thing in the world."[111] Piloting is both a "wonderful science" and "a very high art."[112] In the installment subtitled "Official Rank and Dignity of a Pilot," the hyperbole reaches a telling crescendo: Twain declares that an antebellum steamboat pilot "was the only unfettered and entirely independent human being that lived in the earth." While "every man and woman and child has a master, and worries and frets in servitude [. . .] in the day I write of, the Mississippi pilot had *none*." He was "an absolute monarch who was absolute in sober truth and not by a fiction of words."[113] And he was, of course, also a wonderful storyteller: "All pilots are tireless talkers, when gathered together."[114]

This extraordinary aggrandizement of the pilot was, inevitably, also the aggrandizement of Mark Twain. And Twain went one better, positioning himself as a hybrid figure who transcended even the extraordinary capabilities of a Mississippi pilot. At the end of his third article on the river, Twain meditated on the meaning of his pilot's education in ways that had implications for his future as a writer. Despairing at ever mastering the Mississippi, Bixby had assured him that in time he would come to understand its moods by "instinct," "but you never will be able to explain why or how you know them apart."[115] "It turned out to be true," Twain tells the reader, revealing some of his hard-earned river arcana:

> The face of the water, in time, became a wonderful book—a book that was a dead language to the uneducated passenger, but which told its mind to me without reserve, delivering its most cherished secrets as clearly as if it uttered them with a voice. And it was not a book to be read once and thrown aside, for it had a new story to tell every day. Throughout the long twelve hundred miles there was never a page that was void of interest, never one that you could leave unread without loss, never one that you would want to skip, thinking you could find higher enjoyment in some other thing. There never was so wonderful a book written by man; never one whose interest was so absorbing, so unflagging, so sparklingly renewed with every re-perusal.

Yet there was a price to pay. The devil's bargain of piloting, Twain claimed, was a stark one: "When I had mastered the language of this water [. . .]. I had made a valuable acquisition. But I had lost something, too. [. . .] All the grace, the beauty, the poetry had gone out of the majestic river!" Remembering a sunset he had seen on the river before his education, Twain recalls his "speechless rapture. The world was new to me, and I had never seen anything like this at home." Yet after his education, the view was purely utilitarian: "All the value any feature of it had for me now was the amount of usefulness it could furnish toward compassing the safe piloting of a steamboat." Of course, Twain was being disingenuous. The implicit revelation of this passage is that while Sam Clemens the steamboat pilot might have lost the "romance and the beauty" from the river, Mark Twain the writer could resurrect it at will—and much more besides.[116] It was a different kind of mastery, a different kind of value, but one whose potential was no less potent—a new expression of the ancient "language of this water."

"I Work like a Pilot on a Mississippi River Steamboat"

In later years, particularly in *Life on the Mississippi*, which appeared in 1883, Twain's thoughts on the significance and meaning of experience would change. In 1875 , in his writing for the *Atlantic*, its value was pushed aggressively to the fore. As the series developed, his claim to the river's bragging rights became more aggressive. Echoing his earliest thoughts on the series to Howells about the "virgin subject" of the Mississippi, he told readers in the fourth installment, "I feel justified in enlarging upon this great science for the reason that I feel sure no one has ever yet written a paragraph about it who had piloted a steamboat himself, and so had a practical knowledge of the subject."[117] Responding to the praise of Howells's Uncle Alec, Twain again asserted his special status: "There's something charming about the lonely sublimity of being the prophet of a hitherto unsung race. [. . .] I haven't any rivals; my people will have to take me or go prophetless."[118]

When other members of that "unsung race" did begin to put pen to paper themselves, they were often swift to point out that their "prophet" might not always have been a true one. According to fellow pilot Emerson Gould in 1889, for example, "it is very apparent [. . .] that Mr. 'Twain' [. . .] magnified the authority he possessed as a pilot very largely."[119] Clearly, however, there were deeper significances to the appeal of Twain's performance, which also picked up on ideas that had been implicit in other portraits of the pilot and the river in the preceding years. For Howard Horwitz, Twain's "romance of the free and independent pilot" was "an exercise in historical fantasy, its aesthetic values deriving from an idealized vision of free enterprise and *laissez-faire* property rights," in opposition to "the corporate trend the railroad typified and accelerated."[120] As Lawrence Howe has suggested, Twain's investment of the "riverboat pilot that he had aspired to be" with a quality of "epic identity" was related, on some level, to his desire "to embody personally the idea and experience of America."[121] Though his understanding of that pose would shift, its expression in "Old Times" was a vital stage in Twain's development as a writer and in his—and our—wider understanding of the river. Another effect of this performance was to enshrine the idea that the view of the Mississippi from Twain's pilothouse was the only view that mattered. In large part, it was a claim that stuck.

Such postures—particularly the sense that "Old Times" was as much about writing as steamboating—certainly struck a nerve in his immediate group. As Edgar J. Burde has asserted, during the composition of this series, "the river of the Mississippi steamboat pilot gave Clemens a metaphor [. . .] of writing."[122] This was a significant discovery, for himself and others. Michael Davitt Bell has argued that Howells's support for a certain kind of literary realism was linked to his anxieties about the gendered status of literature in its relationship to "the world of men's activities": "The problem, for Howells as for many of his contemporaries and successors, was that the 'artist' was by accepted definition *not* a 'real' man."[123] As Brodhead has described, this was also the moment of emergence for an "idealized" image of the writer as a "single-minded devotee of a highly specialized craft whose work derives value from its mastery of its art."[124] Twain's simultaneous performance of the roles of pilot and author in "Old Times on the Mississippi"—and his apparent equation, on some level, of the acts of piloting and writing—spoke directly to those ideas, providing himself and others with a model amalgamation of apparently contradictory worlds. So compelling did Howells find the juxtaposition that when asked about his own writing habits in 1886, he replied with a very pointed image: "I work like a pilot on a Mississippi river steamboat, with certain landmarks to shape my course by; I keep a phrase, and attitude, a situation in mind, from the beginning, and steer by those successive points to the end."[125]

In these years of personal flux and change, the river emerged for Twain as his central subject. Like the Mississippi itself, his conception of the river would constantly shift course, but also like the river, whatever else changed, it would remain a constant, flowing through the heart of his work in the decades to come. In 1875, with "Old Times on the Mississippi" near its end, at least one thing was now clear. Twain wrote to Howells on May 22, still enthused about his "virgin subject," "There is a world of river stuff to write about."[126]

"The Mighty River Lay like an Ocean"

AQUATIC ADVENTURES FOR TRANSATLANTIC BOYS

I do not know why my boy's associations with Delorac's Island
were especially wild in their character, for nothing more like outlawry
than the game of mumble-the-peg ever occurred there. Perhaps it
was because the boys had to get to it by water that it seemed
beyond the bounds of civilization.

—WILLIAM DEAN HOWELLS, *A Boy's Town*, 1890

It's very odd how almost all English boys love danger.
You can get ten to join a game, or climb a tree, or swim a stream,
when there's a chance of breaking their limbs or getting drowned,
for one who'll stay on level ground, or in his depth.

—THOMAS HUGHES, *Tom Brown's School Days,* 1857

Go with me to the great river Mississippi. [. . .]
Go with me to this majestic river.

—CAPTAIN MAYNE REID, *The Boy Hunters,* 1853

F lush with the excitement of rediscovering the river in "Old Times on the Mississippi," Twain set about rounding up companions for a journey back to his source. As early as November 1874, he had written to James Redpath: "I have a notion of going west [. . .] to make a lagging journey down the Mississippi, dining pilots & pumping stuff out of them for a book [. . .]. I should want you yourself to stay right *with* me from the first day to the last, & *talk, & lie, & have a good time.*" But really it was Howells, the most significant and enthusiastic audience for his river writings thus far, whom Twain wanted by his side; he spent the next seven years attempting to coax him to the river valley that flowed through both of their early experiences, real and imagined. At some point, Howells must have hastily agreed to the trip—and then repented at extended leisure. On December 18, 1874, Twain declared, "Mrs. Clemens dreads our going to New Orleans, but I tell her she'll have to give her consent this time." The next day, Howells was already backtracking: "Mrs. Howells [. . .] is saying that I ought not to go to New Orleans without her [. . .] but I don't give it up yet, and don't *you*. We will keep this project alive if it takes all winter." On January 10, 1875, though, he wrote to Twain apologetically: "Speaking of Mrs. Howells brings me to New Orleans,—or rather it doesn't." In tortured detail, Howells explained that he had previously promised to take Winifred on holiday to Bethlehem, Pennsylvania: "I can't do both these things, so, without referring the matter to her, I must be a man for once in my life, and say No, when I'd inexpressibly rather say Yes." Twain was obdurate, writing back on January 12: "We *mustn't* give up the New Orleans trip. [. . .] We can *put off* New Orleans until March 1st, & then that would do in place of Bethlehem. You just persuade her." On January 26, still brimming with river material, Twain tried a more wheedling approach: "I do hope you will decide to make the steamboat trip. Of course you mustn't go if Mrs. Howells's desire should remain in any degree against it."[1] The coaxing didn't work either.

On February 12, Twain still kindled a small hope that things would turn his way. He wrote to James R. Osgood: "Howells said [. . .] he would take steamboat at St. Louis with me, in March, & go to New Orleans & back. He is not sure, now, whether he can go or not, but I hope he *will*. [. . .] I wish you would go. Think of the gaudy times you & Howells & I would have on such a bender!" But a week later, on February 20, he temporarily gave up the fight. Writing to Howells, he lamented: "What grieves me [. . .] is, that I have to give up the river trip [. . .]. So I'll trim up & finish 2 or 3 more river sketches for the magazine (if you still think you want them), & then buckle in on another book for Bliss, finish it the end of May, & then either make the river trip or drop it indefinitely." Howells was suitably disconsolate: "Your giving up that river-trip has been such a blow to me." When May arrived, the trip was still on indefinite hiatus, but Twain was no less committed to the prospective bender. Indeed, this journey and its potential meaning for Twain's life and career seemed to be coming into clearer focus: "If I live a year," he wrote to Howells, "I will make one more attempt to go down the river, for I shall have lived in vain if I go silent out of the world and thus lengthen the list of the 'lost arts.' Confidentially, I'm 'laying' for a monument."[2]

In the end, he found another way to get back to the Mississippi: childhood memories. While he contemplated the literary potential of the river in the wake of "Old Times on the Mississippi" and as he tried to strong-arm Howells and others into new escapades, *The Adventures of Tom Sawyer* (1876) took final shape. Evoking Twain's boyhood in Hannibal, the Mississippi flows through the heart of the text—at turns nostalgic and pressingly contemporary in its symbolism. Indeed, the river's ambiguous presence is established in the fluvial name of its eponymous hero: Sawyer, a term used to describe a fallen tree stuck in the riverbed, gently floating up and down with the current, a hidden danger for steamboat pilots. This was a book that had been incubating for a number of years. Twain had apparently begun the composition of *Tom Sawyer* in 1872, returning to it in 1873 and again in 1874, just before composing "Old Times on the Mississippi." He finally completed it in the summer of 1875— the book that he told Howells he was about to "buckle in on" for Bliss. On July 5, he announced to Howells: "I have finished the story & didn't take the chap beyond boyhood. [. . .] I perhaps made a mistake in not writing it in the first person. If I went on, now, & took him into manhood, he would just be like all the one-horse men in literature & the reader would conceive a hearty contempt for him. It is not a boy's book, at all. It will only be read by adults. It is only written for adults." Yet that decision was less firm than it sounded, and he also asked Howells a favor: "I wish you would promise to read the MS of Tom Sawyer some time, & see if you don't really decide that I am right in closing with him as a boy—& point out the most glaring defects for me." By November, plans had changed. "It is glorious news that you like Tom Sawyer so well," Twain wrote to Howells. "I mean to see to it that your review of it shall have plenty of time to appear before the other notices. Mrs. Clemens decides with you that the book should issue as a book for boys, pure & simple—& so do I. It is surely the correct idea."[3]

In all those ambiguities, *Tom Sawyer* was a book of its moment. It was understood from the start that Tom was a character who fitted into a recent fashion in literature for children, particularly adventure books for boys that also spoke to adult readers. Moreover, it was clear that this was an essentially transatlantic trend. In his review of *Tom Sawyer* in the *Atlantic*, Howells pronounced, "Tom Brown and Tom Bailey are, among boys in books, alone deserving to be named with Tom Sawyer."[4] His gestures were to Thomas Hughes's *Tom Brown's School Days* (1857) and Thomas Bailey Aldrich's *The Story of a Bad Boy* (serialized in 1869, published as a single volume in 1870). Both books established a fresh manner of writing about boys at this pivotal moment, mixing a new kind of realism with a celebration of youthful hijinks and a relative diminution of didacticism and moralizing. Also implicated in this process was a concern for shaping new gender identities (in America, a process given new impetus by the Civil War). As Tim Prchal describes, this new type of boy hero "provided its original readers a view of masculinity that, if adopted by grown men, might begin to counterbalance a culture feared to be too ladylike in its level of refinement."[5] As Howells put it as late as 1911, in a preface to a new edition of *Tom Brown's Schooldays*, Hughes "was not only the best sort of Englishman, but he was the making of the best sort of American."[6]

Both of those books also established the central importance—and the important peril—of watery play in this new genre of boy books. Symbolically significant rivers flow through the experiences of both Toms, just as they do through the adventures of Tom Sawyer. They are the scene of Tom Brown's first acculturation into the world of men when, in a powerfully nostalgic vision of English country life, the young protagonist escapes from his nurse Charity to enjoy the company of old retainer Benjy, "a cheery, humorous, kindhearted old man, full of sixty years of Vale gossip": "It was he who bent the first pin with which Tom extracted his first stickleback out of 'Pebbly Brook,' the little stream which ran through the village. [. . .] Charity had appealed against old Benjy in the meantime, representing the dangers of the canal banks; but Mrs. Brown, seeing the boy's inaptitude for female guidance, had decided in Benjy's favour, and from thenceforth the old man was Tom's dry nurse. And as they sat by the canal watching their little green-and-white float, Benjy would instruct him in the doings of deceased Browns." At Rugby itself, the River

Avon—"a capital river for bathing," Hughes notes—is a prime site for misadventure; Tom and his friends spend "a large portion of the day in nature's garb by the river-side," swimming "like fishes" and tussling with gamekeepers on the opposite bank. These kind of hijinks are, Hughes asserts, a vital part of the national character: "It's very odd how almost all English boys love danger. You can get ten to join a game, or climb a tree, or swim a stream, when there's a chance of breaking their limbs or getting drowned." More than that, rivers serve a wider symbolic purpose in the book. Tom's pious friend Arthur—a "timid weak boy" at the beginning of his Rugby career—becomes the means of reform for Tom, and many other boys, transforming him by his devout example from a "scapegrace" with "wild, out-of-bounds habits" to a figure of "manly piety," fit for future work in "country curacies, London chambers, under the Indian sun, and in Australian towns and clearings." When Arthur almost dies from fever, he receives a very specific heavenly vision that becomes a crucial moment in Tom's reformation: "We rushed through the bright air, which was full of myriads of living creatures, and paused on the brink of a great river. And the power held me up, and I knew that that great river was the grave, and death dwelt there, but not the death I had met in the black tomb. That, I felt, was gone for ever. For on the other bank of the great river I saw men and women and children rising up pure and bright, and the tears were wiped from their eyes, and they put on glory and strength, and all weariness and pain fell away."[7]

For Aldrich's bad boy Tom Bailey, rivers were of no less import. Upon the moment of his early removal from New Orleans and the Mississippi to attend school in Rivermouth in New England, the river becomes a crucial locus of childhood play. Establishing "the pleasantest possible [. . .] social relations with my new schoolfellows," Bailey is always up to "some exciting excursion," such as "an exploration of a group of diminutive islands" residing in the river, "upon one of which we pitched a tent and played we were the Spanish sailors who got wrecked there years ago." A Rivermouth boy, Aldrich declares, understands the water to be "mixed up with his destiny": "He burns for the time when he shall stand on the quarter-deck of his own ship, and go sailing proudly across that mysterious waste of waters." Yet the river also becomes the site of the emotional climax of the book. Inspired by these visions of the sea, Bailey and his friends club together to buy a boat, the Dolphin. Bailey's grandfather allows him to row, but not to sail the boat: "The river was dangerous for sailboats [. . .] scarcely a year passed that six or seven persons were not drowned under the very windows of the town." So warned, the boys set out on an excursion to "Sandpeep Island, the last of the islands in the harbour," at the point where the river meets the sea. To begin with, the boys disport themselves merrily in "Robinson Crusoe" fashion. Yet not for long: "What a joyous thing was life, and how far off seemed death—death, that lurks in all pleasant places, and was so near!" A storm swiftly moves in, and Bailey's comrade Binny Wallace ends up floating out to sea in the Dolphin as the boys watch him hopelessly drift to his doom: "Poor little Binny Wallace! Always the same to me. The rest of us have grown up into hard, worldly men, fighting the fight of life; but you are forever young, and gentle, and pure." Even though Binny Wallace's death doesn't have the evangelical effect of Arthur's near-death experience, it marks a shift in tone in the narrative. Inducted into the harsh realities of life, Bailey and his friends "seldom cared to go out into the river now." The narrative ends with the death of Bailey's father and the taking up of adult responsibility in the shape of his uncle's "counting-house."[8]

Mark Twain was well versed in these trends. His friendship with Aldrich blossomed in the 1870s, yet despite their association and Twain's own investment in the changing fashions of books for children (not to mention his debt to Aldrich's book), he was apparently no fan of Tom Bailey's adventures. He professed to Livy in 1869: "I started to mark the Story of a Bad Boy, but for the life of me I could not admire the volume much."[9] Twain met Thomas Hughes numerous times in London in 1872 and owned a copy of Tom Brown's Schooldays.[10] Yet for all that Tom Sawyer was clearly a boys' book in the same vein as these other popular and influential texts, it was also a strange bedfellow. As John Seelye notes, "We may [. . .] list all the points Tom Sawyer shares with the boys' books already in circulation by 1876, but it is the difference that is most important." By this, Seelye means Tom's transformation in the book "from rapscallion to rich boy" without having, as in other boys' books, "to assume the responsibilities normally attending the transformation from bad to good—quite the reverse."[11] Yet if we broaden the frame further, we can see plenty of other differences between Tom Sawyer and its analogues in the work of Hughes and Aldrich. As Alan Gribben has helpfully summarized, "The curious assortment of what we loosely define as 'Boy Books' (or sometimes 'Bad Boy Books') embraces an amazingly heterogeneous collection of writings—sentimental autobiography, juvenile romance, quasi-sociological documentary, comic slapstick, literary burlesque—that mainly have in common a reverence for boyhood, an autobiographical flavor, a setting in the past, and a code of behavior alien to most adults." And as Gribben also highlights, "In most Boy Books the climactic test of courage involves a large, dangerous body of water."[12] Yet not even that comprehensive list contains all the elements that are found within Twain's book. *Tom Brown's School Days* and *The Story of a Bad Boy*, for example, hardly contained the degree of violent crime that Twain conjured in his book for boys: murder, blood, robbery, buried treasure—real as well as imagined—animate the text, even though, unlike in the work of Hughes and Aldrich, no child actually dies in Twain's book.

Tom Sawyer's adventures on the Mississippi must therefore also be understood as another branch of a powerful stream flowing through transatlantic popular culture in these years. Tom Brown and Tom Bailey were hardly the only boys messing about on rivers at this moment. Adventure stories were experiencing a new vogue, with writers and readers on both sides of the Atlantic. Frequently, their thrilling escapades also focused on waterways. The Mississippi loomed large in this arena, establishing itself as a space characterized by a variety of flavors and types of adventure. This trend can largely be traced to the work of influential British—really transatlantic—writers like R. M. Ballantyne and Mayne Reid or the pages of an important story paper like Edwin Brett's *Boys of England* (launched in 1867). Featuring tales of boy protagonists undertaking dangerous escapades in disparate locations around the globe, these stories were often closely implicated in a developing ethos of imperialism: in Bradley Deane's words, "Their boy heroes learned in the school of empire how to master their instincts and, by externalising this trajectory of self-discipline, how to control territories and subdue natives."[13] They were also, in Lisa Honaker's words, largely "aesthetically and ideologically at odds with nineteenth-century domestic Realism."[14] At the same moment in America, other voices were initiating complementary publishing trends that also often linked boyhood to watery adventure. Stimulated by the Civil War, authors like Oliver Optic and Harry Castlemon began to shape a new style of American book for boys that—whether focusing on martial exploits or educational travel narratives featuring plucky young protagonists—often integrated elements of social and economic uplift. Nor were children's books the only place that influential river adventures were being narrated: the same kinds of tropes and concerns bled into and out of other stories of exploration and conquest that circulated widely at this moment. While Twain was planning his own new adventures on the Mississippi, one of the defining stories of the era was Henry Morton Stanley's ongoing exploration of the Congo River. Stanley was a figure who kept the colonial importance of waterways front and center in the world's imagination during this period—and who also happened to be a friend of Twain who knew the Mississippi well, thanks to his own youthful experiences on the river. Closer to home, a figure like Ernest Morris, the so-called boy explorer, gained a fleeting fame for his exploits on the Mississippi and the Amazon.

Water, then, sat at the heart of these new, cross-pollinating, international narratives of boyish adventure, real and imagined—a heady brew of proto-imperialism, self-definition, shifting gender norms, and changing fashions in the production of books for children. On both the page and the world's stage, water was apparently the vital element for adventure at this moment, whether ocean or river—a borderline for shifting standards, a conduit for testing values, the necessary gateway for entry into an imagined world of serious play where childhood games of life and death were often mixed with matters of national identity and colonial policy. In the popular imagination, the waters of the Mississippi mingled with the waters of oceans and rivers from around the world. Looked at in such company, *The Adventures of Tom Sawyer* is a hybrid text that contains within it, perhaps uniquely, the different transatlantic trends and tensions of boyhood fiction at this moment—in ways that coalesce in the Mississippi, on Jackson's Island, and in McDougal's Cave. For in *Tom Sawyer,* the Mississippi is a uniquely multiple river, both domestic in its relationship to the daily life of the boys but also, in its ability to transport, "like an ocean."[15]

It was William Dean Howells who perhaps best expressed the transformative dynamic between boys and bodies of water, big and small, in his own meditation on youth, *A Boy's Town* (1890). "It seems to me," Howells declared, "that the best way to get at the heart of any boy's town is to take its different watercourses and follow them into it." His own childhood home he felt to be "peculiarly adapted for a boy to be a boy in": "It had a river, the great Miami River, which was as blue as the sky when it was not as yellow as gold; and it had another river, called the Old River, which was the Miami's former channel, and which held an island in its sluggish loop; the boys called it The Island; and it must have been about the size of Australia; perhaps it was not so large." As it would for Tom Sawyer—and so many other fictional boys at this moment—the island loomed large in its significance as a richly symbolic space. Howells's island was a space where his "boy's associations [. . .] were especially wild in their character," even though "nothing more like outlawry than the game of mumble-the-peg ever occurred there." "Perhaps," he pondered, "it was because the boys had to get to it by water that it seemed beyond the bounds of civilization."[16] Following Howells's lead, then, let us track the different watercourses that flowed beyond the bounds of civilization through boys' books, adventure fiction, and other imperial imaginings, to get back to the Mississippi and play pirates with Tom Sawyer on Jackson's Island.

"His Favorite Literature"

The Adventures of Tom Sawyer is a book that wears its relationship to antebellum sensation stories—yellow-covered, crime-filled, parentally censured penny dreadfuls "about various types of wanderers or outcasts such as corsairs, freebooters, pirates, criminals," to quote David Reynolds—on its sleeve.[17] Tom's "favorite literature" supplies him with a constant source of inspiration throughout the book: "He would be a soldier, and return after long years, all war-worn and illustrious. No—better still, he would join the Indians, and hunt buffaloes and go on the warpath in the mountain ranges and the trackless great plains of the Far West, and away in the future come back a great chief, bristling with feathers, hideous with paint, and prance into Sunday-school, some drowsy summer morning, with a blood-curdling war-whoop, and sear the eyeballs of all his companions with unappeasable envy. But no, there was something gaudier even than this. He would be a pirate! [. . .] 'Tom Sawyer the Pirate!—the Black Avenger of the Spanish Main!'" Explaining how to be a robber to Huck at the end of the book, unreformed in his reading habits, Tom makes clear his continuing debt: "It's so in all the books."[18] His—and Twain's—immediate and most obvious debt is to Ned Buntline's *Black Avenger of the Spanish Main: or, The Fiend of Blood: A Thrilling Tale of the Buccaneer Times,* first published in 1847—a story, according to its preface, "striking, terrible and bloody."[19] In 1897, Twain noted of his own childhood reading, "Pirates and Knights preferred to other society."[20] Yet other popular antebellum narratives of crime and punishment, situated much closer to home on the Mississippi, also echo through the text.

Most notable was the legend of John A. Murrell, the famed "great western land pirate" whose bad reputation resounded up and down the Mississippi and throughout antebellum popular culture. Murrell was, in David Reynolds's words, "the most prominent example of the likable criminal in antebellum culture," rampaging across the cultural spectrum from penny dreadfuls and the popular stage to the work of diverse writers on both sides of the Atlantic like William Gilmore Simms, Friedrich Gerstäcker, and Herman Melville.[21] In *Tom Sawyer*, when Injun Joe and his partners in crime locate the buried treasure that Tom and Huck eventually claim as their own, its provenance is clear:

> "'Twas always said that Murrel's gang used to be around here one summer," the stranger observed.
>
> "I know it," said Injun Joe; "and this looks like it, I should say."[22]

In his own foundational paean to frontier boyhood, *The Hoosier Schoolmaster* (1871), Edward Eggleston also touched on some of the same themes as Twain yet to instructively different ends. In the climactic trial scene of that book, Eggleston asserts that Walter Johnson, a "mean-spirited" young man who becomes involved with a gang and a robbery, was "the victim of [. . .] such novels as 'The Pirate's Bride,' 'Claude Duval,' 'The Wild Rover of the West Indies,' and the cheap biographies of such men as Murrell."[23] Tom, of course, fares rather better than the imprisoned Walter Johnson.

In the 1870s, the same themes that had piqued the interest of Tom Sawyer—war, the West, pirates, highwaymen—were still engaging young readers, but a clear shift had taken place in the nature of adventure writing for children. On the one hand, the development of the dime novel throughout the 1860s provided a popular new outlet for sensational stories of adventure, though one that attracted a significant amount of parental opprobrium. Far more respectable were the adventure stories crafted by two British writers who both had transatlantic popularity, regularly utilized transatlantic themes, and lived transatlantic lives. R. M. Ballantyne and Captain Mayne Reid were at the forefront of the new wave of adventure writing that proved very influential on young Britons and Americans from the 1850s onward. As J. S. Bratton notes, they shared "a common core of subjects, but Mayne Reid specialised in colourful pioneering adventures in the Americas, while Ballantyne, in producing [. . .] volumes for several decades, ranged over every possible setting." What's more—similar to the advent of the bad boy books—their "didacticism" was "less marked" and their "morality easier" than the work of their predecessors and rivals in the field, as they acted out a "fantasy life of daring action, triumph and adventure."[24] Also sitting on the borderline of respectability was the emergence of a new kind of story paper for children best exemplified by Edwin J. Brett's enormously popular *Boys of England,* founded in 1866, which, in Louis James words, "was to influence every boys' journal that followed." Predominantly aimed at "upwardly mobile lower middle classes" with "strong middle-class aspirations," *Boys of England* combined "patriotism, social mobility and violent adventures" in a winning formula.[25] By the 1870s, it was selling 250,000 copies a week.

The disparate publications of Ballantyne, Reid and Brett shared a number of other commonalities that were significant for the development of adventure writing at this point. First, they aimed themselves firmly at a boy readership; their genesis represented a gendered bifurcation in writing for younger readers that would only grow throughout the rest of the century. Second, they shared a loose sense of politics. On the one hand, they were hardly the virulent voice of empire that some of their successors would prove to be. As Patrick Dunae describes, at this moment the boy heroes of these texts "could not be regarded as conscientious empire builders [. . .] they showed no appreciation of imperial needs or policies. The empire was simply a bizarre backdrop for their quixotic escapades." Yet even though the imperial ideal remained "inchoate in boys' literature until the closing decades of the nineteenth century," the tensions of empire were certainly apparent throughout these texts, and the significance of waterborne journeys to far-flung corners of the globe was still profound.[26]

If there was one overseas location for which these British authors and periodicals shared a particularly affinity, it was America. Partly, this was biographical, given Ballantyne's and Reid's early experiences in North America. But this was an association that went deeper. As Christopher Banham has perceptively highlighted, in reference to the publications of Edwin Brett: "Throughout its entire lifespan *Boys of England* was preoccupied with the USA. Stories set in America outnumbered those set in all the formal white dominions combined. They were also at least as common as stories set in Africa, India and China. The quantity, and more importantly the outlook, of these stories demonstrates that Britain's informal ties with the United States were more significant to

Boys of England than its governance over both white and non-white territories."
Partly this was a sense of shared Anglo-Saxon identity—the idea that Britons and Americans "held common traits which made them the highest of the
world's racial orders, and natural allies." Yet there was also, at least for Brett
and *The Boys of England*, a class consciousness borne out of his Chartist youth
that positioned America as "a model of freedom, affluence, and democracy."
As Banham outlines: "Admiration for America was particularly strong amongst
working-class children. Youngsters working in monotonous or even dangerous
occupations in overcrowded and unsanitary towns and cities frequently looked
towards the States to relieve their drudgery."[27] America was by far the most
popular destination for British emigrants throughout the later decades of the
nineteenth century—60 percent of those leaving Britain by the 1890s.[28] At
one point, Brett even established a column for British readers seeking American pen pals. As such, all of these authors—Mark Twain too—had an awareness that they wrote for a shared transatlantic audience. That this sense of the
shared affinities of transatlantic boyhood inflected the reception of a text like
Tom Sawyer is clear. It's vividly apparent in an early review of *Tom Sawyer* by
an American living abroad in London: "Many a boy and girl here will feel an
agony of envy when they contemplate the scene of Mark Twain's three boys
painted with mud to look like Indians racing up and down the beach to their
heart's content. Many other scenes and notions, too, will correspond to the
familiar feelings of the healthy British boy and girl."[29]

What visions of youth, America and watery adventure did these transatlantic readers receive in the pages of these thrilling tales? In a career spanning
decades, Robert Ballantyne played a central role in redefining adventure stories for boys. The New World was at the heart of his own early experiences,
and it remained at the heart of his fiction until the end of his life. At the age
of sixteen, he related in his autobiography, "I found myself in the heart of that
vast North American wilderness which is variously known as Rupert's Land,
The Territories of the Hudson's Bay Company, and the Great Nor'west, many
hundreds of miles north of the outmost verge of Canadian civilisation." Ballantyne's memories of his time with the Hudson's Bay Company are stamped with
the same kind of cheerful pragmatism as his books for boys: "My comrades
and I spent the greater part of our time in fur-trading with the Red Indians;
doing a little office-work, and in much canoeing, boating, fishing, shooting,
and skylarking. It was a 'jolly' life, no doubt, while it lasted."[30] When that jolly

life was over, Ballanytne turned to books. A memoir documented his own youthful experiences in the New World: *Hudson's Bay; or, Every-Day Life in the Wilds of North America* (1848). His first novel, *The Young Fur Traders* (1856), drew directly on that experience too. Thereafter, in many subsequent books, Ballantyne took his readers on journeys to North America—mainly Canada, though with occasional detours to the United States, like *Digging for Gold; or, Adventures in California* (1869). Not that Ballantyne limited himself to those arenas—he ranged widely across time and space in his adventures. Twain, for example, owned a copy of *Erling the Bold* (1869), a Viking romp that he mentioned reading in a letter to Olivia in 1872.[31]

Arguably the most significant of Ballantyne's books, though—and the one that fixed him, albeit a little reluctantly, on the path of writing explicitly for young readers—had ostensibly nothing to do with North America. Yet Ballantyne's *The Coral Island* (1858) was a signal publication in the history of adventure writing. Even though his three young protagonists cross an ocean, not a river, to reach the site of their adventures, their exploits provide an instructive counterpoint to Tom Sawyer's experiences on Jackson's Island. Ballantyne's book was the most popular of a small boom in "Robinsonades" in the Victorian era—books that, like Defoe's *Robinson Crusoe* (1719), strand their protagonists in remote locations. As Susan Naramore Maher explains: "In the nineteenth century, *Robinson Crusoe* became a prized nursery book, favoured by children for its details and adventure, by parents for its religious sentiment and work ethic. [. . .] As *Robinson Crusoe* became codified by its Victorian audience, so, too, did its offspring, adventure books. *Crusoe's* boys'-book imitators simplify its interplay of romance and realism in order to articulate the myth of cultural superiority. They recast their Crusoes into quintessential empire builders, create islands that signify a hierarchy of culture and race, and ultimately mirror a conquering people's mythology."[32] The island also represented, as Bristow notes, "an appropriately diminutive world in which dangers can be experienced within safe boundaries. Boy heroes can act as the natural masters of these controllable environments. Islands provide an appositely 'childlike' space which boys can easily circumnavigate without revealing any lack of manful maturity."[33] The vogue was profound. Thomas Hughes, in a preface to *Tom Brown's Schooldays*, described "the sight of sons, nephews, and godsons, playing trap-bat-and-ball, and reading 'Robinson Crusoe.'"[34] Aldrich also listed the book as a particular favorite of his bad boy. In 1869, Louisa May Alcott sardonically pictured a boy—another Tom—"reposing on the sofa with his boots in the air, absorbed in one of those delightful books in which boys are cast away on desert islands [. . .] where the young heroes have thrilling adventures."[35] In 1887, when Twain was asked for his recommendations for youthful readers, *Robinson Crusoe* made his list for boys—but for girls he recommended "striking Crusoe & substituting Tennyson."[36]

Ballantyne's book developed the genre in a number of important ways. First, Ballantyne's protagonists are three unaccompanied boys—Ralph Rover, Jack Martin, and Peterkin Gay, the only survivors of a shipwreck on their coral island in the South Seas. Second, Ralph Rover narrates their story to us himself (as an old man, not as a youth, yet his first-person narration still provides an immediacy that is significant). "I was a boy when I went through the wonderful adventures herein set down," begins the preface, in which Ralph also declares, "I present my book specially to boys," while also ambiguously addressing his imagined reader as "boy or man."[37] Third, despite the book's evangelical ending, the narrative itself places less emphasis on the moral lessons of island life than its predecessors in the genre. To quote Maher again, *The Coral Island* was "a turning point" in this respect: "From the 1860s on, the Robinsonade is less a didactic or pedagogic vehicle than a formulaic, secular adventure."[38] As David Agruss describes, whereas in *Tom Brown's School Days*, "the antidote to the contaminating encroachment of femininity is the all-boy public school," in Ballantyne's book—and many other Robinsonades—"the guarantor of normative boyhood masculinity is the all-boy island adventure."[39]

Yet there are still ambiguities to their play—and their paradise. To begin with, the boys' experience of their island is one of largely unalloyed delight, mediated by their different personalities. Ralph Rover himself occupies a middle ground between the characters of his comrades. Jack Martin is the group's de facto leader, thanks to age, courage, and, crucially, his store of knowledge gleaned from his reading habits. "I have been a great reader of books of travel and adventure all my life," Jack lectures Peterkin early in their island sojourn, "and that has put me up to a good many things that you are, perhaps, not acquainted with." Where Tom Sawyer's pleasure reading inspires fantasy, Jack's book learning means that the boys' basic needs are met with ease. Armed only with a motley selection of the kind of schoolboy detritus that Tom Sawyer keeps in his pockets—"a small penknife with a single blade broken off about the middle," "an old German-silver pencil-case without any lead," "a piece of whipcord about six yards long," "a sail-maker's needle of a small size," "a ship's telescope," and "a brass ring"—the boys quickly survive and thrive. Even though Peterkin—the youngest of the castaways and the least practically minded of the boys—declares that he "would not give *tuppence* for a man of books," he still seems well versed in certain kinds of imperial narrative. As such, while Ralph frets about the threats of cannibals and starvation, the island holds no terrors for Peterkin either: "I have made up my mind that it's capital,—first rate,—the best thing that ever happened to us, and the most splendid prospect that ever lay before three jolly young tars. We've got an island all to ourselves. We'll take possession in the name of the king; we'll go and enter the service of its black inhabitants. Of course, we'll rise, naturally, to the top of affairs. White men always do in savage countries."[40]

For much of the book, the boys' main concern is not for survival, escape, or conquest but for play and adventure. They explore the island, frolic in the water, discover underwater caves, and establish a society of male companionship that is the moral and emotional heart of the narrative: "We three on this our island, although most unlike in many things, when united, made a trio so harmonious that I question if there ever met before such an agreeable triumvirate. There was, indeed, no note of discord whatever in the symphony we played together on that sweet Coral Island." Peterkin declares, "It must be the ancient Paradise." Yet soon enough, other forces intrude on their island utopia. Bloody violence marks the second half of the narrative. First, warring tribes of native people arrive on their island: the boys are witness to acts of murder and cannibalism. Second, pirates discover their island and capture Ralph. Throughout these events, Ralph's narration draws a line of connection between these apparently disparate groups. Ambiguities abound. On the one hand, he meditates on the initial disruption to their island home: "We had lived for many months in a clime for the most part so beautiful, that we had often wondered whether Adam and Eve had found Eden more sweet; and we had seen the quiet solitudes of our paradise suddenly broken in upon by ferocious savages, and the white sands stained with blood and strewed with lifeless forms; yet, among these cannibals, we had seen many symptoms of a kindly nature." Contrastingly, Ralph laments, as the boys hide from the pirates in a hidden cave that they have prepared as a refuge in case of disaster, "Little did we imagine that the first savages who would drive us into it would be white savages, perhaps our own countrymen."[41] The boys remain the moral heart of the book, caught between these different renderings of savagery. As Bristow notes, the boys—naturally good and brave—tread an idealized middle ground: they "get as close as possible to being both pirates (defiant, daring, individualistic) and savages (survivors taming nature) but without turning into them."[42]

At the book's climax, the reunited trio attempt to rescue a young native girl from a choice between forced marriage and cannibalism. They fail and are themselves imprisoned, facing execution and consumption: "Here they thrust us into a species of natural cave in a cliff, and, having barricaded the entrance, left us in total darkness. [. . .] It was an unusual sight for me to see our once joyous companion in tears." Like *Tom Sawyer*, their narrative ends with a shift from despair to escape—but the boys don't secure their own release. During the month of their imprisonment, the local chief is converted to Christianity by a visiting missionary: "After they embraced the Christian faith, they sought, by showing us the utmost kindness, to compensate for the harsh treatment we had experienced at their hands." Even though these missionary successes are intended to provide an emotional climax to the text and despite the violence that has beset them, the boys' inevitable return to civilization at the end of the book still seems like an expulsion from paradise: "A thrill of joy, strangely mixed with sadness, passed through our hearts,—for we were at length 'homeward bound,' and were gradually leaving far behind us the beautiful, bright, green, coral islands of the Pacific Ocean."[43]

Though radically different in many of their concerns, the boy heroes of Captain Mayne Reid's many books shared affinities with Ballantyne's harmonious trio. Reid was born in Ireland in 1818 and, by any standards, lived a profoundly transatlantic life. He first left for America in 1839—enchanted, at least according to his wife and biographer, Elizabeth Hyde Reid, with a vision of "the vast prairies and deep forest of the Western United States, about which he had often read." He, in turn, would become the defining chronicler of frontier life for a new generation of young readers. Since Reid arrived in the New World in New Orleans, the Mississippi defined his early experiences of the country—as it would his popular fictions. First employed at "a large commission house" where "gangs of slaves" were auctioned, Reid soon left New Orleans and its "distasteful" trade. Moving upriver to Natchez, he "acted as a clerk in a store," at a time when the Mississippi town was "the resort of river gamblers, thieves, and desperate characters." But Natchez was "also the rendezvous of trappers and Indian traders," and from those characters, Reid "absorbed many a tale of adventure and hair-breadth escape, thereby increasing his own desire for a taste of wild."[44] A series of frontier adventures followed—if Reid and his wife were to be believed. Following his service, and near-fatal wounding, in the Mexican-American War, Reid again crossed the Atlantic. Setting aside plans to involve himself in the European revolutions of 1848, he began to achieve fame as a writer. Even at the time, some of the wilder aspects of his adventurous biography were questioned. Edgar Allan Poe, a friend of Reid in Philadelphia in the mid-1840s, apparently described him as "a colossal but most picturesque liar. He fibs on a surprising scale [. . .] but with the finish of an artist, and that's why I listen to him attentively."[45]

When Reid turned to fiction in earnest, the Mississippi River was foregrounded as the prime arena for his tales of adventure. His first tale for boys was *The Desert Home* (1851)—appropriately, a Robinsonade set in what Reid termed the "Great American Desert" of the Southwest.[46] The father of this "English Family Robinson" had previously been disappointed in a land investment at Cairo on the Mississippi River, echoing Dickens in *Martin Chuzzlewit*. Building on that formula, Reid followed *The Desert Home* with a deeply influential book, *The Boy Hunters* (1852). The dedication highlighted the transatlantic nature of Reid's conception of his audience: "For the Boy Readers of England and America This Book Has Been Written, And To Them It Is Dedicated." The opening sentences of a narrative detailing the dramatic adventures of three boys on a hunting expedition, from Louisiana to Texas in search of a fabled white buffalo, conjure a potent spell of the Mississippi River: "Go with me to the great river Mississippi. It is the longest river in the world. A line that would measure it would just reach to the centre of the earth,—in other words, it is four thousand miles in length. Go with me to this majestic river." The adventures that follow that enticing invitation climax, like *The Coral Island*, with the boys' capture by "fifty tall savages." Just as they are about to be killed—"It was their intention to tie their prisoners to the stake, and use them as a target for their arrows!"—it becomes clear that the boys' father had been a friend of Tecumseh. Now bound in fellowship, the boys spend days "in hunting with the Indians" until their mission is accomplished.[47]

The glamour of the Mississippi was only amplified in Reid's *The Quadroon* (1856), the basis for Dion Boucicault's popular stage play *The Octoroon* (1859). Reid's novel, broadly critical of slavery and the South even though Reid declared his intention "neither to aid the abolitionist, nor glorify the planter," opens with an extraordinary incantation to the river:

> Father of Waters! I worship thy mighty stream! As the Hindoo by the shores of his sacred river, I kneel upon thy banks, and pour forth my soul in wild adoration! Far different are the springs of our devotion. To him, the waters of his yellow Ganges are the symbols of a superstitious awe, commingled with dark fears for the mystic future; to me, thy golden waves are the souvenirs of joy, binding the present to the known and happy past. Yes, mighty river! I worship thee in the past. My heart thrills with joy at the very mention of thy name! [. . .] I gaze upon lovely landscapes ever changing, like scenes of enchantment, or the pictures of a panorama. They are the loveliest upon earth—for where are views to compare with thine?[48]

In the varied adventures that follow—through steamboat races and explosions, from gamblers to slaves—the Mississippi looms large. The Civil War did little to change the vogue for Reid and his work. If anything, he was more in demand during the 1860s and 1870s. In America, he started to write for the Beadle publishing company, at the forefront of the dime novel revolution. In 1868, he wrote *The Planter Pirate: A Souvenir of the Mississippi* for the publisher, subsequently rereleased by Beadle & Adams in 1874 as *The Island Pirate*. The novel begins with a portrait of "Murrell [. . .] the great pirate and robber of the Mississippi," before weaving a new story of crime and punishment along the river.[49]

For a generation, then, Mayne Reid defined a certain spirit of adventure along the Mississippi—a heady blend of boyish heroes, river pirates, lynch law, slavery, and Native American life that circulated widely for decades. Anne Windholz has described the way that public schoolboys in Britain "often amused themselves by reading works such as Captain Mayne Reid's exciting wild west novels for boys."[50] Across the Atlantic, one youthful fan was Theodore Roosevelt. In his *Autobiography*, Roosevelt paid repeated tribute to the significance of Reid's work to his development: "The novels of Mayne Reid [. . .] strengthened my instinctive interest in natural history. I was too young to understand much of Mayne Reid, excepting the adventure part and the natural history part—these enthralled me." (He also enjoyed "reveling in such tales of adventure as Ballantyne's stories.")[51] And in spite of Reid's pointed ad-

dresses to boy readers and an apparently general assumption of a male readership for all of these stories of adventures, it is clear that young female readers
could be equally susceptible to the visions conjured by Reid and his contemporaries. Frances Hodgson Burnett—who also crossed the Atlantic as a young
woman—declared that the "spell" of Mayne Reid "transformed the sofa-arms
[. . .] to 'untamed mustangs' and the Nursery into a boundless prairie across
which troops of Indian warriors pursued the Doll upon her steed."[52]

In 1867, Mayne Reid moved back to America for a number of years. There
he founded his own story paper, *Onward, for the Youth of America,* which declared itself to be "a guide to conduct the youth of America along that path
leading to the highest and noblest manhood."[53] In trying his hand at editing
a short-lived story paper, Reid was himself attempting to capitalize on a new
trend in publishing for younger readers—a trend established in large part by
Edwin J. Brett's *Boys of England,* published from 1866 to 1899. After his youthful experiences of Chartism as an artist-engraver, Brett moved into publishing and spent the early part of the 1860s publishing "London 'low-life' penny
dreadfuls," titles like *The Wild Boys of London.*[54] With *Boys of England,* though,
Brett established a more respectable format and a formula—"exciting fiction,
informative non-fiction, vivid illustrations, and free gifts and competitions, all
delivered with refreshing conviviality"—that would provide him with significant success and a host of rivals on both sides of the Atlantic.[55]

In turn, *Boys of England* and its fascination with America was itself predicated precisely on Reid's brand of adventure narrative. Reid's name appeared
constantly in the paper's first few years, from clamoring readers and anxious
editors alike. His centrality to the cultural world that *Boys of England* inhabited
is clear from the correspondence pages. In August 1867, for instance, a letter
from an A. Redmond suggested, "I think an original tale by Captain Mayne
Reid would be liked very much by your readers." In response, *Boys of England*
replied, "We think so too, and have been in communication with the gallant
captain on the subject."[56] Ultimately, Reid contributed a number of stories of
American frontier life to the paper. In "The Fatal Cord: A Tale of Backwoods
Retribution" (1867), for example, Reid set his (now familiar) scene in "the Mississippian forest [. . .] upon the Arkansas side of the great river [. . .] a quarter
of a century ago, when this district of country contained a heterogeneous population, comprising some of the wildest and wickedest spirits to be found in
all the length and breadth of the backwoods border."[57] As central as Reid's ac-

counts of the American river frontier were to Brett's young readers, they were not the only visions of the Mississippi to appear in the paper. Mark Twain featured periodically as a source of humorous filler material: "Mark Twain says—'To the poor whites along the Mississippi river, chills are a merciful provision of Providence, enabling them to take exercise without exertion.'"[58]

Perhaps the most compelling image of the river to emerge in the pages of *Boys of England* at this moment, however, in ways that resonate with *The Adventures of Tom Sawyer,* was a long forgotten story titled "British Jack and Yankee Doodle." This apparently run-of-the-mill tale of frontier life and adventure along the Mississippi is revealing about the transatlantic dynamic of boyhood adventure in ways that illuminate Twain's river. Though advertised as being "from the pen of one of the most admired Authors of the day," the story was published anonymously.[59] On the surface of things, it is hack work, cobbled together from a series of stock characters and situations, defying the realities of American geography in the movement of its characters, wearing its popular influences (Cooper, Reid, Harriet Beecher Stowe, Bret Harte, probably Twain himself) so broadly that at times it verges on pastiche. Yet its broad brush-strokes serve to effectively highlight the popular image of the Mississippi at this moment, and in spite of its clichés and convolutions, it has the ability to surprise in the fate that it weaves for its youthful transatlantic heroes.

The first installment of "British Jack and Yankee Doodle" establishes its extraordinary cast of template characters, mixing together (as Twain does in *Tom Sawyer*) domestic scenes of boyish fun and frontier adventure in the vein of Mayne Reid. Gathered together on an American farm situated somewhere in an undefined West are three young boys: the American "Master Jonathan Squash Melon" and British heroes "Jack Briton" and Briton's "great chum" Keith Ashbrook. This apparently standard transatlantic setup is more complicated than it first seems, however. Jack and Keith have actually been raised on the frontier by a "tall Indian dressed in full war regalia [. . .] known by two names. Amongst the gamblers of Euchre Gulch he hailed to Fire Water Jim. On the plains his enemies had learned to dread the war-whoop of Grey Wolf." Grey Wolf had discovered the pair of boys floating in a canoe as small children fifteen years earlier—one of the motivating mysteries of the plot. When Jonathan's father encounters this makeshift family on his travels, he comes to the conclusion that Jack Briton may be a distant relation—"'cause I once had a cousin in England of his name"—and so brings the boys and their adoptive father to live with him on the farm: "I wanted him to go to school and learn a white men's ways." Providing comic relief are Zeke Whiffles, a blundering farmhand and Revolutionary War veteran, and "Zip," clearly inspired by Harriet Beecher Stowe's "Topsy," a "black imp of the female sex." The story's notorious antihero—and the figure with the key to Jack and Keith's childhood traumas—is a charming gambler and robber named "Skyer Slug," Grey Wolf's mortal enemy. Also present, alongside scores of gold miners, various outlaws, and other standard American types, is Lord Ashbrook, a lisping British aristocrat—"What a horrid barbawous countway!"—in America for the bear hunting, and his "obsequious toady" Lawyer Smithers, secretly Skyer Slug's father.[60]

The first half of "British Jack and Yankee Doodle" blends scenes of boyish hijinks—in stock settings like corn shuckings and in the schoolroom—with frontier peril. The second half of the narrative, and the ultimate revelation of the text's animating secrets, plays out along the Mississippi River. An extraordinary flood hits the town when its inhabitants are attending a meeting in the schoolhouse; so powerful is this freshet that it seems to carry our heroes from the gold fields of the West to "the bosom of the Mississippi."[61] The youthful heroes float on top of the schoolhouse itself, a structure that they manage to convert into a raft. Various thrilling incidents beset them as they travel—wild boars attack, snakes attack, alligators attack, bears attack, an alligator attacks a bear—until their raft is skewered by a snag. "'Well, that puts an end to our cruise down the river,' Jonathan said, ruefully. 'Darn it, I kinder regret that we have to go ashore.'"[62] And so the motley crew decides to carry on downriver in a new craft: "'There's our canoe,' and he pointed to the tree [. . .]. 'By hickory, that's so,' said the enthusiastic Jonathan. 'We can have a dug out in three shakes of a lamb's tail.'"[63] Prefiguring Tom's plan at the conclusion of *Adventures of Huckleberry Finn*, they intend to "come back by steamboat from New Orleans [. . .] we can work our way as deck hands and roustabouts."[64]

Yet their plans are interrupted. Paddling downriver, they are confronted with a steamboat explosion: "There is a mighty roar. The steamboat is blown into the air. The sky is turned blood-red. The air writhes with the mad horror of human agony."[65] After helping to rescue the wounded and drowning, the cast is gathered together on board another steamboat, where the plot reaches its climax and secrets are revealed (fig. 4). Not only does the river serve as a space of self-determination and adventure for its young characters; it becomes

FIGURE 4. "Grey Wolf Stooped Down and Caught Her by the Arms,"
"British Jack and Yankee Doodle," *Boys of England*, September 17, 1880, 312.

the place where they literally discover who they really are. Grey Wolf and
Skyer Slug fatally wound each other in a knife fight. The source of the animus
of these two surrogate father figures is finally revealed: many years ago, Grey
Wolf had found Slug injured in the forest and brought him back to his tribe;
Slug had fallen in love and eloped with Grey Wolf's daughter Owaissa; they
had a daughter, Wenonah, whom Slug had sent to a boarding school in St.
Louis after Owaissa's death: "She pined for the woods, and died in a city."[66]
The secret of Jack and Keith's origins is also exposed. Slug explains that he is
actually "Charles Smithers [. . .] an Englishman by birth."[67] Having fled Britain
having forged a check, Slug uncovered and foiled a plot by his nefarious father

to disinherit the "last heirs of Lord Ashbrook"—the boys discovered in the canoe by Grey Wolf. If the giddying twists and turns of that summary sound conventionally convoluted enough, the resolution of the tensions of the narrative are perhaps surprising. Jack Briton, now the rightfully reinstated Lord Ashbrook, travels back to England to claim his birthright, but he does not travel alone. He leaves America with "his beautiful wife Wenonah, the grandchild of Grey Wolf. In the castle they have promoted Zeke Whiffles to be butler, and faithful Zip turned out a most useful servant."[68] The future of this text's ideal of white boyhood, then, turns out to be an extraordinary hybridity: British aristocracy, seasoned on the American river frontier, joined in marriage with indigenous America, maintaining a social hierarchy.

"The Great Step of My Lifetime"

While the heroes of British adventure fiction were discovering themselves on desert islands and Mississippi River excursions, American writers were crafting their own new narratives of boyhood. This was a trend that began in the antebellum years and clearly drew on British examples. As Alice Fahs outlines: "These novels drew less on the antebellum literary tradition of exemplum literature than on the 1850s rise of a new fashion in juvenile fiction: adventure novels featuring boy heroes. [. . .] Reid's and Ballantyne's work signalled the beginnings of a fashion in boys' fiction."[69] Like their British counterparts, these American writers also frequently positioned water at the center of their narratives. In contrast, a narrative of economic uplift was also central to their tales: the river didn't just provide these American boys with adventure; it frequently gave them respectability and social status too.

Sitting squarely at the intersection of adventure, the Civil War, and the river were the early works of Charles Austin Fosdick, better known to young readers as Harry Castlemon (along with Oliver Optic, Edward Ellis, and Horatio Alger, one of a quartet of American writers who dominated the landscape of boys' books in the latter half of the nineteenth century). "Boys don't like fine writing," Castlemon famously declared when quizzed about "how to write stories for boys" by the *Writer* magazine in 1896. "What they want is adventure, and the more of it you can get into 250 pages of manuscript, the better fellow you are." Following that formula for decades, Castlemon became one of the most widely read authors of the period. By his own account, a familiar figure was an early inspiration. At the age of sixteen, at the moment that he determined to become an author, he "was reading [. . .] one of Mayne Reid's works which I had drawn from the library."[70] So inspired, Castlemon began work on what would become the first of a series of books featuring boy-hero Frank Nelson that ultimately encompassed the Civil War on the Mississippi—adventures that would remain ubiquitous for decades. As Franklin P. Adams reminisced in 1941: "One Christmas morning in the late Eighties I found, under the tree, three brown-covered, gold-lettered volumes. I finished reading 'Frank on a Gunboat' before dark. [. . .] 'Frank Before Vicksburg' and 'Frank on the Lower Mississippi' were wonderful. They were Adventure and they were History."[71]

The vicissitudes in the series reflected Fosdick's own experiences. The first book that Castlemon completed became *Frank, the Young Naturalist* (1864), finished in manuscript while Fosdick was still a schoolboy. It established his hero as "a handsome, high-spirited boy, about sixteen years of age [. . .] whose highest ambition was to be called the best scholar in his class."[72] But then, the Civil War disrupted his literary plans. At first, Castlemon put books aside: "I was in a fever of suspense, and I wanted to take a hand with the defenders of my country; so at last I enlisted in the navy." That step took him to the Mississippi River: "I went down to Cairo as landsman, served on several boats, getting my promotion as fast as I learned my duties, and was finally ordered to the navy yard as assistant to Fleet Paymaster Dunn." Still, Castlemon "could not forget the manuscript I had left behind."[73] So, with the war still raging, Castlemon found a publisher for *Frank, the Young Naturalist* and in short order dramatically changed the nature of his literary interests to produce a number of sequels detailing Frank's wartime experiences on the Mississippi River. To emphasize the author's youthful, biographical stake in this endeavor, Castlemon's publishers billed their author as "The Gun-Boat Boy" and described him in marketing copy as "a youth who is serving his country on one of our Western gunboats."[74]

In *Frank on a Gun-Boat* (1864), like Castlemon himself, Frank and his cousin Archie exchanged the fun of hunting and sailing on their boyhood river for other kinds of watery adventure in the navy. At first, though, the boys are unhappy with their posting: "The boys were a good deal disappointed [. . .] for the idea of serving out their year on the Mississippi River was not an agreeable one. They had hoped to be ordered to the coast."[75] Yet in the experiences that follow, the river proves to be more than a suitable testing ground for martially minded young men. Frank is captured and imprisoned by the Confederates, only to effect a daring escape; he is present when Vicksburg falls; he commands his own ship; he tangles with spies and single-handedly breaks up a nest of guerrillas terrorizing river traffic on the Lower Mississippi. Throughout, his bravery along the river is rewarded with increasing social and economic status. The end of *Frank before Vicksburg* (1866) finds our hero with a "well-earned reputation as a gallant young officer, waiting to be ordered to new scenes of excitement and danger further down the Mississippi and up her tributary streams."[76] At the end of the war itself, in *Frank on the Lower Mississippi* (1867), Frank is honorably discharged: "He was reluctant to part from his crew [. . .]. One by one the sailors came into the cabin [. . .] they wished their commander 'plain sailing through life' [. . .]. Frank and Archie are proud of the part they have borne in the war of the Rebellion, and will never forget their varied and eventful experience in the Mississippi Squadron.'"[77] In overlaying the narrative of boyhood adventure on the Mississippi onto the contemporary military life of the river, Castlemon was indelibly changing the meaning of both the fictional river and the fictionalized war. As Alice Fahs has described, "Directly influenced by antebellum juvenile adventure literature, Castlemon in turn conceptualized the war as a boys' adventure."[78] As the *American Literary Gazette* put it, "In introducing the young reader to scenes on the Mississippi River and the western country, they possess an element of novelty in this class of works."[79] Many other adventures followed for Frank—in the woods, on the prairies, with the *rancheros*—and countless other characters would flow from Castlemon's pen, but in large part, their genesis lay on the Mississippi River in wartime. Castlemon returned to the river periodically, too, in texts like *George at the Wheel; or, Life in the Pilot-House* (1881).

William Taylor Adams—best known as "Oliver Optic"—was an equally dominant voice in the world of American children's literature, both before and after the Civil War, up to his death in 1897. As Sarah Wadsworth describes, across his influential career Oliver Optic produced "approximately 126 titles," the most popular of which "sold at a rate of more than 100,000 a year. [. . .] By the time of his death an estimated two million copies of his books had been sold."[80] Alongside all that, he edited a series of popular weekly story papers for children. The Mississippi was at the root of his writing career too. His first novel, *Hatchie, the Guardian Slave* (1853, published under the pseudonym

Warren T. Ashton and clearly written to capitalize on the vogue for *Uncle Tom's Cabin*), was explicitly a product of his time on the river. "In the summer of 1848," Adams explained, "the author of the following tale was a passenger on board a steamboat from New Orleans to Cincinnati. During the passage— one of the most prolonged and uncomfortable in the annals of western river navigation—the plot of this story was arranged."[81]

Very swiftly, though, Adams changed his focus and began writing explic- itly for children. In 1875, he gave a speech (reprinted in *Oliver Optic's Maga- zine*) in which he elucidated his motivations in this field. Remembering his own youthful reading—echoing Tom Sawyer's tastes—he lamented: "The hero of these stories was a pirate, a highwayman, a smuggler, or a bandit. He was painted in glowing colors; and in admiring his boldness, my sympathies were with this outcast and outlaw. These books were bad, very bad; because they brought the reader into sympathy with evil and wicked men." Admitting that his own books "have sometimes been rather more 'sensational' than I now wish," Adams remained confident that "I have never made a hero whose moral character, or whose lack of high aims and purposes, could mislead the reader."[82] That moral streak was immediately apparent in his first book for children, *The Boat Club; or, The Bunkers of Rippleton* (1854)—a story largely concerned with boys messing about in boats on a lake in a New England town.

Throughout the torrent of children's books that followed, the Mississippi remained a recurrent setting in the stories that Optic published in his mag- azines and in his series books. None was more telling than *Down the River; or, Buck Bradford and His Tyrants*, first serialized in Optic's *Our Boys and Girls* magazine throughout 1868, before being published as the sixth volume in *The Starry Flag* series in 1869. *Down the River* opens in Wisconsin. Orphaned hero Buck Bradford and his "poor, dear, deformed, invalid sister," Flora, are stuck in abusive lodgings with a "brute" of a landlord. Also suffering is Buck's friend Sim Gwynn—though "stupid," a "great, stout, bow-legged fellow, as good- natured as the day was long"—who is slowly being starved by the farmer for whom he works. Meditating on their problems, Buck finds a release in the wa- ters of the Western Rivers: "I had a taste for river scenery. Every night, when I went for the mail, I used to see the steamboat on the river; and I often thought I should be 'made' if I could make a trip in her. Ever since my brother wrote that he should take us down to New Orleans in the fall, I had looked forward with intense joy to the voyage down the river." So inspired, Buck formulates a plan. With Sim's help, he determines to "build a big raft, with a house on it,—a place to live in,—where we can cook, and sleep, and eat" and float down to New Orleans to find Buck's older brother. Soon the "cozy" construction is complete, and the trio pushes off into the waters of the Wisconsin: "the great step of my lifetime [. . .] the final triumph over my tyrants." Heading to the Mississippi, they experience the usual perils of a river journey while making sure to stop on a Sunday to attend church. Reaching the Mississippi itself opens up "a new world" to the young travelers: "The scene became more lively and exciting as we advanced. [. . .] We had never seen the great world before, and we were overwhelmed with surprise."[83]

Confronted with a ubiquitous steamboat explosion—"we saw one of them suddenly fly in pieces, torn, rent, shivered, the atmosphere filled with fragments"—Buck rescues a young girl from the river. Emily Goodridge, the daughter of a rich New Orleans merchant, joins the group on their raft. This moment of bravery makes Buck's fortune. When they finally arrive at their destination, Emily's father is so grateful to Buck that he becomes his benefactor. Recognizing that he is "noble," while his own sons are all "bad boys," he provides a legacy of ten thousand dollars each to Buck and his sister. Before long, Buck marries Emily and settles into comfortable respectability: "My wife—whom I picked up one day on the Mississippi River—is joy enough for this world, though I have another, and almost equal joy, in dear Flora, whose home is also mine. We are blessed of God, and blessed in ourselves, for we are as loving and devoted to each other as when, years ago, on the raft, we journeyed DOWN THE RIVER."[84]

"The Humours of Rivers"

Fictional escapades along the world's waterways may have been a staple part of popular culture for young readers in the wake of the Civil War, but they also shared shelf space, literary tropes, and an affinity for rivers with a new wave of exploration narratives. Chief among this new generation of imperial adventurers was Henry Morton Stanley. Late in life, looking back in his ultimately unfinished (and unreliable) autobiography, it is clear that Stanley understood his own life through the lens of adventure and uplift as defined by contemporary boys' books. His intention in writing his autobiography was, he explained to his wife, to provide an "example" to "the poor boys in these islands [. . .] and also all the poor boys in Canada, the States, and our Colonies [. . .]. I believe the story of my efforts, struggles, sufferings, and failures, of the work done, and the work left undone,—I believe this story would help others." So much of what Henry Morton Stanley had done with his extraordinary life revolved around rivers. First came the Mississippi. His arrival in the New World in the late 1850s was the first of many reinventions that he effected throughout his life. After a childhood in Wales marked by poverty, hardship, and neglect, young Stanley's first encounter with the Mississippi at New Orleans was profoundly significant: "Though about thirty-five years have elapsed since I first stood upon the levee of the Crescent City, scarcely one of all my tumultuous sensations of pleasure, wonder, and curiosity, has been forgotten by me. [. . .] I was nearly overwhelmed with blissful feeling that rises from emancipation. I was free!—and I was happy, yes, actually happy, for I was free—at last the boy was free!" Stanley's transformative time in America took him far along the Mississippi, providing impressions that would stay with him in the decades and the expeditions to come. Steaming to St. Louis in 1859, the "grand pictures" that Stanley encountered "were likely to remain with me forever": "The intensity of everything also surprised me, from the resistless and deep river, the driving force within the rushing boats [. . .]. A feverish desire to join in the bustle burned in my veins." He came back downriver by flatboat, "a lazy life [. . .] smoking, sleeping, and yarning." All told, Stanley concluded, during his years on the Mississippi, he "gained valuable experience of the humours of rivers. The fluvial moods had considerably interested me."[85] The study would serve him well.

After spending time as "assistant to the cook on a Mississippi riverboat," as a clerk in a "country merchant's business" on the Arkansas River, in military service for the Confederacy, in military service for the Union—and desertion from both—Stanley started to make a name for himself as a journalist.[86] He reported from the field in disparate locations, from "General Hancock's expedition against the Kiowas and Comanches" to the British expedition to Abyssinia in 1868.[87] It was during this postwar period that Stanley first met Mark Twain—in St. Louis, on the Mississippi River. Initially, Stanley angered Twain when he "stenographically reported a lecture of mine" so accurately that Twain was unable to deliver it again in the region.[88] Yet that animosity swiftly grew into friendship. From London, in 1872, Twain confided to Olivia that "Stanley lacks a deal of being a gentleman" and swiftly saw through Stanley's pretense that he was American by birth, yet Twain also noted, "We have been intimate & I have been of assistance to him & he has been of assistance to me."[89] It was a friendship that lasted across the decades and through the extraordinary vicissitudes of fortune experienced by both men. "How far he stretches across my life!" Twain marveled to Stanley's widow, Dorothy, after his death in 1904. "It is 37 years. I have known no other friend and intimate so long, except John Hay—a friendship which dates from the same year and the same half of it, the first half of 1867."[90] Stanley also became close with others who knew—or were soon to know—the Mississippi River well. Edward King first met Stanley in Spain in 1869, when both men were young reporters covering revolutionary violence, just before King went to investigate "the Great South" and the Mississippi River for *Scribner's*. To King, Stanley seemed "the very perfection of activity. He would overcome any obstacle that proved too much for me. [. . .] He is not one of those who get lost."[91] In this prediction, King was prescient. At the end of their time together in Europe, Stanley was to embark on his first great journey to Africa to find the missing missionary David Livingstone. If that expedition secured his fame, his later exploits on Africa's rivers seemed, to his contemporaries, to guarantee him immortality.

In the early 1870s, the geography of Africa's rivers remained one of the most pressing global questions. As *Scribner's Monthly* put it in 1874: "One source after another of the Nile has been reached by one after another of the various explorers who have risked life in their adventurous efforts. And yet the great river is a mystery still, and waits for one more enterprise, at least, to give a complete and conclusive answer to the question of its source."[92] It was this and other mysteries that Stanley would seek to solve during his return to Africa from 1874 to 1877. Ultimately, he would cover seven thousand miles, answering all those pressing geographical questions and opening the Congo to exploitation, and fix the attention of the world on rivers and their wider significance. A glowing profile of Stanley by John Russell Young in *Harper's New Monthly Magazine* provided a useful summary of what his river explorations were felt to have achieved: "Before he went out on this mission we knew there were two rivers—the Congo and the Lualaba. [. . .] What Stanley did was to show that the Congo and the Lualaba were one and the same; that the Congo, instead of losing itself among the rapids, was to force itself into the very heart of the continent; that the Lualaba, instead of going north and submitting to the usurping waters of the Nile, was to turn to the west and force its way to the sea; that these two rivers were to disappear from the map, and be known as one river."[93]

The wider implications of that discovery were tantalizing. *Harper's* elucidated: "This work opens new fields of missionary labor, new channels of trade [. . .]. The possibilities of Africa are made known to us, and the fancy is bewildered as we think what may be done with a country so rich in land, time, and metals."[94] In no uncertain terms, *Harper's* declared that Stanley's journey of discovery "was perhaps the noblest and most intrepid that had ever fallen to one man since Columbus"—and they were not alone in this kind of assessment.

Yet through all Stanley's travels and travails, the memory of the Mississippi remained with him; the river of his youth served as a benchmark by which to measure the African waterways that he encountered. In *How I Found Livingstone* (1872), sick with fever, Stanley's imagination drew him back to his (partly invented) American youth: "I remembered how one day, after we had come to live near the Mississippi, I floated down, down, hundreds of miles, with a wild fraternity of knurly giants, the boatmen of the Mississippi."[95] In *Through the Dark Continent* (1878), Stanley's account of his successful descent of the Congo, the Mississippi made numerous appearances. When he reached the confluence of the rivers Luama and Lualaba, Stanley "likened it even here to the Mississippi, as it appears before the impetuous, full-volumed Missouri pours its rusty brown water into it." Farther downriver, beset by difficulties, Stanley's companion Frank Pocock asked his leader about the prospects of their mission: "Do you really believe, in your inmost soul, that we shall succeed?" In his affirmation, Stanley reached for a very particular predecessor, and a previous age of exploration, in language that would not be out of a place in any adventure book for boys: "It is true that our prospects are as dark as this night. Even the Mississippi presented no such obstacles to De Soto as this river will necessarily present to us. [. . .] Now look at this, the latest chart which Europeans have drawn of this region. It is a blank, perfectly white. [. . .] Never has white paper possessed such a charm for me as this has, and I have already mentally peopled it, filled it with most wonderful pictures of towns, villages, rivers, countries, and tribes—all in the imagination—and I am burning to see whether I am correct or not. Believe? I see us gliding down by tower and town, and my mind will not permit a shadow of doubt." Unlike De Soto, of course, Stanley would not be buried in the river that he laid claim to, even though many of his companions—including Frank Pocock—would find their final resting place in its waters. As his journey progressed, the commercial and colonial potential of the Congo seemed ever more clear. As the "great river grew sea-like in breadth," Stanley noted, "there was water sufficient to float the most powerful steamers that float in the Mississippi."[96] As Stanley brought the Congo to the world's attention, so, too, did he keep the Mississippi in view.

Stanley, though, was hardly alone in feeding the world's new fascination with adventure and exploration along exotic river systems. In the 1870s, for example, a young adventurer from Indiana captured a brief moment of fame as the so-called boy explorer (sometimes "boy naturalist" or "boy traveler") whose feats of aquatic exploration were publicized across the nation. Ernest Morris's first exploits, however, took place on familiar waters. In August 1874, the *Indianapolis Sentinel* reported on the departure of "the young voyagers" (explicitly echoing the title of a Mayne Reid book) who had just embarked on an epic journey down the western waters—from the White River to the Wabash, the Ohio to the Mississippi: "Yesterday morning young Morris, with his companion, Barrett Paine, a youth of about the same age as himself, started on the trip [. . .]. It is the intention of Morris and Paine to push on as rapidly as possible to the Mississippi. From there the voyage will be slow, the main object being to collect as many varieties of birds as possible." The goal was to reach Florida: "The hunters will not probably return home before next summer or fall."[97] Morris kept readers updated with dispatches from the river. In October, the "young voyager" wrote home from "the muddy Mississippi" about the journey so far.[98] By December, the Mississippi was conquered, and Morris was in New Orleans—"a sight nowhere surpassed in the United States"—promising updates from Florida.[99]

Very soon, though, Morris was looking to a new river for adventure. Like Twain before him, he had dreams of the Amazon. In July 1875, the *Indianapolis Sentinel* noted briefly: "Ernest Morris writes to his father announcing his arrival at Para, in South America. He is in good health and full of enthusiasm with the strange sights and prospects of his trip up the Amazon."[100] As Jerry Kuntz explains, there was another significant motivation spurring on Morris's trip: "While planning the route for his first voyage to the Amazon valley, Ernest Morris ignored the east-to-west course taken by many English and American scientists who had published books on the Amazon. Instead, Morris' preferred route was to follow a fictional trail described by a popular writer of boys' adventures stories: 'Captain' Thomas Mayne Reid."[101] According to Kuntz, it was none other than Reid's 1855 novel, *The Forest Exiles; or, The Perils of a Peruvian Family amid the Wilds of the Amazon,* that initially dictated Morris's route. "Our new journey shall have its pleasures and advantages," Reid exhorted his readers at the start of that book, "now we shall pass under the shadows of virgin forests, and float lightly upon the bosom of broad, majestic streams, whose shores echo with the voices of living Nature."[102]

Heeding Reid's call, Morris's escapades on various trips to the Amazon, bringing back rare plants and other intriguing specimens, established his fame in the national press. The reactions to Morris's youthful expeditions highlight the degree to which boyish adventure, exploration, imperialism, and scientific endeavor were blurred at this point. "The agony is over," crowed the *Indianapolis Sentinel* about its hometown hero. "The juvenile Hoosier naturalist, Ernest Morris, has actually arrived [. . .]. He is full of enthusiasm as ever, and satisfied with the result of his trip as a whole."[103] Romantic stories about his travels circulated widely, clearly attempting to transform Morris from boy explorer into the hero of a book for boys. Relating a story that "reads like a chapter from the 'Arabian Nights,'" one frequently reprinted newspaper account described the way that Morris had rescued a "a young Indian maiden" from drowning: "The old chief overwhelmed him with kindness and gifts, has taken him into the family, and now offers him the hand of Miss Princess, who is extremely beautiful and wears a diamond-studded girdle that would ransom a king."[104]

Yet there was a darker element to his travels than those accounts of gumption and pluck suggest. While much of Morris's work on the Amazon revolved around the collection of rare plants, they were not the only specimens that he was busy accumulating. In August 1877, he was profiled by *Frank Leslie's Illustrated Newspaper* and pictured with some of the "ghastly trophies" that he had recently brought back with him: "Upon his return to Brooklyn from this trip, fearing that some might doubt the narrative of his journey, he exposed to exhibition the heads of ten South American Indians that had been preserved by the Mundurucu nation as trophies of war. They are the first that have ever been brought to this country" (fig. 5).[105] Clearly attempting to capitalize on the sensation generated by these artifacts, Morris also endeavored, unsuccessfully, to publish a book about his travels entitled "In Search of Human Heads." At such moments, the violence and exploitation underlying the patina of boyish adventure in these kinds of narratives, real and imagined, was laid bare. Mor-

FIGURE 5. "Ernest Morris, the South American Explorer,"
Frank Leslie's Illustrated Newspaper, August 18, 1877, 409.

ris's portrait in *Frank Leslie's* emphasized both his youth and its uncanny contrast with the horror of his collection. It made for a striking image: Morris as
terrible boy-king, the brutal whims of boyhood incarnate, Tom Sawyer in the
heart of darkness.

"Gazing Longingly across the Wide River"

There might not be any ritual decapitations in *The Adventures of Tom Sawyer,*
but there are plenty of other deaths, real and imagined. Incorporating a variety
of the tropes that animated the spectrum of new books for boys in this period
(as well as a hint of the explorer narratives of the likes of Stanley and Morris),

The Adventures of Tom Sawyer is a text in which Twain uses the iconography of the river to subvert well-established templates of boyish adventure. Returning to Tom Sawyer's Mississippi from the international waters of boys' books, its hybridity is immediately apparent. On one level, the adventures that are described in Twain's book take place on the domestic scale of childhood: St. Petersburg and its immediate environs circumscribe the action of the plot. In this regard, *Adventures of Tom Sawyer* operates in a similar way—and with a familiar nostalgia—to *The Story of a Bad Boy* or *Tom Brown's School Days;* like those bad boys, Tom is certainly not "the Model Boy of the village." Unlike those bad boys, a river doesn't mend his ways. At the same time, the river undergoes multiple imaginative metamorphoses in the text, becoming an "ocean" that can transport Tom and his friends to various adventures that chime with other familiar narratives.[106] At those moments, the book is clearly in dialogue with the wealth of adventure narratives saturating the popular market at this point. On Jackson's Island, for example, the boys engage in their own Robinsonade—an episode that has not hitherto been read as a reworking of that common trope. In the cave, Tom and Becky undergo the kind of frontier peril of a Mayne Reid thriller. While Twain disrupts the expected tropes of adventure fiction in this book—the Robinsonade, for example, leads to boredom and homesickness—he also arguably takes his readers to yet darker places. By mingling the domestic and the sensational, he brings the legacies and possibilities of crime and death along the river home to roost; here violence and mortality are not displaced onto an abstracted frontier, national or colonial, but play out on a Mississippi that is both home and uncannily unfamiliar in the text. The river, therefore, becomes a multivalent symbol that reflects the perhaps unexpected tensions of the streams of influence flowing through the text.

Even before Tom reaches Jackson's Island, those tensions are apparent in the way that the river winds its way into the consciousness of the young characters. The first sense of the river that we receive in the book comes from boyish play. Ben Rogers imagines himself to be the *Big Missouri,* a fantasy of power and authority of the kind that Twain recorded in "Old Times on the Mississippi": "He was eating an apple, and giving a long, melodious whoop, at intervals, followed by a deep-toned ding-dong-dong, ding-dong-dong, for he was personating a steamboat. As he drew near, he slackened speed, took the middle of the street, leaned far over to starboard and rounded to ponderously and with laborious pomp and circumstance [. . .]. He was boat and captain and engine-bells combined, so he had to imagine himself standing on his own hurricane-deck giving the orders and executing them." Tom himself seems to have no interest in the steamboat economy on his doorstep—his tastes are far less prosaic. Soon after, Tom is to be found sulking by the river, looking for "desolate places that were in harmony with his spirit. A log raft in the river invited him, and he seated himself on its outer edge and contemplated the dreary vastness of the stream, wishing, the while, that he could only be drowned, all at once and unconsciously, without undergoing the uncomfortable routine devised by nature." It is the first, but hardly the last, time that the reader is asked to imagine Tom or one of his comrades "brought home from the river, dead, with his curls all wet, and his sore heart at rest."[107]

As John Seelye has described, the boys' trip to Jackson's Island is "the literal as well as the symbolic midpoint in the book."[108] The mini-Robinsonade that sits at the heart of the book clearly plays with the tropes of adventurous island fiction established by Ballantyne's *The Coral Island*. Like Ballantyne, Twain assembles a triumvirate of boys—Tom, Joe Harper, and Huck Finn—away from adult supervision. Though the boys are barely out of surveillance range, Tom's imagination completes the metamorphosis of their journey: "Three miles below St. Petersburg, at a point where the Mississippi River was a trifle over a mile wide, there was a long, narrow, wooded island, with a shallow bar at the head of it, and this offered well as a rendezvous. It was not inhabited; it lay far over toward the further shore, abreast a dense and almost wholly unpeopled forest. So Jackson's Island was chosen. [. . .] The mighty river lay like an ocean at rest. [. . .] It was but a small strain on his imagination to remove Jackson's Island beyond eye-shot of the village." At first, the runaways engage in the same kind of fun as their *Coral Island* counterparts. They set up camp and cook a meal: "It seemed glorious sport to be feasting in that wild, free way in the virgin forest of an unexplored and uninhabited island, far from the haunts of men, and they said they never would return to civilization." Yet even in the first moments of their adventure, the pleasure is undercut by their commitment to artifice: "They could have found a cooler place, but they would not deny themselves such a romantic feature as the roasting campfire." Twain soon further undermines the romantic pretense of their endeavor. Again, like the boys on *The Coral Island,* they set off "through the woods on an exploring expedition," yet though they "found plenty of things to be delighted with," they find "nothing to be astonished at." Moreover, they discover that their island is barely an island at all: "The shore it lay closest to was only separated from it by a narrow channel hardly two hundred yards wide."[109] Soon the bloom fades from their island paradise. The "sense of loneliness" and "budding homesickness" leaves them "gazing longingly across the wide river to where the village lay drowsing in the sun," in self-imposed exile.[110]

Yet here Twain shifts registers. When the boys realize that the village is searching in the river for their corpses, the adventure livens up. "Boys, I know who's drownded," Tom declares, "it's us!" Suddenly, then, they realize that "it was worth while to be a pirate, after all." Their island becomes not just an imagined South Sea atoll but a kind of limbo, catching them between life and death (prefiguring, perhaps, Peter Pan) and positioning the Mississippi as a very different kind of river. Apparently liberated by their imagined deaths, the "three dead boys" start to have fun again. A sudden storm provides enough of a sense of danger that "they sat by the fire and expanded and glorified their midnight adventure until morning." And when imagined piracy starts to drag, they find another game to play: "This was to knock off being pirates, for a while, and be Indians for a change. They were attracted by this idea; so it was not long before they were stripped, and striped from head to heel with black mud, like so many zebras—all of them chiefs, of course—and then they went tearing through the woods to attack an English settlement. By and by they separated into three hostile tribes, and darted upon each other from ambush with dreadful warwhoops, and killed and scalped each other by thousands. It was a gory day. Consequently it was an extremely satisfactory one."[111] The contrast to the boy books that Twain is clearly burlesquing in this island sequence is profound. Long before William Golding reworked Ballantyne's *The Coral Island* into *Lord of the Flies*, Twain had, albeit in a milder way, hinted at the essential brutality at the heart of boys when transported by water beyond the bounds of society. In *The Coral Island*, Ralph and his friends consciously avoid the violent extremities of both pirates and natives; in *The Adventures of Tom Sawyer*, it is precisely those roles that the boys adopt.

Before long, it is time to return to St. Petersburg in time to interrupt their own funerals, one of the many resurrection moments in the book. Yet there are no lessons learned from their time in limbo either; unlike Arthur's vision of heavenly peace across the river of death in *Tom Brown's Schooldays*, no evangelical improvements result from their trip across the Mississippi, despite the occasional guilty twinge. Instead, Tom and Joe learn how to smoke a pipe. If anything, it is the ghost and example of John Murrell that the island sequence resurrects—the semi-mythical river pirate who, in the popular record, loved disguises and pranks and grandiose conspiracies as well as "bloody deeds," while he swept up and down the Mississippi haunting its islands and caves. In the most influential penny dreadful account of his life and crimes, published in 1848, the base of his criminal operations and his "Mystic Clan" of criminal confederates was also depicted as an island in the river—"the Marauder's Paradise."[112]

Though Tom leaves his own Marauder's Paradise behind, he soon finds another suitable home for his imagined criminal conspiracies. To get to it, he has to go through a rather more serious ordeal. At the climax of *The Adventures of Tom Sawyer*, when Tom and Becky are trapped with Injun Joe in McDougal's Cave, the river also plays a crucial role in events. Setting off for a picnic, the youth of the town board the "old steam ferry-boat" and head downriver. When Becky and Tom get separated from the rest of the party during an expedition to the cave, again the town presumes that the children must have died in its vast recesses: "It was said that one might wander days and nights together through its intricate tangle of rifts and chasms, and never find the end of the cave; and that he might go down, and down, and still down, into the earth, and it was just the same—labyrinth under labyrinth, and no end to any of them." Added to those terrors, the pair are also trapped with Injun Joe, already well established as the villain of the book—and demonized as a "murderin' half-breed" and an "Injun devil." Jackson's Island may have been uninhabited, but in McDougal's Cave, at least Tom has to wrestle with the ghost of an indigenous presence. Even then, their encounter is vanishingly brief: "At that moment, not twenty yards away, a human hand, holding a candle, appeared from behind a rock!"[113] For Brander Matthews, writing in 1885, "the vision of the hand in the cave in *Tom Sawyer* is one of the very finest things in the literature of adventure since Robinson Crusoe first saw a single footprint in the sand of the seashore."[114] As Matthews hints here, their time in the cave is itself another kind of Robinsonade and one with far more peril than Tom's voluntary exile on Jackson's Island. Yet Twain swerves direction again. Injun Joe swiftly disappears again after this moment of terror, and there is no story paper confrontation between the pair. Though Tom shares a responsibility in his death, he hardly triumphs over his native nemesis. Instead, his presence lingers, and in death, Injun Joe becomes a figure—a "bloody-minded outcast," another mixture of Indian and pirate—with whom Tom can experience some identification: "Tom was touched, for he knew by his own experience how this wretch had suffered."[115]

The symbolic resonance of Tom and Becky's entrapment and eventual escape from the cave has attracted a number of interpretations. For Harold Aspiz, "The children's descent into the cave becomes a descent into the nether world of sheer terror and the shadow of death."[116] If Tom and Becky's dynamic in the cave seems to prefigure "Twain's affectionate sketches of Adam and Eve," still "the cave episode involves no fall from Paradise: only a resurrection from the cave and from what the St. Petersburg folk fear to be the deaths of the young pair."[117] For Larry Howe, this "trial in the underworld" turns the book into "a kind of bildungsroman-epic hybrid" in which Tom "metamorphoses from an irritating yet amusing juvenile delinquent into something like an American epic hero."[118] For Robert Tindol, this moment is an "anti-captivity narrative" in which "Tom abjures the long-standing choice of appealing to divine powers for salvation, and instead decides to emulate the ethos of his tormentor."[119] Certainly, what this near-death experience doesn't do is prompt Tom to any further reformation. When the *Coral Island* boys are released from their cave prison, it's thanks to English missionary zeal. "It seems to me," Ralph declares, watching the burning of the island's idols, "that the object we came here for having been satisfactorily accomplished, we have nothing more to do but get ready for sea as fast as we can, and hurrah for dear old England!"[120] When Tom emerges from the cave, however, his rebirth is watched over by the presence of a different kind of idol: "He glimpsed a far-off speck that looked like daylight; dropped the line and groped toward it, pushed his head and shoulders through a small hole, and saw the broad Mississippi rolling by!"[121]

So sanctified, Tom takes on a clear destiny. He does not, like Jack Briton in *Boys of England* or Oliver Optic's Buck Bradford, marry Becky Thatcher and settle down into adult responsibility, though he does soon equal them in wealth. Instead, he jumps into a stolen boat with Huck Finn to return to the cave that he has just escaped. With Injun Joe dead, it is time for Tom to take on his legacy. First, he plans to adopt his cave hideout in order to establish his own criminal enterprise: "It's the snuggest hole in this country. You just keep mum about it. All along I've been wanting to be a robber, but I knew I'd got to have a thing like this, and where to run across it was the bother. We've got it now, and we'll keep it quiet, only we'll let Joe Harper and Ben Rogers in—because of course there's got to be a Gang, or else there wouldn't be any style about it. Tom Sawyer's Gang—it sounds splendid, don't it, Huck?" And it's not just Injun Joe's bequest that Tom receives either: the shadow of John Murrell falls over the narrative again, since it is Murrell's treasure that ends up as Tom's inheritance—"a little over twelve thousand dollars." Rather than ending with Tom's slide into respectability, St. Petersburg itself is corrupted by Tom's discovery of Murrell's blood money: "So vast a sum, all in actual cash, seemed next to incredible. It was talked about, gloated over, glorified, until the reason of many of the citizens tottered under the strain of the unhealthy excitement."[122] While the transformative river journeys of other adventurous boy-heroes at this moment attempted to bring a series of apparent dichotomies into sharper focus—boyhood and manhood, civilized and savage, adventure and responsibility, salvation and corruption—the Mississippi in *The Adventures of Tom Sawyer* gleefully blurs all those boundaries and reveals just how permeable they are, just as this book blurs the generic boundaries between small town realism and penny dreadful fantasy. On the island and in the cave, Tom's adventures on the Mississippi place him in the lineage of very different river adventurers. In Twain's America, Tom can evoke a figure from the river like John Murrell, inherit his ill-gotten riches and Injun Joe's hideout, and still end up respectable. Rather than putting away childish things at the end of the book, Tom is empowered to remain happily free in his river playground.

"Huck Finn's Autobiography"

Like Tom at the end of the novel, Twain himself was hardly done with adventuring on the river. In the same year that *Tom Sawyer* was published, Twain began a new book of boyish escapades on the Mississippi—though these exploits would soon have a rather different import. On August 9, 1876, he wrote to Howells: "I have written 400 pages on it—therefore it is very nearly half done. It is Huck Finn's Autobiography. I like it only tolerably well, as far as I have got, and may possibly pigeonhole or burn the MS when it is done." Beginning this new book was not just a way to remain in the company of his boyish characters; it was a way to stay on the river, too, in lieu of a return to the Mississippi——to leave Tom Sawyer playing pirates in order to travel with Huck and Jim on their raft. Rather than staying put in St. Petersburg, this would be a river odyssey that would take in the Mississippi's epic sweep. For many years, it was believed that Twain paused composition in the summer of 1876, at the end of chapter 16, when the steamboat had crashed into Huck and Jim's raft. But actually, as Tom Quirk summarizes, the rediscovery of the first half of Twain's manuscript in 1991 made it clear that "Twain's first stint of composition got him well beyond this point, to that part of chapter 18 where Buck Grangerford asks Huck, 'Don't you know what a feud is?'"[123] Either way, both images remain resonant: from "Old Times on the Mississippi" through the composition of *Tom Sawyer* and the genesis of *Huckleberry Finn*, Twain paused his river writings with a diorama of the tensions that would animate those river writings yet to come: the steamboat and the raft, slavery and freedom, the shifting image of the South. In the coming years, Twain would peck at the manuscript intermittently.

Before its completion, though, he would turn his attention to another river book—the long-planned *Life on the Mississippi* (1883), a powerful blend of memory, travel, and research in which Twain would again tangle with his time on the river. A prompt to some of the darker memories from that era arrived in October 1876, from an unidentified correspondent who had met Twain in Memphis in the immediate aftermath of the explosion of the *Pennsylvania* and the death of his brother Henry. Twain apologized for not remembering her: "That week in Memphis was so terrible that I have never liked to think about it." Yet turning to *Life on the Mississippi*, he would need to think of it, and much more, deeply. He assured this nameless messenger from the past, "I have planned a journey down the Mississippi for the spring of 1878."[124] It would take him longer than that, but he would get there. One thing soon became clear: the completion of these two new books, the dual hearts of his river corpus, would ultimately be closely intertwined. And in order to finish them both, Mark Twain finally needed to go and have some long-delayed river adventures of his own—and not just on the Mississippi.

3

"This Ain't That Kind of a River"

LIFE, DEATH, AND MEMORY ON THE MISSISSIPPI

Mark is a queer fellow. There is nothing that he so delights in as a swift,
strong stream. You can hardly get him to leave one when once
he is within the influence of its fascinations.
—JOSEPH TWICHELL, letter to his family, 1878

~~~~~~

"How did the Mississippi River strike you?" [a reporter asked].
"Well, I think no well-behaved river would overflow as it has done."
—OSCAR WILDE, interview in *Chicago Tribune*, 1882

~~~~~~

We turn his pages and we see / The Mississippi flowing free.
—ANDREW LANG, "For Mark Twain," 1886

I n 1880, a twelve-year-old schoolboy from Dallas, Texas, wrote a letter to Mark Twain on a "lark." Wattie Bowser, required to write a composition on "some man among the living great ones," had chosen Twain (other popular selections among Texas schoolboys in 1880: Edison, Longfellow, Tennyson, Oliver Wendell Holmes). He and some classmates then decided to write to the objects of their admiration in the hope of getting a response to a particular question: "to ask them if they would 'Be a boy again.'" Wattie, with an eye to the main chance that must have appealed to Twain, worked hard to get a reply: he declared himself to be a fan of Tom Sawyer, assured Twain that Longfellow and Whittier wouldn't be able to "stand a joke like you," and dropped in a carefully timed postscript to let Twain know that his teacher was none other than Twain's youthful sweetheart Laura Wright (now Laura Drake).[1] Perhaps it was the mention of Laura that helped to shape Twain's lengthy answer. He had first encountered Laura Wright in New Orleans in 1858. "She wasn't yet fifteen when I knew her," Twain remembered in 1906. "It was in the summertime, and she had gone down the Mississippi from St. Louis to New Orleans as guest of a relative of hers who was a pilot on the *John J. Roe*, a steamboat whose officers I knew very well [. . .]. I could see her with perfect distinctness in the unfaded bloom of her youth, with her plaited tails dangling from her young head and her white summer frock puffing about in the wind of that ancient Mississippi time."[2]

Whether it was memories of Laura or some other impetus, Twain's reply to Wattie demonstrates how significant memories of that "ancient Mississippi time" still were at this moment. Yes, Twain responded, he would be willing to be a boy again—as long as a certain number of conditions were met: "The main condition would be, that I should emerge from boyhood as a 'cub pilot' on a Mississippi boat, & that I should by & by become a pilot, & remain one." There were plenty of minor conditions too: "Summer always; the magnolias at Rifle Point always in bloom [. . .] the river always bank full, so we could run all the chutes—how heavenly that would be! [. . .] I would rule out the middle watch in the night except on moonlight nights [. . .] especially if the boat steers like a duck, & friends have staid up to keep one company, & sing, & smoke, & spin yarns [. . .] & I would have the trips long, & the stays in port short [. . .] & her crew should never change, nor ever die." There was one final clause: "And when strangers were introduced I should have them repeat 'Mr. Clemens?' doubtfully, & with the rising inflection—& when they were

informed that I was the celebrated 'Master Pilot of the Mississippi,' & immediately took me by the hand & wrung it with effusion, & exclaimed, 'O, I know
that name very well!'"[3] At arguably the high-water mark of his life and career,
Twain could still be transported by reveries of the river: the desire to abandon
family and books and kill off Mark Twain to ensure a different kind of fame
for Samuel Clemens, the Mississippi's clubbable Flying Dutchman, gazing out
on the river for eternity from a warm and sociable pilothouse. Twain's public
persona was increasingly implicated in the lingering memory of the river too.
For Twain's fiftieth birthday, Andrew Lang "warmly congratulated" Twain in
the pages of *Longman's Magazine* in pointed terms: "Persons of extremely fine
culture may have no taste for Mark. When he gets among pictures and holy
places perhaps we feel that he is rather an awful being. But on a Mississippi
boat [. . .] Mark is all himself, and the most powerful and diverting writer, I
think, of his American contemporaries."[4]

Some of the same motivations—the retreat into memory and male company, to be "all himself [. . .] on a Mississippi boat"—clearly lay behind Twain's
long struggle to get back to the river. Still frustrated in his search for companions after the completion of *The Adventures of Tom Sawyer* and the development of the partial manuscript of *Adventures of Huckleberry Finn*, he lit out
in other directions. His circuitous return to the Mississippi would only come
by way of many other river journeys—some real, some literary. His extended
travels in Europe in this period resulted in *A Tramp Abroad* (1880) and the
completion of *The Prince and the Pauper* (1881), yet they also (as those texts
reflect) brought Twain into close conversation with other resurgent river cultures. At the moment when his most significant Mississippi writings were
fermenting, Twain encountered the Rhine and the Thames, rivers that were
playing a crucial role in the reshaping of their nations' cultures. If nothing
else, the meandering route that Twain took back to the Mississippi meant that
when he encountered the river again, he brought with him a new transatlantic
understanding of the role that rivers could play in popular culture.

By July 1881, the Mississippi was finally on the horizon again. Seven years
after first floating the idea of the trip, Twain was still optimistic that Howells
would travel to the river with him. He wrote to George Washington Cable,
himself a crucial figure in the literary life of the river at this moment and
indicative of things to come: "Howells is still in the mind to go to New Orleans with me in November for the Mississippi trip, & we shall hope to see

you then."[5] Yet Howells pulled out again, this time due to ill health. And so, in April 1882, with Osgood (and Roswell Phelps, a stenographer) in tow, Twain finally started the journey that would take him back to the river that he had been imaginatively revisiting and reshaping throughout the intervening years. Safe in his sickbed, Howells wished them bon voyage: "I am sorry that Osgood is with you on this Mississippi trip; I foresee that it will be a contemptible half-success instead of the illustrious and colossal failure we could have made it. [. . .] *Ah,* how I should like to be with Osgood and you! Give my love to the young willows (not widows) along the Mississippi shore, and good bye and good luck to you both."[6]

Yet Twain's long-delayed Mississippi odyssey—inevitably, inescapably— could not carry him into the dreamworld that he had outlined to Wattie. Even in those effusions, there had been undercurrents dragging Twain back to deeper waters. The world of his youth was gone, he knew. "One such crew I have in mind," he told the schoolboy, "& can call their names & see their faces, now: but two decades have done their work upon them, & half are dead, the rest scattered, & the boat's bones are rotting five fathom deep in Madrid Bend." Death would haunt his trip back to the river. He remembered that the pilothouse could be a lonely place too: "It makes one feel so dreary & lowspir- ited & forlorn [. . .] in the midst of the wide darkness, with apparently nobody alive in the deserted world but him."[7] Memories of his first meetings with Laura Wright were inextricably tied up with the death of Henry in the explo- sion of the *Pennsylvania.* The complex of emotions that haunted Twain in 1880 made their presence felt on the river itself and made their way into *Life on the Mississippi*—the long-deferred book that turned out to be one of the most painful writing experiences of his career. Grinding out the words throughout the rest of 1882, Twain would dive into the literary history of the river that he was still trying to claim as his own, dredging transatlantic travel accounts old and new, history books, the literature of his contemporaries, and a wealth of other texts attempting to define the Mississippi. Out of the confluence of memory, experience, and intertextuality would come a book that stands as a unique portrait of the river—a fractured and disjointed panorama, a broken mirror, reflecting back both Twain and the meaning of the Mississippi, cele- brating the river when it was most contrary, least controllable. It would also be a portrait of the river that was out of step, in many ways, with other visions of the Mississippi being constructed at this point, particularly in relation to the river's racial histories. But first came Europe.

"Streams of Fame and Song"

In 1879, as part of volume 25 of Henry Wadsworth Longfellow's massive collection of *Poems of Places*, Sarah Josepha Hale's antebellum effusion to the Mississippi was the standout representative of one of only five poems dedicated to the river (including one by John Hay). Hale framed her tribute to the Mississippi with a rhetorical dismissal of "Europe's royal rivers":

> The castled Rhine, whose vine-crowned waters flow,
> The fount of fable and the source of song; [. . .]
> And Thames, that bears the riches of the world: [. . .]
> Our Mississippi, rolling proudly on,
> Would sweep them from its path, or swallow up,
> Like Aaron's rod, these streams of fame and song!

The poem emphasized the degree to which rivers were being newly positioned as carriers of national culture, an idea that was only intensifying in the latter part of the nineteenth century. Her claims for the river's supremacy—"It reigns alone"—were somewhat undercut by the fact that in the same collection, the Thames warranted eighteen poems, the Rhine thirty-two.[8] In cultural terms, at least, the Mississippi still seemed a junior partner.

For Twain, Europe and its rivers provided an escape in 1878, not least from Longfellow himself: on December 17, 1877, Twain had given his famously disastrous speech at the celebration of John Greenleaf Whittier's seventieth birthday, apparently insulting Longfellow, Emerson, and Oliver Wendell Holmes. Feeling like he had alienated all of literary Boston, lighting out for Europe in April 1878 for roughly seventeen months seemed like a good way to hide from the ignominy. "Ah, I have such a deep, grateful, sense of being 'out of it all,'" he wrote to Howells soon after arriving in Germany. "I think I foretaste some of the advantages of being dead." The Rhine and its tributaries were central to his flight: "From this airy perch [. . .] we look down upon Heidelberg Castle, & upon the swift Neckar, & the town, & out over the wide green level of the Rhine valley—marvelous prospect."[9] Europe would hardly prove to be an idyll, but it did bring Twain into contact with certain conspicuous "streams of fame and song" at a crucial moment in the development of his own river writings; each had their own stories to tell and lessons to teach about the ways that rivers snaked their way through national identities. The Rhine and the Thames, in turn, exerted a significant and largely unacknowledged influence on Twain's literary development at this crucial moment in his relationship with the Mississippi and featured centrally in the books that followed these international adventures.

Germany had played a role in Twain's imaginative life for years, back to his river days. As Albert Aron put it, "He picked up German as best as he could, from a shoemaker in Hannibal, from a fellow-printer in Keokuk, Iowa, in a school of languages in St. Louis, during his career as a pilot on the Mississippi."[10] Even before his arrival in Germany, in 1878, the legends of the Rhine loomed over his journey: traveler and writer Bayard Taylor, perhaps the leading interpreter of German literature for American audiences, was aboard the same ship as Twain and his family. He rehearsed a variety of German songs for his fellow passengers, including Heine's "Lorelei," the Rhine legend that would feature prominently in A Tramp Abroad.[11] Twain arrived in Germany at a signal moment in the river's history. The river had long been at the center of political and economic tensions in Europe, and in recent decades, those tensions had been readily manifest—from the creation of the Rhine Province, in 1815, to the Rhine Crisis of 1840 (when France tried to assert ownership of the river) to the Franco-Prussian War of 1870. Throughout, the Rhine had been a significant symbol of burgeoning German nationalism. Bradshaw's tourist guide for travelers on the river explained in 1876: "This river [. . .] is regarded by every German with a kind of reverence and affectionate interest, their poetry calling it 'King Rhine.'"[12]

As the existence of Bradshaw's guide itself makes clear, the river had also long been an established tourist route—a key part of any European tour. The Rhine became the idealized Romantic river par excellence, though as Hagen Schulz-Forberg has pointed out, in "an ironic twist of history," the fashion for the river was "a particularly English invention."[13] Just as it had for the Mississippi, it was the introduction of the steamboat that really opened the river to tourism. Yet whatever its roots, its vogue was long lasting and widespread. For popular novelist Edward Bulwer Lytton, in The Pilgrims of the Rhine (1834), the river's influence on German literature and character was profound: "As the Rhine flows, so flows the national genius, by mountain and valley, the wildest solitude, the sudden spires of ancient cities, the mouldered castle, the stately monastery, the humble cot,—grandeur and homeliness, history and superstition, truth and fable, succeeding one another so as to blend into a whole."[14]

Such was the fashion for a tour on the river that lampooning eager tourists headed for a romantic encounter with the Rhine itself became a hackneyed topic. William Makepeace Thackeray, for example, produced multiple comic accounts of the river, starting with "A Legend of the Rhine" in 1845, a burlesque of Rhine lore that begins with a mordant look at touristic trends: "Do you know in what year the fairies left the Rhine?—long before Murray's Guide-Book was wrote—long before squat steamboats, with snorting funnels, came paddling down the stream."[15] Most influential, though, was Thomas Hood's *Up the Rhine* (1840), a comic epistolary travelogue exploring the adventures and misadventures of a rich, elderly, hypochondriac bachelor; his recently widowed sister; her maid; and his young nephew, on a touristic journey along the river. The party starts in high hopes. At the beginning of what he terms their "Pilgrim's Progress," nephew Frank Somerville declares exuberantly to his correspondent, "WE ARE GOING UP THE RHINE!!! You who have been long aware of my yearning to the abounding river, like the supposed mystical bending of the hazel twig towards the unseen waters, will be equally pleased and surprised at such an announcement." But servant Martha succinctly expresses the difficulties that soon beset their party: "I am tired of steemin [. . .] for forrin traveling is like a deceatful luvver, witch don't improve on aquaintance."[16] Twain himself was very familiar with this heritage. In March 1861, on the cusp of leaving the Mississippi, he had written to brother Orion from St. Louis, noting, "I have been reading lately [. . .] Tom Hood's letters to his family"—presumably a reference to *Up the Rhine*. Even if Twain wasn't a fan in 1861—"Tom Hood's wit, (in his letters) has a savor of labor about it which is very disagreeable"—*Up the Rhine* clearly established the potential of a comic journey organized along a symbolically rich river.[17] It seems that he knew Thackeray's parodies too. According to Franklin Rogers, Twain reworked a moment from Thackeray's *Legends of the Rhine* when writing *Innocents Abroad* (1869).[18]

In *A Tramp Abroad* itself, the travel book that resulted from his European exile, Twain followed a middle path between these two poles in his account of the river. The Rhine takes a central role in the early part of Twain's narrative, and its significance is multiple. Apparently unironic appreciation of the romantic Rhine landscape is put alongside the same kind of satire that others had engaged in decades earlier. As Twain makes immediately clear, he understood the Rhine—as he understood the Mississippi—to be an intertextual river. In the opening chapter of *A Tramp Abroad*, he explains the way that he made himself familiar with the mythic history of the river he was traveling along: "In one of the shops I had the luck to stumble upon a book which has charmed me nearly to death. It is entitled 'The Legends of the Rhine from Basle to Rotterdam' [. . .]. All tourists *mention* the Rhine legends—in that sort of way which quietly pretends that the mentioner has been familiar with them all his life, and that the reader cannot possibly be ignorant of them—but no tourist ever *tells* them. So this little book fed me in a very hungry place." That seriocomic fascination with the mythology of the Rhine—and with Garnham's erratic translation of those myths—winds its way throughout *A Tramp Abroad* itself.

Twain was also confronted by another very rich source of Rhine material on his travels. In *A Tramp Abroad*, Twain plays his encounter with the opera of Richard Wagner for laughs: "The banging and slamming and booming and crashing were something beyond belief. The racking and pitiless pain of it remains stored up in my memory alongside the memory of the time that I had my teeth fixed."[19] A decade later, though, in 1891, Twain would express a different kind of appreciation for Wagner's art. Visiting Bayreuth, Twain still described feeling "strongly out of place" when confronted with the devotion that Wagner's art inspired but also expressed his profound enjoyment of at least some of what he heard: "music to make one drunk with pleasure, music to make one take scrip and staff and beg his way round the globe to hear it."[20] Either way, Wagner's art was steeped in the Rhine, a profound model of river art. The Rhine shapes the narrative of the *Ring* cycle: from the birth of the river in the opening movement of *Das Rheingold* to its apocalyptic, cleansing flood at the climax of *Götterdämmerung*, the Rhine is the central organizing locus of Wagner's epic—the fountainhead of both German identity and humanity more broadly. As Daniel Foster describes, for Wagner, the Rhine is "the cosmogonic wellspring of all life [. . .] the origin of civilization itself."[21] It was a potent example—a totalizing vision of the power of river imagery.

It's not just the Rhine that flows through *A Tramp Abroad*, though. The Mississippi, never far from Twain's thoughts, makes its presence felt early in the narrative, in a supposed memory of childhood embarrassment: "One evening on board a Mississippi steamboat, a boy of ten years lay asleep in a berth—a long, slim-legged boy, he was, encased in quite a short shirt; it was the first time he had ever made a trip on a steamboat, and so he was troubled, and scared, and had gone to bed with his head filled with impending snaggings, and explosions, and conflagrations, and sudden death." Believing the boat to be on fire, the boy bursts into the ladies' saloon, dressed only in his nightshirt, "wild-eyed, erect-haired, and shouting, 'Fire, fire! Jump and run, the boat's afire and there ain't a minute to lose!' All those ladies looked sweetly up and smiled, nobody stirred." "I was that boy," Twain confesses. Here the Mississippi is figured as an original source of trauma.[22]

Turning from that distressing steamboat memory, Twain found an imaginative release in the narration of the most significant river journey in *A Tramp Abroad*: the raft trip down the Neckar undertaken by Twain and "Harris"—the fictionalized Joseph Twichell, who joined Twain in Europe for six weeks in the summer of 1878. Though the raft episode itself is, in Peter Messent's words, "evidently an invented rather than an actual event," it still becomes a creative escape in which Twain plays with themes that were occupying him at this moment.[23] It begins with Twain gazing out on the Neckar, like the Lorelei, hoping for disaster: "I used to sit for hours [. . .] watching the long, narrow rafts slip along through the central channel, grazing the right-bank dike and aiming carefully for the middle arch of the stone bridge below; I watched them in this way, and lost all this time hoping to see one of them hit the bridge-pier and wreck itself sometime or other, but was always disappointed." Then, in a Tom Sawyerish mood, Twain makes a "daredevil" suggestion to his "comrades": "I am going to Heidelberg on a raft. Will you venture with me?"[24]

In the journey that follows, Twain clearly rehearses some of the important leitmotifs that he was exploring with Huck and Jim. He glories in the idea of raft travel: "It is gentle, and gliding, and smooth, and noiseless; it calms down all feverish activities, it soothes to sleep all nervous hurry and impatience; under its restful influence all the troubles and vexations and sorrows that harass the mind vanish away, and existence becomes a dream, a charm, a deep and tranquil ecstasy. [. . .] We went slipping silently along, between the green and fragrant banks, with a sense of pleasure and contentment that grew, and grew, all the time." As it also does for Huck and Jim, the sense of remove from civilization prompts some disrobing (though not quite into the state of nature that Huck and Jim manage): "We took off our outside clothing and sat in a

FIGURE 6. "A Deep and Tranquil Ecstasy," from Mark Twain, *A Tramp Abroad*
(Hartford, Conn.: American Publishing Co., 1880), 129.

row along the edge of the raft and enjoyed the scenery, with our sun-umbrellas
over our heads and our legs dangling in the water. [. . .] Every now and then
we plunged in and had a swim" (fig. 6).[25]

Yet on this raft trip, too, modern technologies intrude. They encounter a
steamboat, which seems to signal the end for the golden age of this stretch
of river: "The Neckar has always been used as a canal, and thus has given
employment to a great many men and animals; but now that this steamboat
is able, with a small crew and a bushel or so of coal, to take nine keel-boats
farther up the river in one hour than thirty men and thirty mules can do it in
two, it is believed that the old-fashioned towing industry is on its death-bed."
The reverie of the raft trip ends (again, echoing Huck and Jim's experiences)
with a vision of destruction: "I saw a raft wrecked. It hit the pier in the center
and went all to smash and scatteration like a box of matches struck by light-
ning."[26] Yet even with the "deep and tranquil ecstasy" of a raft trip down the
Neckar, nothing in *A Tramp Abroad* was able to capture the enjoyment that
Twain could take from waterways better than a note from his friend and traveling companion, Joseph Twichell. Writing to his family during his time in
Europe with Twain, Twichell concluded fondly that "Mark is a queer fellow":

There is nothing that he so delights in as a swift, strong stream. You can hardly get him to leave one when once he is within the influence of its fascinations. To throw in stones and sticks seems to afford him rapture. To-night, as we were on our way back to the hotel, seeing a lot of driftwood by the torrent side below the path, I climbed down and threw it in. When I got back to the path Mark was running down-stream after it as hard as he could go, throwing up his hands and shouting in the wildest ecstasy, and when a piece went over a fall and emerged to view in the foam below he would jump up and down and yell. He said afterward that he hadn't been so excited in three months.[27]

There's no evidence that the Thames gave Twain quite so much pleasure when he returned to London in the summer of 1879, but the river was certainly on his mind. The Thames, like the Rhine, was also experiencing a renaissance of its symbolic relationship to national culture. In a new way, Britons were looking to the river as a mythic space essential to their national identity. In part, this was because of efforts to clean up the river—an industrial open sewer earlier in the century, rather lacking in the Rhine's romance—in the 1860s and 1870s. From a place of Dickensian neglect and abjection, the river became a vital space of recreation and imaginative escape for Londoners. As Alison Byerly writes, a journey up the Thames became "a timeless journey into the heart of England [. . .] a route into some essential but generalized aspect of England itself [. . .] that transcends the specific geography of the landscape traversed, and becomes a journey into the past, into the future, or into an idealized England."[28] It was a trend that manifested itself in a number of vivid ways, from a boating craze on the Upper Thames that reached extraordinary proportions to a series of literary and artistic productions that sought to redefine the river as the nation's mythic stream (sometimes seriously, sometimes ironically).

Americans had a significant part to play in this process, none more so than James McNeill Whistler. In 1859, when Whistler permanently decamped to London, he located himself in Wapping, at the heart of rough river life in a way that proved to be revolutionary for American art and for ideas of the river. As Karl Beckson notes, in both etchings and on canvas, Whistler "focussed on a world relatively untouched by native artists," and did so in a manner that experimented with tone, color and abstraction in pioneering and controversial ways.[29] For his friends and biographers Joseph and Elizabeth Robins Pennell, "He saw the river as no one had seen it before, in its grime and glitter, with its forest of shipping, its endless procession of barges, its grim warehouses, its huge docks, its little waterside inns. [. . .] It was left to the American youth to do for London what Rembrandt had done for Amsterdam."[30] Twain met Whistler at a dinner in London in 1879 and might have visited the artist in his studio too.[31] Either way, he was certainly aware of Whistler's river pictures. Later that summer, staying in Windermere, Twain wrote to his English publisher Andrew Chatto with a request: "In a picture-shop alongside the Haymarket Theatre there is an etching by Whistler of a View from his window on the Thames in Chelsea—price 7 guineas. We have concluded we want it for the young lady who is with us" (Clara Spaulding, Livy's friend and traveling companion).[32]

Other famous American commentators were looking to the river as an index to England and the English character at this moment. At the same dinner party where Twain and Livy met Whistler, they also made the acquaintance of Henry James. Livy preferred the writer to the artist and found him "exceedingly pleasant and easy to talk with. I had expected just the reverse, thinking one would feel looked over by him and criticized."[33] James understood the symbolic power of the Thames at this moment. As he expressed it in a sketch of London life for the Century, one of many American accounts of the river that would emerge in the following years, the Thames was "an adjunct of London life, an expression of London manners. [. . .] I know of no other classic stream that is so splashed about for the mere fun of it." For James himself, the prospect of splashing about in boats held only so much charm. It was, like Whistler before him, the urban and industrial city river that charmed him most: "I like it best when it is all dyed and disfigured with the town and you look from bridge to bridge—they seem wonderfully big and dim—over the brown, greasy current, the barges and the penny-steamers, the black, sordid, heterogeneous shores."[34]

Twain's vision of the Thames—reaching back into English history—struck its own distinctive notes. He had been writing The Prince and the Pauper (1881) since 1877, but he turned to the manuscript in earnest again early in 1880, in the wake of his return to America from Europe—"with an interest which amounts to intemperance," as he described it to brother Orion.[35] The story of the adventures of two youthful, mismatched doppelgängers in sixteenth-century England—groundbreakingly respectable for Twain—was also a book that dwelt heavily on the role of the Thames in English life and the English imaginary. The river sits at the heart of the geography of the novel. It forms a crucial part of the first conversation between Tom and Edward—a moment at which the distance between the Tudor Thames and the antebellum Mississippi seems surprisingly close: "'In summer, sir, we wade and swim in the canals and in the river, and each doth duck his neighbour, and spatter him with water, and dive and shout and tumble and—' 'Twould be worth my father's kingdom but to enjoy it once! Prithee go on.'"[36] In short order, both boys are undergoing their own symbolically charged journeys across and along the river.

As John H. Davis has written of Edward, Tom, and the Thames: "Twain plays their experiences against each other by giving each boy a domain, geographically dividing the areas with the Thames River and figuratively separating them by labelling the land of Edward's adventures south of the river the Kingdom of Dreams and Shadows and declaring Edward its monarch."[37] The liminal world of London Bridge—"a sort of town to itself"—suspended above the waters of the river, is a vital space in this process, serving as a crossing point that takes Edward south of the Thames and begins his education.[38] As Davis describes, "Never touching the water, Edward undergoes a symbolic baptism by walking over the river."[39] The inhabitants of London Bridge are imagined as a kind of amphibious creature, eternally yoked to its intermingling of land and water: "History tells of one of these who left the Bridge at the age of seventy-one [. . .]. He fled back to his old home, a lean and haggard spectre, and fell peacefully to rest and pleasant dreams under the lulling music of the lashing waters and the boom and crash and thunder of London Bridge." Similarly, the elaborate river pageants that Tom experiences, a vivid symbol of the river's symbolic significance in British history, provides its own kind of baptism: "The whole vast river-front of the palace was blazing with light. [. . .] The massed world on the river burst into a mighty roar of welcome; and Tom Canty, the cause and hero of it all, stepped into view and slightly bowed his princely head."[40] Yet this river journey has its educative aspect too: if the first river pageant carries Tom into reveries of royalty, the second, to quote Davis, forces him to reenter "the real world."[41] The Thames, then, becomes a deeply symbolically charged space in the text, one that effects significant change on the boys who cross and travel along it. Soon after completing this river-centered book, Twain began adding to Huck and Jim's adventures again—and was finally poised for a return to the Mississippi.

"The Most Sinister, the Most Perfidious River in the World"

While Twain was physically and metaphorically exploring Europe's river culture, transatlantic currents were also flowing in the other direction. Kenneth Rose has argued that the years after the Civil War were actually "the golden age for European travel in the United States."[42] It is also true that the frequency of commentators who included the Mississippi in their itineraries in America—not least because of the dominance of the railroad—dwindled profoundly, highlighting the river's marginalization. Yet though they hardly equaled the flood of prominent European travelers who took stock of America from the deck of a Mississippi steamboat in the antebellum years, a slow trickle of travelers still made their way to the river. Some, like David Macrae's *The Americans at Home* (1870), simply gave a boilerplate account of the river, repeating tropes from the antebellum years. But two particular narratives—Ernest von Hesse-Hartwegg's *Mississippi-Fahrten* (1882) and George Augustus Sala's *America Revisited* (1882)—were more revealing, echoing each other in their experiences of life on the Lower Mississippi and in their attitudes to the issue of race along the river.

Ernst von Hesse-Wartegg was one of the most prolific world travelers of his day. According to Frederic Trautmann, this aristocratic cosmopolite and part-time diplomat "may have journeyed farther and written more than any other travel memoirist in modern times." In the 1870s and 1880s, he turned his attention to America and made his way to the Mississippi. Though the subtitle of his *Mississippi-Fahrten* gives the dates 1879–80, Hesse-Wartegg's introduction confusingly claims, "Matters caused me to travel twice during four years, each time for several months." Either way, his composite account of the Lower Mississippi was a rare beast. Focusing on the river in this way and at this length was unusual in the latter part of the nineteenth century, as was Hesse-Wartegg's claim that the subject matter of his book was "an essential part of America."[43] In its review, the *New York Times* acknowledged that Hesse-Wartegg brought a different perspective to bear on the river: "A foreigner certainly sees things more picturesquely here than we can. He is more shocked by the special features of low life in the great Mississippi Valley towns. He is more impressed by the hugeness and majesty of the Mississippi steamboat."[44] In many ways, this was a nostalgic exercise for Hesse-Wartegg, inspired in large part by his youthful consumption of the river writings of Friedrich Gerstäcker and Charles Sealsfield: "What enchantment, what romance it seemed to hold then!"[45] (He had other romantic attachments to the river too. During the course of his transatlantic wanderings, Hesse-Wartegg had met and, in 1878, married the world-famous soprano Minnie Hauk, the singer who popularized the role of Carmen and who had spent a portion of her childhood in a houseboat on the Mississippi.)[46]

Some of those romantic influences survived Hesse-Wartegg's own contact with the river. As the *New York Times* suggested, steamboats and steamboat culture delighted him. The Mississippi presented "a singular riverscape," Hesse-Wartegg wrote, and, ever the booster, declared the river "the most important artery of commerce in the giant nation." The steamboat itself Hesse-Wartegg pronounced "the most practical and beautiful conveyance afloat in the world." It drove him to flights of fancy: "Cleopatra's barge could not have been more cheerful, more luxurious, or more elegant than the Mississippi's waterborne palaces. [. . .] It boggles the imagination, this floating, glittering palace in scintillating white, this phantasmagoria. [. . .] What a spectacle!" New Orleans evoked no less hyperbole. Declaring the city "the world's largest river port," he found the levee to be "one of the wonders of the New World [. . .] so overpowering, so magnificent." In all this, Hesse-Wartegg was clearly inspired by Twain too: his familiarity with "Old Times on the Mississippi" is evident, as is his knowledge of Edward King's *The Great South* and Charles Dickens's antebellum account of the river.[47]

Hesse-Wartegg certainly followed Dickens's lead in his assessment of the river itself. Apparently attempting to outdo antebellum commentators in his invective, he declares, "The Mississippi [. . .] is the most tedious, most ennui-producing river in the world." Moreover, it is an active agent of malignity: "The Mississippi ranks as the most sinister, the most perfidious river in the world." Near Memphis—"after traveling to the four corners of the world, I cannot remember impressions anywhere as disagreeable"—he frames "this sluggish Mississippi, the slimy pool," as the pestilential source of the recent outbreak of yellow fever. Unusually, Hesse-Wartegg also attacked the cultural profile of the river, in explicitly transatlantic terms. Noting that the Mississippi "must have caused Longfellow trouble with his anthology, *Poems of*

Places," Hesse-Wartegg exclaims: "What poet ever found words to sing of this dilatory puddle? European waters have nymphs and sirens and mermaids, but could such poetic features be found hovering and flitting about the slowest and most tiresome of rivers?"[48]

At the root of much of this invective lay Hesse-Wartegg's apparent hatred for the black Americans whom he encountered on the Mississippi. An apologist for slavery and a supporter of the Ku Klux Klan, Hesse-Wartegg transforms a steamboat roustabout whom he encounters on the river into what he considers to be a representative type and a moral about emancipation: "A lively bundle of rags with some spots of brilliant white, turns out to be a human being marked by the whites of the eyes and the double row of teeth. The back is crooked, the head bends forward, and the hands tremble at the sides. The clothing consists of loose rags, dangling where they please. [. . .] A crust of dirt covers the face, neck, and hands: the skin looks like an alligator's. Behold a consequence of the Civil War! Look upon the Freed Man, the liberated Negro, the white man's equal at the ballot box and before the law! See what freedom has given him!" Yet behind the hatefulness of these and other images, Hesse-Wartegg ironically provides compelling glimpses of the abiding and intimate connection between the black Americans whom he encounters and the Mississippi that they live and work on. "They drink out of the Mississippi," he marvels, and despite the clear sarcasm in his intent, there is a symbolic truth in his invective: "Yet what king has sipped the finest vintage from a golden goblet with more relish than these stout and sturdy Ethiopians imbibe Mississippi Yellow? Has nectar tasted better to gods than this nectar to those who dip it for themselves out of the river?"[49]

George Augustus Sala's account of New Orleans chimed with Hesse-Wartegg's in a series of important ways. As the title of his 1882 account of his journey, *America Revisited*, made clear, this was not Sala's first time in America. He had covered the Civil War for the *Daily Telegraph*—at the time, a newspaper that was in possession of a daily circulation of around 250,000, the largest in the world.[50] During that sojourn, Sala confessed that he had only "fringed the garment of the North American continent," adding shamefacedly, "I have never seen the Mississippi."[51] In 1879, Sala was frank about the prejudices that had animated his time as a correspondent for the *Telegraph* and still underlay his experiences in postbellum America. Back in 1863, Sala admitted, he had been a "a young man:—very prejudiced, very conceited," who "took, politically, the wrong side; that is to say, I was an ardent sympathiser with the South in her struggle against the North. [. . .] My partiality for 'Dixie's Land' was simply and solely due to a sentimental feeling."[52] That sentimental effusion masked the profound racism of Sala's Civil War correspondence. "I believe that this is the negro," he had told his readers. "I believe that he is naturally inferior to the white man in mental organisation; that his defects and his vices are not to be eradicated by education; that he will always (in the aggregate: of course there are individual exceptions) be lazy, indolent, and slovenly."[53] Despite his apologies, in 1882 Sala also confessed that he remained, essentially, unreconstructed: "My heart is still in the South:—with her gallant sons and daughters."[54] As Peter Blake has outlined, Sala's position—like Hesse-Wartegg's—was indicative of the "shifting cultural and scientific racial climate" informed by the rhetoric of "the age of African exploration": "Significant portions of English middle-class opinion began to gradually move away from a position of abolitionism to one whereby not only the wisdom of emancipating American slaves was challenged, but so too was their essential humanity."[55]

Sala's closest communion with the Mississippi River took place in New Orleans. Significantly, he was unequivocal that the Crescent City, in February 1880, was "the most interesting city that I have yet set eyes upon in this vast continent." As a sign of the times, his journey to the city avoided the river entirely; instead, Sala traveled by rail. He only gestures to the river in his obligatory glance at the levee—"a prodigious embankment fifteen feet wide and fourteen feet high, constructed for a long distance along the river bank, and forming a delightful promenade"—and in his complaints (echoed in *Life on the Mississippi*) about the quality of the city's water supply, hinting at disease and unease about contamination of one kind or another: "The water which they give you here for washing purposes is of the colour, and nearly of the consistency, of pea-soup. That is the kind of tap which the magnificent Mississippi provides for you. [. . .] Perhaps after a long course of bathing in liquid mud you will find your skin pleasantly fertilised. I know that the pea-soup water has turned the linen fronts of all my shirts to a deep yellow. Well, it is better to wear yellow shirts than to have the yellow fever."[56] Far more congenial to his tastes is the contemplation of the picturesque aspects of the city—the already established itinerary for travelers to New Orleans: the French Quarter, Jackson Square, Canal Street, Mardi Gras (he borrowed some of his illustrations from Edward King's *The Great South* too). Ironically anticipating Twain's critiques of both the city and the South in *Life on the Mississippi*, Sala recommends that any of his readers who should find themselves in New Orleans "should take pattern by the pilgrim to Melrose Abbey as advised by Sir Walter and visit it by the pale moonlight." Thanks to Scott's influence, Sala is drawn into a romantic rendering of colonial history in the region and the history of the Mississippi itself—also themes for Twain in *Life on the Mississippi:* "Come back, ye Dead; Come back, doughty Hernan de Soto, first discoverer of the Mississippi. Come back, Fathers Marquet and Joliet, most pious of monks, most enterprising of merchants, come from far-off Quebec, down the St. Lawrence, through Lake Ontario, up Niagara, through Erie, by St. Clair, through Huron, by Mackinaw Straits, through the Fox river, to the Wisconsin river, to the Upper Mississippi. And the daring French soldier, La Salle, and the noble Canadian brothers, Herville and Bienville, have not their wraiths a right to mingle in the shadowy throng?" The romantic transportation is only temporary, though, highlighting the push and pull of the past, present and future of this moment: "I return to Young America, telegraphing, telephoning, and phonographing, and electric-lighting the world out of its mind [. . .] and making dollars all day and all night long for ever and ever."[57]

"W'ere You Fin' Sudge a Reever Lag Dad Mississippi?"

Sala and Hesse-Wartegg were both prescient in their regard for the Crescent City. New Orleans, for all its economic and social problems, was experiencing something of a cultural renaissance in the early 1880s. The city was about to take center stage in a new flourishing of southern literature—and in the nation's engagement with the river. For all that railroad connections facilitated the new wave of tourism to the city, the Mississippi remained vital to its fortunes. Optimistic visions of the inevitable—yet always deferred—prosperity of a city so situated still flared up intermittently. Envisaging a "grand future" for New Orleans, Hesse-Wartegg made it clear that the "Father of Waters prevails as ever: not only the main artery but also the bearer of prosperity and the agent of destiny, the alpha and omega of New Orleans."[58] It is ironic, perhaps, that much of the romantic fascination with New Orleans at this moment can be traced to the work of George Washington Cable—a writer who was singularly out of step with many of the mores of his city. Cable's emergence as the most important translator of New Orleans at this moment was itself rooted in another signal moment in the life of the postbellum river: Edward King's tour of the Great South for *Scribner's* in the early 1870s. When King arrived in New Orleans for Mardi Gras in 1873, Cable was a part-time journalist and employee of the New Orleans Cotton Exchange. He had fought for the Confederacy in the Civil War, but by the 1870s, his views on the issues that were roiling the South were already unconventional. While covering the carnival parade of the Mistick Krewe of Comus for the *New Orleans Picayune*, Cable met King. This was an encounter that would have profound implications.

The travel writer soon apprehended Cable's value to him as a tour guide, and the two traversed the streets together. While shepherding King around New Orleans, Cable also shared a number of short stories with his visitor. Enthusiastic about what he heard—"you are a genius," he wrote to him privately—King left New Orleans with a selection of Cable's work.[59] Back east, he assiduously shopped the stories around the editorial offices of the major publications of the day. Before long, *Scribner's* agreed to publish "'Sieur George: A Tale of New Orleans" in its October 1873 issue, and the world was introduced to Cable's peculiar vision of the city. Decades later, associate editor of *Scribner's* Robert Underwood Johnson likened the story to "a fresh and gentle southwest wind that blew into the office."[60] Yet Cable's aesthetic was hardly fresh or gentle. "'Sieur George" was a dark and tangled story evoking decay, ruin, corruption, poverty, and death. Far from the visions of future prosperity outlined by travelers and New South promoters, Cable's New Orleans was a city sinking into the mud under the weight of its history. Still, readers responded enthusiastically, and the fashion for the Creole culture that he evoked was widespread. A collection of his stories, *Old Creole Days,* was published in 1879; *The Grandissimes*, his first and most significant novel set in the wake of the Louisiana Purchase in 1803, appeared in 1880. Their significance was apprehended immediately. Reviewing the novel for *Scribner's*, Hjalmar Boyesen declared: "Mr. Cable is a literary pioneer. He has broken a path for the daylight into the cane-brakes and everglades, and into the heart of Creole civilization. He is the first Southern novelist [. . .] who has made a contribution of permanent value to American literature."[61] Others noticed too. "Yesterday I was at Mark Twain's," Howells wrote to Cable in March 1882, "and we read aloud from the Grandissimes. [. . .] Clemens and I went about talking Creole all day."[62]

If Cable was primarily a writer of the city, he was also, as Boyesen's review hinted, a writer of the river and its margins too. While Twain was exploring

Europe, Cable was bringing a new sensibility to bear on the Mississippi—
one that was profoundly interested in the history of enslaved people. Cable
had significant personal connections to the river. The vicissitudes of life on
the Mississippi were intertwined with his extended family's fortunes, particularly those of his father. Married in Indiana, George Washington Cable Sr. and
Rebecca Boardman left their home on the Ohio to make a new life in New
Orleans in 1837. One of Rebecca's brother-in-laws had been "a trader on the
Mississippi" and may have encouraged the move.[63] Cable was born in the city
in 1844. In the years that followed, George Sr. gained interests in a number
of steamboats, and a variety of Cable's cousins and other assorted relatives
worked on the river as pilots. As a young cub on the river, Twain knew them—
and noticed their absence when he returned in 1882, remarking in his notebook, "All the Cables are dead."[64] Yet prosperity remained elusive for George
Sr., and in the final years of his life, he took a number of jobs on the river,
before his early death in 1859. Cable, then, like Howells, was well acquainted
with what the river meant for the men who lived—and died—on it. As Arlin
Turner has asserted: "The glories and the tragedies of steamboating grew into
George's childhood memories. [. . .] He could draw on knowledge and impressions almost as vivid as if he had been himself a follower of the river."[65]

In other ways, Cable's childhood memories of New Orleans were intimately bound up with the Mississippi. In later years, writing for children in *St.
Nicholas* magazine in 1893 (the same moment that Twain's *Tom Sawyer Abroad*
was being serialized), Cable described why "Children love New Orleans" with
reference to his own memories of childhood in the city—memories that were
intertwined with the river and, particularly, black life on the Mississippi. On
the levee, Cable explained, "it is fascinating to watch, from the upper guards
of some great packet-boat, this distribution of huge treasure by the hands
of these ragged black Samsons." "I could tell you of a certain man," he told
his young readers, clearly meaning himself, "who, when a boy, used to waste
hours watching the negro 'gangs' [. . .] singing lustily and reeking to their na-
ked waists [. . .]. Don't miss the weird, inspiring scene, if ever you go to New
Orleans." He described, too, the way that "boys pull out in skiffs to 'take the
waves' which rise in the wakes of their great paddle-wheels; for a Mississippi
river side-wheeler 'tears the river wide open,' as they say." Yet Cable was also at
pains to warn of the dangers of the river: "In the warm months many fellows

swim out instead of rowing; but believe me, the 'Father of Waters' is dangerous enough even for a skiff; it is no fit place for a swimmer."[66]

The same kind of fascinations and ambiguities are reflected in the way that the river featured in his work. Though never quite foregrounded, the river is a profound presence in the lives of Cable's characters. At the melancholy denouement of "'Sieur George," Cable evokes a vision of the Mississippi and its overarching influence on the life of the city: "Far away southward and westward the great river glistened in the sunset. Along its sweeping bends the chimneys of a smoking commerce, the magazines of surplus wealth, the gardens of the opulent, the steeples of a hundred sanctuaries and thousands on thousands of mansions and hovels."[67] It can be a more active and implacable agent in the lives of New Orleanians too—a deus ex machina that can be severe in its punishments. This is vividly felt at the dramatic climax of "Belles Demoiselles Plantation." Like a dark fairy tale, the titular dwelling, its ownership entangled with the complex racial history of the region, disappears beneath the waters of the river as retribution for the duplicity of its Creole inhabitant: "Belles Demoiselles, the realm of maiden beauty, the home of merriment, the house of dancing, all in the tremor and glow of pleasure, suddenly sunk, with one short, wild wail of terror—sunk, sunk, down, down, down, into the merciless, unfathomable flood of the Mississippi."[68]

Merciless, unfathomable—but also a source of life and a site of refuge and escape. In *The Grandissimes,* the river is a pagan spirit that flows throughout the text, binding together all of the disparate protagonists of this panoramic text. "W'ere you fin' sudge a reever lag dad Mississippi?" boasts Aurora about the fertile "paradize" of Louisiana, before noting, in tactful French, "It is said [. . .] that its waters have the property of contributing even to the multiplication of the human species." Not just a source of existence, it is the space to which all characters trace their New World lives. It has a hand in the foundation of the family lineages that drive the plot of the novel, when, in 1699, "two overbold young Frenchmen [. . .] ventured away from their canoes on the bank of the Mississippi into the wilderness." Emigrant Frowenfeld ("American by birth, rearing and sentiment, yet German enough through his parents") arrives at the city via the Mississippi at the beginning of the novel, and it seems like returning to the moment of creation and "the half-built world. [. . .] How dream-like the land and the great, whispering river!" Yet this moment also introduces a different aspect of the Mississippi—the "funereal swamps," the marginal and abject hinterlands of the river system, that prove to be a vital space in the text. Those liminal places are themselves intimately connected to the legend of Bras-Coupé, the story of the defiant slave that, like the river, flows through the novel. While the Frowenfelds steam into the city, his story is given its first, brief retelling: "in the shadow of the cypress forest, where the vessel lay moored for a change of wind, told in a patois difficult, but not impossible, to understand, the story of a man who chose rather to be hunted like a wild beast among those awful labyrinths, than to be yoked and beaten like a tame one."[69] Troping the swamp as a site of resistance against slavery was nothing new in the 1880s—Harriet Beecher Stowe, for example, had explored that space in her sequel to Uncle Tom's Cabin, Dred: A Tale of the Great Dismal Swamp (1856). But in the legend of Bras-Coupé, Cable pushed that idea further than most.

Cable tried to tell Bras-Coupé's story, itself adapted from New Orleans folklore, many times, initially as a short story entitled "Bibi." It was the first story that Edward King pitched to Scribner's, but the magazine rejected it, as did Appletons' and the Atlantic (the last citing its "distressful effect").[70] Ultimately, Cable placed the story of Bras-Coupé ("a type of all Slavery, turning into flesh and blood the truth that all Slavery is maiming") and his defiance as the animating centerpiece of The Grandissimes, in a way that yoked it intimately to the river. Bras-Coupé comes to New Orleans via the Mississippi on a slave ship. His exile becomes a kind of homecoming, as the river acknowledges his arrival: "The anchor slid with a rumble of relief down through the muddy fathoms of the Mississippi, and the prince could hear through the schooner's side the savage current of the river, leaping and licking about the bows, and whimpering low welcomes home." As Bras-Coupé's relationship with his master, Don José Martinez, develops in unexpected ways, the river becomes a space of strained equality between white and black—a strange counterpoint to the image of Huck and Jim on the river that Twain was incubating: "Many a day did these two living magazines of wrath spend together in the dismal swamps and on the meagre intersecting ridges, making war upon deer and bear and wildcat; or on the Mississippi after wild goose and pelican; when even a word misplaced would have made either the slayer of the other."[71]

After his escape from slavery, the relationship between Bras-Coupé and the river's marginal spaces becomes profound. Escaping to the swamps, like many real and imagined enslaved people before him, Bras-Coupé does more than hide; he transforms the swamp into a subversive space—a power base from which formidable curses emanate and from which a new America might grow: "Bras-Coupé was practically declaring his independence on a slight rise of ground hardly sixty feet in circumference and lifted scarce above the water in the inmost depths of the swamp."[72] As Anthony Wilson argues, Cable "offers the swamp, as terrifying as it might be, as a more moral environment than New Orleans society itself. There is no picturesque romanticization here: Cable foregrounds the swamp's horrors, only to emphasize the greater horrors that face Creole society's dispossessed."[73] Cable does more, though: his narrative also transforms this abject and neglected space into an aesthetic environment marked by hidden life, hidden history, beauty, and peace, which is described in rich detail:

And what surroundings! Endless colonnades of cypresses; long, motionless drapings of gray moss; broad sheets of noisome waters, pitchy black, resting on bottomless ooze; cypress knees studding the surface; patches of floating green, gleaming brilliantly here and there; yonder where the sunbeams wedge themselves in, constellations of water-lilies, the many-hued iris, and a multitude of flowers that no man had named; here, too, serpents great and small, of wonderful colorings, and the dull and loathsome moccasin sliding warily off the dead tree; in dimmer recesses the cow alligator, with her nest hard by; turtles a century old; owls and bats, raccoons, opossums, rats, centipedes and creatures of like vileness; great vines of beautiful leaf and scarlet fruit in deadly clusters; maddening mosquitoes, parasitic insects, gorgeous dragon-flies and pretty water-lizards: the blue heron, the snowy crane, the red-bird, the moss-bird, the night-hawk and the chuckwill's-widow; a solemn stillness and stifled air only now and then disturbed by the call or whir of the summer duck, the dismal ventriloquous note of the rain-crow, or the splash of a dead branch falling into the clear but lifeless bayou.

Bras-Coupé himself becomes, in the popular tongue, part and parcel of the swamp itself: "*C'est ce maudit cocodri' là bas* (It is that accursed alligator, Bras-Coupé, down yonder in the swamp)." At the scene of his final capture at Congo Square, he himself has fully taken on its trappings (and, too, the trappings of the river's original inhabitants): "his feet in moccasins, his tight, crisp hair decked out with feathers, a necklace of alligator's teeth rattling on his breast and a living serpent twined about his neck." If Bras-Coupé's escape from slavery is only temporary, his time in the swamp indelibly affects all of those who come in contact with his legend and with the marginal spaces of the river. The Mississippi remains a source, too, of subaltern power and the central locus of the syncretic folk culture that has grown up in the city. Fearing himself to be under another voodoo curse, for example, arch-Creole Agricola Fusilier "slipped down every day to the levee, had a slave-boy row him across the river in a skiff, landed, re-embarked, and in the middle of the stream surreptitiously cast a picayune over his shoulder into the river."[74]

Cable himself evidently found a different kind of personal escape in the river's byways at this moment. In December 1881, at the beginning of a storied career as an artist and illustrator, Joseph Pennell received his first major commission: to illustrate, as his wife and frequent collaborator, Elizabeth Robins Pennell, remembered in later years, "a series of papers on Louisiana and the Creoles by George W. Cable" that were due to appear in the *Century Magazine*— the articles that would become *The Creoles of Louisiana* (1884). Arriving in New Orleans in January 1882, his time in the city was an extraordinary experience. Pennell, not the easiest company, immediately struck up a friendship with his host: "Cable is just jolly. I was with him from eight o'clock yesterday a.m. till night—This is really living down here." Together, they explored the city. As Elizabeth narrated, "He discovered the picturesque down by the river."[75]

Indeed, during his time in New Orleans with Cable, the river featured centrally in his experience of the city and his new collaborator. On commission for *Harper's Weekly*, the pair went to witness the swollen Mississippi threatening to break through the city's levee. When it finally broke through farther down the river, Cable and Pennell spent "a long day [. . .] watching the water tumbling, roaring, rushing through the crevasse and spreading out over the cane fields."[76] Yet perhaps the most revealing moment of their time together didn't make it into print. Cable and Pennell hired a schooner, picking it up on Lake Pontchartrain with the intention of sailing "up and down the bays and bayous" and along the Mississippi itself—"but the wind and tide did not mean us to, and we spent days amongst islands inhabited only by distant flamingoes and near pelicans with everlasting alligators on the shore. [. . .] I recall [. . .] the big seas in the river down by Eads Port and Pilot Town." Still, this was its

own kind of river escape, one that opened up Cable's imagination and materials. "In the evenings," Pennell reported, "we would pull up by an island
and the captain would make wonderful gumbo soup and mix rice and toma-
toes and things out of cans [. . .]. Then Cable would sing and sometimes tell a
new story [. . .] and all this was before he sang or talked in public. But at last
we gave in to the head winds, boarded a steamer coming up the river and it
brought us back to town." Many decades later, Pennell would still assert that
his "Cable work was as interesting as any I ever did." The illustrations had a
long second life. Elizabeth noted that despite local opposition to Cable's writings, Pennell's engravings "were so approved in New Orleans as to be pirated
for a guidebook in 1885, a fact of which Pennell knew nothing until his next
visit in 1921. [. . .] His language was not repeatable when he discovered not
merely the piracy, but the fancy wreaths, orange branches, the easel, the ga-
bled window by which the pirates thought to add attraction to the drawings."
Pennell's connection to the river almost had another significant second act:
at one point, it was suggested that he would be part of "a book on the Mississippi, with Mark Twain author and Osgood for publisher."[77] Pennell, then, was
almost the illustrator for *Life on the Mississippi*.

"As Brand New to Me as If It Had Been Built Yesterday"

At the end of *A Tramp Abroad*, missing America, Twain included a list of foods
that he was looking forward to devouring after more than a year of the "monotonous" fare of European hotels. Two of them were river related: "Sheep-
head and croakers, from New Orleans. Black bass from the Mississippi."[78] In
April 1882, it was finally time for him to sample those delicacies again. On
April 20 (with Osgood and Phelps in train), he boarded the steamer *Gold Dust*
and began the eight-day journey downriver to New Orleans. There he spent
significant time in the company of George Washington Cable. After a week
in the Crescent City, the party headed back up the Mississippi on May 6, this
time on the *City of Baton Rouge*, piloted by none other than Horace Bixby. Back
in St. Louis on May 12, Twain headed for the Upper Mississippi, pausing for a
few days in Hannibal to revisit his childhood haunts, before leaving the river
again at St. Paul on May 21.[79]

In 1895, speaking in Australia, Twain remembered the significant emotional investments of this journey: "I had not seen that river for I don't know

how long—perhaps for a quarter of a century—and I went there with a sort of longing. One sometimes has a yearning to see again the scenes that were dear to him in his youth, in his prime, in the time when he had the heart to feel, and I thought I would like to see that river and what was left of that steamboat life exactly as I saw it long, long, long ago."[80] Yet the prospect of this river trip also floated up anxieties. Just before leaving, he had recorded in his notebook, "My nightmares, to this day, take the form of running down into an over-shadowing bluff, with a steamboat—showing that my earliest dread made the strongest impression on me (running steadily down into the deep shadows of Selma Bluffs & head of Hat Island)." That complicated duality made its way into the journey. He knew, too, that on this literary journey, he would need to address a moment of his life on the Mississippi that he had hitherto avoided—the death of his brother. "Tell, now," he instructed himself in his notebook, "the events preceding & following the Pennsylvania's explosion."[81]

Fresh from the Rhine and the Thames, at a moment when other writers were implicating the river in a variety of contradictory statements about life, and particularly race, in America, what did the Mississippi look like to Twain? His experience of the trip as it appeared in notebooks, letters, and newspaper interviews provides a compelling counter-text to *Life on the Mississippi*. To begin with, being back on the river buoyed him up. "We are having a powerful good time & picking up & setting down volumes of literary stuff," he wrote to Livy on April 22.[82] He clearly relished this return , but more particularly, he savored the male bonhomie that the Mississippi always represented to him: "I have felt as much at home and as much in my proper place in the pilot house as if I had never been out of the pilot house." The notebooks recorded details of boat talk—language, lifestyles—that *Life on the Mississippi* couldn't capture but which must have better reflected the tenor of conversation. One of the mates on the *Gold Rush*—"old-fashioned [. . .] affable"—pointed out a large "country residence" that they were passing: "There, that's a God damned fine place. [. . .] The old bitch that owns that place has the biggest whore house in St. Louis."[83]

Twain's half-hearted attempt to travel on the river incognito was vanish-ingly brief. Almost as soon as he was on board the *Gold Dust*, he was "betrayed by one of the boys."[84] John Henton Carter—the steamboatman-turned-writer who went by the pseudonym Commodore Rollingpin—interviewed Twain during this trip and gave a more ribald version of the beginning of his journey downriver. As Carter had it, the pilot of the *Gold Dust*, when asked if he remembered Sam Clemens, gave an answer that cut to the heart of Twain's river identity: "Well I should say I did! Sam left here 'bout twenty years ago, an' has been writin' books ever since. He's better at that'n he was steerin' for he wasn't much of a pilot. [. . .] To tell you the truth, to look at Sam Clemens, he wasn't worth sweepin' up!"[85] Whatever the source of this version of events, and though played for laughs, it still chimed with some of the uncertainties that the Mississippi soon began provoking for Twain.

The change in river life assaulted him immediately. First, mortality pressed in: "Had a great deal of talk about the river and the steam boat men, most of whom are dead now." And he was lost, literally, a situation not helped by the fact that the river was in flood: "I found that the river was as brand new to me as if it had been built yesterday and built while I was absent. I recognized no single feature of it." The pilot's memory, that most wonderful thing, had left him: "I can't bring it back to mind even when the changes have been pointed out to me. It is like a man pointing out to me a place in the sky where a cloud has been. I can't reproduce the cloud." The scene of primal steamboating terror that still haunted him now only lived in his nightmares: "I didn't find Hat Island and upon inquiry learned that it has utterly disappeared." If Twain had planned to travel to the Mississippi to praise the river of his youth, he ended up looking to bury it—at least, that aspect of it that he knew and valued. "The romance of boating is gone, now," he wrote in his notebook. "The steamboatman is no longer a god. The youth don't talk river slang any more."[86] Life on the Mississippi had changed inexorably in his absence, as had Twain himself. The prodigal son of the river was out of step with new times on the Mississippi.

In New Orleans, Twain found himself happily trapped in a "whirlpool of hospitality."[87] George Washington Cable's services as a tour guide were in demand again. Also in town was Joel Chandler Harris, already famous as the author of *Uncle Remus: His Songs and Sayings* (1880). He was there at the explicit invitation of Twain, who was trying to get him onto the lecture stage. "Suppose you meet Osgood and me in New Orleans early in May?" he had cajoled earlier in the year.[88] It was a telling gathering, flagging up the increasing significance of the South to the trajectory of American literature. The socializing continued apace—"breakfasts, dinners, lunches, cock-fights, Sunday schools, mule-races, lake-excursions, social gatherings, & all sort of things"—

and included a short tugboat journey following a reunion with Twain's old mentor Horace Bixby.[89] Writing in 1885, to mark Twain's fiftieth birthday in the pages of the *Critic*, Joel Chandler Harris vividly remembered this moment: "I saw Mr. Twain not so very long ago piloting a steamboat up and down the Mississippi River in front of New Orleans, and his hand was strong and his eye keen. [. . .] The fact that he was bordering on fifty years never occurred to me."[90] Yet unlike Sala and Hesse-Wartegg, Twain wasn't wholly charmed with his return to the city, where he had experienced Mardi Gras decades earlier. Walking through the French Market, a picturesque delight for most travelers, Twain dwelled on other details: "One woman trying to brush flies from leg of mutton. Mutton covered with mashed flies; must be very nutritious mutton. [. . .] The sights here are bad, but the smells heart-rending. Stick to a fellow's clothes all day."[91]

Twain's time in New Orleans also resulted in one of the most compelling portraits of him at this moment, which further meditated on the relationship of his identity to the river that he was revisiting. Lafcadio Hearn (occasional friend of Cable) was making a name for himself as a journalist and writer in New Orleans. His florid evocation of Twain and the Mississippi was published in the *New Orleans Times-Democrat* on May 2, 1882. "The romance of river-life is not like the romance of the sea," Hearn wrote, asserting the distinctness of river culture at this moment. "But it is perhaps sweeter." Delighting in florid visions of "marvelous nights upon the Mississippi, nights filled with the perfume of orange blossoms under a milky palpitation of stars in amethystine sky, and witchery of tropical moonlight," Hearn turned his attention to "an illustrious visitor," never explicitly named as Twain, "who reminded us of all these things [. . .] having once himself turned the pilot's wheel." Despite the fact that "his name is a household word in the English-speaking world," Hearn asserts that the romance of the river still clings to him:

> There is still something of the pilot's cheery manner in his greeting, and the keenness of the pilot's glance in his eyes, and a looking out and afar off, as of the man who of old was wont to peer into the darkness of starless nights, with the care of a hundred lives on his hands. He has seen many strange cities since that day, sailed upon many seas, studied many peoples, written many wonderful books. Yet, now that he is in New Orleans again, one cannot help wondering whether his heart does not sometimes

prompt him to go to the river [. . .] to watch the white boats panting at the wharves, and listen to their cries of welcome or farewell, and dream of nights beautiful, silver-blue, and silent, and the great Southern moon peering into a pilot-house.[92]

The voyage back upriver with Horace Bixby on the *Baton Rouge* took him back into memory in multiple ways, both his youthful piloting and the years of his childhood in Hannibal. There nostalgia tipped into melancholy. In a letter to Livy, Twain described these as "delightful days [. . .] loitering around all day long, examining the old localities and talking with the grey-heads who were boys and girls with me 30 or 40 years ago."[93] Yet in his notebook, he lamented that "everything was changed in Hannibal."[94] The trip finally climaxed in a wail of despair: "Livy darling, I am desperately homesick. [. . .] That world which I knew in its blossoming youth is old and bowed and melancholy, now; its soft cheeks are leathery and wrinkled, the fire is gone out in its eyes, and the spring from its step. It will be dust and ashes when I come again. [. . .] Now I am under way again, upon this hideous trip to St. Paul."[95] The same spirit would tip over into the writing of *Life on the Mississippi*.

"The Crookedest River in the World"

"The Mississippi is well worth reading about"—so begins *Life on the Mississippi*.[96] The *New York Times* agreed in its review of the book: "Any book that Mr. Mark Twain might write with the Mississippi River for a subject would be sure of public welcome."[97] But was it still worth writing about? Finally getting the river on paper was perhaps the most painful writing experience of Twain's life. Unlike the thrilling ease of composing "Old Times on the Mississippi" for Howells, building a book around those sketches was slow and arduous work. Once he had incorporated the *Atlantic* sketches in the manuscript, framed by a number of introductory chapters exploring the history and geology of the river, there was still a lot of river to travel. "I have never had such a fight over a book in my life before," he wrote to Howells in November 1882. (Howells himself was in London, having some rather unfortunate river experiences of his own: "We *did* do a few miles of the Thames," he wrote to Twain, "in a sort of big steam launch, and if it had not rained all the way, and Osgood hadn't had the rheumatism, and another fellow the diarrhoea, we should have enjoyed it.")[98] Near the end of the composition process, Twain exclaimed to Charley Webster, "I will not interest myself in *anything* connected with this wretched God-damned book."[99] Yet as counterpoint, Howells would later write, "Upon the whole I have the notion that Clemens thought this his greatest book."[100] It quickly gained other fans. Not long after its publication, Howells would write to Twain: "One night I met Thomas Hardy, the novelist, at dinner; and he said, 'Why don't people understand that Mark Twain is not merely a great humorist? He's a very remarkable fellow in a very different way,' and then went on to praise your Mississippi in a manner that justified all the admiration I had ever felt for his books."[101] Certainly, there are profound tensions straining through the book—the same ambiguities that animated Twain's journey back to the river. As Jeffrey Alan Melton has described: "Throughout *Life on the Mississippi,* Twain struggles between his multiple perspectives [. . .]. This tension derives from the intrinsic problem for the travel writer who is too close to his subject and the tourist who expects to be at home."[102] Larry Howe has also persuasively argued that Twain is clearly working through anxieties relating to the Civil War throughout the book: "Twain begins by reshaping his personal history so that he assumes an allegorical role in the national crisis and ends by rewriting national history as a conflict of literary kinship in which he emerges as the representative of American value." The "narrow channel of his experience" in relation to the war becomes instead "a national allegory."[103]

The tensions that animate the text are certainly the source of its rich multiplicity. Balancing memory and experience, *Life on the Mississippi* is also a polyphonic performance that absorbs (and rejects) a wealth of other river narratives. Even before Twain began composition of the book, he was reading around the river. In the summer of 1882, he wrote to his publishers with a request: "I wish you would set a cheap expert to work to collect local histories of Mississippi towns & a lot of other books relating to the river for me." They supplied bountifully: "We send you by American express, a bundle containing the seven 'Atlantics' containing the Mississippi articles, and a number of 'Emerson's Magazine' with 'Up the Miss.' by J. A. Dallas in it. We also enclose a lot of books relating to travels in the U.S. by English people in the first half of this century; twenty-five volumes in all." Ralph Keeler's articles on the river for *Every Saturday* from 1871 were sent to Twain in September 1882. He had Hesse-Wartegg's book to hand as well as Francis Parkman's histories, John Disturnell's tourist's guide, Henry Rowe Schoolcraft's Indian legends, and a wealth of newspapers. When George Washington Cable came to visit in October, he asked the New Orleanian to write home with a request for some books from his own collection.[104] Twain paid as much attention—perhaps more—to the printed river as the thing itself.

Out of that rich, muddy soup of emotion and influence emerged a hybrid text that presents its reader with a unique, at times abstract, portrait of the Mississippi. Like the river it describes, *Life on the Mississippi* is a contrary narrative—by far the "crookedest" book written about the river at this moment. Implicitly, it is a text that also seeks to undermine the other narratives being woven around the Mississippi. Like the river that undercuts its banks at unexpected moments, cleaving a meandering path from source to sea, provoking unexpected diversions and digressions, *Life on the Mississippi* makes its own unpredictable path. Though it echoes them at points, Twain's Mississippi ultimately jars with the travel accounts of writers like Hesse-Wartegg and Sala and their Lost Cause picturesque. It is a palpably different river than that evoked by Cable, consciously looking away from the racial difficulties that he confronts; it resists the nationalist effusions surrounding the Rhine and the Thames. Instead, it revels in the idea of the Mississippi at its most uncontainable and indefinable; it dwells, incessantly, on death. *Life on the Mississippi* becomes a text about the futility of other attempts to encompass the river, literally or literarily. Its exceptionalism is the quality that Twain stresses right from the start: "It is not a commonplace river, but on the contrary is in all ways remarkable."[105]

Much of the ambiguous layering at work in this rendition of the river is apparent from the opening chapters of *Life on the Mississippi*. Indeed, the intertextuality is evident from the epigraph: Twain took his description of the Mississippi Valley forming the "body of the nation" from the "Editor's Table" of *Harper's New Monthly Magazine* in February 1863, itself framed around Lincoln's Annual Message to Congress. In the midst of war, *Harper's* was evoking the popular antebellum trope that figured the Mississippi as a symbol of union, framing the river as a symbol of American exceptionalism and supremacy. Yet the rest of the *Harper's* piece went much further than that, defining a very particular vision of Manifest Destiny in the Mississippi valley. "The land was kept open for them for ages after it had become habitable by man," it argued. "Only a few wandering tribes were allowed to approach and hold temporary possession of it. Mound-builders and hunters came and disappeared, leaving behind them no historic traces, because they had no history worthy of perpetuation." Slavery, too, was defended: "The slaves, taken in a mass, are far in advance of their grandfathers who were brought from Africa." Moreover, in *Harper's* vision, the future of the newly emancipated must lay far outside the "Body of the Nation" represented by the valley of the Mississippi because the "whole United States [. . .] will in due time be wanted by the whites."[106] What does this uncomfortable context do to the final sentence of Twain's epigraph? "*As a dwelling-place for civilized man it is by far the first upon our globe*": Twain added the italics—but do they suggest emphatic agreement or irony?[107] How does that statement square with Twain's early reference to Frederick Marryat—perhaps the rudest of all the rude Europeans who reached the river in the antebellum years—and his description of the Mississippi as a "Great Sewer"?[108] Almost immediately, the triumphalist, segregated vision of *Harper's* is questioned and undercut.

Twain's use of history—and historians—in the opening chapters of *Life on the Mississippi* is equally ambivalent. As Twain's notebooks make clear, even before his trip to the Mississippi, he had been reading Francis Parkman's wildly popular accounts of the Mississippi valley. During his time on the river in 1882, he wrote a reminder to himself: "Get statistics of width, length & volume of Misspi out of Cyclopedia. [. . .] And something about La Salle's trip out of Parkman." And he repeated that note not long after: "Get La Salle's discovery of Mississippi."[109] He was referring particularly to Parkman's enormously influential *La Salle and the Discovery of the Great West* (1869), the third volume in his epic account of France and England in North America and a work that placed the explorer who claimed Louisiana for France in 1682 in a heroic role (also situating the Mississippi valley at the root of American identity). In defining what Parkman's La Salle represented, an illuminating contrast can be drawn to the interpretation of the explorer that can be found in a series of paintings by George Catlin. Though more famous for his Indian paintings, in 1847 Catlin produced a sequence of images detailing La Salle's journey through America and along the Mississippi. As Kate Elliott has argued, the narrative and focus of those paintings largely "shuns the message of conquest" in order to "reclaim a moment of purity"—to witness a vision of the Mississippi River valley at the moment that it was about to be lost forever. In so doing, Catlin frequently shifted the focus of his paintings from "the human actors to the environment—the wide, sparkling blue river with its flat banks, thick with lush vegetation." Such a vision had encoded within it a sense that "Native American life and culture [. . .] were important and worthy of being saved."[110]

Parkman, on the other hand, was famously hostile toward Native Americans—as he was to most other groups who were not white, Anglo-Saxon, protestant, and male. As Nicholas Carr has argued, "Fearing national emasculation, Parkman devoted himself to depicting a healthier past in which great men, heroic deeds, and moral grandeur held their rightful place at the center of American life."[111] Not unlike the repositioning of the Thames and the Rhine in their respective national cultures, Parkman's valorization of La Salle was an attempt to place the Mississippi center stage in national life. As Parkman had it, La Salle was the first America visionary, "a grand type of incarnate energy and will," and the Mississippi was "the object of his day-dreams, the destined avenue of his ambitions." According to Parkman, "America owes him an enduring memory; for, in this masculine figure, she sees the pioneer who guided her to the possession of her richest heritage."[112] This was clearly an intoxicating vision in the postbellum decades. Patricia Kay Galloway notes that "popular writers and historians rushed" to the subject matter that Parkman had unleashed (Theodore Roosevelt and Frederick Jackson Turner among them), and "with each retelling La Salle garnered new accolades," becoming "a folk hero whose adventurous and spirit and fearlessness had acquired legendary proportions."[113]

Twain, though, seems dubious about this kind of rhetoric. Yet neither, with his usual antipathy to indigenous people, does he echo Catlin's sentiments about the meaning of this moment of conquest. Though he uses Parkman to narrate La Salle's story, his own commentary is sardonic. Breezing through colonial history in a couple of brief chapters—dismissing the river's "slumbrous first epoch"—Twain summarizes millennia of Native culture and the endeavors of the French colonists in a short précis: "The priest explained the mysteries of the faith 'by signs,' for the saving of the savages; thus compensating them with possible possessions in Heaven for the certain ones on earth which they had just been robbed of. And also, by signs, La Salle drew from these simple children of the forest acknowledgments of fealty to Louis the Putrid, over the water. Nobody smiled at these colossal ironies."[114]

Or perhaps the river did. For Twain, there was a sting in this tale beyond La Salle's untimely death. Throughout the text, Twain discusses the fate of the town of Napoleon, Arkansas, and in so doing he emphasizes the river's ability to resist all human attempts to define its history. Napoleon, Twain avers, was the place where Hernando De Soto first saw the river and where La Salle claimed the river for France. Twain also notes the irony that it was Napoleon Bonaparte himself who would sell Louisiana to America. But returning to the river in 1882, he discovers that Napoleon, Arkansas, no longer exists, having been "emptied [. . .] into the Mississippi [. . .] years and years" ago. The "self-complacent" town had been "swallowed up, vanished, gone to feed the fishes": "It was an astonishing thing to see the Mississippi rolling between unpeopled shores."[115] This apocalyptic vision of the river's implacable ability to erase human endeavor pushes against the confident sense of Manifest Destiny explicit in the predictions of the *Harper's* editorial, dwarfing the history of Parkman and those who followed in his train.

Turning from history, *Life on the Mississippi* gives way to Twain's visions of the river, literary and autobiographical—first with the flatboat episode taken from the manuscript of *Huckleberry Finn*, then through the articles that made up "Old Times on the Mississippi," grafted wholesale into *Life on the Mississippi*. But the operation shifts the meaning of those articles, too, and as James Cox notes: "Enclosed in the travel book, their historical perspective gains force. In their original form, history stood forth as autobiography; in their new context, autobiography stands forth as history."[116] That epoch also seems dead and gone by 1882. The narration of his brother Henry's death—"we bore him to the death-room, poor boy"—serves as an epitaph to the golden age of steamboating. It also domesticates the destruction of Napoleon, Arkansas. The town, the erstwhile site of world historical moments, was also the place where Twain was "handed the first printed news of the 'Pennsylvania's' mournful disaster a quarter of a century ago."[117] If the river erases all trace of human effort, it also expunges human tragedy too.

Just as Twain's river pushes against historical readings, the same subversive, nihilistic spirit is discernible in his discussion of river improvements. Twain himself makes clear that questions of flood control were deeply pressing in the Lower Mississippi valley in the 1880s: "Mississippi Improvement is a mighty topic, down yonder. Every man on the river banks, south of Cairo, talks about it every day, during such moments as he is able to spare from talking about the war."[118] Hesse-Wartegg, for example, devoted a chapter to debating the most plausible methods for containing "the capricious river."[119] The debate played out in the national press too. In *Scribner's*, in July 1881, for example, William Law Murfree (father of author Mary Noailles Murfree, who herself would turn to the river as a topic in the decades to come) profiled "the levees of the Mississippi" to debate the question of how to teach a river with "exceedingly inconvenient peculiarities [. . .] to deport itself like other respectable rivers."[120] In September 1882, David A. Curtis pondered, "What shall be done to the Mississippi River?" for *Harper's:* "The Father of Waters is, in his poetic personality, one of the most valuable individuals on earth, and one of the most troublesome as well as dangerous. What shall we do to encourage his beneficence, and divert his wrath?"[121] N. S. Shaler declared in the *Atlantic,* in May 1883, "that the perfect control of the Mississippi system of waters is perhaps the greatest engineering problem that our race has ever had to attack."[122] In the *North American Review,* in March of that year, Robert S. Taylor also pondered methods for "the subjugation of the Mississippi."[123] Even Oscar Wilde, in New Orleans shortly after Twain, was asked for his opinion on the Mississippi. He scolded, "No well-behaved river would overflow as it has done."[124]

One answer to the question of river control seemed to come in the familiar form of James B. Eads, that other Master of the Mississippi. Eads's attempts to deepen the channel at the mouth of the Mississippi, occupying his attention since the completion of his bridge at St. Louis, had finally borne fruit. His wooden jetties had caused the river to cut a channel to the depth of thirty feet at its South Pass, ensuring that New Orleans was open for shipping and open for business. To recognize his latest triumph over the river, a banquet was held in his honor in New Orleans in December 1882. All the speeches that night, published shortly thereafter, paid deep tribute both to Eads's achievements and the significance of the river for the city. Eads was, according to one speaker, "the great engineer, whose name will stand unforgotten as long as the Mississippi flows." For another, Eads had triumphed in "correcting the eccentricities of the great river with which his name has become so completely identified." Eads himself set out a millennial vision for the Mississippi Valley in which "river improvements" would guarantee its future as "the most prosperous, wealthy and powerful empire on the face of the globe."[125]

Throughout *Life on the Mississippi,* though, Twain is also largely averse to this kind of optimistic boosterism. He gives Eads an admiring mention in relation to the success of his jetties—"a work at the mouth of the Mississippi which seemed clearly impossible." But the overall tone of his attitude to river improvement is skepticism: "One who knows the Mississippi will promptly aver—not aloud, but to himself—that ten thousand River Commissions, with the mines of the world at their back, cannot tame that lawless stream, cannot curb it or confine it, cannot say to it, Go here, or Go there, and make it obey; cannot save a shore which it has sentenced; cannot bar its path with an obstruction which it will not tear down, dance over, and laugh at. [. . .] The Commission might as well bully the comets in their courses and undertake to make them behave, as try to bully the Mississippi into right and reasonable conduct." Again, Twain emphasizes—indeed, revels in—the river's unreasonableness, its refusal to submit to the imposition of a narrative. This is compounded by the invective of Uncle Mumford, the semi-fictional steamboatman "thirty years a mate on the river," who reasserts the Mississippi's independence with another statement of its superiority to biddable European streams: "You turn one of those little European rivers over to this Commission, with its hard bottom and clear water, and it would just be a holiday job for them to wall it, and pile it, and dike it, and tame it down, and boss it around, and make it go wherever they wanted it to, and stay where they put it, and do just as they said, every time. But this ain't that kind of a river." By the time that the commission succeeds in taming the river, Mumford concludes, there won't be "any boats left at all." It is ultimately this vision of the Mississippi—one that "no power on earth can stop"—that leaps from the page throughout the meanders of this sprawling text.[126]

Certainly, Twain resists the new trend for picturesque southern readings of the river, encapsulated in the celebration of New Orleans by travelers like Hesse-Wartegg and Sala. Twain pivots from a critique of Mardi Gras and its "girly-girly romance" to a wider denunciation of "the Sir Walter disease" and the South's love of "sillinesses and emptinesses, sham grandeurs, sham gauds, and sham chivalries of a brainless and worthless long-vanished society." Instead, he promotes Cable's aesthetic, over and above the experience of the city itself: "With Mr. Cable along to see for you, and describe and explain and illuminate, a jog through that old quarter is a vivid pleasure. And you have a vivid sense as of unseen or dimly seen things—vivid, and yet fitful and darkling."[127] Yet at least at this point, Twain did not follow Cable's example in confronting the racial history of the river and its intimate connection to slavery. To a striking extent, black inhabitants of the river are largely erased from *Life on the Mississippi*. Slavery and its legacies are the one narrative that is excluded from Twain's multitudinous text. The closest that Twain came to a direct statement about the issue was in the so-called suppressed chapter that was ultimately left out of the manuscript of *Life on the Mississippi*. "I missed one thing in the South," Twain began, mock-nostalgically, "African slavery. That horror is gone, & permanently."[128] Why the offending chapter was removed is unclear, given the other critiques that Twain makes about the South, but as Guy Cardwell concluded, "If anxiety about the sensitivities of Southerners who were potential buyers of books dictated the omission [. . .] the anxiety was as much Twain's as it was Osgood's."[129]

Either way, no such direct accounting of slavery ultimately featured in this book. The fleeting images of black life on the river that do make their way into the narrative are abject and comic in turns, "a few scattering handfuls of ragged negroes, some drinking, some drunk, some nodding, others asleep." The closest he comes to engaging with the experiences of the emancipated is near Memphis, a place he defines as "the migrating negro region," but there, too, he undermines the desire of black Americans for self-determination, seeing in their desire to leave the South only whim: "These poor people could never travel when they were slaves; so they make up for the privation now. They stay on a plantation till the desire to travel seizes them; then they pack up, hail a steamboat, and clear out. Not for any particular place; no, nearly any place will answer; they only want to be moving."[130]

Instead, the defining aspect of the river in *Life on the Mississippi* is its essential removal from temporal concerns and its symbolic value as both eternal presence and scene of constant flux. Twain peremptorily kills off steamboating as soon as he returns to the river at St. Louis in 1882: "Mississippi steamboating was born about 1812; at the end of thirty years, it had grown to mighty proportions; and in less than thirty more, it was dead! A strangely short life for so majestic a creature."[131] Hesse-Wartegg, by way of comparison, was enraptured by the busy scene that he encountered on the St. Louis waterfront: "dozens of palatial steamboats [. . .] a singular riverscape with thousands of figures: laborers, freight wagons, spectators and tourists."[132] That serves to emphasize the degree to which, with no little irony, *Life on the Mississippi* is a text obsessed with death: dead explorers, dead Indians, dead pilots, dead steamboats, dead towns, dead industries, dead travelers, dead babies, dead brothers, dead childhood friends. It dwells on cemeteries, pontificates about modes of disposal of the dead, and contemplates the work of spiritualists. Even when Horace Bixby reappears in the narrative—"the man whom, of all men, I most wished to see"—he seems like a ghost, uncannily unchanged since Twain's departure from the river, and barely makes an impression: "A curious thing, to leave a man thirty-five years old, and come back at the end of twenty-one years and find him still only thirty-five." The only escape seems to come in the contemplation of the eternally changing, eternally static river: "League after league, and still league after league, it pours its chocolate tide along, between its solid forest walls, its almost untenanted shores, with seldom a sail or a moving object of any kind to disturb the surface and break the monotony of the blank, watery solitude; and so the day goes, the night comes, and again the day—and still the same, night after night and day after day—majestic, unchanging sameness of serenity, repose, tranquillity, lethargy, vacancy—symbol of eternity, realization of the heaven pictured by priest and prophet, and longed for by the good and thoughtless!"[133]

The apparent emptiness of the river in comparison to its golden age in Twain's youth is framed as the completion of a cycle: "The river was an awful solitude, then. And it is now, over most of its stretch." Here there are no grand visions of future prosperity. Death gives the book—a scattershot narrative that models the implicit idea that the river cannot be contained in narrative form—its essential constant. Yet *Life on the Mississippi* still ends on an image of rebirth and renewal. Twain, inevitably, dismisses Indian legends from the river throughout the book—"threadbare [. . .] idiotic [. . .] exceedingly sorry rubbish"—but the final appendix in the book is a Native story, "The Undying Head," borrowed, tellingly, from the work of Henry Rowe Schoolcraft, discoverer of the source of the Mississippi.[134] It is a creation story that begins with death and ends in rebirth and immortality: "They were told that, since they had all died, and were restored to life, they were no longer mortal, but spirits, and they were assigned different stations in the invisible world."[135]

"The Genial, Big-Hearted, Big-Voiced Mississippi Steamboat Captain"

If *Life on the Mississippi* in many ways represented Twain's last sustained engagement with the piloting years of his youth, the figure of the steamboat pilot would enjoy a vivid life in popular culture beyond Twain's works. As he faded into history, he would come to be a representative American type—oftentimes, particularly at the tail end of the nineteenth century, a representative southern type. A telling tribute can be found in Jeannette H. Walworth's

1887 collection, *Southern Silhouettes* (first serialized in the *New York Evening Post*). Walworth's intention, as she described it, was to record "the old order of things in the South [. . .] rapidly passing into the realms of legend and tradition [. . .] the story of a day that is dead."[136] Howells, writing in *Harper's*, described the sketches as "reflexes of a faded civilization [. . .] but one feels that the negatives have been touched, and that is always to be regretted."[137] Others were more effusive, though. The *Critic* delighted in her "graceful and touching" portraits of the "old state of things in the South," which "cast here and there a sunset glimmer over departing institutions [. . .] to show of what strong fibre they were wrought." For particular praise, it singled out her sketch of "Captain Tom"—a figure the magazine "recognized [. . .] instantly as an old acquaintance: the genial, big-hearted, big-voiced Mississippi steamboat captain, who even now, in the flesh, walks the deck of his great steamer."[138]

The "Captain Tom" in question was clearly a thinly veiled portrait of Thomas P. Leathers of the *Natchez*, still a notorious river figure after his 1870 race with the *Robert E. Lee*. In Walworth's hands, Leathers becomes a mystic representative of the river; Twain's vision of the pilot takes on a transcendent tone. A figure of continuity and perseverance—"he still holds the helm stiffly against all adverse currents"—Tom is an explicitly sentimental construction in other ways: "this great rugged Captain Tom, with the voice of a lion and the heart of a girl [. . .] his heart-strings inextricably tangled up with those that beat under the various familiar roof-trees he sees from his hurricane deck twice every week." He is, like the river, the binding agent of this community—its historian and folklorist—and a potent benevolent presence: "In the holidays, that is, in the week that falls just before Christmas, his boat and himself become the dispensers of a solid stream of comfort that is only exhausted when he reaches the wharf boat and Vicksburg." Tom and the river community over which he presides "stand or fall together."[139]

Ultimately, Tom—this extraordinary mixture of the Father of Waters, Old Father Time, and Father Christmas—rises above earthly concerns and becomes an explicitly mythic figure, pushing at the boundaries of the human and approaching the divine. At such moments, Halworth's portrait represents a remarkable eulogy for the pilot—a closing of the circle opened by "Old Times on the Mississippi" that also elides the ambiguities of Twain's portraits of river life. Tom seems to approach immortality, a river spirit who has grown "as near achieving ubiquity as mortal can," infused with the "subtle forces" of the elements "by an alchemy known only to themselves": "Nor wind, nor rain, nor heat, nor cold hold any terrors for him; they pay him tribute in rich blood and boundless vigor."[140]

Though still all too mortal, Twain was also apparently reinvigorated by his last great river odyssey—his journey through the underworld of memory, mutability, and mortality on the river. But he was also ready to leave the pilot-house. He was prepared, in fact, to rejoin Huck and Jim on their raft, to follow the Mississippi to a new reckoning with its racial history. In time, the world would travel with him.

"Sometimes We'd Have That Whole River All to Ourselves"

RUNAWAYS, ROUSTABOUTS, AND THE LIMITS OF FREEDOM

Possibly to him the Song of Steam is the sweetest of all musical sounds,
only as a great tone-record of roustabout memories—each boat whistle,
deep or shrill or mellow, recalling some past pleasure or pain in
the history of a life spent along the broad highway of brown
water flowing to the Crescent City of the South.
—LAFCADIO HEARN, "A Child of the Levee," 1876

A cruise down the Mississippi River had been my early boyhood dream.
[. . .] Not till the warning hand of nature knocked sternly at the door
and demanded a change and a rest from a busy business life,
could I spare the time.
—BEN C. WILKINS, *Cruise of the "Little Nan,"* 1881

Twain's voice has the resonance of a cracked steamboat whistle.
—*St. Louis Daily Globe Democrat,* January 1885

On January 9, 1885, Mark Twain was back on the Mississippi River. Or rather, he was suspended above it, stuck on James Eads's bridge on his way into St. Louis as part of a reading tour with George Washington Cable. This was an excursion, underway since November, carefully timed to coincide with the release of *Adventures of Huckleberry Finn* (already released, in December 1884, in Britain and Canada; still forthcoming in the United States, eventually to be published on February 18). Things had hit a snag. "We had," Twain explained to a local reporter, "just reached that portion of the bridge which overhangs the crystal waters of the Mississippi River when a misunderstanding arose between the forward and rear portions of the train. [. . .] If we had not been going very slowly at the time, the whole train would have left the track." Twain described a "sense of crumbling—something crumbling beneath us [. . .]. I fully expected the bridge to break down—I always have done so when I crossed it." It was his near immersion in the Mississippi, though, that the journalist pushed him on, and Twain was happy to oblige:

> "Personally, I suppose, you had no fears, being familiar with the river currents?"
>
> "Not in the slightest. It would not have discommoded me in the least to have been tossed into the Mississippi. I know the river thoroughly. It was the other people I was thinking of."
>
> "I noticed you seemed very anxious about the other people," Mr. Cable remarked with a quiet smile.[1]

If Twain had been dunked into the freezing waters of the Mississippi that January, with Cable by his side, as Eads's bridge collapsed around him, the river would have reclaimed him at his apex. On the one hand, *Life on the Mississippi* had performed less well financially than Twain had hoped—"the publisher who sells less than 50,000 copies of a book for me has merely injured me, he has not benefitted me," he blasted Osgood, his erstwhile river travel companion—but completing that book had clearly unlocked something.[2] To Howells, he expressed a new sense of freedom in very particular terms: "I do not believe I ever so greatly appreciated and enjoyed and realized the absence of the chains of slavery as I do this time. [. . .] 'I belong to nobody, I have ceased from being a slave.'" Throughout the summer of 1883 at Quarry Farm, buoyed up by his emancipation, he picked up the manuscript of *Huckleberry*

Finn that he had been pecking at for the previous seven years and barely let it go until it was finished. "I haven't piled up MS so in years," he wrote to Howells in July 1883. "Why, it's like old times, to step straight into the study, damp from the breakfast table, & sail right in & sail right on, the whole day long, without thought of running short of stuff or words." "The children are booming," he declared, using a word that Huck continually uses to describe traveling down the river. "I'm booming, these days." By September, he felt he was finished, but still he tinkered. In April 1884, he was trying to hand off a portion of the editing process to Howells: "It took my breath away [. . .] the generosity of your proposal to read the proofs of Huck Finn. [. . .] I cannot conceive of a rational man deliberately piling such an atrocious job upon himself." Howells, kindly, in response: "I shall have the pleasure of admiring a piece of work I like under the microscope."[3] Twain's own editing process was complicated by his plans to branch out into a new field: by establishing the company of Charles L. Webster & Company, *Adventures of Huckleberry Finn* was to be the inaugural volume from his own publishing house. At the same time, he was attempting to lure General Grant—the humiliated hero of Vicksburg, bankrupt, dying, and discredited by his presidency—to publish his memoirs with Webster & Company too.

Then there was the tour. For a number of years—seen in his courting of the bashful Joel Chandler Harris in New Orleans, for example—Twain had been incubating plans for a new lecture excursion. Howells later described the "magnificent scheme" that he imagined: Twain, Aldrich, Cable, and Howells himself "touring the country [. . .] in a private car, with a cook of our own, and every facility for living on the fat of the land. [. . .] He would be the impresario, and would guarantee us others at least seventy-five dollars a day, and pay every expense of the enterprise, which he provisionally called the Circus, himself."[4] As Anthony Berret pointed out, the tour "might just as well have been called a minstrel show."[5] As it turned out, Howells and Aldrich "both abhorred public appearances," and the tour went ahead with just Cable and Twain, traveling, as Howells put it, on "a far less stupendous scale."[6] Still, at least to begin with, Twain remained delighted by what he saw in the New Orleanian. Their friendship had developed after Twain's trip to the Crescent City in 1882. When he was a houseguest at Hartford in November 1883, Twain gushed to Howells: "He's just a rattling reader now [. . .] with 2 seasons of *public* practice, I guess he'll be the best professional reader alive."[7]

While Twain's impatience—ultimately fury—with Cable's personal piety would overwhelm their friendship as the long months of the tour took their toll, their combination at this moment was symbolically compelling. They were repeatedly yoked together in the popular press. A vote for "our 'forty immortals,'" published in the *Critic* in April 1884, with a view to forming the "membership in a possible American Academy," ranked Cable twelfth and Twain fourteenth among living American male writers (Henry James separated them at thirteen; Aldrich was seventh, Howells fifth).[8] Sarah Bolton's profiles of *Famous American Authors* (1887) juxtaposed chapters devoted to the two men.[9] Even more tellingly, at the moment that they were suspended above the Mississippi, halfway through the tour, they were also both featured in the January 1885 edition of the *Century Magazine* (as was James B. Eads, providing his memories of ironclad gunboats and his role in the fight for the Mississippi during the Civil War).[10] Twain was serializing three extracts from *Huckleberry Finn* in advance of its American publication. This month, it was "Jim's Investments, and King Sollermun"—one of the readings that Twain would give on the road and one of the moments of both book and tour that came closest to minstrelsy; next month, it would be "Royalty on the Mississippi," with its beatific vision of watery escape: "Sometimes we'd have that whole river all to ourselves for the longest time."[11]

Cable, though, had published something rather different. "The Freedman's Case in Equity" was the first of several public statements in which Cable would confront, head-on and without the mask of fiction, the ongoing racial injustices of life in the South for black Americans. He had already provoked controversy in the novel that he was ostensibly touring to promote. In *Dr. Sevier* (1884), serialized in the *Century* throughout 1884, Cable fictionalized the Union capture of New Orleans in the Civil War. He used the Mississippi as a symbol of southern despair at the moment of invasion: "The huge, writhing river, risen up above the town, was full to the levee's top, and as though the enemy's fleet was that much more than it could bear, was silently running over by a hundred rills into the streets of the stricken city."[12] What got him in trouble was his assertion that the Union cause had been "just."[13] Unbowed by southern criticism for that slight moment, he doubled down on the controversy with his new essay. As he proclaimed in "The Freedman's Case in Equity," "There rests [. . .] a moral responsibility on the whole nation never to lose sight of the results of African-American slavery until they cease to work mischief and injustice." His central argument hinged on the question that he put to his readers: "Is the freedman a free man?" His conclusion was blunt and unambiguous: "No."[14] The resulting debate—virulent condemnation of Cable in the city of his birth and across the South, "letters full of tender expressions of gratitude and admiration" sent to Cable personally—formed the backdrop of the tour. What Twain thought about Cable's lonely public stance goes unrecorded, though it's certainly plausible that he might not have been thrilled that, in Stephen Railton's words, "for the tour's final six or eight weeks Cable's notoriety eclipsed his partner's."[15] At least one commentator understood that despite the difference in their methods, there was a cognate interest at the heart of both writers at this moment that bound them together. Reviewing the January issue of the *Century,* the *Critic* noted: "Mr. Cable writes of the negro problem, without doubt the most important question before the American people [. . .]. Mark Twain dips into the negro problem, too."[16]

If this tour ultimately highlighted the differences between these two men, it also made one point of connection clear. Major James B. Pond, the lecture circuit impresario who managed Twain and Cable's appearances in 1884 and 1885 (and would go on to organize, among many others, Henry Morton Stanley's tour of America in 1890, not to mention the American engagements of Twain's global, post-bankruptcy lecture expedition in 1895), certainly understood the way that the Mississippi proved to be vital connective tissue between these disparate writers and performers: "Both were Southerners, born on the shores of the Mississippi River, and both sang well. Each was familiar with all the plantation songs and Mississippi River chanties of the negro, and they would often get to singing these together when by themselves, or with their manager for sole audience."[17]

That Pond should focus particularly on their shared love of the black musical culture of the Mississippi was itself telling and timely. It highlighted the degree to which mimicry of the black voice sat at the center of the life and work of both writers (and this tour particularly). Black music from the river of one form or another was a lingua franca that patched over the differences between Twain and Cable. Twain himself had recently come into close contact with this musical legacy: in 1882, on the *Baton Rouge,* his notebooks pay testament to the presence of "Minstrels": "Two colored cabin hands; one *more* colored than other. One played banjo & both sang."[18] They might not have made their way into *Life on the Mississippi,* but the notebook pages assiduously record their songs all the same. Cable, too, had a large repertoire of songs that came from black life in New Orleans and on the river—and he wasn't shy about sharing them either. In October 1882, at a party at Richard Gilder's house, Cable had spent an evening in the company of Clara Louise Kellogg, the famous South Carolinian soprano. "She sang negro melodies and accompanied herself on the banjo," he wrote home excitedly. "What delighted her most was the song of the steamboat roustabouts—'Rock me, Julie, rock me.' She made me sing it over & over."[19] On the one hand, Cable's introduction of this music into his portion of the tour certainly served to amplify the echo of the minstrel show that surrounded the enterprise. Yet it also, ironically, pointed away from minstrelsy and toward a new fashion for—albeit mediated and appropriated— black music from the Mississippi. The *Brooklyn Daily Eagle*, hinting at a growing sense of a diasporic musical tradition that flowed along rivers, pushed the roots of that music farther back, reporting that Cable "sang a Creole song that had been first heard on the banks of the Congo."[20]

Stuck on Eads's bridge above the waters of the river that flowed through their life, their work, their conversation, Twain and Cable sat at the heart of a confluence of currents swirling around the ongoing debate about the meaning of freedom along the Mississippi River—and the rest of America. They were hardly alone in that debate. This was a moment when a host of questions about slavery and liberation, black and white, were being asked and answered along the river in a variety of ways. Huck and Jim might have found "solid lonesomeness" on their raft, an image of freedom that would soon become consecrated in the American imagination, but in wider cultural terms, they traveled on a busy river populated by a diverse cast of Mississippi characters whose own journeys, real and imagined, spoke to many of the same concerns as Twain's most iconic creations.[21] They were all runaways, of one kind or another. On the one hand, in ways that we have not previously considered, the ongoing representation of black life on the river generated a wealth of counterpoints to Jim's experiences, many of which (as suggested by Twain's and Cable's separate passions) focused on the musical life of the river—from a new and lasting vogue for the figure of the roustabout and his songs to the last public work of antislavery campaigners like William Wells Brown. At the same time, the idea of heading to the river for escape and adventures of a different kind was also gaining in popularity. In increasing numbers, urban dwellers (mostly white men) took to canoes and other recreational river craft at all points along the

Western Rivers, in extraordinary numbers. In their concerns, they both prefigured and, eventually, directly emulated Huck's flight from civilization toward a loosely imagined freedom somewhere along the Mississippi—temporary runaways from responsibility and the rigors of respectability.

At the heart of all these endeavors was the image of the river itself. This was something that was understood by an early reviewer of *Adventures of Huckleberry Finn* in the *Hartford Courant*, who emphasized the particular significance of the Mississippi in this narrative, even within Twain's wider bibliography: "The scene of his romance is the Mississippi river. Mr. Clemens has written of this river before specifically, but he has not before presented it to the imagination so distinctly nor so powerfully. Huck Finn's voyage down the Mississippi with the run away nigger Jim, and with occasionally other companions, is an adventure fascinating in itself as any of the classic outlaw stories, but in order that the reader may know what the author has done for him, let him notice the impression left on his mind of this lawless, mysterious, wonderful Mississippi, when he has closed the book."[22] Lawless, mysterious, wonderful, home to outlaws and runaways of all stripes: this was an image of the river that spoke deeply to many Americans, then and now. But whose freedom did it ultimately celebrate, and how far did that freedom stretch? The different trajectories in the cultural life of the Mississippi at this moment, and the different answers to that question, lead us inevitably back to Huck and Jim's raft, again.

"Oh, Ain't I Gone, Gone, Gone, Way Down de Ribber Road"

Minstrelsy's fixation with the Mississippi River hardly went away after the Civil War. Continuing stage adaptations of *Uncle Tom's Cabin* alone meant that the association remained at the heart of popular culture. In 1876, for example, Henry Conway's 1852 adaptation of the novel was revived in Boston. Much of act 2 took place on board a steamboat. Audiences were presented with "a panorama view of the banks of the Mississippi" featuring: "Cotton and sugar plantations with their buildings, negros huts, &c. Wind mills at work &c., &c., with every variety of prospects incidental to its scenery near New Orleans."[23] Yet the war clearly did mark a shift in the meaning of the minstrel show. For David Monod, minstrelsy, like many other American art forms, particularly changed its relationship to the South and to slavery after the Civil

War: "Postwar minstrel shows became sites of mourning for the lost South. [. . .] By claiming authenticity and then portraying happy black slaves, minstrelsy in the late nineteenth century therefore [. . .] became an instrument of southern revanchism over a lost war." Such shows implicitly and explicitly argued that the "Civil War [. . .] had been a mistake; black folks had not been improved by freedom; rather, the security of their perpetual childhood had been destroyed."[24] The Mississippi—already implicated in the postwar culture of reunion and nostalgia—continued to hold a central place in the medium.

Yoked to the changes in minstrelsy during these years was the emergence of the roustabout in popular culture. On the postbellum stage, roustabouts became veritably synonymous with minstrelsy. Luke Schoolcraft—who grew up in New Orleans and "spent much of his boyhood leisure along the docks"— claimed that his postbellum minstrel act "portrayed a type of colored man that was indigenous to the South after the war [. . .] the negro of the levee, the roustabout, with his queer dialect, and shuffling manner and happy-go-lucky ideas."[25] Well into the twentieth century, an article in the *New York Clipper* mourned the passing of the minstrel show in particular ways: "The bell tolled the requiem for our old time favorite [. . .] the quaint antics of the river roustabout."[26] Even in 1912, James Weldon Johnson would complain that "no manager could imagine that audiences would pay to see Negro performers in any other role than that of Mississippi River roustabouts."[27]

The largely forgotten avatar of the roustabout would come to prominence in ways that would far transcend the minstrel role—even if he remained closely linked to it. His emergence as a multivalent and ambiguous figure in popular culture itself reflected the changing nature of black life on the Mississippi in the years after the Civil War. As Thomas Buchanan has demonstrated, the Mississippi and its tributaries had been vital spaces for black Americans, both enslaved and free, in the years before emancipation. As much as the Mississippi was the artery of slavery, it was also a conduit for black networks of resistance, conferring particular privilege and power on those who were able to move along the river. After the war, however, the relationship of black workers to the river changed. African American men came to dominate the roustabout trade. In his account of his life as a steamboat pilot, echoing many others, George Byron Merrick asserted that even on the Upper Mississippi, this change was evident: "In old times the steamboat crews were comprised principally of white men—that is, deck hands and roustabouts (or stevedores).

[. . .] Now, the deck crews are all colored men."[28] Yet in Buchanan's judgment, this new position in the trade was an ambiguous one, and the wider meaning of river life also shifted for those workers. In the years after the Civil War, "river work no longer provided the only source of mobility for African Americans." Moreover, steamboats became "one more place where southern whites effectively stifled African American efforts to expand their rights." By the beginning of the twentieth century, river work was "marginal to African American communities," and those who remained on the river were "among the most exploited laborers" in America.[29] In 1874, even the *New York Times* would describe them as "a class that is poorly treated, and is made to suffer much."[30] Roustabouts were subject to acts of racial violence too. In August 1869, the *New-York Tribune* reported on a "Mississippi steamboat outrage": "Five negroes, deck hands, were victims of the prejudices and ferocity of a crew of raftsmen, and were beaten, cut and drowned."[31]

Yet through these years of exploitation and decline, the roustabout was reborn in popular culture. He was clearly understood to be a timely representative of black American life during and after Reconstruction—in accounts both sympathetic and condemnatory—and came to represent a new vision of freedom on and along the river. If one thing united depictions of the roustabout, it was a belief in and fascination with his musical abilities. When black steamboat workers were mentioned, it was almost always in relation to their songs. In a collection of *Slave Songs of the United States* (1867), for example, one composition—"I'm Gwine to Alabamy"—is described as "a very good specimen, so far as notes can give one, of the strange barbaric songs that one hears upon the Western steamboats [. . .] wild and strangely fascinating."[32] It was a commonplace in travel accounts too. In *The Great South*, Edward King approvingly described "the cheery songs of the boatmen [. . .] scrambling among the freight and singing."[33] Ernst von Hesse-Wartegg noted that "the 'roustabouts' [. . .] ease the travail by singing their exotic songs."[34] Even the *New-York Tribune* reproduced a series, "Quaint Snatches of Song from Cotton-Boat and Levee."[35]

From the 1870s onward, certain observers began playing closer attention. First among them was Lafcadio Hearn. Half-Greek, half-Irish, half-blind, Hearn was packed off to the New World in 1869, at the age of nineteen, by one set of unsympathetic relatives only to paid off by another when he got there: they gave him five dollars and sent him on his way. Stuck in Cincinnati, Hearn spent some time in a precarious state of poverty before finding his way to employment at the *Cincinnati Enquirer* in 1872. He soon established his distinctive literary voice, wedding a Gothic sensibility to a pioneering style of first-person reportage that saw him venture where many of his fellow Cincinnatians feared to tread. Hearn visited slaughterhouses and asylums, murder scenes and brothels. He made his beat the city's demimondes and underworlds and presented them to his respectable readers with a lurid delight for unsettling detail. Like other abandoned waifs who found their way to the Western Rivers, he purposefully set himself against the mores of polite society. "Carpets—pianos—windows—curtains—brass bands—churches! how I hate them!! And white shirts!" he would later rage to a correspondent, sounding like Huck Finn. "Would I had been born savage; the curse of civilised cities is on me—and I suppose I can't get away permanently from them."[36] As part of this quest to escape modern civilization, Hearn would soon head down the Mississippi to New Orleans, before finally and most famously lighting out for Japan in 1890, the place where he would find a lasting home and a lasting legacy.

In Cincinnati in the 1870s, however, that desire for liberation from conventionality led him inexorably to particular parts of the city: Bucktown and the Levee, home to the city's black population and, in particular, a transient population of roustabouts. Hearn's sketches of black life on and along the river were unquestionably pioneering. As Jonathan Cott has described, they were his "most important journalistic pieces during this period [. . .] one of the few depictions we have of black life in a border city during the post–Civil War period."[37] More than that, they set the tone for depictions of roustabout river life that would follow. To quote Cott again: "He experienced a perilous, vital world of comings and goings, piety and lawlessness, gaiety and misery," which he documented with "a kind of inchoate, improvised folkloristic perspective," attempting to celebrate "an African American culture and its rich tradition of songs, dances, stories, poetry, charms, superstitions, proverbs, customs."[38]

To be sure, Hearn's accounts of the men and women he met on the levee were heavily exoticized and couched in the racist terminology of the day. "It is a very primitive kind of life," he described in one of his most significant sketches, "its lights and shadows are alike characterised by a half savage simplicity; its happiness or misery is almost purely animal." While some of his readers may have understood this to be condemnatory, Hearn himself clearly reveled in observing what he felt to be this "grotesquely-picturesque roustabout life." "There is an intense uniqueness about all this pariah existence," he marveled.[39] For all that he projected his own desire for escape from "the curse of civilised cities" onto his portraits of these men and women (much like the minstrels before him and much like many white aficionados of black American culture who would follow), he also took the people and the places that he encountered on the levee seriously, recording much about black river life—and music particularly—that would otherwise have gone unrecorded.

Most of the music that he recorded revolved around life on the Western Rivers (particularly "the popular steamboats running on the 'Muddy Water'"), and Hearn noted both the rich multiplicity of this music and the way that it was largely protected from the oversight of the white community that it lived alongside: "To collect these curious songs, or even all the most popular of them, would be a labor of months, and even then a difficult one, for the colored roustabouts are in the highest degree suspicious of a man who approaches them with a note-book and pencil." Hearn's tactic, he explained, was to "induce an intelligent steamboatman to sing a few river songs by an innocent bribe in the shape of a cigar or a drink." The songs themselves—however arbitrated by Hearn, his editors, and the limitations of what these roustabouts wanted to tell him—were an extraordinary, enigmatic, sprawling mix blending street life and river life, celebrating steamboats and sweethearts, reaching back into history and reveling in the movement still afforded by the western waters. "Number Ninety-Nine" Hearn declares to be "at one time immensely popular with the steamboatmen":

> Yonder goes the Wildwood.
>   She's loaded to the guards,
> But yonder comes the Fleetwood,
>   An' she's the boat for me.

> [. . .] Chorus—Oh, ain't I gone, gone, gone,
> Oh, ain't I gone, gone, gone,
> Oh, ain't I gone, gone, gone,
> Way down de ribber road.

Another song "in vogue among the roustabouts" was "Limber Jim," a composition so rambling that it was only known in full by "a colored labourer [. . .]

who 'run on the river' for years." One verse from a song "popular with the loose women of the 'Rows'" made it past the censors:

> I hev a roustabout for my man—
> Livin' with a white man for a sham,
> Oh, leave me alone,
> Leave me alone,
> I'd like you much better if you'd leave me alone.[40]

Perhaps something in that song struck a chord with Hearn himself, as he developed more intimate ties to the city's black community: during his time in Cincinnati, he married (unlawfully and briefly) the previously enslaved Alethea Foley.

Most resonant, though, was his sketch of Albert Jones—"a child of the levee," as Hearn described him in the article's title. Hearn pictures him as a degraded kind of river spirit. When the sketch begins, Jones is literally fished "out of the river [. . .] insane from poisonous whisky." But Jones is a creature of the river in other ways too. He has a particular talent: Jones can "imitate the whistle of any boat on the Ohio or the Mississippi River" and treats Hearn and his arresting officers to an impromptu performance: "He suddenly threw up both his hands, concave-fashion, to his mouth, expanded his deep chest, and poured out a long, profound, sonorous cry that vibrated through the room like the music of a steam-whistle. He started off with a deep nasal tone, but gradually modulated its depth and volume to an imitation of the steam-whistle, so astonishingly perfect that at its close every listener uttered an involuntary exclamation of surprise." For Hearn, Jones's talent, for all of its peculiarities, was simply an extreme development of the sensibilities common to all of those who lived along the levee, a testament to the intimate centrality of the river and the steamboat trade to these apparently marginal men and women: "All along the rows there indeed dwell many who know by heart the whistle of every boat [. . .] dusky women, whose ears have been trained by rough but strong affection, as well as old stevedores who have lived by the shore from infancy, and wonderingly watched in their slave childhood the great white vessels panting on the river's breast." It was the steamboat whistle that narrated Jones's life—from a lullaby to his "ears in babyhood" to "his requiem some night"—just as it had narrated the life of this community on the edge of Cincinnati and the edge of the river, from slavery to Reconstruction.[41]

Albert's female counterpart was the eponymous "Dolly"—a "pantheress," a "little savage," with "a strong tinge of African blood"—who is as much a creature of the river as Jones. Dolly could, Hearn tells us, "swim like a Tahitian, and before daybreak on sultry summer mornings often stole down to the river to strike out in the moon-silvered current." Like Jones, though, her intimate immersions in the Western Rivers are patrolled by the symbols of white authority. "Ain't you ashamed to be seen that way?" asks a police officer, encountering a semi-clad Dolly on the levee. Dolly's life is also intimately linked to the steamboat trade. It forms a catechism that she teaches to an orphan on the Row, in a numinous passage that opens up the question of what it means to know the river. Instead of the patriarchal hierarchy of *Life on the Mississippi*, Hearn portrays Dolly's river lore as sacred maternal knowledge and the river as a female space, no less vital to these marginal figures than to the men in the pilothouse:

> Then she taught him the names of all the great white boats, and the names of the far cities they sailed from, and the odd symbolism of the negro steamboat slang. When a long vessel swept by, plowing up the yellow current in curving furrows about her prow, and leaving in her rear a long line of low-hanging nimbus-clouds, Dolly would cry: "See, Tommy, how proud the old gal is to-day; she's got a fine *ruffle* on. Look at her *switch*, Tommy; see how the old gal's curling her hair out behind her." Dolly could not read the names of the boats, but she knew by heart their gleaming shapes, and the varying tones of their wild, deep voices. So she taught the child to know them, too, until to his infantile fancy they became, as it were, great aquatic things, which slept only at the levee, and moved upon the river through the white moonlight with an awfully pulsating life of their own.

If this account seems to echo Twain's comic portrait of the slave baffled by the steamboat in *The Gilded Age*, its imprint on the reader is strikingly different. When it's Dolly's time to die—neglected by "a rather good-looking yellow roustabout known along the levee as Aleck"—the Mississippi appears to spirit her soul away: "The river reflected its shining ripple on the whitewashed walls," and a "sound deeper and sweeter and wilder than the hymned melody or the half-savage music below, filled all the moon lit levee—the steam-song of the Maysville packet coming in."[42]

For all the limitations of Hearn's portrait of the people he met on the levee, no other writer of the period paid as much attention to the relationship of black men and—almost uniquely—women to the Western Rivers in the postbellum years. No other white writer took as seriously the unique and deeply influential culture that black Americans had developed around river life and the steamboat trade. Many others, though, were similarly attracted to what they perceived in roustabout life. Throughout the period, accounts of roustabout life appeared in journals and magazines, which, like Hearn, clearly found in black river life a symbol of liberated American blackness. Some of those commentators were bohemian wanderers like Hearn, who projected onto the roustabout their own desire for escape from convention. When Joseph Pennell headed to New Orleans to serve as Cable's illustrator, for example, he carried with him another commission. He wrote to wife-to-be, Elizabeth: "Mr. Davis [from Albion Tourgée's short-lived *Our Continent* magazine] asked me to get up an article on the Mississippi boatmen (roustabouts I believe they are called) making a sort of character sketch."[43] Finally seeing the light of day in the *Century* in 1883, Pennell's account, "The Trip of the 'Mark Twain,'" produced images of roustabout life that chimed with Hearn's sketches. It was, of course, their music that first caught his ear: "Before long one of them began to sing in a [. . .] clear baritone"—a song of water, of slavery and freedom, of repetition and improvisation, individual imagination and communal response:

> Oh, Moses he stretch out he's rod,
>> Oh-o-o-oh de Red Sea.
> And de Childern's Isr'el pass ober dry shod,
>> Oh, de R-e-d Sea.
> An' Pharaoh come follerin' down
>> By de Re-e-d Sea.
> Wid all de sojers in de town
>> By de R-e-d Sea!
> An' dar de Lord confounded 'em
>> By de R-e-d Sea!

An' all de waters drownded 'em
In de Re-e-d Sea!
Dis de way dat folks begin
By de Re-e-d Sea,
An' dat's de way dey tumble in
In de R-e-d Sea![44]

Out of the chorus, Pennell was drawn to one particular roustabout, Billy, who becomes the spokesman for his colleagues—and, as Pennell clearly intends, for black America more broadly: "'I's jist nobody,' he said. 'I's de most lone man dere is. I's got no fre'n's. Fo' de war I was a slabe, now I's free; but, as de preacher says, "Whar's de use o' being free ef you's a slabe to yourse'f."' Here he paused, and stared as if he had made a point. I could not see it, but I shook my head, and said: 'Yes, indeed.'" "Now," Billy concluded, "I's a slabe to dis hyar steam-boat." This characterization of life on board the *Mark Twain* as a continuance of slavery for Billy and his fellow roustabouts was a trope that would dominate depictions of river life for black Americans in the postwar years. "Is the freedman a free man?" Cable had asked. Not according to Billy. There are certainly echoes of minstrelsy in Pennell's characterization of Billy's voice, and there is an apparent absence of sympathy in his subsequent description of "Billy at work": "Now the lonely slave appears to be the lively demon."[45] What transcends those limitations is Pennell's portrait of Billy—an extraordinarily vivid rendering of this emblematic inhabitant of a Mississippi abyss (fig. 7). It is one of the most significant images of life on the Mississippi to appear in the popular press at this moment, free from minstrel stylings, a statement of Billy's individuality and identity that was absent from most other depictions of roustabout life.

Wandering, cosmopolitan bohemians like Hearn and Pennell were not the only figures to pay attention to the roustabout at this moment. Neither was George Washington the only member of the Cable family to write about black life on the Mississippi. In 1884, his now-forgotten brother James Boardman Cable was reaching the rather smaller pinnacle of his own writing career. He had been commissioned by a new Chicago journal, the *Current*, to write a series of short articles about the South. The first of his "southern silhouettes," "Mammy," set the tone for the series that followed. Though James described slavery as "odious," he also made a case for "the mitigating tie of mutual af-

FIGURE 7. Joseph Pennell, "Billy," from "The Trip of the 'Mark Twain,'"
Century Magazine, January 1883, 400.

fection" that it engendered: "a face black, glossy, and radiant from reflected
contentment within; eyes keen, yet kindly; surmounting all a Madras kerchief
[. . .]. Memory hugs tender recollections of her lovingly to her breast; wondering little ones listen to tales of what she was."[46] His portrait of the roustabout
a few months later was similarly freighted with the same attitudes, a mixture
of pernicious racial stereotypes, social Darwinism, and sentiment—a harbin-
ger to the literature of the Lost Cause that would build across the following
decades.

The roustabout, in James Boardman Cable's account, was an enigmatic,
chthonic product of the Western River system: "Whether he is the outcome
of certain conditions, a growth of the humid atmosphere, a generation of the
great river's muddy waters, or whether he just is, and would be, independent
of all these cannot be known." While Hearn hinted at the social iniquities—
the poverty, the racism—that underpinned some of the life that he found on

the levee and frankly admired much about the community that clung onto the riverbank, for James Boardman Cable the roustabout was a telling example of inferior genetics and problematic proclivities. "The true habitat of the roustabout is the steamboat," he begins, in pernicious pseudoscientific terms, "a negro of greater or less blackness of skin and corresponding thickness of skull [. . .] obeying the vague dictates of natural selection." "Easy of life and morals," he continued, now in judgment, "the embodiment of recklessness and irresponsibility, a Bohemian of the river, he is willingly and persistently landless, houseless, homeless." For James Boardman, the roustabout was no marginal musical artist but was instead a creature of purely animal instinct, "the idiot offspring of ignorance and debasement": "He is not a man, but man's shadow thrown out beyond the light."[47] For James Boardman Cable, then— and for many who would come after him—the roustabout became a template of what unchecked black freedom looked like, doomed by "natural selection" to debasement, disease, and death. While Hearn and Pennell found in the roustabout an image onto which they could project their own desires for freedom, couched in the language of paternal concern, James Boardman's vision of black life on the Mississippi was an implicit refutation of Emancipation and all that it had wrought.

"Away from Misery and Despair!"

Against the overwhelming tide of the minstrel stage and the flood of white male authors appropriating roustabout culture for their own ends, a few African American voices who had known the river in the antebellum era were still busy in the postwar years arguing for their own visions of the Mississippi and its ambiguous meaning for black Americans. Twain's apparent familiarity with slave narratives, at least on some level, clearly filtered into the conception and texture of Adventures of Huckleberry Finn. Lucinda MacKethan, arguing for Twain's "rather extensive exposure" to slave narratives, also noted that many of those narratives—particularly the work of William Wells Brown—evoked a river landscape very similar to that occupied by Huck and Jim.[48] But in the 1870s and 1880s, the slave narrative wasn't simply a historic genre. Josiah Henson and Brown himself—both fugitive slaves and very visible figures in the abolitionist movement in the antebellum years—produced postbellum accounts of their lives and experiences along the Mississippi that stood in opposition to the many depictions of black life on the river that were circulating in the decades after the Civil War. If Huck and Jim traveled on a cultural Mississippi saturated with roustabouts—romanticized and ridiculed in turn—they also journeyed in the company of other runaways still describing the river as a route to freedom.

Josiah Henson escaped from slavery in Maryland to Canada in 1830, before publishing a popular account of his experiences—*The Life of Josiah Henson, Formerly a Slave, Now an Inhabitant of Canada, as Narrated by Himself*—in 1849. With no little controversy, he became known as the real-life inspiration for Harriet Beecher Stowe during her composition of *Uncle Tom's Cabin.*[49] Stowe's Tom may have died enslaved, but Henson himself lived long in Canada after his escape, dying at the age of ninety-three, in 1883. His association with Stowe remained with him throughout. As late as 1877, Henson published a new version of his life story with a title that was at pains to make the connection clear: *"Uncle Tom's Story of His Life": An Autobiography of the Rev. Josiah Henson (Mrs. Harriet Beecher Stowe's "Uncle Tom")*. Stowe herself contributed a preface, and a long editorial note provided, for those who had "expressed doubts," a lengthy "explanation and corroboration" of Henson's association with Uncle Tom.[50]

Like Tom, Henson certainly had significant experience of the Western Rivers during his time as a slave. His account of his voyages on the Ohio and Mississippi provides a compelling contrast to both the minstrel stage and to contemporary descriptions of carefree roustabout life on the Mississippi. Henson's association with river life and its possibilities began in 1825: his master in Maryland was facing bankruptcy and charged Henson, as overseer, with the task of covertly transporting his slaves to his brother's plantation in Kentucky. Henson willingly undertook the task and experienced "immense gratification" at the praise bestowed on him by white men as the party slowly completed its thousand-mile journey. When the group reached the Ohio, however, and started traveling down the river by boat, Henson was "assailed" by a "new and unexpected trouble." At Cincinnati, "crowds of coloured people gathered round us, and insisted on our remaining with them. [. . .] We were repeatedly told by persons conversing with us that we were no longer slaves but free men, if we chose to be so." At this point, however, Henson was not to be swayed from his task. Seeing that "the allurements of the crowd were producing a manifest effect" on his fellow travelers, Henson commanded everyone back to the boat "and ordered the boat to be pushed off into the stream." "Often since that day," Henson remembered years later, "has my soul been pierced with bitter anguish, at the thought of having been thus instrumental in consigning to the infernal bondage of slavery, so many of my fellow-beings."[51]

If that moment was pivotal in Henson's relationship to slavery and freedom, so, too, were later experiences along the rivers. In 1828, the rest of the slaves whom Henson had brought with him to Kentucky were sold away. "From that hour," Henson described, "I saw through, hated, and cursed the whole system of slavery." While the quest for freedom was now uppermost in his mind, his immediate prospects looked bleak. Henson was suddenly informed that in the company of his master's son Amos, he was to travel "down the river to New Orleans, with a flat-boat loaded with produce from the farm." What this meant for Henson himself seemed clear: like Uncle Tom, he understood that he was to be sold when they reached the city. Henson's account of his subsequent journey down the Mississippi was, therefore, an extraordinary odyssey that produced some of the most powerful images of the river to circulate at this moment:

> All outward nature seemed to feed my gloomy thoughts. I know not what most men see in voyaging down the Mississippi. If gay and hopeful, probably much of beauty and interest. If eager merchants, probably a golden river, freighted with the wealth of nations. I saw nothing but portents of woe and despair. Wretched slave pens; a smell of stagnant waters; half-putrid carcases [*sic*] of horses or oxen floating along, covered with turkey buzzards and swarms of green flies,—these are the images with which memory crowds my mind. My faith in God utterly gave way. I could no longer pray or trust. I thought He had abandoned me and cast me off for ever. I looked not to him for help. I saw only the foul miasmas, the emancipated frames of my negro companions; and in them saw the sure, swift, loving intervention of the one unfailing friend of the wretched,—death!

To compound these horrors, at Vicksburg, he encountered some of his former companions from Maryland who had been sold down the river: "It was the saddest visit I ever made. Four years in an unhealthy climate and under a hard master had done the ordinary work of twenty. [. . .] Some of them fairly cried at seeing me there, and at the thought of the fate which they felt awaited me."[52]

Henson's Mississippi journey had a different outcome than the harrowing deaths of his friends, though. If the river threatened to break Henson in body and soul, it ultimately proved to be his salvation. First, he learned the river. Each of the boat's occupants was required to "take our turn at the helm." Henson "learned the art of steering and managing the boat far better than the rest. I watched the manoeuvres necessary to shoot by a 'sawyer,' to land on a bank, avoid a snag, or a steamboat, in the rapid current of the Mississippi, till I could do it as well as the captain." When the captain was struck down by illness, Henson took his place: "I was in fact master of the boat from that time till our arrival in New Orleans." Empowered by his newfound command of the river, Henson began to contemplate drastic action: "I resolved to kill my four companions, take what money there was in the boat, scuttle the craft, and escape to the north." Such an outcome would have radically shifted the meaning of Henson's narrative and its significance for the depiction of the river as a site of resistance for the enslaved. Ultimately, Henson decided against murder. Instead, he made a resolution "to resign myself to the will of God." His prayers were answered when Young Master Amos fell ill from "river-fever." Now the Mississippi that had threatened to condemn Henson helped to save him. As Henson put it, "The tables were now turned." Amos was "the supplicant, a poor terrified object, afraid of death, and writhing with pain." Apologizing to Henson for attempting to sell him, Amos assured him of a return home if he would "dispatch matters" in New Orleans and nurse him through his illness. Soon they were steaming northward: "O my God! how my heart sang jubilees of praise to Thee, as the steamboat swung loose from the levee and breasted the mighty tide of the Mississippi! Away from this land of bondage and death! Away from misery and despair! Once more exulting hope possessed me, and I thought, if I do not now find my way to freedom, may God never give me a chance again."[53] Before long, released from his transformative Mississippi odyssey, Henson and his family were safe in Canada.

William Wells Brown's accounts of life on the Mississippi also stand in powerful complement to Twain's perspective from the pilothouse. Born in Kentucky in 1814, Brown and his family were moved to St. Louis in 1826. His mother and siblings were soon sold away by their master. From then until his escape from slavery, on January 1, 1834, Brown knew the Mississippi and its various trades intimately, in a wide variety of roles. As Ezra Greenspan details:

By his account, he passed through the hands of three different slave masters; had his labour contracted by them to roughly a half-dozen steamboat captains; made multiple traverses of the Mississippi River downstream between St. Louis and New Orleans and upstream between St. Louis and Galena; traveled on the Missouri River westward to its then-navigable limits near Independence, Missouri; labored a hellish year as all-purpose servant to a slave trader preparing slaves for sale in markets along the lower Mississippi River [. . .]. Those years of river travel were to equip him with a breadth of insight into the trans-Mississippi region and the life of the black Mississippi that few ex-slave authors, and few Americans of any background, could match. [. . .] Memory of life on the Mississippi was as inescapable for him as it would one day be for Twain.[54]

Just as it would for Twain, the Mississippi remained one of the central images of his writing life, flowing throughout his extraordinarily varied literary outputs as he told the stories of the black men and women who experienced slavery along the Mississippi and its tributaries.

Accordingly, Brown's visions of the river contrasted markedly with those of Twain. Like Twain, Brown knew about steamboat life, but his multiple perspectives of slavery and steamboats gave him a very different sense of its possibilities and limitations; this was as true in the 1880s as it was in the antebellum years. As Thomas C. Buchanan has described Brown's position: "Mobility had educated him in the horrors of the sugar and cotton plantations of the deep South and the slave markets of New Orleans. But the river was the focus of his dreams, too. The steamboats that moved up and down the Mississippi River carried the tentacles of slavery and racism, but they also carried liberating ideas and pathways to freedom."[55] This animating tension ran throughout his life and his work. Beyond their treatment in his various autobiographies, images of slavery on the Mississippi bled into all aspects of Brown's extraordinary output.

One of the hallmarks of Brown's career—whether in autobiography, travel writing, drama, or novels—was his willingness to play with popular representations of slavery and black American life, including minstrelsy. As Paul Gilmore has outlined, Brown often redeployed "the standard conceits of the minstrel show [. . .] to uncover its antislavery possibilities."[56] This subversive approach clearly informed his use of the river in his work. By placing the Mississippi close to the center of his written output and foregrounding the terrible ironies of river life for black Americans in the antebellum years, Brown was both implicitly and explicitly challenging dominant white visions of the Mississippi as a triumphant artery of manifest destiny, industry, and commerce. The most vivid example was his reaction to one of the most popular entertainments of the antebellum years. When William Wells Brown went to see John Banvard's celebrated moving panorama of the river he knew so well, he had a rather different reaction than most viewers: "During the autumn of 1847 I visited an exhibition of a Panorama of the River Mississippi, which was then exhibited in Boston, United States. I was somewhat amazed at the very mild manner in which the 'Peculiar Institution' of the Southern States was there represented, and it occurred to me that a painting, with as fair a representation of American Slavery as could be given upon canvass, would do much to disseminate truth upon this subject."[57] Understanding the profound absence of slavery in Banvard's universally admired rendition of the river, Brown produced his own panorama of slavery during his time in England in 1849, including vignettes in New Orleans and St. Louis.

In the 1880s, at the peak of Twain's river output, Brown was still writing about the Mississippi too. In 1882, as Twain was back on the river and writing *Life on the Mississippi*, Brown released his final major work, *My Southern Home: or, The South and Its People*. In keeping with his approach throughout the rest of his long career, this was a text that played with tropes that were currently popular in American culture—tropes in which the Mississippi River was clearly implicated. John Ernest has argued that *My Southern Home* subverts "the narrative form and content similar to a great number of publications after the Civil War that approached life on the antebellum plantation with a kind of idealized fascination." Even if Brown's own position in relation to those tropes "is never entirely clear," still *My Southern Home* serves as "an extended examination of the possibilities of literary representation in response to a racist and often threatening culture."[58]

The river had a compelling role to play in this process. Rather than retell the story of the river's influence on his own life, Brown highlighted the central place of the Western Rivers in many stories of liberation through the example of "a brave and manly slave" who "resolved to escape from Natchez." Jerome is clearly an idealized model of enslaved masculinity for Brown, a clear contrast to the still-pervasive model of Uncle Tom and countless minstrel figures, even if his story of escape ultimately echoes Stowe's narrative: "He was brave and daring, strong in person, fiery in spirit, yet kind and true in his affections"; [he "was of pure African origin, was perfectly black, very fine-looking." In Brown's telling, it is the "deep sound of the escape of steam from a boat, which was at that moment ascending the river," that provides Jerome with the inspiration for his own audacious escape: "'If that boat is going up the river,' said he, 'why not I conceal myself on board, and try to escape?' He went at once to the steamboat landing, where the boat was just coming in. 'Bound for Louisville,' said the captain, to one who was making inquiries. As the passengers were rushing on board, Jerome followed them, and proceeding to where some of the hands were stowing away bales of goods, he took hold and aided them." Secreting himself in the hull among the boat's cargo, Jerome remains hidden for days until the need for food and water drives him out of his hiding place. Luckily, "with his lips parched and fevered to a crisp," he stumbles across a box of "bridal cake, with several bottles of port wine" brought on board the boat by a bridal party.[59] This sustains him for the next eight days.

Jumping ship at Louisville, Jerome heads out of the city, keeping "near the Ohio River" and looking for a chance to cross over into Indiana.[60] But one night, he is "pounced upon by three men who were lying in wait for another fugitive." Tortured into revealing the name of his owner, he dissembles: "Jerome gave them a fictitious name in Virginia, and said that his master would give a large reward, and manifested a willingness to return to his "old boss." Jerome is taken by the slave catchers to an inn, on the banks of the Ohio River. When his captors drink themselves into a stupor, Jerome is quick to seize another opportunity for escape—making sure to dress himself in "the best suit" that he can find among the belongings of the men, leaving the "worn-out and tattered garments" of slavery behind him. Starting once more for Canada, Jerome finds himself pursued again. Stuck between two groups of white men— his captors, pursuing him on horseback, and the inhabitants of a farmhouse along the road—he uses knowledge given to him by his time on the river to make a decision about which path of action to take: "The broad-brimmed hats that the farmers wore told the slaves [sic] that they were Quakers. Jerome had seen some of these people passing up and down the river, when employed on a steamer between Natchez and New Orleans, and had heard that they disliked slavery." Trusting that knowledge, Jerome runs to the Quaker farm, where the family hides him in their barn and holds off his pursuers until Jerome has facilitated another escape—this time, his last. According to Brown, this flight to freedom along the river was the originating event in the creation of the Underground Railroad, "that famous highway over which so many of the oppressed sons and daughters of African descent were destined to travel."[61] Neither was Jerome's use of the Western Rivers here as fantastical as it may first seem. As Thomas Buchanan has concluded, "While the precise number of river runaways is impossible to gauge, evidence suggests that thousands of fugitives rode the decks of steamboats to freedom."[62]

Certainly, Brown's originating fable of black liberation along the Western Rivers stands in dramatic contrast to Twain's account of Jim's attempted escape. Though reliant on white assistance in the shape of the Quaker community, Jerome's quest for freedom is predicated on his own ingenuity and bravery and his understanding of the possibilities of liberation along the Mississippi. Josiah, Jerome, and Jim therefore stand as revealing juxtapositions of ways to imagine and express the relationship between black Americans and the Western River systems in the postwar years.

"This New World of Waters"

When Huckleberry Finn first sets out on his adventurous escape from the horrors of Pap Finn and the constrictions of civilization, it's a canoe that helps him on his way: "I got out amongst the drift-wood and then laid down in the bottom of the canoe and let her float. I laid there and had a good rest and a smoke out of my pipe, looking away into the sky."[63] In this, Huck was a boy of his moment: the quest for a good rest in a canoe on the Mississippi preoccupied large numbers of Americans in the 1880s. While others were projecting ideas of freedom onto roustabouts and some were retelling their own too-real stories of escape on the Mississippi, returning to the river became an important part of a wider trend that saw Americans fleeing towns and cities for nature vacations, runaways from the pressures of modern urban life. As Peter J. Schmitt has described, "Enthusiasts claimed the country was in the midst of a full-scale return to nature. [. . .] Urban gentlemen took to forest and stream for temporary outings [. . .]. More and more Americans convinced themselves that they were naturists, claiming closer friends among the woodchucks and warblers than among their country neighbors, and taking as their standard the gospel of the holy earth."[64]

Mark Twain's immediate circle of friends and neighbors was at the forefront of this trend for holidaying in the wild. Neighbors Charles Dudley Warner and his wife Susan and Joseph Hopkins Twichell and wife Julia were regular visitors to the Adirondacks from 1866 onward, inspired to visit by the descriptions of local Hartford landscape artist John Fitch.[65] This put them at the vanguard of the popular vogue for sojourns in the wilderness and just ahead of the enormous fashion for the Adirondacks inspired by the publication of William H. H. Murray's *Adventures in the Wilderness* (1869). As Susan Warner put it in 1866, succinctly describing the appeal of this new passion for the outdoors, "It starts the blood & invigorates the bones; we feel made over & ready to take the brunt of life for another year at least."[66] In the summer of 1870, Twain and Livy were supposed to join them, but the death of Livy's father and her pregnancy (Langdon would be born in November) prevented the trip. But Twain, and many other readers, could follow their adventures through Charles Dudley Warner's accounts of holidaying in the Adirondacks, first in the *Atlantic,* then in a collection of those essays, *In the Wilderness,* published in 1878.

For all that Warner was a devotee of nature excursions, he was also aware of the ironies and foibles of those who had suddenly discovered a passion for the great outdoors; as much as he was alive to the beauties of the wilderness, he also lightly lampooned those (especially himself) who followed the now beaten path to the Adirondacks. On the one hand, he certainly appreciated the motivations that drove people to the woods—at least for those of his social strata. It was, very clearly, another temporary revolt against middle-class respectability: "the instinct of barbarism that leads people periodically to throw aside the habits of civilization, and seek the freedom and discomfort of the woods [. . .] the unconquered craving for primitive simplicity, the revolt against the everlasting dress-parade of our civilization." Like Huck and Hearn, Warner harped on the word *civilization:* "The real enjoyment of camping and tramping in the woods lies in a return to primitive conditions of lodging, dress, and food, in as total an escape as may be from the requirements of civilization. And it remains to be explained why this is enjoyed most by those who are most highly civilized. It is wonderful to see how easily the restraints of society fall off." Yet Warner was also aware of the limitations of this atavism: getting lost in the woods, Warner starts to question the benevolence of the wilderness and the contemporary platitudes surrounding its spiritual munifi-cence: "I had read of the soothing companionship of the forest, the pleasure of the pathless woods. But I thought, as I stumbled along in the dismal actuality, that, if I ever got out of it, I would write a letter to the newspapers, exposing the whole thing. [. . .] It's a hollow sham, this pantheism, I said; being 'one with Nature' is all humbug."[67] Disillusionment was built into Warner's expe-rience of the wild—as it would creep into the accounts of many of those who followed these paths into the wilderness.

The canoe became a particularly resonant American symbol of this mo-ment's return to nature and the Mississippi's role in it. As Jessica Dunkin has described, the late nineteenth century "witnessed an explosion of interest in canoeing as sport, recreation, and leisure in Canada, the United States, and Britain. Greater disposable income, increased leisure time, and a growing be-lief in the ameliorative effects of nature contributed to this 'canoe boom'"—a term used in a *New York Times* editorial in 1880 announcing the inaugural meeting of the American Canoe Association (ACA).[68] It was, of course, pri-marily an "urban middle class"—and white—phenomenon, marked out by "newly formed canoe clubs that dotted urban waterways."[69] The genesis of this explosion of interest in canoeing in America can be traced to the immediate moment after the Civil War. In 1866, John MacGregor—British traveler and explorer—fired the imaginations of would-be gentleman adventurers on both sides of the Atlantic with his account, *A Thousand Miles in the Rob Roy Canoe on Rivers and Lakes of Europe*. It wasn't just the scale of his fluvial feats that im-pressed his readers; it was also his use of a new kind of craft that retained the lightness and portability of a canoe while also adding sail power and a covered deck to limit the amount of water the craft would take on. Moreover, Mac-Gregor was evangelical about the benefits of traveling by canoe rather than the usual touristic methods: "The tourist [. . .] has admired a few yards of the water, and has then left it for ever. He is carried again on a noble river by night in a steamboat [. . .]. But a mine of rich beauty remains there to be explored, and fresh gems of life and character are waiting there to be gathered." A "new world of waters" was waiting to be discovered.[70] Americans heeded the call. Harry Castlemon even capitalized on the fashion by releasing a book for boys, *Snagged and Sunk: or, The Adventures of a Canvas Canoe*, in 1888.[71]

Another sign of the nascent canoe boom was the launch of the *American Canoeist*, a publication of the ACA, in 1882. The pages of that magazine pay ample testament to the fact that the Mississippi loomed large as the ultimate challenge for America's new breed of canoeist. In its inaugural issue, for example, a "Mr. Edwin Lewis" was advertising in the hope of meeting "several canoeists to join him in a cruise from St. Louis down the Mississippi to the Gulf of Mexico."[72] If men dominated the hobby and the pages of the *American Canoeist*, women still staked a claim to the Mississippi. In March 1883, Mrs. A. B. Chapin provided the magazine with an account of "a short canoe trip" on the Mississippi: "We were well satisfied with our boat and trip, and improved in health with appetites tremendous, and faces fairly bronzed [. . .]. I thoroughly enjoyed everything, even the cooking in the tent and out-doors and the many hours of hard work with the paddle; and I think if all gentlemen would but take their *wives* with them, the wives would enjoy it very much."[73]

So central was the image of a canoe voyage on the Mississippi to the nascent sport, the ultimate test of gentlemen hobbyists, that a succession of men closely involved with the foundation and promotion of the American Canoe Association embarked on lengthy expeditions along the Western Rivers in the late 1870s and early 1880s. Nathaniel H. Bishop, Charles A. Neidé, and Ben C. Wilkins all canoed down the Mississippi before publishing accounts of their adventures afloat. These narratives, sharing a similar set of assumptions, preoccupations, and revelations about life on the Mississippi, provide a remarkable index to the river's meaning to those who were driven to head downriver in a series of small, vulnerable river craft—at precisely the moment that Huck and Jim's raft was beginning its own precarious journey in American culture.

In keeping with the wider trends of the moment, all of these canoeists framed their separate journeys down the Mississippi in terms of an escape. As a group, they were explicitly running away, albeit temporarily, from the cares of business, from the travails of civilization, from the responsibilities of class, into nature and health-promoting activity. Bishop, traveling down the Ohio and Mississippi and along the Gulf of Mexico in the winter of 1875–76, foregrounded this spirit: "One of the chief charms in a boatman's life is its freedom, and what that freedom is no one knows until he throws aside the chains of every-day life, steps out of the worn ruts, and, with his kit beside him, his oar in his hand, feels himself master of his time, and FREE." The combination of physical activity and "the mental rest from vexatious business cares, all proved superior to any tonic a physician could prescribe."[74] Wilkins, having dreamed of a cruise down the Mississippi since "early boyhood," only took the plunge in 1881, when "the warning hand of nature knocked sternly at the door and demanded a change and a rest from a busy business life."[75] Neidé—combining a variety of nature crazes by sailing from Lake George in the Adirondacks, via a number of portages, down the Ohio and the Mississippi in 1882—sought merely "a quiet, health-seeking voyage to the Gulf of Mexico."[76] At times, the river did provide the kind of transcendental escape that they sought. "What need had I of companions?" Wilkins asked. "The fields and forests, the rivers and lakes, the birds and fishes, they were all my companions." Transfixed by a sunrise on the river, Wilkins communed with the "vastness and unfathomable mysteries of the boundless space above."[77] Neidé was initially rejuvenated: "I bound out of the tent with the agility of a young buck. How this life is strengthening wind and limb, expanding the chest and developing the muscles."[78] Yet all three men ultimately got more—or perhaps less—than they bargained for out of their voyage down the Mississippi. At one moment, Bishop declares that "river life makes all men equal."[79] Yet implicitly and explicitly, all three accounts speak to the profound inequalities of life in America that they are confronted with along the Western Rivers. They might cast off into an imagined riverscape of physical and mental liberation, but they end up repeatedly confronted with the hard realities of life along the Mississippi. Like Warner's—and, indeed, Huck and Jim's—these are ambiguous voyages into the wilderness. Unexpectedly, and in ways these authors don't always seem to understand or acknowledge, their journeys became descents into America's own dark heart—a land of division, poverty, and violence—in ways that prefigure and echo Huck and Jim's own misadventures on the Mississippi.

Often, it proves more difficult to escape the markers of civilization than these canoeists have imagined. Bishop, for example, is particularly chagrined by the pollution that he encounters on the Ohio: "Clouds [of smoke] rested upon everything. [. . .] All this din and dirt, this ever-present cloud of blackness settling down each hour upon clean and unclean in a sooty coating [. . .]. If this was civilization and enterprise, I should rather take a little less of those two commodities and a little more of cleanliness and quiet." Even away from the spoliations of industry, the constant threat of "molestation by steamboats" remains an ever-present threat—just as it does for Huck and Jim—and one that Bishop doesn't always manage to avoid: "A snorting, screeching, stern-wheel steamer crossed the river with its tow of barges and demoralized all my surroundings, driving me against the flat, and shooting water over the deck of my craft," separating him from his companions. Neidé, too, spends his time "paddling cautiously, with the sense of hearing constantly on the alert, that we may not be run down by a steamer." Wilkins encounters a packet "steaming and snorting like a fiery demon." If Huck and Jim encounter the symbolically significant wreck of the *Walter Scott*, then Neidé meets with his own resonant image of industrial self-destruction: "About the middle of the afternoon we came upon the wreck of the once splendid steamer Robert E. Lee, which a few weeks before had been burned, when forty of its passengers and crew perished in the flames."[80]

Though all men meet with kindness of one kind or another during their time along the river, even from steamboat pilots, crime and violence seem endemic, evidence of a deeper malaise in American life. As Bishop is warned by a German inhabitant of a river town on the Ohio, fearing for the safety of his boat: "Mine friend, in dese times nobody knows who's which. I say, sar, nobody knows who's what. [. . .] Since de confederate war all men is skamps, I does fully pelieve. [. . .] De peoples know de poat is here, and some of dem has told others about it. If you don't hide her down de rivver to-night, she will be stolen by de rivver thieves." At another point along the river, Bishop is warned to hide away at night, since "any feller might put a ball into you from a high bank. [. . .] There is plenty of folks that would do it, too." The Western Rivers come to seem "the grand highway for a large class of vagabonds [. . .] and scoundrels of all kinds." His fellow canoeists agree. Neidé laments the "army of tramps, unprincipled boatmen, and scoundrels of all descriptions [. . .] who prey upon the country as they pass through it." Having encountered a variety of "notorious outlaws" and "desperate men" on one particularly eventful stretch of the river, Wilkins declares, "Surely I had experienced adventures enough in one day to satisfy even the dime novelist." That threat of crime and violence takes other forms too. All men comment on the prevalence of extralegal violence that they encounter. When Neidé steps ashore at one river town, "the first object of interest to meet my view is a long rope with a hangman's noose on the end, swaying in the morning breeze from the branch of a tall cypress tree. Here is the mark of the summary manner in which justice is meted out to the offender against the laws of the land." Far along the Mississippi, Bishop is told that "nothing but lynch law would 'go down' in their

wild region." He comes perilously close to discovering the truth of that assertion when, in New Orleans, he is suspected of "being a national government
spy" in town to influence "the enfranchised negro to vote the 'right ticket'"
and spends an uncomfortable night being verbally abused by a drunken mob.
Bishop escapes, but he meets others who provide evidence of the mob's very
real threats. One man, talking to him about conflict between white fishermen
and "bloody furiners," boasts: "One morning a Chinaman was found dead in
a cabin. Pretty soon after, one or two others was found floatin' round loose, in
the same way; and after that lesson or two the fellers got CIVILIZED." Just as
for Huck and Jim, the river becomes for these canoeists a space of retreat from
the terrors of racialized mob violence that the men encounter on the banks
of the river. As Wilkins puts it, "Again I sought refuge on the mighty deep."[81]

Try as they might, they cannot escape from the harsh realities of life for
those who make their home on and along the river—the markers of inequality
that are all too apparent among the men, women, and children of the Ohio
and Mississippi who are marginalized from society permanently, not just for
the duration of a canoe trip. All three men are fascinated and discomfited,
in turn, by the flotilla of shantyboats that they encounter on the river, the
seasonal homes of those forced onto the river to survive. Their assessment of
this "teeming [. . .] strange, nomadic life," to use Bishop's phrase, ranges from
contempt to pity to admiration. The canoeists are simultaneously repulsed by
and attracted to the life they encounter among these wanderers—true exiles
from civilization as understood by these men:

> Another shanty-boat is built by a party of young men suffering from im-
> pecuniosity. They are "out of a job," and to them, the charms of an inde-
> pendent life on the river is irresistible. Having pooled their few dollars to
> build their floating home, they descend to New Orleans as negro minstrels,
> trappers, or thieves, as necessity may demand. [. . .] In this descent of the
> river, many persons, who have clubbed together to meet the expenses of
> a shanty-boat life for the first time, and who are of a sentimental turn of
> mind, look upon the voyage as a romantic era in their lives. [. . .] And
> so the great flood of river life goes on, and out of this annual custom of
> shanty-boat migration a peculiar phase of American character is devel-
> oped, a curious set of educated and illiterate nomads, as restless and un-
> profitable a class of inhabitants as can be found in all the great West.

If Bishop is alive to the romance of this life, Neidé provides a corrective during his encounter with a near-destitute family on a shantyboat of "the poorest description": "While the wondering children stood about the canoes as the daylight strengthened, I noticed that the shivering, barefooted little girl had but one thin garment, while the eldest boy had a rag of a coat tied about his otherwise unprotected person." Neidé and his traveling companion provide what clothing they can for the children.[82]

The canoeists are no less ambiguous in their attitude toward race. Though all three of these northern men ostensibly, to use Bishop's words, "sympathized strongly" with the "unfortunate race," they slip easily into racist tropes clearly informed by the minstrel stage when describing their encounters with black Americans on the river. Despite the quasi-anthropological tone adopted by Neidé—"meeting with negroes along the shore is now of almost daily occurrence"—the canoeists tend to play their interactions with African Americans for laughs. If an uncertainty about the meaning of black freedom lingers behind their comments, Bishop's summary judgment is typical: "In freedom or slavery, north or south, in sunshine or out of it, ever the same easy, improvident race; ever the same gleaming teeth and ready 'Yes, sah! 'pon my word, sah!' and ever the same tardiness to DO." The spirit of reunion also informs their encounters with the southern landscape; Bishop slips into a standard Lost Cause reverie: "The houses of the planters along the river's bank were enveloped in foliage, and the air was so redolent with the fragrance of flowers that I seemed to be floating through an Eden."[83]

Yet life on the Mississippi also provides some compelling moments of interracial interaction in these narratives, none more so than Neidé's unexpected meeting with four men who appeared by his campfire one night—men who knew the river intimately: "Their story was that they had been employed as roustabouts on one of the St. Louis and New Orleans packets, and one of them, having had a dispute with the mate of the boat, was receiving a sound thrashing, when the other three pitched in and turned the tide of battle." After recovering from his initial surprise, Neidé and the discharged roustabouts share a "merry" evening, "singing plantation melodies and cracking jokes at one another's expense. The bass and tenor were excellent, but the rich falsetto of the largest fellow of the party astonished me with its softness." Neidé's admiration for this "fine, hardy-looking set of fellows" is only matched by his surprise that "they had all been born in slavery." Plantation memories prompt one of the roustabouts to gleefully liken Neidé's canoe to "dat ar coffin ole massa war toted to de burin'-groun' in." Though Neidé still mistrusts his new river companions enough to set a watch in fear that "we might miss some article," breakfast restores some kind of communal harmony: "Daybreak sees all hands at work, the negroes piling wood on the fire, while Barnacle finds a piece of bacon for each of my dark-skinned guests, to which we add a half dozen crackers each and a cup of coffee. They seem very grateful for the light breakfast, and with a shake of the hand all around they disappear into the dense thicket, while we clean up and pack the canoes for an early start."[84] At such a moment, two very different images of freedom on the river stood face to face in fascinating contrast. Bishop, Neidé, Wilkins, and countless other canoeists encountered a very different river than the one they had expected: cast off from the cares of society in the hopes of romantic adventure in sublime river scenery, they had to reckon, instead, with a landscape fraught with inequality.

The canoeists weren't the only ones heading downriver in unusual crafts, though. In contrast to the earnestness of the would-be nature lovers stands the showmanship of a figure who came to fame at this moment. Captain Paul Boyton achieved international celebrity with a canny combination of gimmickry and self-publicity. Boyton, too, spent a boyhood obsessed with the Western Rivers: "He often dreamt of the time when he would be large enough to go down the mighty Ohio and the great Mississippi." Still a child, he ran away from home on a coal barge heading from Pittsburgh to New Orleans. There he learned another important lesson: "The loud commands and fierce oaths of the mate made him feel very grateful that he was not a roustabout."[85] Boyton found a different career on the river—or rather, in the river. Ostensibly with the purpose of promoting its lifesaving potential, Boyton donned a pioneering, inflatable wetsuit and flung himself into a series of waterways around the world. As he noted in his autobiography (a book that Mark Twain rejected for Charles L. Webster & Company in 1887—"Boyton book for babies," he wrote in his notebook—though he eventually owned a copy), the suit "was invented by C. S. Merriman of Iowa, a pants and tunic made of highly vulcanized rubber. [. . .] All portions of the body are covered except the face. There are five air chambers in the costume; one at the back of the head which acts as a pillow and when fully inflated it draws the thin rubber around the face so that no water can wash down. The other chambers are situated in the back, breast, and around each leg from the hip to the knee. [. . .] When voyaging, he propels himself by a light double bladed paddle six feet long."[86] Serving as his very own human canoe, Boyton first achieved fame in Europe, crossing the Channel from France to Dover in 1875, demonstrating his suit for Queen Victoria, and floating along the Thames, always with a press boat in tow. Many other rivers followed, and stories of his exploits circulated around the world.

Eventually, he made his way to the Western Rivers. From February to April 1879, he bobbed down the Ohio and the Mississippi and, at least according to Boyton, was received with much fanfare: "At all towns he passed, crowds of people lined the banks and offers of hospitality were numberless. [. . .] Thousands of people jammed the bridges and thousands lined the shore." When Boyton finally reached New Orleans, it was Captain Leathers and the *Natchez* that escorted him for the last few miles of his journey. Then, after a jaunt to South America, Boyton returned to the Mississippi in May 1881, ready to tackle the Upper Mississippi from St. Paul to Cairo—"more beautiful than [. . .] any river he had yet traversed" (fig. 8).[87] When he arrived in St. Louis,

FIGURE 8. "Boyton Descending the Mississippi," from Nathaniel H. Bishop, *Four Months in a Sneak-Box* (Boston: Lee & Shepard, 1879), 187.

according to the *New York Times,* he was received by an "immense crowd."[88] Having conquered the Mississippi, he lit out for the West—before retiring from the rubber suit business, teaming up with P. T. Barnum, and opening a series of pioneering theme parks, certainly drawing more attention to his Mississippi exploits than the canoeists. Ultimately, though, his success in marketing his daring adventures on the world's rivers still spoke to the same desires for escape and adventure.

The varied experiences of these white men heading back to the Mississippi River in small craft on voyages of escape, self-discovery, and self-publicity formed a crucial part of the cultural backdrop at the moment that *Huckleberry Finn* was coming into existence. And in one particular instance, the nascent vogue for canoeing had a direct bearing on Huck's development. William Livingston Alden was an influential magazinist, a mover and shaker in the New York literary world who founded both the Lotos Club—of which Twain was a member—and the New York Canoe Club, the first such organization in the country. The so-called father of American canoeing, fresh from writing his own sailing and canoeing books for boys, was also one of the first readers of *Adventures of Huckleberry Finn.*[89] In 1881, Twain shared a manuscript-in-progress with his fluvial friend and correspondent; in turn, Alden unequivocally approved: "I have just read Huck through in course. It is the best book ever written."[90]

"Back to the Raft"

When *Adventures of Huckleberry Finn* was finally unleashed upon America, there was little sense of how indelible—and how debated—the image of Huck and Jim on their raft, floating down the Mississippi, would become to the iconography of the river (and indeed, America itself). Examining their river journey in light of the other texts exploring similar problems of freedom and escape on the Mississippi at this moment, however, arguably presents us with a rather different view of the raft and all that it symbolizes. That a man like Alden should respond so warmly to Huck and his adventures should give us some metric about what's really at stake in the representation of the river in this book. As Frederick Woodard and Donnarae MacCann have highlighted, "That Huck's story is about freedom of one sort or another is an essential given."[91] Seen alongside other accounts of liberation along the Mississippi from this period, the freedom that this text ultimately seems most concerned with is that of Huckleberry Finn himself—especially when it speaks to the same desire to run away from civilization that informed both the bohemian fetishization of the roustabout and the dream of a canoe trip downriver. For Walter Blair, at least in part, the composition of this book itself was Twain's response to the pressures of civilized life—his own version of a restorative canoe trip: "On many occasions between 1880 and 1883, Mark [. . .] might have written Huck's rhapsody about the pleasures of returning to the raft and [. . .] a life of contentment and companionship in an imagined world far from the hectic Hartford of the 1880s."[92] That understanding of the journey is present in other classic accounts of what matters in this text. For Leo Marx, "The freedom which Jim seeks, and which Huck and Jim temporarily enjoy aboard the raft, is [. . .] freedom *from* everything for which Miss Watson stands"—namely, "the polite lies of civilization that suffocate Huck's spirit"—and not, apparently, slavery.[93]

Certainly, as soon as Huck decides to head out in his canoe for Jackson's Island—to light out, like his fellow canoeists, from civilization and the more violent oppressions of Pap Finn—he is never happier than when messing about in boats on the river. Jim, terrified by his unexpected appearance on the island, understands him to be a spirit deeply connected to the Mississippi: "You go en git in de river agin, whah you b'longs, en doan' do nuffn to Ole Jim, 'at 'uz awluz yo' fren.'" Unquestionably, Huck is happiest on the river with Jim. He declares, "Everything we had in the world was on our raft"—except of course, as the narrative makes clear, much that is dear to Jim is missing. Readings of the Mississippi in this text that figure the raft as a paradisiacal, liminal space set apart from the social strains of the shore unsurprisingly foreground the halcyon moments of solitude on the river, particularly the period of reunion that takes place after Huck's time with the Grangerfords:

> I never felt easy till the raft was two mile below there and out in the middle of the Mississippi. Then we hung up our signal lantern, and judged that we was free and safe once more. I hadn't had a bite to eat since yesterday, so Jim he got out some corn-dodgers and buttermilk, and pork and cabbage and greens—there ain't nothing in the world so good when it's cooked right—and whilst I eat my supper we talked and had a good time. I was powerful glad to get away from the feuds, and so was Jim to get away from

the swamp. We said there warn't no home like a raft, after all. Other places do seem so cramped up and smothery, but a raft don't. You feel mighty free and easy and comfortable on a raft. [. . .] Two or three days and nights went by; I reckon I might say they swum by, they slid along so quiet and smooth and lovely. Here is the way we put in the time. It was a monstrous big river down there—sometimes a mile and a half wide; we run nights, and laid up and hid daytimes; soon as night was most gone we stopped navigating and tied up—nearly always in the dead water under a towhead; and then cut young cottonwoods and willows, and hid the raft with them. Then we set out the lines. Next we slid into the river and had a swim, so as to freshen up and cool off; then we set down on the sandy bottom where the water was about knee deep, and watched the daylight come.[94]

Free and safe, free and easy: it was this deeply appealing image of an American Eden, the dawn of a new day, that drove canoeists to the Mississippi. Famously for Leo Marx, this was "virtually Arcadian perfection."[95] For Betty H. Jones, "The two cleanse themselves in the waters of the great river-god, waters symbolic of potential redemption and rebirth. [. . .] Scenes such as these remind us of the possibilities of beauty, truth, and grace in a society free of the oppressive burden of racism."[96]

It is this moment that Huck is at pains to recapture and preserve in the narrative too. When the river brings them the duke and the king and a whole host of torments for Jim, Huck goes with the flow and remains primarily committed to the raft and the river: "Because it would a been a miserable business to have any unfriendliness on the raft; for what you want, above all things, on a raft, is for everybody to be satisfied, and feel right and kind towards the others." At the end of the narrative, too, when Jim has been escaped from the Phelps's plantation and they have returned to the raft again—"*Now*, old Jim, you're a free man again, and I bet you won't ever be a slave no more"—Huck's plan is simply to "shove off down the river on the raft with Jim, hiding daytimes and running nights, the way me and Jim used to do before."[97] Yet that is really an attempt to recapture the idyll and the pleasure of the raft, not to secure Jim's escape. It is the same kind of logic that led Louis Budd to declare, "Most of us would rather travel with Jim on a stray raft than with Uncle Tom on a steamboat"—not because Jim is running away from slavery while Uncle Tom remains enslaved but because of the adventures that are promised.[98]

For who is free and safe on this raft? Who is free and easy? Very literally, not Jim. The middle of the Mississippi was hardly a place of safety for a runaway slave—as the narrative itself repeatedly bears out. Any reading of the book that foregrounds the appeal of the raft and its "community of saints" (Lionel Trilling's phrase) marginalizes and sidetracks—as the narrative itself continually does—Jim's escape from slavery and the river's role in his quest for freedom.[99]

Jim and the river have, of course, received plenty of critical attention over the decades. "But for the River," T. S. Eliot felt, "the book might only be a sequence of adventures with a happy ending. [. . .] The River makes the book a great book." Indeed, in Eliot's reading, it is more than just a river: it is a "River God."[100] Lionel Trilling took the conceit even further: "Generally, the god is benign: a being of long sunny days and spacious nights [. . .] like any god, he is also dangerous and deceptive. [. . .] But its nature seems to foster the goodness of those who love it."[101] Leo Marx, on the other hand, rejected such formulations in favor of what he felt to be the central theme of the book: "I do not see that it means much to talk about the river as a god in this novel. [. . .] It provides a means of escape."[102] Arnold Rampersad—himself writing over thirty years ago now—summarized the debate: "Whether one sees the river, according to the debate now some forty years old, as a god or as a morally neutral agency, certainly the Mississippi rolls through Mark Twain's novel as a constant reminder of an ultimate force beyond human beings."[103] Such readings, though, are focused on Huck's relationship with the river—not Jim's.

Similar ambiguities surround Twain's characterization of Jim, especially in relation to minstrelsy. Henry B. Wonham has argued that *Adventures of Huckleberry Finn* narrates Twain's own relationship to the changing nature of minstrelsy across the nineteenth century: "The novel's minstrel sequences intend to recover, through memory and fantasy, some of the dialectical force Twain attributed to early blackface performance within the context of its transformation into a new form of public entertainment," even as Twain understood that his contemporary audience was increasingly "impatient with racial and ethnical ambiguity."[104] In a similar vein, Sharon D. McCoy has attempted to rehabilitate our understanding of Twain's favorite minstrelsy troupes that "reveled in social and political satire and burlesque [. . .] performing skits and songs that transgressed accepted boundaries of race, class, and culture."[105] For other commentators, Woodard and MacCann chief among them, Twain's use of minstrel devices fatally "undercuts serious consideration of Jim's humanity beyond those qualities stereotypically attributed to the noble savage [. . .]. Jim is forever frozen within the convention of the minstrel darky."[106] Bernard W. Bell has argued that even if for much of the book Jim knowingly dons a "comic mask which he wears defensively to conceal his true feelings and thoughts from Huck and other whites who pervert their humanity in demeaning or denying his," ultimately "Twain [. . .] sells Jim's soul down the river for laughs at the end."[107] As Shelley Fisher Fishkin has also noted, many of the passages from *Huckleberry Finn* that Twain selected for his readings on tour with Cable "were passages that strike readers today as the most redolent of the minstrel show." Whatever subversive meanings we might ascribe to those passages, "we do not have the evidence to prove [. . .] that Twain's white lecture audiences got these points; it is quite possible they responded to these pieces precisely as minstrel routines."[108]

What happens, though, if we don't foreground the river as a God or as "an ultimate force beyond human beings" whose main purpose in the text is to provide Huck and the reader with adventure, moral and spiritual instruction, and restorative moments of American pastoral? What does the river look like if we try to see it from Jim's perspective—primarily as the main artery of slavery in antebellum America and still a place of ambiguous freedoms in the 1880s? And what does Jim start to look like if, taking his quest for freedom on the river seriously, we view him less as an inadequate minstrel and more as a runaway or a roustabout—a man fully aware of the potentials and pitfalls of the quest for liberty along the Mississippi—trapped in a narrative that blocks his escape at every turn? From the swampy margins and silences of this text emerges a different vision of the Mississippi, one that hints at the meaning of freedom and escape for black Americans on the river in ways that aren't accounted for by the serene vision of Huck and Jim on the raft. First, we have to assume that the stakes are as high for Jim as they were for other runaways on the river, like Henson and Brown. While he is clearly no rambunctious, roving roustabout, Jim understands the workings of the Mississippi as well as—perhaps better than—anyone in the book. Even though the narrative constantly frustrates his plans, pushing him into minstrel poses in order to perpetuate Huck's voyage, it's not for a lack of river knowledge that he doesn't effect his own freedom.

Almost immediately, Jim's understanding of the river system and its meanings for black Americans becomes clear. One of the motivations for his escape at this moment is that he heard "ole missus tell de widder she gwyne to sell me down to Orleans." As much is Jim is painfully aware of what a voyage down the Mississippi means for the enslaved, he is also aware of how to make his escape via the river. First, he plans—just like William Wells Brown—to steal a skiff, but thinking that its absence would be noticed, Jim comes up with a stealthier strategy: "A raff is what I's arter; it doan' make no track." He can read the river too: "De river wuz arisin' en dey wuz a good current; so I reck'n'd 'at by fo' in de mawnin' I'd be twenty-five mile down de river, en den I'd slip in, jis' b'fo' daylight, en swim asho' en take to de woods on de Illinoi side." And that should have been that: by all rights, Jim should have crossed the river and made a run for it, like many other runaways before him. Yet in what becomes a pattern, Twain frustrates Jim's intentions: "a man begin to come aft wid de lantern," and Jim is forced swim for Jackson's Island. This moment also emphasizes the degree to which, far from a restful idyll, the Mississippi is a space where Jim and those kin to him—like Hearn's sources on the Cincinnati levee—are subjected to almost constant white surveillance. The same is true of his time on the island with Huck. When Huck gets bored of his new freedom—"it was getting slow and dull"—and gets to talking with a woman who lives on shore, it becomes apparent that not only is Jim a wanted man but that he has been under observation all along. She tells Huck, "I was pretty near certain I'd seen smoke over there, about the head of the island, a day or two before that, so I says to myself, like as not that nigger's hiding over there; anyway, says I, it's worth the trouble to give the place a hunt." When the boys escape to Jackson's Island in *Tom Sawyer*, they are able to disappear for days. Runaway Jim is discovered immediately. Awareness of constant scrutiny is also what makes Jim hesitate before exploring the wreck of the *Walter Scott* too: "Like as not dey's a watchman on dat wrack."[109]

After their escape from the island, as Huck and Jim head downriver, a new plan is formulated, though who is responsible for the details is uncertain. Huck tells us: "We judged that three nights more would fetch us to Cairo, at the bottom of Illinois, where the Ohio River comes in, and that was what we was after. We would sell the raft and get on a steamboat and go way up the Ohio amongst the free States, and then be out of trouble." The only time Jim expresses the kind of liberating sentiment that Huck attributes to their time on the raft is here, when he believes the junction of the Ohio to be close at hand: "We's safe, Huck, we's safe! Jump up and crack yo' heels! Dat's de good ole Cairo at las', I jis knows it!" Of course, Jim is far from safe, and events intervene again. They miss Cairo, the steamboat smashes the raft, Huck and Jim are separated, and Huck spends an ultimately traumatic sojourn with the Grangerfords. The reader only catches glimpses of what Jim is up to during this time, but what we can see reinforces how Jim uses his knowledge of the river to aid in his escape. It also hints at the importance of the network of resistance and information inculcated and shared among the enslaved communities who lived along the river. As soon as Jim swims ashore, he is helped in his escape by the enslaved people he meets: "Early in de mawnin' some er de niggers come along, gwyne to de fields, en dey tuck me en showed me dis place, whah de dogs can't track me on accounts o' de water, en dey brings me truck to eat every night, en tells me how you's a gitt'n along." Like Cable's Bras-Coupé, Jim heads for the safety of the swamp. While there, he gets busy: "I ben a-buyin' pots en pans en vittles, as I got a chanst, en a-patchin' up de raf' nights."[110] The river beckons again.

What follows is Huck's halcyon moment of "free and easy" life on the Mississippi—enabled by Jim's unseen labor in the swamp. Yet all that is left for Jim on this journey downriver, his quest for freedom apparently deferred and marginalized in order to keep the river adventures going, is abjection. At one moment, Huck wakes to find Jim "moaning and mourning to himself. [. . .] He was thinking about his wife and his children, away up yonder, and he was low and homesick." Yet despite all that Jim seems to know about the workings of the Mississippi—its hazards but also its potential for liberation—the narrative robs him of his agency and capability at this moment. Jim simply floats farther south. Left alone on the river for days at a time by the duke and the king, made to look ridiculous, this river-savvy runaway still doesn't try to escape. "Jim was satisfied," Huck tells us. When they momentarily flee from the duke and the king, Huck repeats his favorite affirmation: "Away we went, a sliding down the river, and it did seem so good to be free again and by ourselves on the big river."[111] But the duke and the king are close by, in their own skiff, and more misadventures for Jim soon ensue.

Twain doesn't show us Jim's capture on the banks of the river, but he certainly does show us Jim's time on the Phelpses' farm. Like Uncle Tom, Jim's journey down the Mississippi ultimately ends in imprisonment and torture on a plantation, though this time his tormentors include his friends. Also like

Uncle Tom at the end of his river ordeal, Jim sacrifices himself to protect others. If not for Tom Sawyer's deus ex machina announcement that "he ain't no slave; he's as free as any cretur that walks this earth!" a more plausible ending for runaway Jim is hinted at by Huck: "Some of them wanted to hang Jim for an example to all the other niggers around there, so they wouldn't be trying to run away like Jim done, and making such a raft of trouble." As well as a chilling reminder of the racial violence that always lurked along the river, it's an apt phrase: for Jim, if not for Huck, their raft has indeed been a raft of trouble. Holding out the promise of escape, the river—at least in Twain's telling of it— gives Jim only an ambiguous and partial freedom. Like Huck, we are haunted by the ghost of an image of Jim: "I see Jim before me, all the time, in the day, and in the night-time, sometimes moonlight, sometimes storms, and we a floating along, talking, and singing, and laughing."[112] Yet recovering Jim's river story from the marginal marshes of this text highlights the degree to which, hiding away from the terrifying visibility of the middle of the Mississippi, this is a frustrated narrative of agency and escape that chimes in telling ways with other stories of slavery and freedom on the river.

"When We Three Came Back Up the River in Glory"

To ask again the same question Cable pondered, once freed, was Jim a free man? In truth, he remained the property of Mark Twain, and if the final sections of Adventures of Huckleberry Finn saw Jim sold down the river, then what followed saw him sold back up it again. At the end of Huckleberry Finn, Tom Sawyer explains his motivation for keeping the secret of Jim's emancipation. It, too, revolves around the desire for adventure on the river: "What he had planned in his head from the start, if we got Jim out all safe, was for us to run him down the river on the raft, and have adventures plumb to the mouth of the river, and then tell him about his being free, and take him back up home on a steamboat, in style, and pay him for his lost time, and write word ahead and get out all the niggers around, and have them waltz him into town with a torchlight procession and a brass-band, and then he would be a hero, and so would we." Even Huck seems to understand the degree to which this is a fantastic, delusional vision of life on the antebellum river. It evinces a rare moment of sly critique from him: "I reckened it was about as well the way it was."[113] Still, there was to be no family reunion for Jim—no life in the free states, no buying or stealing his wife and children to safety. Instead, Twain chose to make good on Tom Sawyer's dream of the river. *Tom Sawyer Abroad* (1894) begins with an account of the way that Huck, Jim, and Tom returned to St. Petersburg after the end of the *Adventures of Huckleberry Finn:* "You see, when we three came back up the river in glory, as you may say, from that long travel, and the village received us with a torchlight procession and speeches, and everybody hurrah'd and shouted, it made us heroes, and that was what Tom Sawyer had always been hankering to be. [. . .] You see he laid over me and Jim considerable, because we only went down the river on a raft and came back by the steamboat, but Tom went by the steamboat both ways. The boys envied me and Jim a good deal, but land! they just knuckled to the dirt before Tom."[114] Jim, pushed back into the shell of minstrelsy, is doomed to accompany Huck and Tom on further adventures, the images of freedom that he generated on the Mississippi evaporating into river mist. Twain planned other river sequels for Huck too. "Make a kind of Huck Finn narrative on a boat," he wrote in his notebook, "let him ship as cabin boy & another boy as cub pilot—& so put the great river & its bygone ways into history in form of a story."[115]

From the precarious vantage point of Eads's bridge in January 1885, it was impossible to see the turbulent future that lay ahead for Twain's most significant creations or the degree to which the image of Huck and Jim on their raft on the Mississippi would flow through American culture. Even for an old steamboat pilot, it was impossible to see the darker waters that lay ahead. After he got off the bridge in St. Louis, Twain's reading tour with Cable would take him back to Hannibal. This new return to the source would come earlier than he had predicted in 1882, and not everything was quite "ashes and dust" yet—but it was a poignant trip all the same.[116] He wrote to Livy on January 13, 1885: "This visit to Hannibal—you can never imagine the infinite great deeps of pathos that have rolled their tides over me. I shall never see another such day. I have carried my heart in my mouth for twenty-four hours [. . .]. And at the last moment came Tom Nash—cradle-mate, baby-mate, little-boy mate—deaf & dumb, now, for near 40 years, & nobody suspecting the deep & fine nature hidden behind his sealed lips—& hands me this letter, & wrings my hand, & gives me a devouring look or two, & walks shyly away." What was in that letter went unrecorded, though Twain thought enough of it to write in his notebook: "Tom Nash's confidential remark."[117] Nash had lost the power of hearing and speech—like Jim's chimerical daughter—when he fell through the thin ice of the frozen Mississippi River while skating with a young Sam Clemens. It was an enigmatic, even ominous moment—a reminder of the river's cruel power and a portent of dark times ahead. Then Twain was off again, to perform the roles of Huck and Jim for months to come as his new book transmitted a defining vision of the Mississippi to the world.

5

"I Went on A-Spinnin' down de River"

UNDERWORLDS AND UNDERTOWS

It was his opinion that there was as great a river as the Mississippi
flowing directly under it—an underself of a river.
—GRACE KING, "The Little Convent Girl," 1893

I could see the mighty river [. . .] at liberty to forget the rush and bustle
of that raging monster which the French call the *fin de siècle*.
—JULIAN RALPH, "The Old Way to Dixie," 1893

I am 59 years old; yet I never had a friend before who put out a hand
and tried to pull me ashore when he found me in deep waters.
—MARK TWAIN, 1894

In January 1895, bewildered by the extraordinary reversals of fortune that the previous decade had wrought, Mark Twain sat down to write a letter to Henry Rogers, the industrialist who was helping guide him through—and hopefully out of—financial ruin. In an attempt to come to terms with the fact that "my ten-year dream is actually dissolved," Twain tried to explain to Rogers why he had been sure that things would eventually turn his way. When he was a child, the Mississippi had shown him to be especially blessed by providence: "As a small boy I was notoriously lucky. It was usual for one or two of our lads (per annum) to get drowned in the Mississippi or in Bear Creek, but I was pulled out in a 2/3 drowned condition 9 times before I learned to swim, and was considered to be a cat in disguise. When the 'Pennsylvania' blew up and the telegraph reported my brother as fatally injured (with 60 others) but made no mention of me, my uncle said to my mother 'it means that Sam was somewhere else, after being on that boat a year and a half—he was born lucky.'" And so, even as his ill-fated speculations spiraled out of control—his investments in both the Paige Typesetting Machine and his publishing company, Webster & Company—he "couldn't shake off the confidence of a life time in my luck." That luck, though, had definitively dried up. He confided to Rogers, still dwelling on water and destiny, "Nothing daunts Mrs. Clemens or makes the world look bleak to her—which is the reason I haven't drowned myself."[1]

Even before the rising tide of financial ruin crested with the bankruptcy of Webster & Company in April 1894, the years after the publication of *Adventures of Huckleberry Finn* had been marked by sickness, death, and looming economic disaster. Things began auspiciously enough, with Webster & Company's enormously successful publication of the *Personal Memoirs of U. S. Grant* in 1885. Then the tide began to turn. After the death of both his mother and Livy's mother and that of a variety of friends and acquaintances, Twain lamented to William Dean Howells in 1890 (whose daughter Winifred's death in 1889 was one of those painful bereavements), "I have fed so full on sorrows, these last weeks that I seem to have become hardened to them—benumbed." Ill health and the need to economize pushed the Clemenses to an extended sojourn in Europe, from June 1891 to May 1895—an exile from their Hartford home that seemed temporary but would become permanent. Howells only found out about their plans from the newspapers. Twain, in response, tried to make light of the situation: "Mrs. Clemens *must* try some baths somewhere, &

this it is that has determined us to go to Europe. The water required seems to be provided at a little obscure & little-visited nook up in the hills back of the Rhine somewhere." The bitterness still leaked out: "Travel has no longer any charm for me. I have seen all the foreign countries I want to see except heaven & hell."[2] Earlier in 1891, the same sourness had flowed into his notebook as he imagined one possible end for his most famous creations: "Huck comes back, 60 years old, from nobody knows where—& crazy. Thinks he is a boy again [. . .]. Tom comes, at last, 60 from wandering the world & tends Huck [. . .] both are desolate, life has been a failure, all that was lovable, all that was beautiful is under the mould. They die together."[3]

While moving his family around Switzerland, France, Germany, and Italy in this period, Twain himself would also cross the Atlantic repeatedly in an attempt to get his business affairs in order. Still, out of all kinds of necessity, he wrote prolifically—*A Connecticut Yankee in King Arthur's Court* (1889), which featured the image of "a steamboat explosion on the Mississippi"; *The American Claimant* (1892); *Tom Sawyer Abroad* (1894); and *Personal Recollections of Joan of Arc* (1896).[4] At the confluence of all this—swirling personal tragedy, looming economic disaster, extended European peregrinations, and multiple Atlantic crossings—Twain turned again to the Mississippi. *Pudd'nhead Wilson*, his last sustained literary engagement with the river, was serialized in the *Century* from December 1893 to June 1894 before its release as a single volume later in the year (the copyright in Livy's name, thanks to the bankruptcy of Webster & Company).

Throughout this decade, as Twain imaginatively returned to the Mississippi for the final time, rivers continued to swirl around him, mingling and mixing their waters in the popular cultural landscape. The close of the nineteenth century was a moment when rivers had a potent role to play in matters of geopolitics, national identity, and world literature; Twain stood at their nexus. First, Henry Morton Stanley was back in America. Having completed his extraordinary expeditions along the Congo, he had a new book to promote and lectures to give. *The Congo and the Founding of Its Free State* (1885) detailed Stanley's work along the river in the employ of King Leopold II of Belgium as he attempted to establish the Congo Free State—an endeavor that, masquerading under the cloak of philanthropy, would soon become an exemplar of colonial brutality, what Adam Hochschild has described as "the first major international atrocity scandal in the age of the telegraph and the camera"—

resulting in the death and enslavement of millions of Africans.[5] Joseph Conrad, who would provide the defining literary account of the horrors of this time and place in *Heart of Darkness* (1899), worked along the river in 1890 in the service of a Belgian trading company and was traumatized by what he encountered: "I find everything repugnant here. Men and things, but especially men."[6] He had one respite from the misery, though: "Often [. . .] I thought of 'The Mississippi Pilot' and of Twain while I was in command of a steamer in the Congo and stood straining in the night looking for snags. Very often I thought of him."[7] Twain himself would eventually join the chorus of international condemnation of events in the Congo—"his final and most intensive anti-imperialist effort"—with the publication of the satirical pamphlet *King Leopold's Soliloquy: A Defense of His Congo Rule* in 1905.[8]

In 1886, though, Twain was happy to publicly sing his old friend's praises. When Stanley reached Hartford on his tour of America, the explorer stayed with the Clemens family. Twain introduced him for his lecture in Boston, too, and was not faint in his admiration: "When I contrast what I have achieved in my measurably brief life with what he has achieved in his possibly briefer one, the effect is to sweep utterly away the ten-story edifice of my own self-appreciation and leave nothing behind but the cellar. When you compare these achievements of his with the achievements of really great men who exist in history, the comparison, I believe, is in his favour."[9]

The Mississippi had another role to play in this moment too. Stanley's laudatory—really propagandistic—account of *The Congo and the Founding of Its Free State* was marked by an insistent comparison between the rivers of Africa and the American rivers that Stanley had known in his youth. In attempting to extol the colonial potential of the Congo, he frequently pictured the Mississippi as a tired and inferior competitor. Surveying the Congo's place in the pantheon of world rivers and assuring his readers, "You would express a preference for it to any river known to you," Stanley immediately dismissed the Rhine as a "microscopic miniature of the Lower Congo." The Nile, the Danube, the Volga, and the Amazon were dispatched as swiftly. The Mississippi, though, deserved more consideration: "The Mississippi? The Congo is one and a half times larger than the Mississippi, and certainly from eight to ten times broader. You may take your choice of nearly a dozen channels, and you will see more beautiful vegetation on the Congo than on the American river. [. . .] And as for the towns, why, I hope the all-gracious Providence will bless our labour, and they will come by-and-by; meantime there is room enough, and to spare, to stow the half of Europe comfortably on its spacious borders. [. . .] But what is of far more value, it possesses over 40,000,000 of moderately-industrious and workable people, which the Red Indians never were."[10] In such an image, the seeds of the Congo's role as a new Mississippi, complete with the enslavement of the Africans along its banks, were sown. At the same time, Twain's vision of the Mississippi in *Pudd'nead Wilson* would be touched by a darkness that itself reflected the contemporary horrors taking place along the Congo.

The Thames, too, continued to make ripples that reached Twain. In 1889, Jerome K. Jerome published *Three Men in a Boat (To Say Nothing of the Dog)*, a humorous account of a trip up the Thames by three friends that simultaneously capitalized on and lampooned the popular vogue for boating on the river. But this definitive river text also poked fun at other popular narratives of the moment. As the boating comrades are preparing to set off for their pleasure cruise, burdened with a "good deal of luggage," onlookers poke fun at their excessive preparations:

> "They ain't a-going to starve, are they?" said the gentleman from the boot-shop.
> "Ah! you'd want to take a thing or two with you," retorted "The Blue Posts," "if you was a-going to cross the Atlantic in a small boat."
> "They ain't a-going to cross the Atlantic," struck in Biggs's boy; "they're a-going to find Stanley."[11]

As William J. Scheick has noted, this and other moments in which Jerome frames the misadventures of his protagonists in the light of imperial adventure narratives "suggest that civilization along the Thames can be strange and barbaric—as exotic as the land and people Stanley encounters in the Dark Continent."[12] Commingling the waters of the Thames and the Congo, Jerome also implicated the Mississippi. His debt to Twain and his river books was immediate to his early reviewers. The *Atlantic*, for example, described the book as an "English extravaganza upon the America model, the boat journey being up the Thames, and the characters young men who had received their intellectual training principally through a course of Mark Twain."[13] Their paths crossed, personally and professionally, at this moment. Following the success of *Three Men in a Boat*, Jerome was appointed coeditor of the newly founded *Idler* magazine in 1892—a position previously offered to, and rejected by, Twain himself. Twain was still an animating presence in the magazine, though, since the first issue opened with his full-page portrait before beginning the serialization of the *American Claimant* (1892). The pair met in London not long after, and Jerome invited Twain to dinner: "We sat talking, looking out upon the silent park, till pretty late," he remembered, "and it struck me as curious [. . .] that neither of us had made a single joke nor told a funny story."[14]

Early in his European banishment, Twain attempted a familiar escape from troubles: a river jaunt. In September 1891, he embarked on a ten-day boat voyage down the Rhône. Unlike previous such excursions, Twain traveled alone, accompanied only by a courier and a boatman. The trip failed to coalesce into the travel account—"Innocents Adrift"—that Twain had hoped to produce, however many times he returned to it over the coming years. Yet what he did write suggests that this river outing offered at least a modicum of relief from the torments of the moment. As Arthur L. Scott notes, Twain's account of the Rhône voyage is a "peaceful idyll—largely descriptive—of three men floating lazily down a river."[15] Twain himself certainly framed the trip as nostalgic escape: "In old times a summer sail down the Rhône was a favorite trip with travelers. But that day is long gone by. [. . .] The main idea of the voyage was, not to see sights, but to rest up from sight-seeing. There was little or nothing on the Rhône to examine or study or write didactically about; consequently, to glide down the stream in an open boat, moved by the current only, would afford many days of lazy repose, with opportunity to smoke, read, doze, talk, accumulate comfort, get fat, and all the while be out of reach of the news and remote from the world and its concerns." The trip proved to be not just an escape from the world—it was even an escape from narrative. Unlike the Rhine, the Rhône apparently had no legends to offer: "One's first impulse was to be irritated; whereas one should be merely thankful." Instead, it offered "infinite peace."[16] To Joseph Twichell, whose company Twain missed, he reiterated the sense of pleasurable annihilation that the river had given him: "You ought to have been along—I could have made room for you easily—& you would have found that a pedestrian tour in Europe doesn't begin with a raft-voyage for hilarity, & mild adventure [. . .] & extinction from the world & newspapers, & a conscience in a state of coma, & lazy comfort, & solid happiness. In fact there's *nothing* that's so lovely." "But," he lamented to Twichell, "it's all over."[17]

Above all, though, the Mississippi still insistently made its presence felt.

Twain returned to the river in June 1886, with family in tow, to visit his aging and ailing mother. Fourteen-year-old Susy recorded the trip in the notebook she devoted to telling her father's story; indeed, it is the last entry in the journal, stopping abruptly on the Mississippi, midsentence: "We are all of us on our way to Keokuk to see Grandma Clemens, who is very feeble and wants to see us. And pertickularly Jean who is her name sake. We are going by way of the lakes, as papa thought that would be the most comfortable way. July 4. We have arrived in Keokuk after a very pleasant"[18]—what Susy and her sisters, or indeed Livy herself, thought of either their first sight of the Mississippi or their steamboat experiences, so central to the personal and professional identity of their father and husband, respectively, went unrecorded. Twain, though, gave an interview in Chicago in which he mused about the demands of entertaining his daughters while Livy was unwell: "There is no place for loafing more satisfactory than the pilothouse of a Mississippi steamboat. It amuses the children to see the pilot monkey with the wheel." The reporter calculated that it would be "worth going fifty miles on foot" for the experience of hearing Mark Twain "unravel the word Mississippi."[19]

The river came to him in other ways too. In 1888, an old river acquaintance, Major "Jack" Downing, wrote to him unexpectedly. "I supposed that you were dead, it has been so long since I heard your name," Twain replied. He also hinted at other plans: "Possibly I may see you, for I shall be in St. Louis a day or two in November. I propose to go down the river and 'note the changes' once more before I make the long crossing, and perhaps you can come there. Will you? I want to see all the boys that are left alive." But those plans came to nothing. As Albert Bigelow Paine concluded, "He had always hoped to make another steamboat trip with Bixby, but one thing and another interfered and he did not go again."[20] When Twain returned to the river in 1890 for Jane Clemens's funeral, he traveled alone.

Less gloomily, his association with the Mississippi still brought Twain international renown of the sort that he relished, across the social and cultural spectrum. In February 1892, Twain had dinner with Kaiser Wilhelm II: "I was greatly pleased to perceive that his Majesty was familiar with my books [. . .]. In the course of his talk he said that my best and most valuable book was 'Old Times on the Mississippi.'" That evening, returning to his Berlin lodgings, he was surprised to find that the usually surly *portier* was delighted to see him return, despite the late hour. Dragging him over to "a row of German translations of my books," the *portier* exclaimed: "There—you wrote them! I have found it out! By God, I did not know it before, and I ask a million pardons! That one there, the 'Old Times on the Mississippi,' is the best book you ever wrote." Even in 1906, the "picturesqueness" of this coincidence—that "the very top of an empire and the very bottom of it, should pass the very same criticism and deliver the very same verdict upon a book of mine"—still delighted him.[21]

Yet perhaps the most significant prompt to Mississippi memories during this period came in a rather different shape than old river comrades and crowned heads—and in a form rather more to the liking of the Clemens women. In 1885, while Twain and Cable had been rolling around the country on their fractious tour, much of the rest of literary America headed to New Orleans and the Mississippi. Ostensibly, they were in town to comment on the World's Industrial and Cotton Centennial Exposition that ran from December 1884 to June 1885, a grand undertaking that was supposed to kick-start New Orleans's industrial rebirth—before it closed in bankruptcy. Whatever else the ill-fated World's Industrial and Cotton Centennial Exposition achieved, it launched the career of Grace King. Working with Julia Ward Howe, who was appointed head of the exposition's Woman's Department, King was well placed to mingle with the literary figures who flocked to the city. At "a little gathering in one of our clubs," she met Richard Watson Gilder, editor of the *Century*, who quizzed her about the "inimical stand taken by the people of New Orleans against George Cable and his works." After outlining the litany of complaints leveled against Twain's tour mate—"his preference for colored people over white," most particularly—Gilder challenged her: "'Why,' he said, 'if Cable is so false to you, why do not some of you write better?'" Disturbed by the "rankling taunt," King "resolved to do at least my share in our defense."[22] Gilder himself rejected her first (anonymously submitted) story.

Yet at the same moment, King also met Charles Dudley Warner, Twain's neighbor and *Gilded Age* collaborator—currently occupying the "Easy Chair" of *Harper's Monthly*—and in him she found a champion. When he returned home from the exposition, he sold her first short story, "Monsieur Motte" (1886), which was extended to novel length in 1888. Despite the racial politics that underpinned her writing, Grace King was embraced by literary Hartford ("You needn't fling your being a Yankee and Abolitionist at me," she wrote to Warner, "if you can stand it, I can").[23] The Warners invited her for a visit in 1887, at which point she also met the neighbors. "Mark Twain!" King exclaimed in her autobiography, "He was our household friend at home, as I told him [. . .] in the darkest days of reconstruction." That was more than enough to establish an attachment between the pair. As Cable, with his public condemnations of race relations in the South, was pushed out of Twain's orbit, King came to occupy a treasured place in the bosom of the Clemens family. Livy, particularly, became her close confidante.

King also offered Twain something significant as he imaginatively returned to the river for the last time: memories of the Mississippi. When Grace King visited with the Clemens family in Florence in 1892, during their European exile—at the moment that Twain was writing *Pudd'nhead Wilson*—talk turned to home. Admiring a sunset from the terrace of the Villa Viviani, Mark Twain declared, "It cannot be compared to the sun on the Mississippi River." King and her sister enthusiastically agreed with him, "although it did seem incongruous to mention the Mississippi River in Florence." Incongruous it may have been, but it opened up a vein of memory that took Twain back to the source of his river life again. King narrates:

> I had made a trip up the Mississippi from New Orleans to St. Louis and back again with Captain Bixby, who had, or claimed to have, taught Mark Twain how to pilot. I told him about it. He took the pipe from his mouth, and his gray eyes glistened under their shaggy brows as he listened, and the soft expression of his boyhood came, an expression that Florence could not have called forth. We talked of Bixby and life on a steamboat; of the cursing, swearing mate and the tumbling, rushing deck hands; of how good the hot rolls tasted for supper, and the fragrant cup of coffee served at any hour of the night by the good-natured steward; of the bells and noises that prevented sleep at night; of the various stopping places, always interesting, picking up a traveler here and there who insisted upon getting on intimate terms of friendship with one by the time we reached New Orleans. No other life seemed worth living. Mr. Clemens grew excited with us over the memory of its recollection, adding his humorous comments.[24]

Twain might not have made it back to the river for another trip with his mentor, but in Florence, Grace King gave him something close. And yet the river book that Twain was working on at this moment would hardly reflect these burnished memories.

At the same time, King was also developing her own portrait of the Mississippi, in ways that were prescient for Twain's own concerns. Her enigmatic short story "The Little Convent Girl" was published in the *Century* in August 1893, just before the serialization of *Pudd'nhead Wilson* began. It explored the same ambiguities as Twain's novel, though to different ends. The story details the journey of a timid young girl, used to convent life, on board a steamboat from Cincinnati to New Orleans. She is traveling to meet her estranged mother after the recent death of her father. At first, her timidity is crippling: "She could not do anything of herself; she had to be initiated into everything by some one else." As the journey develops, though, the boat accommodates itself to her presence, and she, in turn, begins to experience the river: "Every one learned to know her shyness, and began to feel a personal interest in her, and all wanted the little convent girl to see everything that she possibly could"—especially the roustabouts: "And it was worth seeing—the balancing and *chasséeing* and waltzing of the cumbersome old boat to make a landing. [. . .] And then what a rolling of barrels, and shouldering of sacks, and singing of Jim Crow songs, and pacing of Jim Crow steps; and black skins glistening through torn shirts, and white teeth gleaming through red lips, and laughing, and talking and—bewildering! entrancing!" The pilot, too, coaxes the girl into the pilothouse, where he "would talk of the river to her": "It was his opinion that there was as great a river as the Mississippi flowing directly under it—an underself of a river, as much a counterpart of the other as the second story of a house is of the first; in fact, he said they were navigating through the upper story. Whirlpools were holes in the floor of the upper river, so to speak; eddies were rifts and cracks. And deep under the earth, hurrying toward the subterranean stream, were other streams, small and great, but all deep, hurrying to and from the great mother-stream underneath." Yet the roustabouts and the pilot's vision of the "underself" of the river both prove to be foreshadowing: when the boat arrives in New Orleans and the girl's mother comes to greet her, her acquaintances realize an underlying secret: "All exclaimed audibly, or to themselves, 'Colored!'" When next the steamboat is in town, the girl's mother brings her increasingly morose daughter for a visit—and the girl, whether accidentally or intentionally, falls in the Mississippi and drowns. Though the roustabouts jump in to save her, her body is never seen again. "Perhaps," King concludes, "as the pilot told her whirlpools always did, it may have carried her through to the underground river, to that vast, hidden, dark Mississippi that flows beneath the one we see."[25]

Vast, hidden, dark: King's image of the Mississippi, perilous with undertows and deep water exerting strange pulls, was an apt one for its moment. On the one hand, plenty of other writing about the South at this moment, by locals and tourists, incriminated the Mississippi in sympathetic and picturesque visions of antebellum life in the region—a nostalgic vision, to use David Anderson's words, of "immense wealth, self-sufficiency, honor, hospitality, happy master-slave relations" that swiftly gained national and international popularity.[26] Though frequently perceived as a cultural backwater, far off the beaten track, a wealth of travelers and writers gravitated to the river for this reason, framing it as a telling symbol of the state of the South at the end of a century. Their interpretations of black life on the Mississippi, particularly the perennial and multiple figure of the roustabout, followed suit. Yet King's undercurrents also echoed through the river's other lives in popular culture at this point. Through the memoirs of gamblers and dime novel narratives of crime and corruption, the river came to seem a space of deceit, delinquency, and death stagnating in the heart of the nation—but also a site of play and possibility. Out of this bleak whirlpool of racial inequity, criminality, and violence emerged voices from the river—folklore heroes and deathless ballads—that had long remained hidden. Roustabout culture now became popular culture in ways that had profound ramifications in the decades to come.

Pudd'nhead Wilson—a text in which Twain wrestled most directly with the traumatic racial history of the river and the lives of those who experienced it—was therefore intensely a text of its moment. Taking the reader into an American heart of darkness, Twain crafted a mordant image of the Mississippi marked out by slavery, suffering, crime, and corruption. It was, indeed, an underself of the river that he had imagined over the previous years, an unforgiving space offering almost no place of grace, no chance of escape, and only the bleakest of laughs. As narratives of the Old South elided the realities of antebellum slavery and accounts of the Congo obfuscated the specter of slavery's return, Twain produced a river narrative that challenged both of those deceptions. In the form of Roxy, too, Twain finally created a complex female character who also represented the subaltern life of the river—the obscure world of female steamboat workers and their place in the life of the Mississippi hitherto ignored in Twain's work and barely visible in popular culture more generally. If the world of Dawson's Landing was a desolate end to Twain's river odyssey—an underworld, a despairing counterpoint to the image of Hannibal as the numinous "white town drowsing in the sunshine of a summer's morning," a coming to terms with the inequities of river life for all who were caught up in its deep waters—*Pudd'nhead Wilson* was a text whose vision of the river exemplified the tensions of its moment, in Twain as well as in America and the wider world.[27]

"The Old Way to Dixie"

In 1893, Julian Ralph published an account of a steamboat journey along the Mississippi for *Harper's New Monthly Magazine*—one of a number of articles that would be collected as *Dixie: Southern Scenes and Sketches* in 1895 (Twain owned a copy). Though this kind of sketch had been a magazine staple for decades, something in Ralph's framing of the trip set the template for accounts of the Mississippi for years to come. Immediately, Ralph stressed the recherché nature of his decision to travel along the river in this way. The Mississippi had become, as he phrased it in the article's prescient title, "the old way to Dixie"—an intrinsically nostalgic space. By 1893, traveling by steamboat on the river had become a self-consciously antiquarian activity that took its passengers away from the cares of the modern world and into an imagined, chronologically ambiguous Old South: "It was quite by accident that I heard, while in St. Louis, that I could go all the way down the Mississippi to New Orleans in one of a fleet of packets that differ in no material way from those which figure in a score of *ante bellum* novels like *Uncle Tom's Cabin,* and which illuminate our Northern notions of life in the South when its planters basked in the glory of their feudal importance."[28] On one level, Ralph was only reflecting economic realities by pitching his journey as a relic of times past, as a vanishing curiosity. As early as 1882, Jonathan Baxter Harrison had predicted in the *Atlantic* that "the river will be of less importance henceforward. The dominion is passing to the railroads."[29] In many ways, he was right: the steamboat trade had long been under threat from a combination of the railroads, low water, and other obstructions to navigation; the internal combustion engine was about to hammer the final nail in its coffin. Between 1870 and 1910, there was a 70 percent reduction of steamboat tonnage between St. Louis and New

Orleans; by 1909, there was no longer a direct packet service between those twin poles of the Lower Mississippi, Twain's old beat.[30] What remained was a mere shadow of the steamboat's midcentury apotheosis. As Louis Hunter concluded in his definitive history of the industry: "Steamboat traffic was [. . .] reduced to a minor movement of package freight and farm products to and from the larger river cities and a highly localized, short-distance flow of goods between small river communities, hundreds of which had little or no rail service."[31] For some commentators, there was little romance left in the steamboats that still survived. "The Mississippi steamboat is a glorious craft in history and fiction," explained the *New-York Tribune* in 1895, "but the reality is rather disappointing. [. . .] She looks decidedly topheavy, extremely cheap, and unspeakably dirty."[32]

Yet for Ralph, the declining fortunes of those who worked along the river in the passenger trade (people and boats) were precisely what made his journey along the Mississippi "the laziest, most alluring and refreshing, journey that one tired man ever enjoyed." The world might have "forgotten that they are still running," but that only seems to add to Ralph's delight at being able to watch "roustabouts at work with the freight; [. . .] gossip and swap stories with the same sort of pilots about whom I had read so much; [. . .] see many a slumbering Southern town." In short, Ralph anticipated that if a steamboat on the Mississippi could not quite transport him to the antebellum South, it could do the next best thing. In very explicit terms, then, Ralph framed his journey into the South along the river as a retreat into the past, away from all trappings and pressures of modernity. Steamboat life, he argues, demonstrates an "absolutely charming disregard for nineteenth century bustle": "I could cast my lines off from the general world of to-day to float back into a past era, there to loaf away a week of utter rest, undisturbed by a telegraph or telephone, a hotel elevator or clanging cable-car, [. . .] and at liberty to forget the rush and bustle of that raging monster which the French call the *fin de siècle*."[33] Ralph's backward-looking vision of the river set the template for the next two decades of magazine travelogues on the river. As the twentieth century dawned, the Mississippi became busy with travelers basking in its emptiness. In January 1903, Willis Gibson took "the old route to New Orleans" for *Scribner's Magazine*; in August 1905, illustrator Thornton Oakley produced "Mississippi sketches" for *Harper's New Monthly Magazine*; as late as September 1915, William J. Aylward went "steamboating through Dixie,"

also for *Harper's*. Clifton Johnson took a steamboat trip as part of his exploration of the *Highways and Byways of the Mississippi Valley* (1906). As it had
been for Ralph, the river world that these travelers encountered and evoked
was a premodern, anti-industrial southern space par excellence; its waters
carried them into a South that seemed both trapped in the past and outside of
time entirely. In opposition to Twain's blistering historical vision of the river
in *Pudd'nhead Wilson*, the value of the Mississippi in these varied accounts
became understood primarily as a pathway to a nostalgically rendered Old
South. Their understanding of the romance of the steamboat itself exemplified
this; the dilapidated craft that they encountered on the Mississippi seemed a
perfect synecdoche for their sentimental sense of the South as a whole. For
Oakley, the Mississippi steamboat was "a straggler in the march of time [. . .]
a creature of the past [. . .] outworn and archaic in the face of progress."[34] Gibson waxed equally lyrical in his attempts to explain "how wonderful a being is
the steamboat. She has a romance clinging to her every timber": "There is no
sadder sight than a steamboat whose day is done. I came across one tied at the
bank below Vicksburg, a stern-wheel packet. Her wheel was gone, her chimneys awry, her rotted woodwork protruding through gaps in her faded paint.
So she was waiting the end—either dismantling or dissolution—with the river
she had known so many years mournfully caressing her decrepit hull." Gibson
felt that the steamboat on which he traveled was a "queenly ghost of some
champion-of-the-waters of the days before the war."[35] For Oakley, when the
"*Sarah Lane* slipped away from her moorings," the modern world disappeared:
"Cotton-bales and levee and town drifted slowly away into a dim perspective
like other things that have passed into memory."[36]

If there was one figure who particularly crystallized these travelers' sensations of steaming into the past, it was, of course, the roustabout. The roustabout allowed travelers to discuss (and largely support) the wider racial hierarchies of the South, compounding racial stereotypes that were pervasive in
the early twentieth century. There was little of Lafcadio Hearn's bohemian
appreciation of these men in their portraits. As Gibson put it: "There is an impression that the roustabout is a much-abused individual [. . .]. This is wholly
wrong." Instead, in Gibson's eyes, "the roustabout is traveller, nomad, autocrat, man of leisure." He was also very particularly a signifier of the Lower
Mississippi and the South: in Gibson's words, "He is little seen on the upper
river, but in St. Louis, Memphis, and Orleans, there are enough of him to man

five times as many boats as touch at those ports." Almost all of these accounts worked hard to emphasize what they saw as the racial otherness of these river workers. Gibson avers, "He works day and night—a sort of work no white man could stand for even twelve hours."[37] Aylward repeats the same truism: "No foreign competition has been able to supplant him. [. . .] The most powerful European laborer breaks down under the strain."[38] A steamboat captain tells Clifton Johnson that "as far as their work was concerned he preferred them to whites; for none but negroes would contentedly 'eat hardtack' and snatch such sleep as the exigencies allowed, 'with a lump of coal for a pillow.'"[39] The toughness of these men was interpreted in similarly dehumanizing ways. For Gibson, the roustabout was "a powerful machine, answering to the slightest inclination of a mate's will."[40] Oakley, nakedly racist, likened them to "mere beasts of burden [. . .] toiling animals"; one worker is "misshapen, huge, with knotted muscles and apelike arms and the strength of a gorilla"; another has an "apelike face." Oakley depicts roustabouts "gripping the treacherous earth with prehensile toes" at a difficult landing.[41]

Despite their feats of strengths, almost all of these accounts were agreed on another point: roustabouts were lazy. Ralph described "the old barbaric instinct to loaf, or to move by threes at one man's work."[42] Oakley describes "groups of negroes stretched out on the cotton-bales and basking in the torrid glare."[43] For Gibson, the roustabout is able to "shirk with consummate cunning." And so these commentators were also agreed that the degree of surveillance and discipline to which they were subject by the steamboat's white mate was a matter of necessity—apparently turning the roustabout into a figure on whom they could project a wider sense of race relations in America. Gibson explained: "A strong mate with fifty blacks can accomplish astonishing results. But he must exercise unceasing vigilance and complete physical mastery." Gibson found it to be "a good system."[44] Oakley depicts his steamboat's mate "cracking a whip and shouting oaths and orders." Yet despite such signifiers, in Oakley's terms at least, this was not an exact replaying of slavery, though it certainly seemed close. Apparently untroubled by the violence, this was, he justified, a necessary middle ground: "The mild man who would request the negro politely to 'hurry up' would probably be left with all his freight waiting on the wharf. The driver who would affect the brutality of the slavery days, and who would kick and best the toiling rousters, would find himself in a little while left with nobody to work for him; but a big, roaring, cursing, whip-cracking fellow like our mate appears to stimulate the blood and tone up the nerves of the black man so he will load a packet full of cotton in no time."[45] Only Clifton Johnson struck a different note. Condemning the brutality of steamboat life, he praised the roustabouts' "celerity and deftness in the heavy labor" as a "wonder" and noted, with evident disapproval: "Though to me the roustabouts seemed so alert and willing, they were not at all satisfactory to the mate, who, puffing viciously at a cigar, was constantly urging them to greater haste, and once in a while he let off an explosion of oaths." Little surprise, then, that Johnson concluded that his voyage along the river "was not all pleasure" and advised his readers that "few people would [. . .] enjoy being on a Mississippi steamboat more than a day."[46]

Where these travelers agreed, like so many before, was in their appreciation of the music that the roustabouts made as they worked. Johnson recorded the "strange chant" that accompanied the roustabouts' work, "a monotone consisting of an improvised sentence shouted each time a bag or box was lifted [. . .] to which the other responded like an echo."[47] Aylward was also captivated by their songs. He focused particularly on the figure of "Preacher"—"a jewel," as Aylward described him, "an old-time shanty-man of the rare breed who improvise as they go along." Even Aylward understood that Preacher's improvisations served multiple purposes: as along with accompanying work, they also "lampooned the people on the bank, the passengers hanging over the railing, and, more guardedly, the steamer, the captain, and even the mate." This subtle form of protest, Aylward notes, "was done in such a way that nothing offensive was overheard, but the roars of African laughter in the hold sometimes told us that a particularly sharp barb of 'Preacher's' had gone home."[48] This kind of resistance, though not often noticed by travelers, was a crucial part of the roustabout's art: as Buchanan notes, "As they had been during slavery, roustabout songs continued to be an important way in which African Americans controlled the pace of their work and allowed them to comment on the abusive aspects of their labor."[49] For Aylward, it was "a bit of the real Mississippi by one of the old river's own untaught bards"—and it, too, seemed to be a remnant of another time.[50]

The most sustained investigation of black life on the Mississippi at this moment came in an article entirely devoted to "the Mississippi roustabout" by Stoughton Cooley in the *New England Magazine* in November 1894, the same month that *Pudd'nhead Wilson* was finally published in America. Cooley was

himself the son of a steamboating family, intimate with river life, and the author of a river novel, *The Captain of the Amaryllis* (1910). He began his profile
by lamenting that "the roustabouts of the Mississippi steamboats are left in
obscurity by the writers of fictions," despite the fact that "his manners, customs, sayings and doings are [. . .] unique." In the main, Cooley's perspective
on these men was as demeaning as most other accounts of roustabout life from
this moment, and in both tone and content might have been an antebellum
apologia for slavery; but, as in other accounts, the distinctive, inventive culture of roustabout life still appears through the cracks. The roustabout, Cooley
declared, was "stupid and brutal [. . .] his own great enemy. Indolent and
shiftless [. . .] an abject slave to gambling, women and whiskey." Yet, Cooley
declared, "he has his good points. He is generous to a fault and forgiving in
his nature [. . .]. Nor is he lacking in courage or faithfulness." And of course,
there was the music: "The sense of rhythm in the roustabouts, like that in all
negroes, is very acute. Though they have a limited vocabulary, they readily
construct songs for any and all occasions. [. . .] No event in river history is so
complicated that it cannot be told in musical rhyme." Cooley, too, admits that
there was an extreme precariousness to these lives: "The white people sometimes have an unpleasant way of dealing with 'niggers' whom they think re-
miss in their duty."[51] Accompanying his text was a series of photographs of the
men behind the stereotypes, one of the most significant records of roustabout
life ever recorded (fig. 9). Thomas Buchanan rightly notes that these images
"reveal that in many ways working on the deck of southern steamboats had not
changed much since slavery," nor had conditions: "Though most of the young
workers photographed would never have known slavery, their lives were intimately structured by the legacy of bondage."[52] Still, Cooley's images give us
the most palpable sense of the lives of these men who helped define this era
on the Mississippi—and who, through the river, defined themselves.

"Stacker Lee Is Lookin' fo' the Bully"

Stoughton Cooley concluded his portrait of roustabout life with an assertion that "the day of the roustabout is passing," which also meant that "the
songs of the boatmen [. . .] seem destined to pass away."[53] In so many ways, he
couldn't have been more wrong. Roustabout culture, particularly roustabout
song, was about to explode into popular culture in ways that would echo down

FIGURE 9. "Partners," from Stoughton Cooley, "The Mississippi Roustabout,"
New England Magazine, November 1894, 293.

the years. In 1895, two cultural artifacts from the life of the river—one song, "The Bully"; one murder that inspired a wealth of songs—both experienced extraordinary journeys through American popular culture. Both, too, chimed in compelling ways with Twain's late vision of the river. Just as *Pudd'nhead Wilson* was a text that meditated on race and crime on the river, so, too, did these roustabout-rooted accounts of violence and murder on the Mississippi explore the same themes, attracting an extraordinary audience along the way. In itself, this was a seminal moment in the history of American music, particularly in cities along the Mississippi. Ragtime was about to soundtrack the death of one century and the birth of another; blues and jazz were fermenting along the river. In different ways, the fragments of roustabout culture that emerged in 1895 catalyzed the development of those vital art forms. In turn, in "The Bully" and the story of Stagolee, decades of vibrant roustabout life and culture from the Mississippi River took shapes that resonate down to the present day. Even though both of these songs emerged in the same place at the same moment, their very different journeys through American popular culture are profoundly revealing.

Though its origins are obscure, "The Bully" was a song that clearly owed its genesis to roustabout life. It narrates a fight between a roustabout and the song's narrator for dominance on the levee. As early as 1894, it received mention in the *Leavenworth (Kans.) Herald*: "Kansas City girls can't play anything on pianos except 'rags,' and the worst kind of 'rags' at that. 'The Bully' and 'Forty Drops' are their favourites."[54] This was also the first printed reference to the musical movement—ragtime—that would come to dominate popular culture. Yet there is other evidence to place the birth of the song on the river. W. C. Handy, so-called and self-proclaimed father of the blues, knew the song in his youth. During a period of destitution in St. Louis in 1893, when Handy was forced to sleep "on the cobblestones of the levee of the Mississippi," he specifically remembered having "heard *Looking for the Bully* sung by the roustabouts [. . .]. I had watched the joy-spreaders rarin' to go when it was played by the bands on the *Gray Eagle*, or the *Spread Eagle*."[55] Similarly, in the preface to the *The Book of American Negro Poetry* (1922), James Weldon Johnson described "The Bully"—the first ragtime song "to become widely known"—as "a levee song which had been long used by roustabouts along the Mississippi."[56]

It was, apparently, a short journey from the river and the levee to the brothel. At some point, "The Bully" apparently became part of the repertoire at one of the most musically significant venues in fin de siècle America. Sarah "Babe" Connors's famous bordello the Castle Club boasted two pioneering musicians: Tom Turpin, the pianist with a good claim for the invention of ragtime; and Letitia Lula Agatha Fontaine, better known as "Mama Lou," a singer who developed and popularized a variety of street songs for performance on the stage ("Ta-ra-ra Boom-de-ay," "Frankie and Johnny," "Hot Time in the Old Town Tonight") before they filtered through into mainstream popular culture.[57] Mama Lou made "The Bully" one of her numbers. Its popularity exploded in extraordinary and unexpected ways when it reached the ears of May Irwin, a Canadian-born singer and comic actress who would become one of the biggest stars of the American stage—thanks, in large part, to "The Bully" itself. Quite how Irwin came across the song is unclear. Most accounts place Charles Trevathan, a sportswriter involved in horse racing, as the point of connection (and Trevathan is listed as the composer on the sheet music copies of the song that also bear Irwin's name). According to one version, recounted by Paul Oliver, they met "while on a train en route to Chicago from San Francisco," and Trevathan sang her the song that he had learned in Babe Connor's place.[58] However she came across it, Irwin's enthusiasm for the song—the song that had traveled to her from roustabout on the levee to sportsman in the brothel—was such that she immediately inserted it in *The Widow Jones,* a farce that opened in Brockton, Massachusetts, in 1895 before transferring to New York. The song, as Susan Ammans notes, "had little, if anything, to do with the play."[59] But audiences didn't mind: and so, in the hands of a vaudevillian with—to borrow David Wondrich's description—a "clear, slightly fruity soprano," "The Bully" became a national phenomenon.[60] In Irwin's mediated version, played for laughs, audiences far and wide were introduced to the violent pleasures of levee culture:

> I'm a Tennessee nigger, and I don't allow,
> No red-eyed river roustabout with me to raise a row.
> I'm lookin' for dat bully, and I'll make him bow
> When I walk dat levee round, round, round.[61]

Propelled by the popularity of "The Bully," *The Widow Jones* ran for two years, with revivals in 1901 and 1902. Its popularity in print also meant that middle-class music makers eagerly transplanted the levee into their homes: in 1896, the *New York Sun* envisaged "every family piano and every family vocalist throughout the land [. . .] playing and singing it."[62] Irwin also recorded a version of the song for Victor in 1907 that remained in their catalogs for a decade.[63]

There were other consequences, too, beyond the reinforcement of an already worn path of cultural appropriation. Just as the river had been crucial to the development of minstrelsy in earlier eras, so the popularity of "The Bully" helped to define a new era of minstrelsy, one dominated by the "coon song" and its vivid racism. At the moment that Irwin took to the stage as an ersatz levee bully, in James Dormon's words, "coon songs proliferated in music hall and vaudeville performances and in sheet music form. Over six hundred of them were published during the decade of the 1890s, and the more successful efforts sold in the millions of copies." "The Bully" was a defining text in this process. Closely linked to the popular emergence of ragtime, coon songs were marked out by a new abrasiveness—a textual violence matched by the virulence of their racial portraits. As Dormon defines it, in these songs, "blacks began to appear as not only ignorant and indolent, but also devoid of honesty or personal honor, given to drunkenness and gambling, utterly without ambition, sensuous, libidinous, even lascivious [. . .] razor-wielding savages." Taken from the river and the levee, where such songs had helped to define a roustabout subculture formed in the face of increasing inequities, "The Bully" became the prime exhibit in a new, wildly popular permutation of minstrelsy that telegraphed the message that black Americans, at the moment that Jim Crow laws were being enshrined by the Supreme Court in *Plessy v. Ferguson*, "must be controlled and subordinated by whatever means necessary."[64]

Stagolee, on the other hand, stayed closer to the river—and, indeed, gained legendary status precisely because of his refusal to be controlled and subordinated. At the heart of his legend lay a Stetson hat. William Lyons, a levee hand in some accounts, was drinking with his friend Lee Shelton in a St. Louis saloon on Christmas evening 1895. At some point, the pair began to argue—perhaps about politics. Then Lyons snatched Shelton's hat from his head. When he wouldn't return it, Shelton shot Lyons dead. From those scant details, a legend emerged, wrapped up in Shelton's nickname: Stagolee (or Stack O'Lee, Stackerlee, Staggerlee, or whatever permutation was preferred by whoever was telling his tale) killed Billy Lyons over the mistreatment of his Stetson hat, and he never repented for that act.

In a host of ways, the river was woven deep into the heart of Stagolee's story as it developed in the popular imagination. Lee Shelton himself, as Cecil Brown has elucidated, did a variety of manual jobs—waiter, carriage driver—but was also likely involved in the St. Louis underworld as a dandyish pimp and the owner of a "lid club," which "catered to gambling and prostitution."[65] Yet most of the oral accounts of Stagolee's story placed him in close relation to the river and the roustabout world. In 1910, a version of the Stagolee song was sent to John and Alan Lomax by Ella Scott Fisher from San Angelo, Texas. According to Fisher, who placed the story's origins in Memphis: "The song is sung by the Negroes on the levee while they are loading and unloading the river freighters, the words being composed by the singers. The characters were prominently known in Memphis, I was told, the unfortunate Stagalee belonging to the family of the owners of the Lee line of steamers, which are known on the Mississippi from Cairo to the Gulf."[66] Another version of the song quoted by the Lomaxes placed the action in New Orleans. Yet the ongoing confusion about the location of the originating murder only highlights the degree to which it clearly filtered along the whole river.

Whether or not the real Stagolee was related to the famous Lee steamboat line, some connection is clearly discernible in his nickname. There certainly was a member of the famous (white) Lee steamboat dynasty called Stacker Lee, born in 1848, who, at the time of his death in 1890, was vice president of the Lee line.[67] From 1901 to 1916, the steamboat *Stacker Lee* worked along the river, named for his memory. The Lomaxes offered up a variety of conflicting voices to explain this connection: "'His real name was Stack Lee and he was the son of the Lee family of Memphis who owned a large line of steamers that ran up and down the Mississippi.' . . . 'He was a nigger what fired the engines of one of the Lee steamers.' . . . 'They was a steamer runnin' up an' down de Mississippi, name de Stacker Lee, an' he was one o' de roustabouts on dat steamer.'"[68] According to Mary Wheeler in *Steamboatin' Days* (1944), her anthology of roustabout songs collected in the early decades of the twentieth century, there was a clear lineage for Stagolee, and it was through female steamboat workers: "Some of the Negroes say that his mother was for many years a chambermaid on the Lee boats"—like Roxy in *Pudd'nhead Wilson*—while "others will tell you that he was born while his mother was a cook on board the *Stacker Lee*."[69]

Even if Lee Shelton didn't have a deep connection to the Mississippi beyond the resonance of his nickname, all of those voices who connected him to the river were speaking a deeper truth. Stagolee fitted so well into roustabout culture and mythology that it is unsurprising that the black men and women who made their lives on and along the river should make him one of their own. When his actions were enshrined in song—according to George Eberhart, the originating ballad was "likely [. . .] first written in the summer of 1896," probably "as a ragtime composition," perhaps by (Shelton's friend) Tom Turpin at the Castle Club—it soon spiraled out into a plethora of adaptations, black and white.[70] It's also clear that the roustabouts helped to develop the song as it flowed out "along the Mississippi River and throughout the rural South as an African American folk ballad."[71] Mary Wheeler certainly found his myth thriving on the riverbanks as late as the 1930s and 1940s. In a fitting culmination of the roustabout's art, Wheeler noted the way that steamboats and badmen were often conflated: "There are many Stacker Lee songs. Some of them can be connected with the packet boat; others center around the personality of a lawless character who was known and feared along the Ohio until a conviction for murder put an end to his career about forty years ago."

The versions that Wheeler collected from the old roustabouts also blurred the lines between "The Bully" and "Stagolee," hybridizing these popular songs. One version pitted them against each other, a perfect distillation in the dying years of the roustabout world:

> Stacker Lee is lookin' fo' the Bully,
> The Bully can't be found,
> Now we're going to walk the levee roun'.

In another, the brutality of Stagolee merged with the brutality of steamboat life for the roustabouts still on the river:

> Oh, Stack in the rivuh, turnin' all roun' an' roun',
> An' I am prayin' fo' the long tall Stack to go down.
> When the women hollerin' "Oh Mr. Stacker Lee,
> Have taken my husban', an' made a trip fo' me."
> Oh, Stack has got ways jes' lak a natural man.[72]

W. C. Handy was steeped in this lore just as much as he was intimate with the cult of "The Bully":

Clarksdale was eighteen miles from the river, but that was no distance for roustabouts. They came in the evenings and on days when they were not loading boats. With them they brought the legendary songs of the river.

> Oh, the Kate's up the river, Stack O' Lee's in the ben',
> Oh, the Kate's up the river, Stack O' Lee's in the ben',
> And I ain't seen ma baby since I can't tell when.[73]

"The Bully" might have metastasized into the popular obsession with the coon song, while "Stagolee" remained the property of the demimonde, but both songs were part and parcel of the same cultural moment occupied by *Pudd'nhead Wilson*. Musically and attitudinally, they helped pave the way for the blues musicians who would soon pick up the roustabout's musical legacy—

as well as their oppositional, rambling, hyper-gendered poses—and take it to the heart of modern American culture. As R. A. Lawson has described, "The men who became blues musicians took on the role of the outsider, the castaway, the drifter" and were "countercultural not only in their often licentious and restless lifestyles but also in their ability to communicate publicly through veiled and coded language."[74] So were the roustabouts—and it is evident, at least, that at the end of the nineteenth century, their songs were the sound of the future as much as an echo of the past. Their importance to W. C. Handy alone was enough to provide them with a certain kind of immortality. When Handy was writing the song that would truly break the blues into America's consciousness in 1914, he was spurred into action by wandering alone along Beale Street in Memphis to absorb the attitude of the "powerfully built roustabouts from river boats" who "sauntered along the pavement, elbowing fashionable browns in beautiful gowns." He witnessed, too, "pimps in boxback coats and undented Stetsons"—reminiscent of Stagolee.[75] And he remembered the songs of the roustabouts, "The Bully" and the song of "Stack O'Lee" chief among them. Then he sat down to write "Saint Louis Blues" and changed the course of American music once again.

"The Measure of His Astonishing Fraud"

Tales of crime and punishment on the Mississippi and river narratives featuring a wide variety of ne'er-do-wells flowed widely through popular culture at century's end. In particular, the figure of the steamboat gambler experienced a remarkable rebirth. These currents certainly found their way into *Pudd'nhead Wilson*, not just in Tom's gambling but also in the general air of corruption, deceit, and hypocrisy that permeates the text. The idea that the river could be a space for dishonesty, double-dealing, and other forms of depredation had been well established in the antebellum years. As early as 1838, Benjamin Drake defined a new "race of modern gentlemen" who could be "found in the valley of the Mississippi," professional gamblers, colloquially known as "blacklegs": "They dress with taste and elegance; carry gold chronometers in their pockets; and swear with the most genteel precision."[76] Instructive narratives warning travelers about the peril of sitting down to gamble with steamboat professionals circulated widely. In particular, the tableaux of a rich planter carelessly gambling away his slaves became a popular abolitionist trope, a defining image of the social ills of the antebellum South. William Wells Brown lamented, from his own experiences on steamboats: "Such is the uncertainty of a slave's position. He goes to bed at night the property of the man with whom he has lived for years, and gets up in the morning the slave of some one whom he has never seen before!"[77]

Twain was certainly aware of this heritage, real and imaginary. According to old river character W. H. Davis—an alleged acquaintance of Twain who was arrested for drunkenness in 1912, at the age of eighty-nine, and interviewed by the *Washington Post*—Twain "wouldn't gamble with them fellers on the boats [. . .]. Mark liked a little game as much as any the rest of us, maybe, but he was mighty particular about who he played with."[78] While in Hannibal in 1882, Twain had made a note to himself in his notebook: "Tell how I once saw a planter gamble a negro away.—Make it realistic.—The negro appeals dumbly to the passengers. Or put this tale in another man's mouth."[79] This story didn't make it into *Life on the Mississippi*—or, indeed, anywhere in print during Twain's lifetime. But in the 1890s, he did address this classic trope of river life in two unpublished sketches, "Newhouse's Jew Story" and "Randall's Jew Story." The first was reportedly told to Twain on the steamboat *Alonzo Child* in 1860 by "an ancient pilot [. . .] George Newhouse" as a memory of the "old time of much poker and high gambling on the boats," when the "professional card-sharp was always in evidence." The second he placed in the mouth of a narrator remembering back to the 1850s, when he was "a brisk young man [. . .] away down the Mississippi, passenger on a steamboat bound for New Orleans." Both stories shared the same essential details: a planter gambles with a professional blackleg, eventually gambling away not only his own slaves but also his daughter's maid: "Mr. Newhouse went into the social hall, and found the passengers packed together around the gaming table, holding their breath for interest. The maid was standing there crying. The gambler had just won her, and was chewing his toothpick nonchalantly and gazing across the table in an amused way at the white-headed planter [. . .]. Then there was a stir in the crowd, and the young mistress came flying down the long cabin with her hair down her back and tears flowing, [. . .] and as the crowd fell apart she swept through and stopped before the gambler and began to plead wildly and pathetically for the maid, saying she was the same to her as a sister." When such pleas avail little with the gambler, a Jewish passenger unknown to the gambler's victims steps forward to challenge the blackleg to a duel. To the acclaim of the boat, the gambler is killed, the maid is returned to her original owner, and the heroic stranger is hailed as "a man; an all-round man; a man cast in a large mould."[80]

Yet by the 1890s, that kind of story was out of favor. In 1896, Tom Ellison, a superannuated blackleg still "tottering about Vicksburg on warm days," would assert, "The river used to be the place for gambling, but that's been dead for over twenty years." Yet the gambler had been rejuvenated in popular culture. Far from being a figure of antebellum censure, he had become something of a hero, expressive of his moment. In response to this cultural shift, another old steamboatman on the St. Louis levee lamented: "It's very pretty to read about, but the real thing was not so nice. The black-eyed, black-mustached hero gambler that you read about was anything but a hero. There was no chivalry in his nature, and he was ready for any dark deed that would profit him."[81] Popular culture warmed to him accordingly. In large part, this was thanks to dime novels. As Ann Fabian has described, "Dime novelists writing in the 1880s used the Mississippi Valley's surviving myths of easy wealth to create the fictional river gamblers who lived by graceful airs and careful ruses, and they sold their tales to the northern readers who were increasingly confined to the small and uncertain gains of wage labour."[82] Rather than their victims, readers now identified with the daring, dashing blacklegs themselves.

Heroic gamblers like "Dan, the River Sport," "Gabe Ganderfoot," "Monte Jim," and "Sandycraw" proliferated, but none had the élan of "Flush Fred," the hero of a series of dime novels written by Edward Willett and released throughout the 1880s: *Flush Fred, the Mississippi Sport; or, Tough Times in Tennessee* (1884); *Flush Fred's Double* (1884); *Flush Fred's Full Hand* (1884); and *Flush Fred, the River Sharp; or, Hearts for Stakes: A Romance of Three Queens and Two Knaves* (1888). So charming is Fred—"a tall and handsome young man, with dark eyes and hair"—that those he beat at cards were more charmed than chagrined by the experience: "I like the young fellow's looks, and I like his style, and I was quite willing that he should win my money. Will you join me, gentlemen, in drinking the health of the man who got the best of us?" Nor is Fred only good at gambling. Making a social call on the pilothouse of the steamboat he's working, Fred is shocked when the pilot suddenly drops dead at a dangerous river crossing. Undaunted, he takes the wheel: "Fred Henning was no pilot. In the mere act of steering he was sufficiently an adept, having practiced it on many boats and in the company of various pilots. He had, moreover, an excellent memory, and the amount of river lore he had accumulated was something remarkable. [. . .] Everything depended on his head and his hands; but he did not flinch." Of course, Fred succeeds in steering the boat to safety and is "the lion of the hour"—a position only compounded when Fred donates a purse raised for him by the grateful passengers to the dead pilot's family.[83] At such a moment, the gambler supplanted the pilot as the representative hero of the Mississippi.

In turn, undoubtedly stimulated by the dime novel successes of their fictional counterparts, a generation of professional gamblers, retired from the river, set about writing down their own memories of life on the Mississippi. Chief among them—at least in his own reckoning—was George Devol, "the most daring gambler in the world." He framed his account of his career as an act of rebellion—a knowing rejection of a workaday life building boats in favor of an adventurous one making easy money on board them (not unlike the dream of becoming a pilot): "I concluded to either quit work or quit gambling. I studied the matter over for a long time. At last one day while we were finishing a boat that we had calked, and were working on a float aft of the wheel, I gave my tools a push with my foot, and they all went into the river. My brother called out and asked me what I was doing. I looked up, a little sheepish, and said it was the last lick of work I would ever do. He was surprised to hear me talk that way, and asked me what I intended to do. I told him I intended to live off of fools and suckers. I also said, 'I will make money rain'; and I did come near doing as I said."[84] That there was something Tom Sawyerish about Devol and his quest for quick riches is plain. His biography is filled with tale after tale relating the ways that he separated "fools and suckers" from their money (and the fights that frequently ensued). But the pleasure in his account comes from the pride Devol takes in the inventiveness and audacity of many of his confidence tricks—the disguises, the ruses, that Devol and his confederates often employed. In his hands, mean and grubby tricks employed against innocent travelers are elevated to the level of subversive performance art; the river becomes an anarchic space of play, with the gambler at its heart.

Frequently, chiming with Twain's concerns in *Pudd'nhead Wilson,* Devol's ploys involved playing with the South's racial fault lines. During one misadventure, Devol escapes from an angry mob by posing as a roustabout: "I saw there was going to be trouble, so I made a sneak for my room, changed my clothes, and then slipped down the back stairs into the kitchen. [. . .] I then blackened my face and hands, and made myself look like a deck-hand." Sneaking off the boat at the next landing, shouldering a load with the other roustabouts, Devol successfully makes a run for it: "It was a pretty close call, but they were looking for a well-dressed man, and not a black deck-hand." More commonly, though, Devol would ape the style of the planter class. He recalls, for example, relieving a New Yorker of his money with a marked card trick: "My partner told him that I was a planter; that I owned six plantations, and so many niggers that I did not know the number myself." Often Devol put on a performance when boarding or leaving a boat to establish an image of wealth and propriety—a performance in which roustabouts were complicit, performing the role of loyal servitude in order to facilitate Devol's predation of the planter class: "I had the niggers all along the coast so trained that they would call me 'Massa' when I would get on or off a boat. If I was waiting at a landing I would post some old 'nig' what to say when I went on board, so while the passengers were all out on the guards and I was bidding the 'coons' good-bye, my 'nig' would cry out: 'Good-bye, Massa George; I's goin' to take good care of the old plantation till you comes back.' I would go on board, with one of the niggers carrying my saddle-bags, and those sucker passengers would think I was a planter sure enough; so if a game was proposed I had no trouble to get into it." For Devol, therefore, there was a cynical morality behind all this. Though hardly working to overturn it, he and his gambler colleagues did little more than exploit the hypocrisies and superficialities of a corrupt society. "A gambler's word is as good as his bond," Devol concluded, "and that is more than I can say of many business men who stand very high in a community."[85]

Not that gambling stories or dime novels were always subversively at odds with the wider narratives about life and race along the Mississippi in this period, nor were gamblers always positioned as heroes in the popular narratives that circulated at this point. Published in 1881—and again in 1902—Colonel Prentiss Ingraham's *Darkie Dan, the Colored Detective; or, The Mississippi Mystery* was a unique dime novel that drew together these trends in ways that also used the same ingredients that Twain combined in *Pudd'nhead Wilson*. Also like Twain's book, it was a detective story with a twist. At one and the same time, *Darkie Dan* features a brave and resourceful African American protagonist at its center while also espousing a Lost Cause philosophy that seems at odds with its eponymous hero. Dan is a slave who gains his freedom at the age of fifteen while saving his young mistress from a pack of wolves. Despite his freedom, Dan chooses—indeed, begs—to remain on the plantation of his youth. Thereafter, he becomes a companion to his previous owner, Fenton Delamere. Years later, the scene shifts to "one of those magnificent Floating Palaces" of the Mississippi. A game is underway, "being played for higher stakes than usual, even among the princely sports of the Mississippi thirty years ago." Fenton Delamare is about to lose all of his fortune to a notorious river sport: "a man who had lately flashed like a meteor before the sporting fraternity, and whose constant success with cards had gained for him the name of the King of Diamonds."

Dan fails in his attempts to dissuade his former master from gambling away his plantation, nor can he save him in the duel that ensues. Yet in the wake of his former master's death, Dan turns undercover detective in order to protect the inheritance of Delamere's children and uncover the nefarious plot that really led to his Delamere's death. In so doing, Dan is as inventive as any riverboat gambler. Alongside a knack for subterfuge—like Devol, moving in the racial blind spots of the South—he is a formidable spirit of vengeance, too, killing a variety of disreputable gamblers on his quest for vengeance. The culmination of his revenge comes at a masked ball at the Hotel St. Louis in New Orleans. As the King of Diamonds breathes his last, Dan makes sure he knows "who has slain you":

> *"Great God! You are Darkie Dan."*
> And the gambler shrank away in an agony of dread even in his dying moments.
> "Yes; I am Darkie Dan, and I have avenged my poor master's death, and all that you made me suffer."

Despite the apparently radical nature of these images of righteous black violence being meted out to deserving white villains (villains attempting, no less, to re-enslave free black Americans), the ending of the dime novel effectively sells Dan into the service of the Confederacy. It imagines a future for him following the young Frank Delamere "through the long years of battling for the Lost Cause"; today Dan, "refusing to meddle in politics [. . .] devotes himself to cotton-planting."[86]

The association between the Mississippi, corruption, and confidence tricks could take many forms, sometimes unlikely ones—even unlikelier than Darkie

Dan. Captain Willard Glazier took the sharp practice of the riverboat gambler and applied it, of all things, to geography. Throughout the late 1880s and beyond, Captain Glazier attempted to convince the world that he had made an extraordinary discovery. Glazier was a self-proclaimed soldier-author who released a steady stream of popular autobiographical works. His first books recounted his experiences in the Civil War, including various escapes from Confederate prisons. Having exhausted that material, he sought out other popular subjects, eventually writing a book exposing the "peculiarities of American cities" in 1884 and an account of his experience crossing the country on horseback eleven years later.[87] But it was the Mississippi that would prove his most important—and controversial—subject. In 1881, Glazier headed to the river with a purpose: despite the fact that most people, and all authorities, considered the matter settled after Henry Rowe Schoolcraft's expedition to Lake Itasca in 1832, Glazier felt that there was "still much uncertainty" about the location of the "true source" of the Mississippi River. So he set out to settle the matter once and for all.

Apparently tapping into the popular fascination with the new age of exploration on the Congo, he explicitly set out to evoke a previous moment of discovery on the Mississippi. His account of his voyage to the true source of the Mississippi was doubly framed both by an introduction that placed Glazier in the lineage of De Soto, La Salle, and more recent explorers and an opening chapter in which Glazier traces his own motivation for his expedition to time spent musing "upon the exploits of the heroic old explorers who led the way to this grand and peerless river of North America." The expedition of discovery itself was a quick affair. After a few days travel upriver, mildly bothered by mosquitoes and low provisions, a native guide leads them beyond Lake Itasca to "one of the most pure and tranquil bodies of water of which it is possible to conceive." Glazier had achieved his mission: "I was confident that we were looking at the TRUE SOURCE of the Great River, and that we had completed a work begun by De Soto, in 1541, and had corrected a geographical error of half a century's standing."[88] Then he set about publicizing his extraordinary discovery.

In literary terms, Glazier unashamedly made the most of things. He recounted the discovery first in 1883 in Sword and Pen; Ventures and Adventures of Willard Glazier, (The Soldier-Author,) in War and Literature—a book credited to John Algernon Owens but clearly written by Glazier himself. A glowing preface declared, "His career has been a romance."[89] Then he devoted an entire volume to his experiences along the Mississippi: *Down the Great River; Embracing an Account of the Discovery of the True Source of the Mississippi* (1887). Initially, at least, those unfamiliar with and distant from the Mississippi took his claims at face value. Glazier's account was convincing enough to merit publication in the *Proceedings of the Royal Geographical Society* in January 1885.[90] Then the net started to close in. Those who knew the territory that Glazier described in the various accounts of his discovery swiftly came to realize that "Lake Glazier" was really the body of water already well-known as Elk Lake. Condemnation of Glazier flared up in a variety of publications. Because of Glazier's use of a canoe during his explorations, both *American Canoeist* and *Outing* made moves to distance themselves from any associated ill repute that might attach to the hobby. *Outing* dismissed both Glazier and his claims summarily: "Canoeing has been practically free from frauds and 'beats' up to the present time, but the increasing popularity of the sport has attracted some rogues to it."[91] Inconveniently for Glazier, *American Canoeist* pointed out that not only was his discovery of "Glazier Lake" not a discovery at all but that a fellow canoeist, A. H. Siegfried, had recently published an account of a canoe journey to the very same territory in *Lippincott's Monthly* in August 1880.[92]

The strongest condemnation came from James H. Baker and the Minnesota Historical Society, who in 1887 published an entire pamphlet refuting Glazier in blistering terms. Having carefully laid out the case against him, including the revelation that Glazier had also plagiarized portions of his narrative of discovery from the accounts of earlier explorers, Baker unloaded: "In the face of these facts, the bold assumption of the man Glazier, is without a parallel in the annals of geographical history. His conduct is a total disregard of all the rule and dignities of a true scientist. Scientific knowledge has scarcely before been made the prey of a charlatan. The measure of his astonishing fraud, has not yet fully penetrated the public mind. [. . .] He has perverted the facts of our early history; told stories of imaginary adventures along our noble streams; deluged the country with false and erroneous maps of the Northern portion of our State, and sought to rob us of ancient names."[93] A charlatan, a fraud, a purveyor of imaginary adventures, a perverter: in many ways, Glazier was right at home on a river that was home to a variety of tricky characters and purveyors of tall tales. The Minnesota Historical Society, apparently still furious with Glazier, went as far as hiring a surveyor to conduct a new review of the headwaters of the Mississippi in 1888. His conclusion, in an open letter to Glazier: "You have falsely, and with shameful erroneousness, endeavoured to appropriate to yourself the honour and fame justly due other and more distinguished gentlemen."[94]

Not one to be daunted by widespread personal condemnation and apparently irrefutable evidence, and possibly encouraged by the notoriety, Glazier went back to the well. Perhaps with little more motivation than stoking the continued ire of the Minnesota Historical Society, Glazier undertook another expedition to the source in 1891 and wrote yet another account of his adventures on the river, in which he critiqued his critics and modestly and blithely concluded: "I simply claim to have established the fact that there is a beautiful lake above and beyond Itasca [. . .] in every way worthy of the position it occupies as the Primal Reservoir or True Source of the Father of Waters."[95] And there, unrepentant, Glazier bowed out of life on the river. Mark Twain was getting ready to bow out too—but not before he had made his last major statement on the Mississippi.

"He Was Getting into Deep Waters"

In the midst of southern reveries, roustabout violence, charming gamblers, and corrupt explorers, Twain set to work on his final Mississippi novel. The genesis of Pudd'nhead Wilson, coming at this time of personal turmoil for Twain, was a confused one. Written in various European locales throughout the early 1890s, metamorphosing from a farce about conjoined twins to a darkly comic tragedy about race in America, Twain only hit upon the final shape of the book in July 1893. Delivering the manuscript to Fred Hall of Webster & Company, Twain described his sense of the book's development: "3 people stand up high, from beginning to end, and only 3—Pudd'nhead, 'Tom' Driscoll, and his nigger mother, Roxana; none of the others are important." Twain had also "knocked out everything that delayed the march of the story— even the description of a Mississippi steamboat. There's no weather in, and no scenery—the story is stripped for flight!"[96] Though that might suggest the marginalization of the river in this book, in truth Pudd'nhead Wilson might represent Twain's most sustained reckoning with the meaning of the Mississippi. Stripped of nostalgia, the bleak logic of the river's terrible racial mechanics are laid bare. In so doing, Twain chimed with many of the other conversations surrounding the river at this moment, mingling racial politics with dime novel adventure, murder, and corruption. Yet in one aspect, *Pudd'nhead Wilson* also represents Twain's most complete account of steamboat life—in particular, its meaning for black Americans. For in the character of Roxana, Twain produced not only his most compelling female character but also the character who best expressed the pleasures and perils of the Mississippi for black Americans in the antebellum years and the final decade of the nineteenth century alike. As Chad Rohman has rightly described: "Using the river as an extrinsic and subtle mechanism, Twain's *Pudd'nhead Wilson* further challenges prevailing notions on race and equality while exposing the dubious truths regarding identity in nineteenth-century America that led to overt racism, radically changed fates, rampant and irreversible injustices, and ironic and pathetic conclusions regarding the fate of many African-Americans left straddling the color line."[97]

The genesis of at least one crucial aspect of the novel seems rooted in Twain's experiences on the Mississippi back in 1882. A clear prompt for the creation of Roxy was the steamboat workers whom he had met on that trip. On the Mississippi near Baton Rouge, Twain's notebook records the way that he "lay in berth all the afternoon listening to the big coloured laundress on guard gossiping with a subordinate." After discussing Twain himself—"Who is Mark Twain," "I dun'no"—and the peculiarities of his nightshirts, they turned to other topics of boat life: "They talked of religion; they black-guarded the colored barber [. . .]. They discussed the ways of rich men—how they come to get their shirts & say they haven't got the change." They talked about the past, too, and the way that memories of slavery still fell over their lives, explicitly refuting the Lost Cause romance that was starting to saturate popular culture:

> At one place one of them said: "That's a mighty beautiful plantation."
> The other replied, "Lordy, Lordy, many a poor nigger has been killed there, just for nuffin, & flung into that river thar' & that's the last of-em." [. . .]
> "I come mighty near being sold down here once; & if I had been I wouldn't been here now; been the last of me."
> The other said, "I was sold once down as far as Miss. I was afraid I'd go furder down. If I had I'd never been here."

They sang "strange plantation melodies" and talked about "one of the colored waiters" who had "got himself burnt in a low down house in Cincin" and was now in "pain & suffering"; in response, they declared, "If I was a girl I wouldn't sleep with no stranger, don't care what he'd pay." Having dismissed the attentions of a young roustabout, one concluded, "I don't want anything to do with *boys*. If I want anybody I want a *man*."[98] At least in part, the genesis of Roxy must rest with these independent, confident, resilient, frank, worldly-wise, and world-weary women—and the ghost of the other such steamboat workers that Twain must have encountered on the river of his youth.

From its opening paragraphs, it is clear that the Mississippi river town of Dawson's Landing is markedly different from the burnished Hannibal of "Old Times on the Mississippi." Indeed, it is like a Gothic reflection of that earlier river vision. To begin with, we are farther down the river: "half a day's journey, per steamboat, below St. Louis."[99] On the surface, it wears a similarly bucolic charm. Yet where Hannibal was "a white town drowsing in the sun," Dawson's Landing is specifically "whitewashed"—here there are things to be covered up, and whiteness is something that can be put on.[100] Though the word *slave* appeared nowhere in "Old Times on the Mississippi," slavery is immediately foregrounded in *Pudd'nhead Wilson*: "Dawson's Landing was a slaveholding town, with a rich slave-worked grain and pork country back of it. The town was sleepy and comfortable and contented." The river is central to town life, but here, too, there is a difference. Rather than the occasional steamboat visitations of "Old Times on the Mississippi," Dawson's Landing is a busy village, a small node in a much larger river network:

> The hamlet's front was washed by the clear waters of the great river [. . .]. Steamboats passed up and down every hour or so. Those belonging to the little Cairo line and the little Memphis line always stopped; the big Orleans liners stopped for hails only, or to land passengers or freight; and this was the case also with the great flotilla of "transients." These latter came out of a dozen rivers—the Illinois, the Missouri, the Upper Mississippi, the Ohio, the Monongahela, the Tennessee, the Red River, the White River, and so on; and were bound every whither and stocked with every imaginable comfort or necessity which the Mississippi's communities could want, from the frosty Falls of St. Anthony down through nine climates to torrid New Orleans.[101]

Setting out this national vision of a Mississippi binding the nation together and bringing the world to Dawson's Landing makes one thing clear: we might be in the South, but whatever happens in a small river town like Dawson's Landing implicates the rest of America.

Another defining aspect of life on the Mississippi and its relationship to slavery is also quickly introduced, at precisely the same moment that the reader first meets Roxy. At the novel's opening, Roxy is enslaved, currently in charge of two babies—her own son and the son of her master, Percy Driscoll: "The white child's name was Thomas à Becket Driscoll, the other's name was Valet de Chambre: no surname—slaves hadn't the privilege." "From Roxy's manner of speech," we are told, in an admiring description, "a stranger would have expected her to be black, but she was not. Only one sixteenth of her was black, and that sixteenth did not show. She was of majestic form and stature, her attitudes were imposing and statuesque, and her gestures and movements distinguished by a noble and stately grace." It is Roxy's reaction to a particular disciplinary threat that crystallizes the sense of the river in this novel. Searching for a suspected thief among his slaves, Percy Driscoll promises a punishment that defines the lives of all of the major characters in the novel: "'I give you one minute'—he took out his watch. 'If at the end of that time you have not confessed, I will not only sell all four of you, *but*—I will sell you down the river!' It was equivalent to condemning them to hell! No Missouri negro doubted this."

The threat, and the reality, of being sold down the river is the defining idea of the novel—the animating prompt of the plot, a continual refrain that echoes through the text a dozen times or more in a variety of permutations. Rather than heaven, it situates the Mississippi as a kind of "hell"—as an inescapable destiny, an inexorable doom. Animated by the fear of this prospect for her small baby—"Her child could grow up and be sold down the river!"—Roxy at first gives in to despair. Like many tragic mulattos before her (Grace King's convent girl or the heroine of William Dean Howells's "Pilot's Story," for example), she plans to drown herself in the Mississippi with her child: "Come along, honey, come along wid mammy; we gwine to jump in de river, den de troubles o' dis worl' is all over—dey don't sell po' niggers down the river over yonder."[102] But then she, and Twain, changes the familiar script. Instead of suicide, she enacts an audacious scam: she swaps the babies in her care in their cradles, freeing her child and enslaving her master's son. It is a confidence trick, an act of disguise, a shell game clever enough to impress any gambler. And like those blacklegs, the counterfeit Tom spends the rest of the narrative masquerading, knowingly and unknowingly, as the scion of a rich planter.

Beyond its narrative position as abstract threat, the Mississippi has a significant role to play in the lives of all these characters. The swapped boys grow up side by side and romp in the river. But there is no comradeship between them; unlike in *The Prince and the Pauper*, the river has no lessons to offer these transplanted boys; unlike *Adventures of Huckleberry Finn*, it does not offer a liminal space of kinship between free and enslaved, however fleeting. Instead, it becomes a space for Tom—Roxy's son, now master—to bully Chambers, the Driscoll heir, now enslaved: "Tom always made Chambers go in swimming with him, and stay by him as a protection. When Tom had had enough, he would slip out and tie knots in Chambers's shirt, dip the knots in the water and make them hard to undo." When Chambers saves Tom from drowning, the humiliation tips him into violence—"Tom sprang at him and drove his pocket-knife into him two or three times before the boys could snatch him away"—the first hint that Tom, though a coward, will also become a permutation of the roustabout and the river badman, a spoiled Stagolee in training. Next Tom tries to get his father to "sell the boy down the river"—a malicious act that even manages to offend the sensibilities of Dawson's Landing.[103]

Roxy, though, has rather a different experience on the Mississippi. When Percy Driscoll dies, Roxy is freed and decides to take to the river: "She would go chambermaiding on a steamboat, the darling ambition of her race and sex." During her eight years on the river, she comes close to achieving her aim to "be independent of the human race thenceforth forevermore if hard work and economy could accomplish it." Moreover, she is part of a community that Twain paints as verily utopian, at least in comparison to the alternatives depicted in the novel; the steamboat is the only safe space in her river world. Roxy is swiftly "infatuated [. . .] with the stir and adventure and independence of steamboat life" on board the *Grand Mogul*: "Then she was promoted and became head chambermaid. She was a favorite with the officers, and exceedingly proud of their joking and friendly way with her."[104]

Unfortunately, after a brief stint at Yale, Tom also discovers the appeal of life on the Mississippi. He succumbs to the familiar temptations of river life: "He began to make little trips to St. Louis for refreshment. There he found companionship to suit him, and pleasures to his taste, along with more freedom, in some particulars, than he could have at home. So, during the next two years his visits to the city grew in frequency and his tarryings there grew steadily longer in duration. He was getting into deep waters. He was taking chances, privately, which might get him into trouble some day—in fact, did." Drinking and gambling, the twin pillars of young planter behavior on the Mississippi, leave Tom perilously in debt (a subject close to Twain's heart at this moment) and under threat of disinheritance by his adoptive uncle. Thereafter, the river becomes a vital conduit of corruption for his increasingly desperate schemes to correct his fortunes. Like riverboat gamblers, he adopts disguises in order to rob his neighbors' houses—only, in turn, for his ill-gotten goods to be stolen from him on the crooked river: "A brother-thief had robbed him while he slept, and gone ashore at some intermediate landing."[105]

Events conspire to bring Roxy and Tom back together. Retiring from the river with a small nest egg, Roxy is soon made "a pauper, and homeless," after the bank in which she invested her money collapses (another financial reversal). Her old steamboat colleagues raise a purse for her, and she decides to return to Dawson's Landing. At first, the fame of her steamboat years brings her some pleasure among her old friends (again, perhaps echoing Twain's own experiences): "She was obliged to confess to herself that if there was anything better in this world than steamboating, it was the glory to be got by telling about it." But when Tom, as her old charge, rebukes her request for money and she discovers that he has been gambling, Roxy attempts to take charge of her wayward, one-time son. She reveals to him the secret of his parentage, much to his horror, and eventually devises a scheme to reestablish his fortunes: "Here is de plan, en she'll win, sure. I's a nigger, en nobody ain't gwyne to doubt it dat hears me talk. I's wuth six hund'd dollahs. Take en sell me, en pay off dese gamblers." Roxy intends that Tom should sell her "down in de middle o' Kaintuck somers" before repurchasing her freedom in a year's time; instead, for the sake of expediency, "Tom forged a bill of sale and sold his mother to an Arkansas cotton-planter." Though the planter assures Tom that Roxy won't be aware of her fate until she is safely ensconced on his plantation, she knows the river too well for that subterfuge to work: "She! Why, she had been steamboating for years. [. . .] Her practised eye fell upon that telltale rush of water." Reading the river like any experienced Mississippi worker, the terrible truth breaks upon her: "I's sole down de river!"[106]

The indefatigable Roxy refuses to give in to this turn of events, though. She relates a miniature slave narrative, in which Twain affords her a degree of self-determination largely refused to a character like Jim. Moreover, in outlining the cruelties of Roxy's new experience of slavery down the river, Twain gave his frankest account of the realities of slavery, a significant gesture that was out of step with the sentimental renderings of the Old South that were circulating widely at this moment. Suffering on the Arkansas plantation, "wore out wid de awful work en de lashin's, en so downhearted en misable," Roxy decides to make an escape. Enraged when an overseer beats a child in front of her, Roxy knocks him down with a stick. Seizing her chance, she runs—in the direction, of course, of the river, "as tight as I could go." All too aware of the fate that would come with recapture—either worked to death or sold "furder down de river"—Roxy again turns to thoughts of suicide: "I 'lowed to drown myself en git out o' my troubles." But again, she finds a different kind of salvation in the river. Spotting a canoe, still a symbol of freedom and potential, Roxy heads out onto the Mississippi—still a space of hard-earned liberty and self-definition: "I went on a-spinnin' down de river. I paddled mo'n two hours, den I warn't worried no mo', so I quit paddlin', en floated down de current, considerin' what I 'uz gwine to do if I didn't have to drown myself." Luckily for Roxy, the river still harbors some slight sense of community. She comes across a steamboat making repairs and immediately recognizes "de shape o' de chimbly-tops ag'in' de stars, en den good gracious me, I 'most jumped out o' my skin for joy! It 'uz de *Gran' Mogul*." Quickly, she makes herself comfortable, reclaiming her throne: "I tromped right along 'mongst 'em, en went up on de b'iler deck en 'way back aft to de ladies' cabin guard, en sot down dah in de same cheer dat I'd sot in 'mos' a hund'd million times, I reckon; en it 'uz jist home ag'in, I tell you!"[107] In triumph, she steams past the plantation from which she has just escaped.

Now needing to evade recapture, Roxy disguises herself—as a man: "a wreck of shabby old clothes, sodden with rain and all a-drip [. . .] a black face under an old slouch hat," complete with some "cold steel."[108] In short, she has become a roustabout. Threatened with exposure by Roxy unless he buys back her freedom, Tom also resorts to desperate measures. Blacked-up and disguised as a woman, Tom is caught in the act of robbing his uncle, Judge Driscoll, and murders him. The question of what these separate, ironic minstrel acts (crossing both gender and racial lines) signify is central to most interpretations of the novel. For Henry Wonham, for example, the echoes of "coon song" imagery here and elsewhere means that Tom is marked "unmistakably as a 'coon,' according to the period's rigid vocabulary of racial stereotypes." While the "success of Roxy's revolutionary act of racial inversion might at first appear to suggest that for Twain the color line is deceptively fluid," Wonham argues that Twain ultimately "embraces coon caricature on its own terms as the period's only available discourse of racial identity."[109] The wider context of river life and its popular depictions at this moment complicates this conclusion, though. In the case of Tom, collapsing into coon stereotype as the novel develops, that is certainly a plausible reading—though it is also conceivable that his behavior is the product less of his genetics than his spoiled position as a member of a planter class for whom drinking, gambling, and violence along the Mississippi were central markers of identity in the antebellum years. Either way, his story cuts against comfortable narratives of the Old South. Roxy, though, is a denizen and a product of a different river—the subaltern Mississippi of roustabouts and chambermaids, of a culturally rich steamboat world that celebrated figures like Stagolee and the Bully before they mutated into coon song stereotypes—and remains a genuinely revolutionary character who, though ultimately trapped by the grim logic of the antebellum river world, does her best to use the Mississippi as a space of rebellion and self-definition by any means necessary.

In the end, of course, Roxy's plans come to nothing. At the murder trial that closes the novel, Pudd'nhead Wilson reveals her originating baby swap and proves Tom guilty of the murder of his uncle: "Roxy's heart was broken. The young fellow upon whom she had inflicted twenty-three years of slavery continued the false heir's pension of thirty-five dollars a month to her, but her hurts were too deep for money to heal; the spirit in her eye was quenched, her martial bearing departed with it, and the voice of her laughter ceased in the land. In her church and its affairs she found her only solace." Though beaten by the system, Roxy is at least free. Tom, however, is not so lucky. Found guilty of murder, he escapes execution by being re-enslaved by the creditors of the Driscoll estate. And then, fulfilling the bleak inevitability of the antebellum river, he is "sold down the river."[110]

"Everything's So Solemn"

"Sold down the river": Twain's last major literary statement on the Mississippi leaves the reader with a tragic vision of river life. It was, apparently, the last step in a process of disillusionment in which the celebratory nostalgia of Twain's early statements about river life in the decade after the Civil

War collapsed into a despair that for Twain was both a product of the social shifts of American life in the last years of the nineteenth century and an intensely personal reaction to the vicissitudes of his own fortunes. Twain was in deep water; he was not alone. Unable or unwilling to conjure the dream of the Mississippi again, reaching the end of the arc he had begun with "Old Times on the Mississippi" two decades earlier, he left the river behind. Not entirely: river memories would still filter into his correspondence, and in his final years, it could still provoke him, still haunted him. Indeed, not long after *Pudd'nhead Wilson,* in 1896, he returned to the river again for *Tom Sawyer, Detective.* Like *Pudd'nhead Wilson,* the last published adventures of Huck and Tom also dealt with theft, confidence tricks, and murder along the Mississippi, here played for entertainment without the undertow of that previous book. In spite of the forced fun, the most indelible image in the book comes from its opening, narrated by Huck. It is a vision of the river containing echoes of the famous sunrise in *Adventures of Huckleberry Finn* but now weighted with a profound sense of finality: "The big Mississippi down there a-reaching miles and miles around the points where the timber looks smoky and dim and it's so far off and still, and everything's so solemn it seems like everybody you've loved is dead and gone, and you 'most wish you was dead and gone too, and done with it all."[111] Yet still, Twain wasn't quite done with it all. He toyed with another intriguing story that revolved around the river, set in the same world as *Pudd'nhead Wilson* and with similarly radical implications. It also featured, in a starring role, a female character that transcended social norms. The surviving fragment that survives revolves around the fortunes of two characters—Oscar "Thug" Carpenter and Rachel "Hellfire" Hotchkiss, the titular heroine. Both of these characters push against the gendered expectations of their place and time. As one character describes: "Pudd'nhead Wilson says Hellfire Hotchkiss is the only genuwyne male man in this town and Thug Carpenter's the only genuwyne female girl, if you leave out sex and just consider the business facts."

True to this inversion of roles, when Oscar Carpenter becomes trapped on breaking ice on the Mississippi River while skating with his friends, it is Hellfire Hotchkiss who rides in to save the day: "A trim and fair young girl, bareheaded and riding bareback and astride, went thundering by on a great black horse [. . .] with her welcome roaring about her. Evidently she was a favourite." Rachel swims out to his ice floe with a life preserver and helps him to safety. This is hardly her only accomplishment—she was also the "smartest boxer in town"; she had taught herself to swim in the river; she "fished, boated, hunted, trapped"; she breaks horses for fun.[112] But having created this dynamic heroine who had proven her bravery in the freezing waters of the Mississippi, Twain could apparently take the fragment no further. Hellfire Hotchkiss remains only a tantalizing tributary in Twain's river writings. Yet if Twain couldn't navigate that stream, he still had miles to go before he would follow his Mississippi to its end. He had one river trip left in him and countless journeys to take in memory. And around him, at the beginning of a new century, others were rediscovering the Mississippi—now, in large part, his Mississippi—anew.

Epilogue

"A BLACK WALL OF NIGHT"

The majesty and glory of the Great River have departed;
its glamour remains, fresh and undying, in the memories of those who,
with mind's eye, still can see it as it was a half-century ago. [. . .]
Its glamour is that indefinable witchery with which memory clothes
the commonplace of long ago, transfiguring the labors, cares,
responsibilities, and dangers of steamboat life as it really was,
into a Midsummer Night's Dream of care-free,
exhilarating experiences, and glorified achievement.
—GEORGE BYRON MERRICK, 1909

I wish the Mississippi River were drained. Such a torment as it has been.
—MARK NOAILLES MURFREE, 1908

Ever and anon I hear of the death of some old comrade of the river,
whose name recalls the fragrant memories of other days.
—MARK TWAIN, 1902

A dream and a torment: as the age of Mark Twain became history in the early twentieth century, the polarization of what the Mississippi meant—and continued to mean—became ever more profound. It was, after all, the dichotomy that sat at the heart of Twain's river books. George Byron Merrick was one of a number of writers who attempted to capture the golden age of the Mississippi in print as it passed out of experience and memory. Unlike most of them, Merrick himself had also been a steamboat pilot on the Mississippi; like Samuel Clemens, he had left the river on the eve of the Civil War. Merrick understood the cultural process that was at work in transforming the "commonplace" of river life into "glamour." Yet he was also susceptible to the appeal of this "Midsummer Night's Dream" and lamented the passing of the river's golden age. Along with providing a history of "old times on the Upper Mississippi," personal and general, Merrick looked back longingly to the world of his youth that had gone forever. Proclaiming that "civilization has been its undoing"—just as it had been for the "wild tribes which peopled its banks sixty years ago"—Merrick blamed deforestation for the changes in water level that had reduced the Mississippi "to the dimensions of a second-rate stream." Now, he asserted, to "most men of our day," life on the Mississippi in its golden age "is legendary, almost mythical." To those "few participants who yet remain, it is but a memory." As far as Merrick was concerned, the river's "story is unwritten."[1]

As if in response, a multitude of others took to the theme. Popular histories of the river began appearing in the early years of the twentieth century; their evocation of the now lost world of steamboating and its glamour became ever more romantic. John Habermehl evoked "life on the Western Rivers" in 1901 ("interesting to all classes in learning something of the olden times of this hard life, with some spicy scenes"); in 1910, Julius Chambers explored "the Mississippi River and its wonderful valley" ("Such a theme is worthy of a wondersmith in words"); Herbert and Edward Quick went "Mississippi steamboatin'" in 1926 ("one of our most valuable heritages, gleaming with the sheen of romance"); Garnett Laidlaw Eskew hymned "the pageant of the packets" in 1929 ("Where shall I find it—that strange music, gone, / Of steamboat whistles blowing in the dawn?"); the same year, Irvin Anthony told tales of "paddle wheels and pistols" ("And the river, what does it think of it all? [. . .] quiet at the last, done with its thousand cities and the tales of men").[2] Onward the flood continued.

In many ways, through such books, this was the moment that the Mississippi—to quote Christopher Morris—became a fully "imagined river, frozen in time and place [. . .] trotted out for sentimental reasons," too often the subject of "tiresome and clichéd" commentary.[3] Yet in other unrecognized ways, in story and song, the Mississippi charted a new course through American life in the early decades of the twentieth century; the unpredictable river still had some surprises to offer. *Pudd'nhead Wilson* remained Twain's last major statement on the river. In the sixteen years between the publication of that novel and his death, in 1910, Twain never again centered the Mississippi in his writings. Not that the river had left his thoughts: in his autobiography, the Mississippi remained a topic to which he returned repeatedly. One last time, he would return to the river itself. Yet around him, the Mississippi took on a new life; other waters rushed in to fill the vacuum that Twain left. Across a variety of media, the river was revivified as a quintessentially American symbol, rich in meaning, and not just as romantic Americana (even if that pose predominated). In some ways, this was simply the continuation of stories established in the previous decades. As Twain's Mississippi became increasingly archetypal, other streams of representation and imagination that had bubbled up from the river in the years after the Civil War also widened and broadened through American culture. Canoeists still took to the river enthusiastically, accompanied now by a wealth of houseboaters, looking for similar forms of escape; the music of roustabouts, or at least the image of it, still echoed through popular culture; the river's role as an icon of the South persisted, no less ambiguously. Many writers who had known the Mississippi Valley in their youth—friends of Twain—also came back to the river in old age. All of those who were part of this inundation were conscious that they now traveled on an imagined stream that Twain had powerfully helped to shape. But like the jazz music that it would help to birth, the Mississippi was still a multivocal thing—a chorus of competing and complementary voices, each winding out its own visions of the river.

"We Love the River, Damn It!"

Public discourse around the river in the early years of the twentieth century was not marked by optimism; the river could indeed be a torment. The tensions between industry and wilderness, control and freedom, continued. Ongoing economic misery—the familiar refrains of the railroads, low water, and other obstructions to navigation—was only compounded by a sequence of punishing floods throughout the early years of the twentieth century, with notably bad years in 1903, 1912, and 1913. As Christine Klein and Sandra Zellmer have described, such events "left most Mississippi valley residents physically and economically exhausted."[4] Far from being the iconic artery of internal commerce and American industrial might of the antebellum years or even the recherché path to faded glory of later decades, to many observers the river now seemed to be simply a provincial backwater that was a perennial problem in American life.

Not that everyone had given up on the river: in 1905, boosters from towns stretching along the Mississippi formed a "Lakes-to-the-Gulf Deep Waterway Association" in the quest for a fourteen-foot river channel from Chicago to New Orleans. But hopes were dashed when representatives from the East Coast and Great Lakes "strenuously opposed" such federal intervention.[5] President Theodore Roosevelt—who described the Mississippi, to an audience of New Orleanians, as "at once their most valuable asset and their most dangerous liability"—also made moves to improve the social and economic life of the river on a federal level.[6] He established the Inland Waterways Commission in 1907 in an attempt to develop a comprehensive national water policy that would circumvent such regional rivalries and reinvigorate the nation's water transport systems. It, too, ultimately achieved little. Attempts to control the river were still largely limited to ad hoc levee construction, floods continued, and economic stagnation persisted.

In the *North American Review* in 1914, Speaker Champ Clark (a Democrat from Missouri) labeled the river "a perennial national problem in the United States" and lamented that the "states on the lower river had been struggling, unaided, without cessation against the ruthless enemy, while Congress was doing nothing."[7] But for the *Century Magazine,* and for others, this was a regional matter, and the situation was truly "a duty of the South to itself": "It would be too much to say that the South holds in its hands the power of forever preventing the floods of the Mississippi; but we sincerely believe that it has the unused power of greatly reducing them."[8] British engineer Sir William Willcocks—designer of the Aswan Dam and other feats of water control—visited the river in 1914 and brought a different perspective to bear on the central questions. Willcocks pointedly critiqued the "failure" of American attempts to control the river. "Many millions have been expended," he asserted, "and still the people are disconcerted by the presence of the river's water in their parlors when a high flood comes." Part of the issue, he diagnosed, was "more a problem of your national psychology than of your river. You treat the Mississippi as if it were a river apart, differing utterly from all other streams. It is nothing of the sort. It is just like all other rivers."[9] Americans—southerners in particular—weren't inclined to agree with his attempts to prick the bubble of exceptionalism that had long surrounded conceptions of the river. Certainly, other accounts of the Mississippi at this moment did little to challenge the idea that this river, whatever else it might be, was not like all other rivers.

By 1917, the *Literary Digest* would characterize the river as a "great national highway almost unused."[10] This state of affairs was thrown into even sharper relief by the development of another important waterway. The discussions about the Mississippi's economic future at this moment were given an added impetus by the feverish discussion that surrounded the millions that were being invested in the Panama Canal, from the moment that it was taken into American hands in 1904 until (and after) it finally opened in 1914. It was hoped that the creation of the Panama Canal would improve the fortunes of the Mississippi. As George Blakeslee outlined in the *Outlook* in 1915: "The opening of the Canal has already stimulated an important movement for the adequate development of this river route. The business interests of the Mississippi Valley have now come to realize that they must have cheap all-water communication to the Pacific Coast in order to compete with the low freight charges through the Canal at present enjoyed by the Atlantic seaboard." In 1915, at least, this was still a hope deferred: "At present, however, adequate facilities for shipping cargoes along this route do not exist, and the inland cities which have been looking forward to a great freight movement along the Mississippi towards the Gulf and Panama are complaining bitterly because shipments for the Pacific are going to Panama by way of New York and other Atlantic ports. [. . .] New Orleans [. . .] has received little, if any, gain in traffic movement on account of the Canal."[11] In 1909, the "St. Louis Business Men's League" even chartered the steamboat *Alton* to transport its members to New Orleans with the purpose of campaigning and organizing for "deep water to the Gulf [. . .] and all of the attendant blessings." At the end of their trip, David R. Francis, chairman of the Missouri delegation, gave voice to the assembled frustrations: "I would have Congress, if I had the power, declare for the improving of the Mississippi River, or rather the building of this waterway from the lakes to the Gulf, as it declared itself concerning the Panama Canal."[12]

Raymond S. Spears, writing about the Mississippi in the *Atlantic* in September 1908, crystallized many of these issues, elucidating the ambiguities that surrounded the river at this moment. He was adamant that the Mississippi was "the greatest irritant in the United States. Its fickleness, conscious power, and taunting eddies bring oaths to the lips of the most respectable and law-abiding residents along its lower course." According to Spears, the residents of "St. Louis, Vicksburg, Memphis, and other river towns" longed for "the sight of the river humbled and humiliated and in shackles." But Spears also understood that those who lived alongside it retained a potent emotional investment in the river. "Talk to a Mississippi River man," Spears suggested, "shanty-boater, pilot, raftsman, plantation owner, or city merchant,—and he will brag about the river wonders. Its bigness charms him, and makes him feel large and elated. [. . .] 'We love the river, damn it!' is a literal expression."[13]

The same contradictions lay at the heart of the river's appearances in the late-career work of a pair of southern writers who had risen to fame at the same moment as Twain in the local color boom of the late nineteenth century. Taken together, Ruth McEnery Stuart's *The River's Children: An Idyl of the Mississippi* (1904) and Mary Noailles Murfree's *The Fair Mississippian* (1908) and *The Story of Duciehurst: A Tale of the Mississippi* (1914) represent a small and almost entirely neglected corpus of Mississippi writings. As a group, they can be seen as part of what Jennifer Rae Greeson has described as "a veritable flood of literary portrayals of the Reconstruction South" that "swamped the U.S. cultural marketplace" in the early twentieth century—texts that "retold the Reconstruction South from a variety of ideological perspectives."[14] Though their competing interpretations of the river and Reconstruction diverged dramatically, what links these texts is their conception of the Mississippi as a space that exemplified recent changes to the South; symbolically charged floods and ruined steamboats abound. The Mississippi emerges as part river-god, part southern *grand dame*—capricious, often implacable, occasionally benevolent, and a powerful agent of change and destruction.

As contemporary reviews recognized, Stuart's *The River's Children* was fully engaged with the idea of the Mississippi as a southern deity. For the *Literary Digest*, Stuart "turns the noble old river into a thing of sentient life to its children, endowing it with a soul to appeal to and conjure with."[15] Throughout the book, characters pray to, sacrifice to, and baptize themselves in the waters of the Mississippi (not unlike Cable's *Grandissimes*). Told briefly, the narrative revolves around the reunion of planter Harold Le Duc and his daughter, Agnes. Agnes is presumed to have drowned in a Mississippi flood during the Civil War but, in the intervening six years, has been cared for by Le Duc's former slaves Hannah and Israel. As that précis suggests, the sympathies of the book are firmly with the Old South. Yet in ways that complicate that reading, the novel also represents one of the most sustained meditations on the Mississippi's symbolic value in its depiction of the Reconstruction South.

From its opening scenes of threatened flood (as one nervous Creole planter marvels, "De ruling lady of dis low valley country [. . .] is Old Lady Mississippi!"), the river saturates the text. Agnes is raised on a levee in "the ladies' cabin of an old Mississippi steamboat, still shabbily fine in white paint and dingy gilding, which Israel had reclaimed from an abandoned wreck." In this powerfully emblematic space, Hannah and Israel tell biblical stories to Agnes—"the Eden story was easily favorite"—while reminiscing about life before the war. Le Duc's plantation is itself figured as an antebellum "Eden."[16] When Le Duc is wounded and captured during the Civil War, his paradise collapses, and the flood that is thought to have drowned his daughter destroys his plantation.

The ultimate moment of reunion between master and former slaves takes place on the river itself—in Israel's skiff, as he unwittingly ferries Le Duc across the Mississippi. For Hannah, in the spiritual heart of the novel, this moment exemplifies the "mericle mystery" of the Mississippi: "Look like ef we'd ever went beyan' de river's call, we'd been same as de chillen o'Isrul lost in de tanglement o' de wilderness. All we river chillen, we boun' to stay by her, same as toddlin' babies hangs by a mammy's skirts. She'll whup us one day, an' chastiste us severe; den she'll bring us into de light, same as she done to-night—same as reel mammies does." Nor is the extraordinary image of the Mississippi as Mammy the final word on the river in this novel. Apparently in thanks, Hannah immerses herself in the Mississippi, an act described as a "last communion"; that night, as she and her husband sleep, the river washes away their cabin. Yet their influence—as well as the influence of the Mississippi itself—lives on. As the book closes, the reader encounters an older Agnes, who, having been ecumenically educated "alternately in Louisiana [. . .] and in New England," is steaming toward New Orleans to be crowned Queen of Carnival at Mardi Gras. "My dear old Mammy," Agnes asserts (though whether she means Hannah or the Mississippi itself is unclear), "taught me to love the river, and perhaps I am a little sentimental over it. I hope always to be so." Ultimately, Stuart pictures the Mississippi, not least through Agnes, "uniting while she seems to divide, bringing together whom she appears to separate"— while apparently erasing black life and culture from its banks.[17]

Mary Murfree's conception of the river was more commensurate with the sense of stagnation that colored other accounts of the Mississippi at this moment. Though she forged her career writing about mountain life in Tennessee, her turn to the river in her final novels was really a return to her roots: her family had owned plantations along the Mississippi. This was no happy homecoming, though: Murfree's river—as Benjamin Fisher has described it in almost the only piece of scholarship directed to her Mississippi works—is more "nightmare" than idyll.[18] In a world turned upside down socially and economically ("The rich are the poor; the right are the wrong," as one of her characters despairs), the river is imagined as the central agent of that destruction.[19] Both *The Fair Mississippian* and *The Story of Duciehurst* revolve around tangled inheritance claims to river plantations; in both books, the Mississippi is a constant source of danger.

In *The Fair Mississippian*, much of the peril comes courtesy of Jed Knoxton, an itinerant river rat whose shantyboat (a "dingy and plebeian craft") makes a landing near the plantation of Great Oaks—home of heroine Mrs. Faurie, her son, and her son's tutor, Edward Desmond. Knoxton is a prime avatar of Murfree's Mississippi: he is "a sodden, amphibious, nondescript animal [. . .] hardly frog, hardly fish, hardly water-rat, yet partaking of the characteristics of all three." In an argument over stolen property, Knoxton physically assaults Faurie and Desmond; later, accompanied by his fellow "river pirates," Knoxton cuts Great Oaks's levee during a period of high water and launches an attack on the house that ends only when Desmond shoots him in the head. Though the plantation is finally saved (from flood, the lower orders, and legal challenge), it is little wonder that the river drives Mrs. Laurie to an extraordinary vision of the Mississippi as charnel house, a watery grave running through the South like a festering wound: "I wish the Mississippi River were drained. Such a torment as it has been. What a queer thing its channel would be, though. [. . .] Boats unnumbered, of all sizes and pretensions [. . .]. Then the bones of all the people that have gone down in the fires and collisions and swampings and sinkings to their watery graves! The nations, the races, they are all represented there, and who knows what prehistoric people [. . .] under tons and tons of the ooze and mud of the Mississippi."[20] Murfree was hardly less morbid in *The Story of Duciehurst*. The book begins with a vivid image of southern stasis and stagnation: "Dead low water and there the steamboat lay on the sand-bar, stranded and helpless." And there the *Cherokee Rose* remains for the duration of the novel, slowly rotting while marriages and murders are cemented on its stricken decks. A hurricane begins the dismantling: "The smoke-stacks of the *Cherokee Rose* crashed down [. . .]. The boat yawed over, suddenly smitten." Thereafter, she becomes a "very melancholy [. . .] spectacle" and an image of dilapidation and decay that is a perfect analogue for Murfree's vision of the Reconstruction South: "Waters swirled around her, and fish swam through her cabin doors and the slime and ooze of the river had befouled the erstwhile dapper whiteness of her guards and saloon walls." By the end of the novel, the titular plantation has been washed away by the river, its false claimant with it, yet the *Cherokee Rose* abides, "white and stark, skeleton-wise, like bleaching bones on the sand-bar."[21]

Alongside those images of death, destruction, and decay, the Mississippi could also still serve as a route of liberation—or attempted liberation—from the cares of the world. The legacy of the pioneer canoeists of the 1870s and 1880s was clear. Heading down the river in small craft of various designs was still an escapade apparently worth pursuing. Now, though, these canoeists paddled along Twain's river. Albert S. Tousley, in *Where Goes the River* (1928), traveled the length of the Mississippi from source to gulf. He saw the Mississippi as "the nation's river" but understood his journey to be an individual attempt to "know its moods and moments, loves and hates, beauties and terrors, smiles and frowns," with metaphysical implications: "I wanted to associate with the spirits of Indians and explorers, to traverse the river whereon had gone great personalities, to be one of the few who had known all the river and loved it. [. . .] I learned that the greatest force in America is this river, and that within oneself there is freedom from practically everything. One who has taken this journey need never bicker over creeds and sects: this river becomes to him part of religion, an apostle itself of God." He went looking for something—someone—else too. "We were in Mark Twain's land!" he announced near Hannibal. "We saw Tom and Huck through the trees, as we threaded our way among islands. Then came their shouts of discovery and a rush to their canoe and a paddle to meet us." Just as "a steamboat came puffing upriver," the vision disappeared.[22] Similarly, Major Rowland Raven-Hart paddled his canoe all over the world, but when he set out in his *Canoe Errant on the Mississippi* (1938), there was only one place to begin: "The cruise started at Hannibal [. . .] home of Tom Sawyer and Mark Twain." He pondered, "Is it realized in America how these books are read and loved by British boys?" He quoted "Jim Bludso," too, and lamented the degree to which America had apparently turned its back on a river that was still alive in his imagination. Traveling by rail to St. Louis in advance of his trip, Raven-Hart heard a fellow passenger inquire, "What that river was?" "Had it been a tributary I could have forgiven him, but not to know when one is in the presence of the 'Father of Waters' comes perilously close to *lèse-majesté*—not that the Mississippi seemed to notice the insult."[23]

The canoeists were soon outnumbered by the enthusiasts of another kind of rivercraft—one that also spoke to the desire for escape, from convention as well as the pressures of everyday life. The fashion for houseboats and shanty-boats was significant in the early decades of the twentieth century. Ben Lucien Burman estimated that when he knew the river in the 1920s and 1930s, as many as thirty thousand houseboats were scattered along the Mississippi and its tributaries. Of course, a home on the river had always been a necessity for some; the canoeists of the 1870s and 1880s had testified as much. The steamboat tourists of the late nineteenth and early twentieth centuries framed them in a different, more bohemian light. When William Aylward went "steamboating through Dixie," he recognized that the contemporary river served for many as an escape route from modern life notably distinct from the retreat into nostalgia that flavored other accounts of the river. "It is an interesting phase of Mississippi life," Aylward explained, "the really vast scattered population that makes its home upon either the river or its tributaries." "River People," he felt, experienced "a sort of outlaw life beyond the jurisdiction of bordering states." Such an existence demonstrated a kind of rough equality that stood in stark contrast to the steamboat hierarchy: "He may be of any color, of any nationality, or any creed or none; honest man or thief, mill-hand with children in school, a hopeless tramp seeking quiet pastoral nooks, or an arrant rogue pilfering as he goes." The epitome of this life, for Aylward, was the "New Era Floating Theater": "From all accounts it is a picturesque life not without incident, and offering opportunity galore for him who would hunt and fish as well as strut the boards [. . .] where audiences are easily amused and existence is a simple thing." In this guise, the Mississippi seemed to offer "the undeniable charm of a life of perfect freedom, drifting as fancy dictates from place to place." Moreover, it seemed to Aylward to provide access to the "real America."[24]

The new breed of houseboaters apparently shared Aylward's sentiments as well as the canoeists' propensity to write about their river journeys. In 1904, William Waugh—lamenting that "the great American people reside in the valley of the greatest river in the world, and pay no attention to it"—laid out the pleasures of houseboating as he saw them: "a broad river, the boat lazily floating, children fishing, wife's cheery call to view bits of scenery too lovely for solitary enjoyment, and a long year of blissful seclusion where no tale of woe could penetrate [. . .]. Here was a scheme to make the heart of a city-tired man leap."[25] For unlike the canoe, the houseboat also dissolved the boundaries of travel and everyday life, of wilderness and domesticity, turning a river journey into a liminal, open-ended experience. It was a dream that particularly seems to have held a romantic appeal for newlyweds. In 1911, John Lathrop Mathews described himself and his new wife, Janet, as "gypsies by nature" who "had roamed the woods and fields together in happy freedom." Their houseboat was "was to be a honeymoon boat" as well as an escape from respectability: "We would throw aside our formal, conventional selves, and step for a brief season into the full fellowship of wanderers [. . .] water gypsies in a floating van."

They were hardly the only pair to heed the "mysterious luring whispers of the mighty river."[26] Kent and Margaret Lighty, for example, were also delighted by "the simple miracle of being able to carry our household bodily over the waters." But there was more behind the escape the river offered. For the Lightys, the river had "slipped out of the public consciousness into a fertile kind of obscurity." The Mississippi had "become a frontier once more [. . .] the last frontier of those who will not live by laws other than their own, and for those who have broken laws elsewhere."[27] Harold and Russell Speakman paid similar attention to the river's marginalized communities during their shantyboat river voyage in 1925. Harold, for example, spends time in the hobo jungle outside Baton Rouge, talking to the transient residents about their lives. Though Russell has fewer unconventional tendencies, she is forgiving of her husband's mild bohemianism: "By every rule of conventional matrimony, she should not only have been scandalized but have made me change my clothes on the deck as well. Instead, she said, 'I haven't seen you look so carefree in weeks. Go back and play with them tomorrow.'"[28] Today the river still holds a similar spell for many. As William Least Heat-Moon has noted, "The Mississippi has an encompassing mystique no other American river exerts," and "taking a craft of whatever configuration down the Mississippi" is "a pattern of travel" that has become "an archetype [. . .] so repeated it's on the way to developing into a ritual for a nation shy on communal rituals."[29]

If the image of Huck and Jim on the raft informed—and still informs— the appeal of the apparent freedoms of houseboating, Tom Sawyer's example also continued to exert a pull. Boyish adventures on the river continued to proliferate well into the twentieth century. George Cary Eggleston told the story of the *The Last of the Flatboats* in 1900: "'Let's all go to New Orleans, and don't let's pay any steamboat fare at all except to get back! [. . .] Let's run a flatboat!' [. . .] The boys were all eagerness."[30] It was hardly the last such adventure, though, and boys' books set on the river continued to multiply: Everett T. Tomlinson's *Four Boys on the Mississippi* (1908), Edgar B. P. Darlington's *The Circus Boys on the Mississippi* (1912), Captain Quincy Allen's *The Outdoor Chums on a Houseboat* (1913), Harry Gordon's *The River Motor Boat Boys on the Mississippi* (1913), and Harrison Adams's *The Pioneer Boys of the Mississippi* (1913); even after the First World War, George Halsey detailed *The Adventures of William Tucker in a Shantyboat on the Mississippi* (1927). The river's role as a playground—as a space in which to solve crimes, save drowning strangers, brave floods, encounter flora and fauna, find treasure—was undiminished. The spirit of Tom Sawyer, ossified into generic poses, lived on.

Yet it was the river's musical life—and life in music—that was now most prominent in the Mississippi's meanders through popular culture. Tin Pan Alley's portraits of the river, still bearing traces of the coon song and a long history of minstrelsy, became definitive: in popular song, the image of the Mississippi reached its largest audiences in the early twentieth century. In Karen Cox's words, "Hundreds of songs with 'Dixie' in the title or songs that played on the names of southern states were extremely popular in the decade between 1910 and 1920."[31] Exploring that craze on the other side of the Atlantic, Brian Ward has identified what he terms a "Dixiephilia" at work in Great Britain in these years.[32] The Mississippi—and particularly the steamboat and the roustabout—had a vital part to play in these evocations of the southern imaginary. Even Dixie songs that had little or nothing lyrically to do with the Mississippi commonly featured some aspect of river iconography on their covers as immediately recognizable and appealing symbols of the South.

Perhaps the most notable examples of the trend for Mississippi River songs were two compositions first made famous by Al Jolson in the 1912 Broadway musical revue *The Whirl of Society*—in the performance that represented the debut of "Gus," the blackface alter ego that he would continue to play for the rest of his career. Both "On the Mississippi" and "Waiting for the Robert E. Lee" were extraordinary distillations of the kinds of tropes that were central to the literary and journalistic interpretations of the river. "On the Mississippi" (words by Ballard Macdonald, music by the vaudeville duo Arthur Fields and Harry Carroll) presented listeners with a heavily romanticized portrait of roustabout life:

> In my dreams I seem to hear a whistle shrill,
> Like the whip-poor-willing of the whip-poor-will,
> In my ears I hear it ringing,
> And the past to me it is bringing,
> It reminds me of the dear old Mississipp',
> When I loaded cotton on that stern wheel ship,
> Roustabout, knocked about,
> They were the happy days there's no doubt.[33]

"Waiting for the Robert E. Lee" (words by L. Wolfe Gilbert, music by Lewis F. Muir) tapped a similar vein, evoking the ghosts of steamboat races and dwelling on the persistent mystique of the Mississippi steamboat:

> The whistles are blowin', the smokestacks are showing,
> The ropes they are throwin', excuse me, I'm goin'
> To the place where all is harmonious [. . .]
> If you ever go there you'll always be found there,
> Why dog gone, here comes my baby
> On the good ship Robert E. Lee.[34]

Both songs were enormously popular far beyond the bounds of Jolson's performances on Broadway. Looking back on Harry Carroll's career in 1949, *Billboard* magazine described "On the Mississippi" as a "million-copy seller" that moved "faster than a Mississippi sidewheeler from the country's music counters."[35] "Waiting for the Robert E. Lee" became no less of a standard. Across the Atlantic, both songs featured in the revue *Come Over Here*, which, according to Brian Ward, had been seen by 400,000 Londoners by September 1913.[36] Such interpretations—ersatz, minstrelized fabrications of river and roustabout life—continued to crystallize the Mississippi's magic in the early twentieth century.

Beyond the ongoing minstrel poses of the Tin Pan Alley Mississippi, the river was still proving crucial to the development of African American musical styles that would define the century to come—and which, in many ways, were also still rooted in the roustabout experience. On the one hand, this was the end of an era. The *Washington Post* announced the "passing of the Negro roustabout" in 1910, not least because roustabouts were striking for better working conditions.[37] Writing from Hannibal, a correspondent lamented that "the banishment of the negro roustabout and his soulful song will be turning the Father of Waters into a cemetery. [. . .] The man who has never made a trip down the Mississippi River in the real steamboat days has lost a page of life."[38]

Yet it was also the time for something new. As William Howland Kenney has vividly demonstrated, jazz gave the Mississippi steamboat a last reinvigoration, extending its working life up to the middle of the twentieth century. In Kenney's words, just after the First World War, "steam-driven boats that sold harbor excursions in New Orleans during the winter months began [. . .] to leave town during the summer months to 'tramp' the Mississippi and Ohio rivers, bringing an exotic new music labeled riverboat jazz to the nation's inland waterways." The effects of this new, waterborne dissemination were profound, inaugurating "fundamental changes in instrumentation, repertoire, and style to the small-ensemble New Orleans styles, making them far more accessible to broader popular audiences." Luminaries like Louis Armstrong and Bix Beiderbecke put in their time on the Mississippi. Yet the legacy of the roustabout and roustabout culture was still palpable. Indeed, so significant was the figure of the roustabout to the popular understanding of the river that jazz cruises were still obliged to capitalize on his popular image: boats even "kept a few black entertainers on hand to play the roustabout's role" for tourists who expected his presence. Despite such compromises, the river provided these musicians—as it had the roustabouts before them—with a space in which they could shape an "enigmatic [. . .] culture, one within which they discovered more about themselves, about music, about fashioning new worlds of their own imagining."[39] "I often hear people going wild over jazz," declared Captain Blanche Leathers (daughter-in-law of the venerable Thomas Leathers, one of the only women to receive a license, in 1894, to command her own steamboat), "but I wish they could have heard the negro roustabouts singing as they unloaded cotton. It was jazz pure and simple."[40] Soon the whole world was listening.

If such things can be dated, a new era of life on the Mississippi began somewhere around 1927. In that year, it became clear just how much of contemporary culture had been forged on and around the waters of the Mississippi River—filtered, in large part, through the work of Mark Twain. On the one hand, Edna Ferber's *Show Boat* (1926) and, particularly, its manifold adaptations (and their manifold ambiguities) redefined the river for a new generation. Out of the Mississippi ingredients that were circulating widely in the early twentieth century—steamboats, roustabouts, music, nostalgia, romance, Bohemian escape, and the accompanying entanglements of race and gender—Ferber and her book's adapters (most notably, Jerome Kern and Oscar Hammerstein's musical from 1927) produced visions of the Mississippi that defined the decades to come. Magnolia Ravenal—*Show Boat*'s heroine and, next to Huck Finn and Jim, surely the river's most important representative—is very explicitly a perfect product of this Mississippi *terroir*: "She swam muddy streams [. . .] caught catfish; drank river water out of the river itself; roamed the streets of strange towns alone; learned to strut and shuffle and buck-and-swing from the Negroes whose black-faces dotted the boards of the Southern wharves as thickly as grace notes sprinkle a bar of lively music." Steaming along the Mississippi, Magnolia "came to know her country [. . .]. She learned its people by meeting them, of all sorts and conditions." She was, Ferber tells us, "infinitely more free afloat than [. . .] on land." If others might see river life as "rotten and sordid and dull," her dream of a "divinely care-free existence" on its waters—a dream that was firmly rooted in the cultural artifacts of the early twentieth century—would transcend those earthly cares and indelibly shape the meaning of the Mississippi. As Magnolia understood: "The Mississippi is always interesting. It's like a person that you never know what they're going to do next."[41]

The unpredictability of the river was certainly clear in 1927, when the Mississippi flooded in devastating and unparalleled ways. From January to June, particularly on the lower river from Cairo to New Orleans, communities along the Mississippi and its tributaries experienced the power of the river at its most destructive. As John Barry summarizes the terrifyingly sublime statistics of the damage done:

> Along the Lower Mississippi alone the flood put as much as 30 feet of water over lands where 931,159 people—the nation's total population was only 120 million—had lived. Twenty-seven thousand square miles were inundated [. . .]. As late as July 1, 1.5 million acres remained underwater. Not until mid-August, more than four months after the first break in a mainline Mississippi River levee, did all the water leave the land. An estimate 330,000 people were rescued from rooftops, tress, isolated patches of high ground, and levees. The Red Cross ran 154 "concentration camps," tent cities, in seven states [. . .]. A total of 325,554 people, the majority of them African-American, lived in these camps for as long as four months.[42]

The newspapers struggled to keep up with casualties. "Seven deaths were reported today," reported the *New York Times* on April 17, "Thurman Burris, 17, was drowned at Atkins, Ark., while trying to rescue his father and mother; a baby fell into the water at Paragould, Ark., and died; Ray Rovers, 12, was drowned in Illinois; a negro woman and her new-born babe died in a refugee wagon."[43] On went the litany.

The implications of the flood, practical and otherwise, spiraled out across the decades. Some were literary—like Lyle Saxon's *Father Mississippi* (1927); sections of William Alexander Percy's memoir, *Lanterns on the Levee* (1941); and stories like Richard Wright's "The Man Who Saw the Flood" (1937). Some were functional: again, the nation turned to the problem of how to keep the river between its banks. Yet the most significant creative legacy of the flood was musical. The 1927 floods coincided with the expansion of the music industry's interest in the blues. As Robert Dixon and John Godrich outline, "The years 1927 to 1930 were the peak years of blues recording." In 1927 alone, "500 blues and gospels records" were issued. In search of new voices and new material, "companies made frequent excursions to the major towns in the South: during these four years Atlanta was visited seventeen times by field units in search of race talent, Memphis eleven times, Dallas eight times, New Orleans seven times."[44] Previously invisible voices were now recorded for posterity, producing art that still echoes down the years. The floods were a subject that blues singers came back to time and again. The songs testified to the traumatic experience of the flood for black southerners while also reinforcing the centrality of the Mississippi River for the blues. As with more contemporary disasters, the performers and their songs also highlighted the ways in which natural disasters often simply uncovered long-standing inequities and were made much worse by human action. In his vital *Backwater Blues: The Mississippi Flood of 1927 in the African American Imagination*, Richard Mizelle highlights that "over fifty blues songs were recorded on the 1927 flood," a body of music that "can be read as a counterhegemonic force or corrective impulse that sets the record straight, so to speak, about what the 1927 flood and broader environmental world meant for black folks at the time." Immediately, this meant "the messages of violence, peonage, forced labor, and the misuses of charity [. . .] being spread to overlapping diasporic communities." Its wider message was "rooted in the idea that race and nature were interrelated burdens; the perils of rain, wind, and water only exacerbated existing vulnerabilities of second-class citizenship."[45]

Of course, disaster wasn't the only legacy that the river would have for black art in the twentieth century. Langston Hughes had already enshrined the Mississippi as a central locus of African American identity, connecting its waters—deep waters—with other symbolically vital rivers:

> I built my hut near the Congo and it lulled me to sleep.
> I looked upon the Nile and raised the pyramids above it.
> I heard the singing of the Mississippi when Abe Lincoln
>   went down to New Orleans, and I've seen its muddy
>   bosom turn all golden in the sunset.
>
> I've known rivers;
> Ancient, dusky rivers.
>
> My soul has grown deep like the rivers.[46]

Nor was it only as a symbol of destruction and dislocation that the river made its way into the blues. Of all the records that we could play, let us listen to this one: Henry Spaulding only recorded two songs, both for the Brunswick label in 1929. He is one of the many marginal voices that got caught in a field recording session, alive to us still in a snapshot of a life and a career that is otherwise lost. It seems he spent his life by the river, in one way or another: Don Kent notes, "Although Spaulding is from Mississippi, he is vaguely remembered as having worked in and around the Cairo area, and worked extensively with Henry Townsend in the St. Louis area." That supposed trajectory means that Spaulding was part of the Great Migration, like many other blues and jazz musicians at this moment. Townsend remembered him "as an older man" during their time together.[47] Spaulding's lived experience of the river, therefore, presumably stretched back into the nineteenth century. One of the songs he recorded that day in 1929 was very explicitly a song of the Mississippi: "Cairo Blues." "Cairo," Spaulding begins, swooping down on the note, "Cairo is my baby's home."[48] Cairo: the junction point of the Mississippi and the Ohio—the town that Jim looks for on his raft journey with Huck, the missed beacon of freedom, the fulcrum between slavery and liberation. Spaulding is heading there too: "Going to Cairo, baby, and it won't be long." But that's not the only story he has to offer. Spaulding also has a warning for us. While "women in Cairo will treat you nice," he tells us, not all of the river is so welcoming. Some ears hear the next lines as a cautionary tale about the duplicity of these Cairo women: when you don't expect it, they'll "kick you and knife you."[49] Yet through the static, I hear a different warning, one that echoes down the years in a different way: "Kick you in Natchez," Spaulding is telling us, "beat you and cut you too." Down the river, down South, things will go worse for you. When "they get through" with you, you'll be "ready for the grave." And that's where, for now, Spaulding is stuck—sold down the river, looking for an escape. Telegraphically, it is the entire story of black life on the Mississippi River in the age of Mark Twain. But it's okay—like the river, like the roustabouts before him, Spaulding will just keep moving: "I swear I won't be here long. [. . .] I'm going home, and I swear it won't be long."

"This Is the End of It for Me on the River"

Spaulding wasn't the only one going home. Before the modernists and the musicals and the musicians—and Mickey Mouse, who debuted as *Steamboat Willie* in 1928—made the river their own, a clutch of writers who had been there at the beginning of Twain's Mississippi journey and had been companions throughout that trip looked back to their own watery roots. They chimed with a mood for retrospection along the river. John Hay, in the midst of his work to secure the construction of the Panama Canal, returned to the Mississippi both as site and subject in 1904 at the opening of the "Press Parliament of the World" at the St. Louis World's Fair, itself marking the anniversary of the Louisiana Purchase. Hay, now secretary of state for Theodore Roosevelt and less than a year from his death, took stock of the river that he had put into verse in the shape of "Jim Bludso" so many years ago. "The valley of the mighty river which rolls by the wharves of St. Louis," Hay explained to the assembled members of the press, in a sentimental mood, "can never be considered by me otherwise than as my home": "The years of my boyhood were passed on the banks of the Mississippi, and the great river was the scene of my early dreams. The boys of my day led an amphibious life in and near its waters in the Summer time, and in the Winter its dazzling ice bridge, of incomparable beauty and purity, was our favorite playground [. . .]. We sang rude songs of the cane brake and the corn field; and the happiest days of the year to us who dwelt on the northern bluffs of the river were those that brought us, in the loud puffing and whistling steamers of the olden time, to the Mecca of our rural fancies, the bright and busy metropolis of St. Louis." Broadening out his frame, Hay was no less glowing about the "historical value of the Mississippi"—"not less than its geographical and natural importance": "Its course through the pages of our country's story is as significant as the tremendous sweep of its waters from the crystal lakes which sleep beneath the northern stars to the placid expanse of the Gulf of Mexico." In short, the Mississippi was the "silver bar that binds together the framework of the wedded states." It was, as it had been in the antebellum years, a symbol of Union once more.[50]

George Washington Cable made peace with the Mississippi too. After more than two decades of exile from the city of his birth, just after the death of his only son to survive to adulthood, Cable came back to New Orleans. He had it in mind to write about the river—as his daughter narrates: "Since his wife's health and his own demanded a warmer sun than a New England winter could offer, they went in the late fall of 1908 to spend a few months in New Orleans. Here he gathered material for the new story, while he renewed his acquaintance with the river [. . .]. This was to be a story of the Mississippi river and its steamboats, in the time of their glory. From his boyhood the great river beside which he was born had had its fascination for him, and many were the hours dreamed away on its banks."[51] Cable took another prompt from Alice Crary Sutcliffe's 1909 account of Robert Fulton's invention of the steamboat in the *Century Magazine,* to mark the centenary of that achievement.[52]

Inspired by his return to the river and Sutcliffe's account, Cable wrote enthusiastically to his old editor Richard Watson Gilder about his vision for his new book: "Early this year I became more interested than ever in the history of the navigation of the Mississippi river." He planned to write a novel that would "embrace the history of steamboat traffic on the Mississippi from the days of the first steamboat, through the period of triumph, and wind up with the tragic ending of steamboats in the Civil War, when they were used as transports and gunboats."[53] The result was *Gideon's Band: A Tale of the Mississippi* (1914), a tale that sat uneasily with other narratives of the river and the South at this moment. *Gideon's Band,* on the surface of things, is a heavily burnished—almost utopian—tale of antebellum steamboat life. In the course of one steamboat journey in 1852 (and a coda set eight years later, on the brink of Civil War), Cable narrates a love story between the scions of two rival steamboat dynasties, Hugh Courteney and Ramsey Hayle. The reader encounters the Mississippi primarily through the role that it plays in their triumphant courtship. Both are unabashedly "in love with the river life"; Ramsey declares the *Votaress*—the Courteney boat on which she is traveling—"the most wonderful thing in the world"; life on "this mighty stream" is "exalted, exalting." Despite the opposition of Ramsey's malignant brothers, the pair are inseparably joined together because, as Ramsey puts it, "We both love the river so." Moreover, when they are finally reunited after a separation of eight years, their imagined union is one of relative equality: in the interim, Ramsey has learned the river "like a pilot"—like Blanche Leathers; her father proclaims her to be "a better steamboatman [. . .] than many a first class-one."[54] At the book's end, Ramsey pointedly sits next to Hugh as he takes his position in the captain's chair, ready to steam into a golden future.

For all that Hugh and Ramsey are described as "the first human pair" in a "veritable Eden as Eden was before the devil got in," there is plenty of deviltry on display in the novel. Intertwined with Hugh and Ramsey's courtship are other narratives that address the iniquities of river life (with much resonance for the early twentieth century) for immigrants and the enslaved: cholera rages through the lower decks, and a runaway slave is discovered on board.

But these issues, too, provide Cable with an opportunity to imagine a Mississippi steamboat world that is exempted from the dictates of life on shore. Very explicitly, Hugh woos Ramsey with the distinction between life on the Mississippi and what he describes as "starving plantation life":

> Said Hugh, "It's a life I don't want you to live," and for an age of seconds
> they looked into each other's eyes.
> Then Ramsey—not drooping a lash—"I love the river."
> "For keeps?"
> She nodded, and still they looked.

In the course of the novel, they gather others around them, steamboat pilots and itinerant actors, who "believed in letting the oppressed go free"and face off against the powers of reaction who marshal against them—senators, generals, and Ramsey's brothers. While their enemies lobby for the cholera-stricken immigrants to be stranded on the banks of the river, Hugh, Ramsey, and their friends make sure they are tended to and stage a benefit performance to raise funds for their care. When others plot to return runaway slave Phyllis to bondage, Hugh and Ramsey secure her freedom. In the end, it is those who are creatures of the river—and "powerful queer" because of it— who are triumphant.[55]

Yet the appeal of Cable's countercultural and cosmopolitan view of the Mississippi was undercut by the knowledge of what awaits these characters and their river. They know that a war is coming—Hugh pointedly leaves it an open question whether he will fight for North or South—and the implications of that war for the Mississippi will clearly be profound. Cable gestures to the future not through his human protagonists but through the imagined fates of those craft with whom their lives are intertwined: "Good night, *Votaress!* [. . .] These bends were never again to see you in your beauty—though in tragedy, yes! yes! [. . .] You were to be caught by a great war, a war greater than the great river, and should return to these scenes a transport; a poor, scarred, bedraggled consort to gunboats [. . .]. After all, in recovered decency, honored poverty, you should wear out a gentle old age as a wharf-boat to your unspeakable inferiors."[56] If melancholy therefore dominates, it does not quite kill the hope that Hugh and Ramsey—described by James Robert Payne as "ideal New

South types of ultimately enlightened young manhood and womanhood"—
hint at a future that might transcend parochial, patriarchal, and reactionary
definitions of both the Mississippi and the South.[57]

It was William Dean Howells, though, who returned most insistently to the
rivers of his youth—and he kept returning, up until the end of his life. As the
twentieth century dawned, Howells produced a boutique corpus of works—
travel accounts, memoir, short stories, poetry—that saw him evoke, time and
again, the world of rivers and steamboats that had been part of his inheritance,
with nostalgia and love and friendship and regret. He never did make it to the
Mississippi with Twain, but in 1902, he undertook a river journey of his own.
He took a trip along the Ohio with his brother Joe—a return to the scenes of
childhood in the same year that Twain would return to Hannibal for the last
time. As he described it to his daughter Mildred, it was a "glorious" expedition, a cure for a weariness that had beset him: "I sat on the hurricane deck or
in the pilot house every minute I was not eating or sleeping, and purred away
with the pilots."[58] In print, in an essay titled "Floating Down the River on the
O-hi-o," first published in the "Editor's Easy Chair" of *Harper's,* Howells was
ambiguous about the meaning of his voyage. Yes, it was a conscious exercise
in nostalgia: "Early memories stirred joyfully in the two travellers [. . .]. The
boats and the levee were jointly equal to the demand made upon them by the
light-hearted youngsters of sixty-five and seventy, who were setting out on
their journey in fulfilment of a long-cherished dream." The skills of the pilot
were still "a triumph, a miracle." The passengers, too, Howells found from another time: "They seemed none the worse for being more like Americans of
the middle of the last century than of the beginning of this." They were "well
mannered, if quiet manners are good." He liked the houseboats—"the only
feature of their travel which our tourists found absolutely novel." They "gave
evidence of a tranquil and unhurried life which the soul of the beholder envied within him."[59]

Still, at other moments, he didn't blink in the portrait of the river that he
found. Immediately, the Pittsburgh levee is home to "the smoke of a thousand
foundry chimneys," and Howells found the Ohio spoiled by "new ideals, the
ideals of a pitiless industrialism." He was no less world-weary in his description of the life of roustabouts. Describing a landing at night, Howells narrated:
"Then the work of lading or unlading rapidly began in the witching play of
the light, that set into radiant relief the black, eager faces and the black, ea-

ger figures of the deck-hands struggling up down the staging under boxes of heavy wares [. . .] till the last of them reeled back to the deck down the steep of the lifting stage, and dropped to his broken sleep wherever he could coil himself." "No dog," Howells concluded, "leads such a hapless life as theirs." Yet he wasn't finished. Preempting his readers' response to this gloomy ending to his pleasure cruise—"ah! why should their sable shadows intrude in a picture that was meant to be all so gay and glad?"—Howells found a wider, sadder truth in the roustabouts' situation: "In what business in this hard world, is not prosperity built upon the struggle of toiling men, who still endeavor their poor best, and writhe and writhe under the burden of their brothers above, till they lie still under the lighter load of their mother earth?"[60]

Close to the end of his career and life, throughout 1916 and 1917, while the world was at war, Howells imagined his way back to the river again. If Howells had found the image of steamboat pilot a resonant one for his sense of himself as a writer back in the 1880s, that was no less true when it was time to leave his profession. In "Captain Dunlevy's Last Trip," he returned to his roots in more ways than one, by crafting a poem that was reminiscent of "The Pilot's Story," the first poem he published in the *Atlantic* in 1860. It begins with the vision of a pilot:

> In the midst of talk that was leading up to a story,
> Just before we came in, and the story, begun or beginning,
> Always began or ended with some one, or something or other,
> Having to do with the river.

Prompted by a question from one of the passengers about the art of piloting— "by daylight we see them, / And in the dark it's like as if somehow we felt them," he explained, echoing Twain again—the pilot tells the story of Captain Dunlevy. Dunlevy is a representative figure—one who "had been pretty much his whole life on the river," from the age of keelboats until the end of the "flush times," when "the railroads began to run away from the steamboats." The narrator of the poem, who had been Dunlevy's cub, was now his copilot. One day, relieving him to take his shift, the narrator "couldn't believe my senses." Dunlevy was taking an island on the wrong side, about to ground the boat on a bar. When the cub reluctantly questions his old mentor's course, Dunlevy realizes that he has mistaken upstream for downstream. Though this is "the first time he ever had lost his bearings [. . .] *he* knew, / In such a thing as that, that the first and the last are the same." Immediately, Dunlevy understands what his mistake augurs. "This is the end of it for me on the river," he laments:

> When we had got through trying our worst to persuade him, he only
> Shook his head and says, "I am done for, boys, and you know it,"
> Left the boat at Wheeling, and left his life on the river—
> Left his life on the earth, you may say, for I don't call it living.

When questioned as to why the pilot couldn't return from such a mistake, the narrator himself is unable to answer: "*I* don't hardly believe that I could explain it exactly."[61] It was a mature counterpoint to "Old Times on the Mississippi": where Twain drew youthful mastery and promise, Howells found a metaphor of fallibility, mortality, and retirement.

"The Pearl," also from 1916, was no less inscrutable. Howells framed the story in a familiar way, using the same itinerary as both his formative childhood steamboat trips and his 1902 pleasure cruise: a voyage taken by three "cousins [. . .] going round from Pittsburg to St. Louis on their uncle's boat in the spring of the year sixty years ago." The plot revolves around the alleged theft of a tiepin, in which the autobiographical character of Stephen West, a would-be poet, is implicated. When the missing pin is found in his bag, his cousins immediately believe the cabin boy, Jim, put it there—but Stephen still carries a burden of guilt; he cannot quite believe in his own innocence. Meeting one of the cousins in later life, Stephen explains that the experience has stuck with him across the intervening years: "Every one of us has a grain of sand in him that keeps him a kind of sick oyster. He coats it over with his juice and hides it away in his shell somewhere; and that's what turns into a pearl, they say."[62]

In his final statement on the river, Howells employed the same protagonist and the same setting. In "A Tale Untold," back in the *Atlantic*, where Howells had begun, Stephen takes another steamboat trip, one that represents a similar shift from innocence to experience. But if "The Pearl" was an exploration of Howells's psychological life, then "A Tale Untold" was a meditation on his literary career—and, perhaps, a coming to terms with his friendship with Twain. As the story begins, Stephen is on board a steamboat on "his farthest travel from the village where he had lived in a vision of the world, as he knew

it equally from Tennyson and Longfellow and from Thackeray and Cervantes."
His indoctrination into the world of men, opposed to the world of letters,
comes first in the shape of the boat's pilot. At first, the pilot charms him: "He
had the habit of talking with him about life. Stephen's reading and thinking
had aged him beyond his years, but the pilot was of a worldly wisdom which
he could not hope to gain when the years had made them contemporaries."
Yet the pilot outrages Stephen when he argues that "negroes had no souls
and might be fitly enslaved for their defect." At the same time, Stephen also
encounters a figure known only as the "stranger," who turns out to be a confidence man working in cahoots with a gambler on board the boat. The stranger
tricks him into buying a worthless watch chain for three dollars, promising
him that it is gold. Both of these disillusioning experiences fail to fully erase
the "enchantment of the river."

Yet what stays with Stephen is his "pleasure in the ironical color of his experience and the ending of his wrath for being the prey of a plausible scoun-
drel." And what puzzles him is how he would render the stranger and his
blackleg partner in print. On the one hand, Stephen "thought how he might
turn the adventure to account in the sort of literature which he loved almost
as much as he loved the highest poetry [. . .] like certain of the episodes in
Don Quixote, or like Thackeray in some of those picaresque sketches of his."
But he pauses: "He was aware of a certain crudeness in the setting. Could polite lovers of such fiction be made to care for something that happened on a
stern-wheel steamboat between Pittsburg and St. Louis? At the same time, did
not that very crudeness of the setting give a novel value to the facts?" Before
long, Stephen had imagined these "rascals" ending their story "in a prosperity
defiant of both literary and moral convention." Or, he wondered, would the
material be better if rendered as a tragedy? For he could also imagine the way
that "the field of his rascals' adventures narrowed every year," that they would
be "in constant danger of violence." Eventually, after imprisonment, sounding
like sad echoes of Huck and Tom, "one of them would sicken and die," and
the other "would wander back to the village where he had been a worthless
boy and end there a friendless pauper." Torn between those literary poles and
a sense of his own inadequacy for either task, he leaves their story unwritten:
"As he did not write the comedy of those evil lives, because he rejected it, so
he did not write the tragedy of them, because it rejected him." The echoes of
Twain's art, particularly his river books, are unmistakable, but for Howells,

these were the roads—or the rivers—not taken. Their rejection had defined his life and his art, and so "their story remained with him a tale untold."[63]

"Last Time at the Wheel"

What of Twain through these changes—so many of which he had wrought? Whatever spirit pulled his old friends back to the imaginative river, Twain was apparently immune. Having written so much about the Mississippi, his pronouncements about the river in the last years of his life were relatively few and far between. His most public engagement with the river was his final return to the source in 1902—a jamboree that attracted significant attention. Officially, the purpose of his voyage back to the Mississippi that year was to receive an honorary doctorate from the University of Missouri, but he also wanted to see Hannibal again—for the last time, as he repeatedly stressed. As Paul Sorrentino has described, "What started out as a simply planned trip, however, turned into what ranks among the busiest and most emotional eleven days of his life."[64] It also became a journey back through the landscape and the sentiments of his river books, from *The Gilded Age* onward. Throughout, Twain was frequently rendered mute by sentiment. "Sobs choking him," the *St. Louis Republic* described on one typical occasion, "the man of laughs, in deep, heart-touching seriousness [. . .] wept manly tears." The flood of memory began in St. Louis. Just off the train, Twain met Horace Bixby:

> "You were a good pilot, all right, Mark," said Capt. Bixby. "I don't want it said that I turned out a bum workman."
>
> "Yes, I knew enough to tell when the river was rising or falling."[65]

To the *New York Times,* Twain was more obdurate: "Who is that claims I was a bad pilot? The fellow that said that never was a pilot himself."[66] As for Bixby himself, Twain dubbed him "one of the greatest pilots this old Mississippi has ever known." Bixby would outlive his old pupil, dying in 1912—never having left the river.

Twain departed for Hannibal that evening. The following days were a teary blur of social functions, meetings with old friends and acquaintances, maudlin reminiscences and interviews. Journalists were keen to associate the old residents whom Twain encountered with his characters—Injun Joe, Becky

Thatcher, Huck Finn. Reporters also kept prompting him for thoughts on the river. At times, he was happy to valorize. He had recently seen rivers "in India, Australia, Africa, way up in Iceland, down in South America," he pronounced immediately on his arrival in St. Louis, "but do you know there never was such an old river as the Mississippi?" To Bixby, he admitted that the river "looked new in places."[67] Often, though, he was less than forthcoming: "As his train sped along the elevated tracks and the broad river came within view, he gazed upon it pensively. Asked what he thought of it now, he replied:'It's very natural. It's the same river.'" On another occasion, a journalist inquired, "Does the river look familiar?" "Yes," Twain replied, "just as wet and muddy."[68] Later that year, at a celebration to mark his sixty-seventh birthday, Twain ruminated on his trip to Hannibal at length and gave the most fulsome account of its emotional power for him, but he did so in a way that also recognized the wider significance of the Mississippi Valley for his contemporaries and their influence on America across the decades. Looking out on the New York crowd, Twain noted that "there's a lot of people here who came from elsewhere, like John Hay from away out West, and Howells from Ohio [. . .] and me from Missouri." Reflecting on his visit back to Hannibal, just along the river from Hay's hometown of Warsaw—"it is an emotional bit of the Mississippi"— the tone of nostalgia was profound. Twain declared it to be "a paradise for simplicity [. . .] a delectable land." And at the heart of it was the river, beautiful and melancholy:

> It was a heartbreaking delight, full of pathos, laughter, and tears, all mixed together; and we called the roll of the boys and girls that we picnicked and sweethearted with so many years ago, and there were hardly half a dozen of them left; the rest were in their graves; and we went up there on the summit of that hill, a treasured place in my memory, the summit of Holiday's Hill, and looked out again over the magnificent panorama of the Mississippi River, sweeping along league after league [. . .]. I recognized then that I was seeing now the most enchanting river view the planet could furnish. I never knew it when I was a boy; it took an educated eye that had travelled over the globe to know and appreciate it.[69]

After a quick visit to Columbia to collect his honorary doctorate, Dr. Clemens was back in St. Louis again and back on the river. To mark his visit, a harbor boat was renamed the *Mark Twain* in his honor. As a treat, he was allowed to take control of the boat. "You are all dead safe as long as I have the wheel," he reassured his passengers, "but this is my last time at the wheel."[70] "This is the last time I will ever play pilot," another account had it.[71] It was, a reporter noted, probably his "last trip on the Mississippi river" too.[72] When the leadsman measured "Mark Twain," the spectators shouted it back in chorus. When it was over, the *St. Louis Republic* reported: "Tears stood in the eyes of old rivermen. [. . .] The whistles of the harbor boat answered and the river was sonorous with sound. It was the tribute of the rivermen to the distinguished pilot."[73] Twain trumpeted his success but also acknowledged his fallibility: "'I have piloted that steamboat, and by the grace of God, that steamboat is still safe. I steered it correctly.' He added, however, that when he saw a line in the river which in years back would have been familiar to his formerly experienced eye and he could not decide whether it was caused by sand or a reef, he simply told them he was tired and quit." The *St. Louis Dispatch* waxed lyrical: "The face of Mark Twain at the wheel was a map of joy. It was evident he felt the thrill of the thing. [. . .] Mark Twain was a boy again [. . .] steering straight for Hannibal."[74] Another elegiac account pictured Twain's return to the splendid isolation of "the pilothouse far above the crowd on the decks" as "the river breezes caressed his frosty hair" and "the great wheel moved obediently to his master hand."[75] No one squared the circle better of Twain's era on the river, though, than the unnamed poet who rewrote John Hay's "Jim Bludso" to commemorate his last time at the wheel:

> There was cryin' and cursin', but Mark yelled out,
>   Over all the infernal roar:
> "I'll hold her nozzle agin the bank
>   Till the last galoot's ashore!"

> Through the thick, black smoke of the harbour-boat
>   Mark Twain's loud drawl was heard,
> And they all had trust in his cussedness
>   And knowed he would keep his word.

> But soon as they run the gang plank out
>   They hurried to git ashore,

Fur they knowed Ole Mark hadn't steered a boat
Fur forty years or more.[76]

And with that, it was time to leave—for good, except in memory. "He realized that in human probability many more years will not be his," wrote the *St. Louis Republic,* in mawkish mood, "and he has as much said that this would be his last visit to the land of the Mississippi in which had had lived so long, in which he had drawn the sinews of his fame."[77] The centrality of the river to his identity and his work were now fully cemented. Whatever else Mark Twain and the Mississippi would mean in years to come, their essential identities were now irrevocably intertwined.

For all that Twain had trumpeted this trip as his last homecoming to the Mississippi, he toyed with other returns. The St. Louis World's Fair opened up plenty of unexpected opportunities for more river hijinks. At one point, it was suggested that "Twain's home and the adjacent fence may be transported in a barge to St. Louis and exhibited at the World's Fair."[78] Nor was that the only way in which Twain's conjuration of the river of his youth was considered for enshrinement as an icon of American culture at this international gathering. When famous merchant and yachtsman Sir Thomas Lipton (a friend of Twain) suggested that the St. Louis World's Fair would benefit from "a series of old-time Mississippi steamboat races," Twain himself enthusiastically supported the idea, in perhaps his most publicized final statement on the river. In a letter to the president of the fair, reprinted in the *New York Times* and elsewhere in March 1903, Twain reveled in the idea of bringing back "Old Times on the Mississippi" one last time:

> As to particulars, I think that the race should be a genuine reproduction of the old-time race, not just an imitation of it, and that it should cover the whole course. I think the boats should begin the trip at New Orleans [. . .]. I think they should have ample forecastle crowd of negro chantey-singers, with able leaders to do the solo [. . .]. I should extinguish the Government lights in every crossing throughout the course, for where boats are equally matched in the matters of speed and draught it is the quality of the piloting that decides the race. [. . .] The fair would issue the great War Department map of the Mississippi, and every citizen would buy a copy and check off the progress of the race hour by hour.

Of course, for true authenticity, the race would need "an old-time blow-up as the boats finished the home stretch. But this should not be arranged: it is better left to Providence and prayer."[79]

Twain even planned one last adventure with his most famous creations. As he described the abortive project, "Huck Finn was the teller of the story, and of course Tom Sawyer and Jim were the heroes of it." Instead, he destroyed it; believing "that trio had done enough work in this world," he left them to "a permanent rest."[80] Though Twain never did visit the river again, he sent biographer and companion Albert Bigelow Paine in his stead in 1907. "Coming up the river on one of the old passenger steamboats that still exist," Paine recorded, "I noticed in a paper which came aboard that Mark Twain was to receive from Oxford University the literary doctor's degree." For Paine, it was a timely announcement, allowing him to measure certain achievements with the Mississippi for scale: "That the little barefoot lad that had played along the river-banks at Hannibal, and received such meagre advantages in the way of schooling—whose highest ambition had been to pilot such a craft as this one—was about to be crowned by the world's greatest institution of learning [. . .] was a thing which would not be likely to happen outside of a fairy tale."[81]

The river had always been a multiple thing for Twain, though, and as he dictated his autobiography in his final years, the Mississippi came back to him in different tempers. Some days it was the still the glorious river of "Old Times on the Mississippi," its own kind of fairy tale. "Piloting on the Mississippi River was not work to me," he pontificated on July 7, 1908, "it was play—delightful play, vigorous play, adventurous play—and I loved it." At others, particularly when stoking his animus against those he considered enemies, he channeled the unbiddable river that he imagined in *Life on the Mississippi*. In stark contrast to his alleged comments about river improvements when back on the river in 1902, Twain vigorously attacked the enterprise when Theodore Roosevelt became involved. On September 13, 1907, he noted that "the President is about to start out on another advertising tour [. . .] he is going to review the Mississippi River—that poor old abandoned waterway which was my field of usefulness when I was a pilot in the days of its high prosperity." Then he let rip: "This time he goes as cat's paw for that ancient and insatiable gang, the Mississippi Improvement conspirators, who for thirty years have been annually sucking the blood of the Treasury and spending it in fantastic attempts to ameliorate the condition of that useless river [. . .]. These efforts have never improved the river, for the reason that no effort of men can do that. The Mississippi will always have its own way; no engineering skill can persuade it to do otherwise; it has always torn down the petty basket-work of the engineers and poured its giant floods whithersoever it chose, and it will continue to do this." According to Twain, the mayor of Cairo (and Memphis too) invited him to "come out and join the conspiracy"—even, perhaps, to "steer the President's boat, with my venerable boss, Bixby, standing guard over me in the pilot-house to see that I didn't butt the boat's brains out." He declined the offer, citing age and ill health, though word leaked out that it was a specific snub to Roosevelt. The *Washington Post* accordingly marked the occasion with an ode ("I love poetry," Twain noted approvingly, "at least I love it when it advertises me"):

> Nay, nay! no piloting for me,
> Theodore! O Theodore!
> On board of any craft with thee,
> Theodore! O Theodore!
> I'm rather old and on the shelf;
> I do not care for fame and pelf—
> Say, steer the darned old boat yourself,
> Theodore! O Theodore![82]

The abiding idea of the river that stayed with Twain in his final years was a more troubling one. It was an image that encapsulated the ambiguities that had always flowed in the waters of his Mississippi and that still flow through it now. Was the river a route to freedom or a stream to get sold down? Was it a path to fortune or disaster? Was it safe water that was good for steamboating or treacherous water to drown in? Was it a realm for Samuel Clemens, Master Pilot of the Mississippi, to play in or a space for Mark Twain to conjure more serious games? Was it the triumph of America or its failure? It was always, of course, all of those things and more. Though it has assumed apparently fixed and benign poses in the popular imagination—Huck and Jim on the raft, Tom Sawyer and friends on the island—Twain's Mississippi was as much a threat as a promise. And so, in his final years, it was for him. In dreams, he stayed on the river to the end. In dreams, he conjured an image that encapsulated so many of the hopes and worries that the Mississippi had always held for him: "There is never a month passes that I do not dream of being in reduced circumstances, and obliged to go back to the river to earn a living. It is never a pleasant dream, either. I love to think about those days; but there's always something sickening about the thought that I have been obliged to go back to them; and usually in my dream I am just about to start into a black shadow without being able to tell whether it is Selma bluff, or Hat Island." Or perhaps, he pondered, it wasn't those old triggers of anxiety that he was approaching in the darkness, torn between the pleasures of burnished memory and an inescapable knowledge of the dangers and disappointments that always lurked in the deep water. Perhaps it was an escape of a different kind. Perhaps he was only steaming toward "a black wall of night."[83]

ACKNOWLEDGMENTS

As many voices in this book make clear, any extended journey along the crooked Mississippi necessitates a strong crew and inevitably leaves you in debt. Having finally followed the river to its end, I'm very glad to be able to pay down at least a few of those many obligations. Since this book had its genesis in the completion of my first book, it has been a good number of years in the making. Throughout that time, both the School of Art, Media and American Studies and the Faculty of Arts and Humanities at the University of East Anglia have provided continual backing for this project, including two vital periods of research leave. Thank you, too, to a variety of colleagues, too many to mention by name, but particularly those in the Department of American Studies, for their camaraderie and advice as this book took shape. Much gratitude is due to series editor Scott Romine, James Long, Catherine Kadair, and all at Louisiana State University Press for their enthusiastic support. Michelle Neustrom designed (another) beautiful cover. Elizabeth Gratch was a truly brilliant copyeditor. Kim Lockwood provided indispensable editing and indexing assistance.

Heartfelt thanks go to Joseph Lemak and the Center for Mark Twain Studies at Elmira College. I was lucky enough to be the recipient of a Quarry Farm Fellowship in the summer of 2018 and spent an unforgettable fortnight in that special place, accompanied by my wife and daughters, at a crucial moment in this book's creation. As such, I am enormously grateful to all involved with making that extraordinary experience come to pass. Thank you, too, to Larry Howe and Pete Messent for supporting my fellowship and for reading parts of this project as it evolved. Portions of this book were originally published as journal articles in the *Mark Twain Journal* and *Southern Quarterly*. I would like to thank the editors of those journals both for their permission to reprint elements of those chapters here and for their encouragement of my research. Similarly, parts of this project were given as invited papers at the Mark Twain Boyhood Home and Museum in Hannibal, Missouri; the University of Birmingham; and the University of Hertfordshire. Sincere thanks to the colleagues at those institutions who made those rewarding events happen.

Some more personal appreciation: much love and gratitude to my parents, Kathleen and Peter, who proved once again, as always, to be tireless and enthusiastic early readers; and to my wife's family—Helen and Panos; Katerina, Demetris, and Teddy—for their support. None of this would have been possible without the love and belief of my wife, Arianna, who, almost two decades since its early beginnings, provided tireless companionship for every mile of this river odyssey. Her influence can be felt on every page. And finally, this book is dedicated with all my love to my daughters Delilah and Tabitha, who taught me so much while I wrote this book.

NOTES

Throughout this book, I have used bracketed ellipses to signal omissions I have made from original quotations.

Introduction: "The Mississippi Was a Virgin Field"

1. Scharnhorst, *Mark Twain,* 161.
2. Cady, "Howells on the River," 39.
3. Keller, *Midstream,* 57.
4. Read, *Mark Twain and I,* 7.
5. McIntire-Strasburg, "Mark Twain, Huck Finn, and the Geographical 'Memory' of a Nation," 83.
6. Blair, *Mark Twain & Huck Finn,* 37.
7. Bates, "Mark Twain and the Mississippi River."
8. Dix, "Twain and the Mississippi," 294.
9. Matthews, *Inquiries and Opinions,* 161.
10. McDermott, *Before Mark Twain;* Kruse, *Mark Twain and "Life on the Mississippi."*
11. McMillin, *Meaning of Rivers,* xi.
12. James, *Principles of Psychology,* 1:239.
13. Smith, *Mark Twain,* 72.
14. Bird, *Mark Twain and Metaphor,* 41.
15. "Mad Freaks of the Mississippi," 374–76.
16. Patrick, *Fragments,* 104.
17. Thompson, "Mark Twain," 443–45.
18. Bates, "Mark Twain," 7–8.
19. Twain, *Huck Finn and Tom Sawyer among the Indians,* 88.
20. Quoted in Dempsey, *Searching for Jim,* 167.
21. Paine, *Mark Twain,* 1:64.
22. Dempsey, *Searching for Jim,* 167.
23. Paine, *Mark Twain,* 1:64.
24. Smith, *Autobiography of Mark Twain,* 1:401–2.
25. Twain, *Mark Twain's Letters,* 4:50–51.
26. Twain, *Life on the Mississippi,* 530, 534, 536.

27. Herndon and Gibbon, *Exploration*, 1:176, 186, 189.

28. See Branch, "Proposed Calendar," 2–27.

29. Flint, "Progress of the West," 25–26.

30. Twain, *Mark Twain's Notebooks & Journals*, 1:47.

31. Twain, *Life on the Mississippi*, 92.

32. Merrick, *Old Times on the Upper Mississippi*, 111.

33. Paine, *Mark Twain*, 1:148.

34. Twain, *Mark Twain's Letters*, 1:77.

35. Twain, *Early Tales & Sketches*, 1:128.

36. Twain, *Early Tales & Sketches*, 1:131–33.

37. Scharnhorst, *Life of Mark Twain*, 119.

38. Paine, *Mark Twain's Letters*, 2:496–97. For more on the controversy surrounding the origin of Twain's pen name, see MacDonnell, "How Samuel Clemens Found 'Mark Twain'" ; and Kruse, "Mark Twain's 'Nom de Plume.'"

39. Twain, *Mark Twain's Letters*, 1:97–98, 102.

40. DeVoto, *Mark Twain's America*, 108–9.

41. Johnson, *River of Dark Dreams*, 5.

42. Buchanan, *Black Life on the Mississippi*, 6.

43. Lloyd, *Lloyd's Steamboat Directory*, iii.

44. Marleau, "Crash of Timbers Continued," 18–19.

45. Twain, *Life on the Mississippi*, 217–18.

46. Twain, *Mark Twain's Letters*, 1:77.

47. Twain, *Life on the Mississippi*, 246.

48. Webster, *Mark Twain*, 60.

49. Twain, *Mark Twain's Letters*, 1:108–10.

50. Twain, *Early Tales & Sketches*, 1:64.

51. Quoted in Lorch, "Source," 309.

52. Lorch, "Source," 312.

53. Longfellow, *Evangeline* (1847), 91–93.

54. Longfellow, *Evangeline* (1900), x.

55. Banvard, *Description of Banvard's Panorama*, 17, 9.

56. Dahl, "Mark Twain," 21–22.

57. Dickens, "American Panorama," 314–15.

58. Dickens, *Life and Adventures*, 282, 284.

59. Twain, *Mark Twain's Letters*, 1:104.

60. Dickens, *American Notes*, 2:110–11, 2:147–48.

61. Trollope, *Domestic Manners of the Americans*, 1:2, 19.

62. Marryat, *Diary in America*, 1:225, 234.

63. Dickens, *American Notes*, 1:59.

64. Brown, *Narrative of William W. Brown*, 31, 33–34, 94–95.

65. Krauth, *Mark Twain & Company*, 88.

66. Stowe, *Uncle Tom's Cabin*, 120.

67. Twain, *Mark Twain's Letters*, 4:58.

68. Krauth, *Mark Twain & Company*, 90.

69. Saxton, "Blackface Minstrelsy," 69–70.

70. Emerson, *Doo-Dah*, 71.

71. Hatch, intro.," *Lost Plays of the Harlem Renaissance*, 9.

72. Ludlow, *Dramatic Life*, 392–93.

73. See Meer, *Uncle Tom Mania*, 106.

74. Nevin, "Stephen C. Foster," 609–10.

75. Cockrell, *Demons of Disorder*, 71.

76. Rice, *Jim Crow*, 30.

77. Mahar, *Behind the Burnt Cork Mask*, 13.

78. David Monod gives "1826 or 1827" as the date for the first performance of "Gumbo Chaff." See Monod, *Soul of Pleasure*, 59.

79. "Gumbo Chaff," quoted in Lhamon, *Jump Jim Crow*, 140–41.

80. Gerteis, "Blackface Minstrelsy," 92.

81. Nowatzki, "'Our Only Truly National Poets,'" 368.

82. Mahar, *Behind the Burnt Cork Mask*, 252.

83. Emerson, *Doo-Dah*, 118, 120, 130, 128.

84. Twain, *Autobiography*, 2:294.

85. Twain, *Early Tales & Sketches*, 148–50.

86. Webster, *Business Man*, 48.

1. "There Is a World of River Stuff to Write About": Reconstructing the Mississippi

1. Twain, *Mark Twain's Letters*, 1:210–11, 236, 327.

2. Twain, *Letters*, 1:329, 331.

3. "Letter from 'Mark Twain,'" 1.

4. Twain, *Mark Twain's Letters*, 4:499.

5. Twain, *Innocents Abroad*, 201, 270, 495, 620, 627–28.

6. Twain, *Roughing It*, 203, 293.

7. Twain, *Letters*, 4:58.

8. Twain, *Letters*, 1:358.

9. Twain, *Mark Twain's Letters*, 5:15, 49.

10. Egan, *Mark Twain's Huckleberry Finn*, 60.

11. Twain, *Autobiography*, 3:241.

12. Aldrich, *Crowding Memories*, 150, 160.

13. Howells, *My Mark Twain*, 5.

14. Blair, *Mark Twain & Huck Finn*, 37.

15. Hunter, *Steamboats*, 481.

16. White, *Railroaded*, 50, xxii.

17. Morris, "Only a River," 153.

18. "The St. Louis Bridge," 4.

19. Whitman, *Specimen Days*, 155.

20. Twombly, "Illinois and St. Louis Bridge," 162–63.

21. Ewell L. Newman, quoted in Vlach, *Planter's Prospect,* 113.

22. "River News," 4.

23. "River Intelligence," 7.

24. "Great Race" (July 1, 1870), 1; "Great Race" (July 2, 1870), 1.

25. Betts, "Technological Revolution," 239.

26. "Steamboat Race," 1.

27. Quoted in *Georgia Weekly Telegraph,* July 19, 1870, 4.

28. "River News," 4.

29. "Two Racers," 3.

30. Quoted in *Cincinnati Daily Gazette,* July 4, 1870, 3.

31. "Racing on the Mississippi," 4.

32. Trowbridge, *South,* 383, 389, 348–49.

33. Reid, *After the War,* 569.

34. Silber, *Romance of Reunion,* 67.

35. Brodhead, *Cultures of Letters,* 125.

36. Rainey, *Creating Picturesque America,* 22.

37. Cochran, "Mississippi," 178.

38. Rainey, *Picturesque,* 3.

39. Bryant, *Picturesque America,* 324, 318, 343.

40. Disturnell, *Tourist's Guide,* 43, iii.

41. Bryant, *Picturesque America,* 266, 269.

42. Silber, *Reunion,* 67, 76.

43. *Picturesque America,* 1:269, 275.

44. Jones, *Appletons' Hand-Book,* 244.

45. Jones, *Southern Tour,* 252; Hoyt, *Romance of the Table,* 183.

46. Nichols, "Down the Mississippi," 835–38.

47. De Leon, "Western River-Race," 370–72.

48. Morris, *Wanderings of a Vagabond,* 413, 419–21.

49. King, *Great South,* 60, 71.

50. Silber, *Reunion,* 79.

51. King, *South,* 71.

52. King, *South,* 235, 259.

53. See King, "Great South," 641–69.

54. Blair, *Mark Twain & Huck Finn,* 37.

55. Berkove, "Dan De Quille," 30.

56. De Quille, "Pilot Wylie," 1.

57. Howells, *My Mark Twain,* 15.

58. Cady, "Howells on the River," 28.

59. Wortham, *Early Prose Writings of William Dean Howells,* 109, 112, 119.

60. Howells, "Pilot's Story," 325.

61. Howells, *Their Wedding Journey,* 73.

62. Hay, "Foster-Brothers," 544.

63. Eggleston, *Recollections,* 157.

64. Hay, "Jim Bludso," 5.

65. De Leon, "River-Race," 371.

66. Collins, *George Eliot*, 130.

67. Twain, *Letters*, 4:299–300.

68. Eggleston, *Recollections*, 161.

69. Storey, *Rural Fictions*, 5.

70. Eggleston, *End of the World*, 109, 171, 188, 198.

71. "Recent Literature," 747.

72. Salamo and Smith, *Mark Twain's Letters*, 5:347–48.

73. Sandweiss, *Seeking St. Louis*, 277.

74. Carter, *Log of Commodore Rollingpin*, 43, 110–12.

75. Keeler, *Vagabond Adventures*, 18, 90.

76. Smith and Hirst, *Autobiography* 1:152–53.

77. Keeler, *Vagabond*, 20, 178, 189–90, 209, 296.

78. "Publishers' Announcements," 410.

79. Greenslet, *Life of Thomas Bailey Aldrich*, 10.

80. Keeler, "On the Mississippi" (September 30, 1871), 333.

81. Keeler, "On the Mississippi" (May 20, 1871), 477–78.

82. Keeler, "On the Mississippi" (September 2, 1871), 236–38.

83. Kruse, *Mississippi*, 49.

84. Howells, *My Mark Twain*, 6.

85. Paine, *Mark Twain*, 1:476–77.

86. Hoffman, *Inventing Mark Twain*, 207.

87. Bassett, *Studies in the Novel*, 395.

88. Twain and Warner, *Gilded Age*, 48, 35–36, 41–43.

89. Twain and Warner, *Gilded Age*, 49–52.

90. Twain and Warner, *Gilded Age*, 33, 36–37, 41, 37.

91. Hay, "Jim Bludso," 5.

92. Twain and Warner, *Gilded Age*, 49.

93. "Gilded Age," *Old and New*, 387.

94. "Gilded Age," *Saturday Review*, 223.

95. "Novels of the Week," 53.

96. Warner, *My Winter on the Nile*, 119.

97. Ferriss, "Mark Twain," 16.

98. Twain, *Mark Twain's Letters*, 6:247, 262–63, 266, 294, 295, 301, 358, 312.

99. Twain, *Letters*, 6:303–4, 306, 356–57.

100. Twain, *Letters*, 6:482, 325–27, 423–24, 475.

101. Howells, *My Mark Twain*, 20–21.

102. DeVoto, *Mark Twain's America*, 107.

103. Twain, "Old Times on the Mississippi: I," 69.

104. Twain, "Old Times on the Mississippi: VI," 729–30.

105. Twain, "Old Times on the Mississippi: VII," 192.

106. Twain, "Old Times on the Mississippi: I," 70.

107. Twain, "Old Times on the Mississippi: VII," 190.

108. Twain, "Old Times on the Mississippi: I," 73.

109. Twain, *Letters*, 6:301.

110. Twain, "Old Times on the Mississippi: I," 71.

111. Twain, "Old Times on the Mississippi: V," 571.

112. Twain, "Old Times on the Mississippi: VI," 721; Twain, "Old Times on the Mississippi: VII," 192.

113. Twain, "Old Times on the Mississippi: VI," 721.

114. Twain, "Old Times on the Mississippi: II," 221.

115. Twain, "Old Times on the Mississippi: III," 288.

116. Twain, "Old Times on the Mississippi: III," 288–89.

117. Twain, "Old Times on the Mississippi: IV," 446.

118. Twain, *Letters*, 6:473.

119. Gould, *Fifty Years on the Mississippi*, 490.

120. Horwitz, "'Ours by the Law of Nature,'" 246, 265, 264.

121. Howe, "Transcending the Limits of Experience," 421–22.

122. Burde, "Mark Twain," 882.

123. Bell, *Problem of American Realism*, 27, 22.

124. Brodhead, *Cultures*, 81.

125. "Interviews with William Dean Howells," 284.

126. Twain, *Letters*, 6:482.

2. "The Mighty River Lay like an Ocean": Aquatic Adventures for Transatlantic Boys

1. Twain, *Mark Twain's Letters*, 6:298–99, 325, 327, 348–49, 356–57.

2. Twain, *Letters*, 6:381, 390, 400, 473–74.

3. Twain, *Letters*, 6:49 n. 4, 503–4, 595.

4. Howells, "Recent Literature," 622.

5. Prchal, "Bad Boys and the New Man," 188.

6. Hughes, *Tom Brown's School Days*, xi.

7. Hughes, *Tom Brown's School Days, by an Old Boy*, 28–29, 220–22, 95, 267, 241, 219, 250, 242, 352.

8. Aldrich, *Story of a Bad Boy*, 61, 146, 149, 153, 163–66, 255.

9. Twain, *Mark Twain's Letters*, 3:440.

10. See Twain, *Mark Twain's Letters*, 5:395–96.

11. Seelye, "What's in a Name," 421–22.

12. Gribben, "Manipulating a Genre," 15, 19.

13. Deane, "Imperial Boyhood," 690.

14. Honaker, "'One Man to Rely On,'" 27.

15. Twain, *Adventures of Tom Sawyer* (1876), 115.

16. Howells, *Boy's Town*, 24, 2, 32.

17. Reynolds, *Beneath the American Renaissance*, 208.

18. Twain, *Adventures of Tom Sawyer*, 115, 81, 258.

19. Buntline, *Black Avenger*, 7.

20. Gribben, "Mark Twain's Lifelong Reading," 35.

21. Reynolds, *Beneath the American Renaissance,* 179. Simms riffs on Murrell's myth in *Richard Hurdis* (1838) and *The Border Beagles* (1840); Gerstäcker did the same in the transatlantically popular *Die Flußpiraten vom Mississippi* (1848), translated as *The Pirates of the Mississippi* (1856); Melville mentioned Murrell in *The Confidence Man* (1857). For more on Murrell's extraordinary adventures in antebellum popular culture, see my articles "Independence Day"; and "'Dead Men Tell No Tales.'"

22. Twain, *Adventures of Tom Sawyer,* 205.

23. Eggleston, *Hoosier Schoolmaster,* 205, 207.

24. Bratton, *Impact of Victorian Children's Fiction,* 135, 138.

25. James, "Tom Brown's Imperialist Sons," 89, 90, 92.

26. Dunae, "Boys' Literature," 107.

27. Banham, "'England and America,'" 162–63.

28. Windholz, "Emigrant and a Gentleman," 632.

29. Quoted in Scharnhorst, *Critical Essays,* 28.

30. Ballantyne, *Personal Reminiscences,* 4, 5.

31. Twain, *Letters,* 5:15.

32. Maher, "Recasting Crusoe," 169.

33. Bristow, *Empire Boys,* 94.

34. Hughes, *Tom Brown's Schooldays,* xv.

35. Alcott, *Old-Fashioned Girl,* 90.

36. Gribben, "Mark Twain's Lifelong Reading," 34.

37. Ballantyne, *Coral Island,* iii.

38. Maher, "Recasting Crusoe," 174 n. 3.

39. Agruss, "'Boys Gone Wild,'" 8.

40. Ballantyne, *Coral Island,* 33, 26–27, 33, 24.

41. Ballantyne, *Coral Island,* 133, 35, 196–97, 202.

42. Bristow, *Empire Boys,* 107.

43. Ballantyne, *Coral Island,* 333, 339, 344, 346.

44. Reid, *Captain Mayne Reid,* 7, 9–10.

45. Paul, "Recollections," 556.

46. Reid, *Desert Home,* 1.

47. Reid, *Boy Hunters,* title page, 1, 453, 464.

48. Reid, *Quadroon,* 13, 16.

49. Reid, *Island Pirate,* 10.

50. Windholz, "Emigrant and a Gentleman," 636.

51. Roosevelt, *Theodore Roosevelt,* 18–20.

52. Burnett, *One I Knew the Best of All,* 60.

53. Reid, *Captain Mayne Reid,* 176.

54. Springhall, "'Life Story for the People,'" 224.

55. Banham, "'England and America,'" 151.

56. "Correspondence," 176.

57. Reid, "Fatal Cord," 81.

58. "Mark Twain Says," 128.

59. "New Story," 47.

60. "British Jack and Yankee Doodle," May 8, 1880, 49–51; May 28, 1880, 50–52; July 9, 1880, 148; July 23, 1880, 180.

61. "British Jack and Yankee Doodle," August 13, 1880, 235.

62. "British Jack and Yankee Doodle," August 20, 1880, 250.

63. "British Jack and Yankee Doodle," August 27, 1880, 263.

64. "British Jack and Yankee Doodle," September 10, 1880, 295.

65. "British Jack and Yankee Doodle," August 27, 1880, 263.

66. "British Jack and Yankee Doodle," September 24, 1880, 332.

67. "British Jack and Yankee Doodle," September 17, 1880, 311.

68. "British Jack and Yankee Doodle," September 24, 1880, 333.

69. Fahs, *Imagined Civil War*, 268.

70. Castlemon, "How to Write Stories for Boys," 4–5.

71. Blanck, *Harry Castlemon*, xi.

72. Castlemon, *Frank, the Young Naturalist*, 13–14.

73. Castlemon, "How to Write Stories for Boys," 4–5.

74. Blanck, *Harry Castlemon*, 23.

75. Castlemon, *Frank on a Gun-Boat*, 15.

76. Castlemon, *Frank before Vicksburg*, 256.

77. Castlemon, *Frank on the Lower Mississippi*, 233, 236.

78. Fahs, *Imagined*, 270, 286.

79. Blanck, *Harry Castlemon*, 28.

80. Wadsworth, "Louisa May Alcott," 21–22.

81. Ashton, *Hatchie*, 5.

82. "Juvenile Reading," 478.

83. Optic, *Down the River*, 17, 32, 101, 105, 113, 117, 182, 177, 208.

84. Optic, *Down the River*, 211, 251, 270, 302–3.

85. Stanley, *Autobiography*, v, 81–82, 115–17.

86. Jeal, *Stanley*, 39–40.

87. Stanley, *Autobiography*, 151.

88. Twain, *Autobiography*, 280.

89. Twain, *Letters*, 5:199.

90. Twain, *Mark Twain's Letters*, 2:752.

91. King, "Expedition with Stanley," 106, 112.

92. "Heart of Africa," 504.

93. Young, "Through the Dark Continent," 681, 686.

94. Young, "Dark Continent," 686.

95. Stanley, *How I Found Livingstone*, 274.

96. Stanley, *Through the Dark Continent*, 2:92–93, 194–95, 311.

97. "Afloat," 5.

98. "Down the River," 8.

99. "Down to the Delta," 3.

100. "General City News," 4.

101. Kuntz, *Boy Naturalist in the Amazon*, 17.

102. Reid, *Forest Exiles*, 8–9.

103. "At Home," 4.

104. "Indiana Boy's Romantic Adventures," 6.

105. "Ernest Morris," 409.

106. Twain, *Adventures of Tom Sawyer*, 21, 115.

107. Twain, *Adventures of Tom Sawyer*, 29, 39, 38.

108. Twain, *Adventures of Tom Sawyer* (1986), viii.

109. Twain, *Adventures of Tom Sawyer*, 124.

110. Twain, *Adventures of Tom Sawyer*, 117–18, 123–24, 135.

111. Twain, *Adventures of Tom Sawyer*, 126, 146, 142–43.

112. *Life and Adventures of John A. Murrell*, 5, 36, 69.

113. Twain, *Adventures of Tom Sawyer*, 218–20, 89, 94, 245.

114. Budd, *Mark Twain*, 260.

115. Twain, *Adventures of Tom Sawyer*, 251, 253.

116. Aspiz, "Tom Sawyer's Games of Death," 149.

117. Aspiz, "Tom Sawyer's Games of Death," 149.

118. Howe, *Mark Twain and the Novel*, 73.

119. Tindol, "Tom Sawyer and Becky Thatcher," 118.

120. Ballantyne, *Coral Island*, 343.

121. Twain, *Adventures of Tom Sawyer*, 257.

122. Twain, *Adventures of Tom Sawyer*, 258, 267.

123. Quirk, *Coming to Grips with Huckleberry Finn*, 4–5.

124. Twain, Letter to "Unidentified."

3. "This Ain't That Kind of a River": Life, Death, and Memory on the Mississippi

1. Covici, "Dear Master Wattie," 106.

2. Twain, *Autobiography* 2:149–51.

3. Covici, "Dear Master Wattie," 107–8.

4. Lang, "For Mark Twain," 445–46.

5. Quoted in Kruse, *Mark Twain*, 15.

6. Twain and Howells, *Mark Twain–Howells Letters*, 1:403.

7. Covici, "Dear Master Wattie," 107–8.

8. Hale, "Mississippi River," 114–15. See Longfellow, *Poems of Places*, vol. 3: *England;* and Longfellow, *Poems of Places*, vol. 2: *Germany.*

9. Twain and Howells, *Mark Twain–Howells Letters*, 227, 229.

10. Aron, "Mark Twain and Germany," 67.

11. Twain, *Mark Twain's Notebooks & Journals*, 2:118.

12. Bradshaw, *Bradshaw's Hand-Book*, 96–97.

13. Schulz-Forberg, "Sorcerer's Apprentice," 86.

14. Bulwer-Lytton, *Pilgrims of the Rhine*, 102.

15. Thackeray, "Legend of the Rhine," 119.

16. Hood, *Up the Rhine*, 1, 79–80.

17. Twain, *Mark Twain's Letters*, 1:116–17.

18. Rogers, *Mark Twain's Burlesque Patterns*, 48.

19. Twain, *Tramp Abroad*, 19, 82–83.

20. "Mark Twain at the Shrine of St. Wagner," 21.

21. Foster, *Wagner's "Ring" Cycle*, 89.

22. Twain, *Tramp Abroad*, 95–96.

23. Messent, "Tramps and Tourists," 143.

24. Twain, *Tramp Abroad*, 124.

25. Twain, *Tramp Abroad*, 126, 129–30.

26. Twain, *Tramp Abroad*, 130–31, 183.

27. Paine, *Mark Twain*, 2:628.

28. Byerly, *Are We There Yet*, 86.

29. Beckson, *London in the 1890s*, 258.

30. Pennell and Pennell, *Life of James McNeill Whistler*, 60. See also Pennell and Pennell, *Stream of Pleasure*.

31. See Baetzhold, *Mark Twain & John Bull*, 36.

32. Twain, letter to Andrew Chatto, August 19, 1879.

33. Paine, *Mark Twain*, 2:645.

34. James, "London," 219–39.

35. Twain, letter to Orion Clemens, February 26, 1880.

36. Twain, *Prince and the Pauper*, 44.

37. Davis, "Bridging the Gap," 18.

38. Twain, *Prince and the Pauper*, 133–34.

39. Davis, *Geographical Imagination*, 21.

40. Twain, *Prince and the Pauper*, 185, 103, 106.

41. Davis, *Geographical Imagination*, 28.

42. Rose, *Unspeakable Awfulness*, 1.

43. Hesse-Wartegg, *Travels*, 1, 13.

44. "German Traveler on the Mississippi," 3.

45. Hesse-Wartegg, *Travels*, 225.

46. See Hauk, *Memories of a Singer*.

47. Hesse-Wartegg, *Travels*, 19, 22, 25, 137–38. For echoes of Twain and King, see, e.g., 31, 117, 39.

48. Hesse-Wartegg, *Travels*, 39, 40, 46, 54, 39.

49. Hesse-Wartegg, *Travels*, 49, 184.

50. Blake, "George Augustus Sala."

51. Sala, *My Diary in America*, 2:5.

52. Sala, *America Revisited*, 1:viii.

53. Sala, *My Diary*, 2:39.

54. Sala, *America Revisited*, 1:viii.

55. Blake, "George Augustus Sala."

56. Sala, *America Revisited*, 2:3, 6, 87.

57. Sala, *America Revisited*, 2:44–45.

58. Hesse-Wartegg, *Travels*, 154.

59. Turner, *George W. Cable*, 55.

60. Johnson, *Remembered Yesterdays*, 122.

61. "Cable's 'Grandissimes,'" 159.

62. Turner, *Cable*, 122.

63. Turner, *Cable*, 4.

64. Twain, *Mark Twain's Notebooks & Journals*, 2:528.

65. Turner, *Cable*, 13.

66. Cable, "New Orleans," 44, 46–47.

67. Cable, *Old Creole Days*, 23.

68. Cable, *Old Creole Days*, 84.

69. Cable, *Grandissimes*, 182 ("On dit [. . .] que ses eaux ont le propriété de contribuer même à multiplier l'espèce humaine"), 26, 10, 11, 13.

70. Turner, *Cable*, 54.

71. Cable, *Grandissimes*, 220–21, 230.

72. Cable, *Grandissimes*, 236.

73. Wilson, *Shadow and Shelter*, 97.

74. Cable, *Grandissimes*, 237, 242, 247, 408.

75. Pennell, *Life and Letters of Joseph Pennell*, 1:49, 53, 55.

76. Pennell, *Adventures of an Illustrator*, 95.

77. Pennell, *Life and Letters*, 99, 73–74, 80.

78. Twain, *Tramp Abroad*, 573–74.

79. Twain, *Mark Twain's Notebooks & Journals*, 2:436–37.

80. Fatout, *Mark Twain Speaking*, 294.

81. Twain, *Mark Twain's Notebooks & Journals*, 2:454.

82. Quoted in Kruse, *Life on the Mississippi*, 16.

83. Twain, *Mark Twain's Notebooks & Journals*, 2:530, 526.

84. Twain, *Mark Twain's Notebooks & Journals*, 2:527.

85. Scharnhorst, *Mark Twain*, 41.

86. Twain, *Mark Twain's Notebooks & Journals*, 2:527–28, 530, 450, 489.

87. Twain, *Love Letters of Mark Twain*, 211.

88. Paine, *Letters of Mark Twain*, 224.

89. Twain, *Love Letters*, 211.

90. Harris, "To the Editors of the Critic," 253.

91. Twain, *Mark Twain's Notebooks & Journals*, 2:556–57.

92. Hearn, *Fantastics*, 191–97.

93. Paine, *Letters*, 226.

94. Twain, *Mark Twain's Notebooks & Journals*, 2:556–57.

95. Paine, *Letters*, 226.

96. Twain, *Life on the Mississippi*, 21.

97. "Mark Twain's Latest Book," 3.

98. Twain and Howells, *Mark Twain–Howells Letters*, 1:418, 413.

99. Twain, *Mark Twain's Notebooks & Journals*, 2:435.

100. Howells, *My Mark Twain*, 20.

101. Twain and Howells, *Mark Twain–Howells Letters*, 2:434.

102. Melton, *Mark Twain*, 132.

103. Howe, "Transcending the Limits of Experience," 422, 424.

104. Kruse, *Life on the Mississippi*, 49–50, 94–95.

105. Twain, *Life on the Mississippi*, 21.

106. "Editor's Table," 415, 416–17.

107. Twain, *Life on the Mississippi*, 5.

108. Twain, *Life on the Mississippi*, 23.

109. Twain, *Mark Twain's Notebooks & Journals*, 2:472, 482.

110. Elliott, "Reclaiming the Land," 243, 255, 258.

111. Carr, "'I Have Not Abandoned Any Plan,'" 7.

112. Parkman, *Discovery of the Great West*, 402, 196, 366.

113. Galloway, *La Salle and His Legacy*, 5–6.

114. Twain, *Life on the Mississippi*, 25, 37–38.

115. Twain, *Life on the Mississippi*, 362–63.

116. Twain, *Life on the Mississippi*, 18.

117. Twain, *Mississippi*, 245, 363.

118. Twain, *Mississippi*, 309.

119. Hesse-Wartegg, *Travels*, 129.

120. Murfree, "Levees of the Mississippi," 420, 432.

121. Curtis, "Mississippi River Problem," 609.

122. Shaler, "Floods of the Mississippi Valley," 659.

123. Taylor, "Subjugation of the Mississippi," 212–22.

124. Hofer and Scharnhorst, *Oscar Wilde in America*, 92.

125. Representatives of the Mercantile and Commercial Interests of the City of New Orleans, *Grand Banquet*, 22, 17, 8.

126. Twain, *Life on the Mississippi*, 302, 275, 303, 307, 208.

127. Twain, *Life on the Mississippi*, 467–68, 443.

128. Ticknor, "'Mark Twain's' Missing Chapter," 306.

129. Cardwell, "Mark Twain," 187.

130. Twain, *Life on the Mississippi*, 256, 326.

131. Twain, *Life on the Mississippi*, 256.

132. Hesse-Wartegg, *Travels*, 19.

133. Twain, *Life on the Mississippi*, 475, 292.

134. Twain, *Life on the Mississippi*, 579, 589. Schoolcraft's telling of the legend can be found in *Algic Researches*, 1:96–120.

135. Twain, *Life on the Mississippi*, 624.

136. Walworth, *Southern Silhouettes*, n.p.

137. Howells, "Editor's Study," 321.

138. "Mrs. Walworth's 'Southern Silhouettes,'" 310.

139. Walworth, *Southern Silhouettes*, 29–30, 41.

140. Walworth, *Southern Silhouettes*, 34, 31.

4. "Sometimes We'd Have That Whole River All to Ourselves": Runaways, Roustabouts, and the Limits of Freedom

1. Scharnhorst, *Mark Twain*, 71.

2. Twain, *Mark Twain's Letters to His Publishers*, 165.

3. Twain and Howells, *Mark Twain–Howells Letters*, 1:427, 435–36, 2:482, 484.

4. Howells, *My Mark Twain*, 52.

5. Berret, "Huckleberry Finn," 38.

6. Howells, *My Mark Twain*, 53.

7. Twain and Howells, *Mark Twain–Howells Letters*, 1:451.

8. "Our 'Forty Immortals,'" 169.

9. Bolton, *Famous American Authors*.

10. Eads, "Battles and Leaders," 419–23.

11. Twain, "Jim's Investments," 456–58; Twain, *Adventures of Huckleberry Finn*, 159.

12. Cable, "Dr. Sevier" (September 1884), 711.

13. Cable, "Dr. Sevier" (August 1884), 603.

14. Cable, "Freedman's Case," 413, 409, 418.

15. Railton, "Twain-Cable Combination," 176, 175.

16. "Magazines for January."

17. Pond, *Eccentricities of Genius*, 231.

18. Twain, *Mark Twain's Notebooks & Journals*, vol. 2.

19. Bikle, *George W. Cable*, 83.

20. "Fun on the Stage."

21. Twain, *Adventures of Huckleberry Finn*, 158.

22. *Hartford (Conn.) Courant*, February 20, 1885, 2.

23. Conway, *Uncle Tom*.

24. Monod, *Soul of Pleasure*, 232, 234–35.

25. Monod, *Soul of Pleasure*, 234.

26. Slout, *Burnt Cork and Tambourines*, 251.

27. Johnson, *Autobiography*, 102.

28. Merrick, *Old Times on the Upper Mississippi*, 250.

29. Buchanan, *Black Life on the Mississippi*, 174–75, 179, 175.

30. "River Life. The Roustabouts of the Mississippi," 2.

31. "Mississippi Steamboat Outrage," 2.

32. Allen, Ware, and Garrison, *Slave Songs of the United States*, 89, viii.

33. King, *Great South*, 72, 76.

34. Hesse-Wartegg, *Travels on the Lower Mississippi*, 28.

35. "Roustabouts' Farewell," 12.

36. Bisland, *Life and Letters of Lafcadio Hearn*, 2:199.

37. Cott, *Wandering Ghost*, 98.

38. Cott, *Wandering Ghost*, 98.

39. Hearn, *Children of the Levee*, 61–62, 64.

40. Hearn, *Children of the Levee*, 64–65, 70.

41. Hearn, *Children of the Levee*, 9–12.

42. Hearn, *Children of the Levee*, 13–17, 20–21.

43. Pennell, *Life and Letters of Joseph Pennell*, 1:50–51.

44. Pennell, "Trip of the 'Mark Twain,'" 399–400.

45. Pennell, "Trip," 401–2.

46. Cable, "Southern Silhouettes I," 1:1, 7.

47. Cable, "Southern Silhouettes VII," 1:7, 107–8.

48. MacKethan, "Huck Finn and the Slave Narratives," 253.

49. For a discussion of the vicissitudes and controversies of Henson's status as "Uncle Tom," see Winks, "Making of a Fugitive Slave Narrative.".

50. Henson, *"Uncle Tom's Story,"* 5–6.

51. Henson, *"Uncle Tom's Story,"* 46–48.

52. Henson, *"Uncle Tom's Story,"* 52, 64, 68, 67.

53. Henson, *"Uncle Tom's Story,"* 66–67, 70, 74–75.

54. Greenspan, *William Wells Brown*, 48–49, 58, 85.

55. Buchanan, *Black Life*, 5.

56. Gilmore, "'De Genewine Artekil,'" 758.

57. Brown, *Description*, 3.

58. Ernest, "William Wells Brown Maps the South," 90.

59. Brown, *My Southern Home*, 126–27.

60. Brown, *My Southern Home*, 128.

61. Brown, *My Southern Home*, 128–30, 133.

62. Buchanan, *Black Life*, 102.

63. Twain, *Adventures of Huckleberry Finn*, 59.

64. Schmitt, *Back to Nature*, xxi, 7, 19.

65. Stoll, *Inherit the Holy Mountain*, 103.

66. Courtney, *Joseph Hopkins Twichell*, 133.

67. Warner, *In the Wilderness*, 126, 131, 126–27, 36.

68. Dunkin, "Labours of Leisure," 131.

69. Dunkin, "Producing and Consuming Spaces," 229.

70. MacGregor, *Thousand Miles*, 9.

71. Castlemon, *Snagged and Sunk*.

72. "Drifting," 9.

73. Chapin, "Short Canoe Trip," 29–30.

74. Bishop, *Four Months in a Sneak-Box*, 209, 41.

75. Wilkins, *Cruise*, 9–10.

76. Neidé, *Canoe Aurora*, 53–54.

77. Wilkins, *Cruise*, 71–72, 80.

78. Neidé, *Canoe Aurora*, 53.

79. Bishop, *Four Months in a Sneak-Box*, 150.

80. Bishop, *Four Months in a Sneak-Box*, 35, 37, 38, 154; Neidé, *Canoe Aurora*, 65; Wilkins, *Cruise*, 53; Neidé, *Canoe Aurora*, 155–56.

81. Bishop, *Four Months in a Sneak-Box*, 75, 84, 71, 56; Neidé, *Canoe Aurora*, 65; Wilkins,

Cruise, 53; Neidé, *Canoe Aurora,* 145; Bishop, *Four Months in a Sneak-Box,* 259, 212, 181–82; Wilkins, *Cruise,* 84.

82. Bishop, *Four Months in a Sneak-Box,* 194, 58–59, 61, 64, 66; Neidé, *Canoe Aurora,* 100, 102.

83. Bishop, *Four Months in a Sneak-Box,* 257; Neidé, *Canoe Aurora,* 96; Bishop, *Four Months in a Sneak-Box,* 206, 192.

84. Neidé, *Canoe Aurora,* 130–32.

85. Boyton, *Story,* 5–6, 9.

86. Twain, *Mark Twain's Notebooks and Journals,* 3:347; see also Hellwig, *Mark Twain's Travel Literature,* 184. Boyton, *Story,* 105–6.

87. Boyton, *Story,* 225–26, 296.

88. "Swimming Down the Mississippi," 1.

89. See Munroe, "Modern Canoeing," 217. See also, e.g., Alden, "Perfect Canoe," 754–59; and *Cruise of the Canoe Club.*

90. Quoted in Blair, *Mark Twain & Huck Finn,* 5. Twain had other literary artifacts of this moment's canoe craze in his library too: Thomas Sedgwick Steele's *Canoe and Camera: A Two Hundred Mile Tour through the Maine Forests* (New York: Orange Judd Co., 1880); and *Paddle and Portage: From Moosehead Lake to the Aroostook River, Maine* (Boston: Estes & Lauriat, 1882). See Gribben, *Mark Twain's Library,* 2:661–62.

91. Woodard and MacCann, "Minstrel Shackles," 142.

92. Blair, *Mark Twain & Huck Finn,* 258.

93. Marx, "Mr. Eliot," 427.

94. Twain, *Adventures of Huckleberry Finn,* 67, 92, 155–57.

95. Marx, *Machine in the Garden,* 339.

96. Jones, "Huck and Jim," 157.

97. Twain, *Adventures of Huckleberry Finn,* 166, 344, 294.

98. Budd, "Southward Currents," 237.

99. Trilling, "Huckleberry Finn," 110.

100. Eliot, intro., *Adventures of Huckleberry Finn,* xii, xv.

101. Trilling, "Huckleberry Finn," 107–8.

102. Marx, "Mr. Eliot," 431.

103. Rampersad, "*Adventures of Huckleberry Finn* and Afro-American Literature," 50.

104. Wonham, "'I Want a Real Coon,'" 147, 136.

105. McCoy, "'Trouble Begins at Eight,'" 233.

106. Woodard and MacCann, "Minstrel Shackles," 142.

107. Bell, "Twain's 'Nigger' Jim," 137–38.

108. Fishkin, *Was Huck Black,* 88–89.

109. Twain, *Adventures of Huckleberry Finn,* 69–70, 82, 86, 96.

110. Twain, *Adventures of Huckleberry Finn,* 115, 124, 151.

111. Twain, *Adventures of Huckleberry Finn,* 201, 204, 260.

112. Twain, *Adventures of Huckleberry Finn,* 360, 356, 271.

113. Twain, *Adventures of Huckleberry Finn,* 364.

114. Twain, *Tom Sawyer Abroad,* 9.

115. Twain, *Mark Twain's Notebooks & Journals,* 3:91.

116. Paine, *Letters of Mark Twain,* 226.

117. Twain, *Mark Twain's Notebooks & Journals,* 3:90–91.

5. "I Went on A-Spinnin' down de River": Underworlds and Undertows

1. Twain, *Mark Twain's Correspondence,* 114–15.

2. Twain and Howells, *Mark Twain–Howells Letters,* 2:633, 645.

3. Twain, *Mark Twain's Notebooks,* 3:606.

4. Twain, *Connecticut Yankee in King Arthur's Court,* 355.

5. Hochschild, *King Leopold's Ghost,* 4.

6. Najder, *Joseph Conrad,* 160.

7. Clark, "Joseph Conrad and Mark Twain," 13.

8. Hawkins, "Mark Twain's Involvement with the Congo Reform Movement," 147.

9. Fatout, *Mark Twain Speaking,* 214.

10. Stanley, *Congo,* 2:7–8, 375.

11. Jerome, *Three Men in a Boat,* 73–74.

12. Scheick, "Going to Find Stanley," 408.

13. "Books of the Month," 286.

14. "Mark Twain," *Bookman,* 116.

15. Scott, "*Innocents Adrift,*" 231.

16. Twain, *Europe and Elsewhere,* 129, 139.

17. Bush, Courtney, and Messent, *Letters,* 167.

18. Griffin, *Family Sketch,* 164.

19. "Amusing the Children," 2.

20. Paine, *Mark Twain's Letters,* 2:495–96.

21. Twain, *Autobiography,* 2:310, 316.

22. King, *Memories,* 60–61.

23. King, *Grace King of New Orleans,* 379.

24. King, *Southern Woman,* 75, 172.

25. King, "Little Convent Girl," 547, 549–51.

26. Anderson, "Down Memory Lane," 110.

27. Twain, "Old Times on the Mississippi: I," 69.

28. Ralph, "Old Way," 165.

29. Harrison, "Studies in the South," 751.

30. Hunter, *Steamboats,* 637, 639.

31. Hunter, *Steamboats,* 640.

32. "Mississippi River Steamboats," 26.

33. Ralph, "Old Way," 184, 165.

34. Oakley, "Mississippi Sketches," 455.

35. Gibson, "Old Route to Orleans," 26, 6.

36. Oakley, "Mississippi Sketches," 448.

37. Gibson, "Old Route," 24–25.

38. Aylward, "Steamboating through Dixie," 514.

39. Johnson, *Highways and Byways*, 81.

40. Gibson, "Old Route," 25.

41. Oakley, "Mississippi Sketches," 447, 455, 450, 451.

42. Ralph, "Old Way," 175.

43. Oakley, "Mississippi Sketches," 447.

44. Gibson, "Old Route," 25.

45. Oakley, "Mississippi Sketches," 447–78.

46. Johnson, *Highways*, 79–80, 83.

47. Johnson, *Highways*, 80.

48. Aylward, "Steamboating," 515–16.

49. Buchanan, *Black Life*, 157.

50. Aylward, "Steamboating," 518.

51. Cooley, "Mississippi Roustabout," 290, 299–300, 293.

52. Buchanan, *Black Life*, 171.

53. Cooley, "Roustabout," 301.

54. Abbott and Seroff, *Out of Sight*, 448.

55. Handy, *Father of the Blues*, 27, 118–19.

56. Johnson, *Book of American Negro Poetry*, xi.

57. See Oliver, "Lookin' for 'The Bully,'" 111; and Kenney, *Jazz on the River*, 97.

58. Oliver, "Lookin' for 'The Bully,'" 112.

59. Ammen, *May Irwin*, 35.

60. Wondrich, *Stomp and Swerve*, 99.

61. Trevathan, *May Irwin's Bully Song*, 3.

62. Ammen, *Irwin*, 94.

63. Oliver, "Lookin' for 'The Bully,'" 112. Twain attended a dinner with Irwin, hosted by Augustin Daly, in 1887, at which he spoke. See Fatout, *Mark Twain Speaking*, 222.

64. Dormon, "Shaping the Popular Image," 453, 455.

65. Brown, *Stagolee Shot Billy*, 38–39.

66. Lomax, *American Ballads*, 93–94.

67. Buehler, "Stacker Lee," 190.

68. Lomax, *American Ballads*, 93.

69. Wheeler, *Steamboatin' Days*, 101.

70. Eberhart, "Stack Lee," 407–9.

71. Eberhart, "Stack Lee," 410.

72. Wheeler, *Steamboatin' Days*, 100, 103.

73. Handy, *Father of the Blues*, 75.

74. Lawson, *Jim Crow's Counterculture*, 11, 2.

75. Handy, *Father of the Blues*, 75.

76. Drake, *Tales and Sketches*, 27.

77. Brown, *Clotel*, 70.

78. "Twain's Friend Held," 8.

79. Twain, *Mark Twain's Notebooks & Journals*, 2:480–81.

80. Twain, *Fables of Man*, 280, 285, 281–82, 289.

81. Lillard, *Poker Stories,* 50, 42.

82. Fabian, *Card Sharps and Bucket Shops,* 6.

83. Willett, *Flush Fred's Full Hand,* 1–2.

84. Devol, *Forty Years a Gambler,* title page, 14.

85. Devol, *Forty Years a Gambler,* 54–55, 99, 295–96.

86. Ingraham, *Darkie Dan,* 3, 21.

87. Glazier, *Peculiarities of American Cities;* Glazier, *Ocean to Ocean.*

88. Glazier, *Down the Great River,* 29–30, 72, 75.

89. Owens, *Sword and Pen,* v.

90. Glazier, "Discovery of the True Source of the Mississippi," 23–25.

91. "Editor's Open Window," 580.

92. "Source of the Mississippi," 182–86. See Siegfried, "Canoeing on the High Mississippi," 171–80.

93. Baker, *Sources of the Mississippi,* 13, 17–18.

94. Quoted in Brandon, *Lake to the South of Itasca,* 51.

95. Glazier, *Headwaters of the Mississippi,* 403.

96. Twain, *Mark Twain's Letters,* 2:591.

97. Rohman, "River 'Ready for Business,'" 241.

98. Twain, *Twain's Notebooks & Journals,* 2:546–47.

99. Twain, *Pudd'nhead Wilson,* 17.

100. Twain, "Old Times on the Mississippi: I," 69; Twain, *Pudd'nhead Wilson,* 17.

101. Twain, *Pudd'nhead Wilson,* 19–20.

102. Twain, *Pudd'nhead Wilson,* 33, 32, 39, 41–43.

103. Twain, *Pudd'nhead Wilson,* 59, 62, 65.

104. Twain, *Pudd'nhead Wilson,* 65–66, 93–94.

105. Twain, *Pudd'nhead Wilson,* 69–70, 213.

106. Twain, *Pudd'nhead Wilson,* 94, 97, 215–17, 220.

107. Twain, *Pudd'nhead Wilson,* 229, 231–34.

108. Twain, *Pudd'nhead Wilson,* 226, 244.

109. Wonham, "Minstrel and the Detective," 130–31.

110. Twain, *Pudd'nhead Wilson,* 301, 303.

111. Twain, *Tom Sawyer Abroad, Tom Sawyer, Detective and Other Stories,* 115–16.

112. Twain, *Mark Twain's Satires,* 185–87, 195.

Epilogue: "A Black Wall of Night"

1. Merrick, *Old Times on the Upper Mississippi,* 13–14.

2. Habermehl, *Life on the Western Rivers,* iv; Chambers, *Mississippi River and Its Wonderful Valley,* xvi; Quick and Quick, *Mississippi Steamboatin',* vii; Eskew, *Pageant of the Packets,* xiii; Anthony, *Paddle Wheels and Pistols,* 327, 329.

3. Morris, "Only a River," 149–65, 153–54.

4. Klein and Zellmer. *Mississippi River Tragedies,* 55.

5. Pisani, "Water Planning in the Progressive Era," 393.

6. "Federal Control of the Mississippi River," 117.

7. Clark, "Perennial National Problem," 29, 31.

8. "Duty of the South to Itself," 631.

9. Klein and Zellmer, *Mississippi River Tragedies*, 57.

10. "Trouble with Our Waterways," 22.

11. Blakeslee, "Results of the Panama Canal on World Trade," 494.

12. Stevens, *Log of the Alton*, 7–8, 64.

13. Spears, "Moods of the Mississippi," 382.

14. Greeson, *Our South*, 274.

15. "Postbellum Sketch of Mississippi River Life," 558.

16. Stuart, *River's Children*, 11, 34–5, 32, 53.

17. Stuart, *River's Children*, 117–18, 124, 151, 156, 179.

18. Fisher, "Other Mary Murfree," 134.

19. Craddock, *Story of Duciehurst*, 56.

20. Craddock, *Fair Mississippian*, 96, 99, 143, 146.

21. Murfree, *Story of Duciehurst*, 1, 113, 123, 390, 438.

22. Tousley, *Where Goes the River*, n.p., 131–32.

23. Raven-Hart, *Canoe Errant on the Mississippi*, 1, 5–6, 8.

24. Aylward, "Steamboating through Dixie," 521–22.

25. Waugh, *Houseboat Book*, 5–6.

26. Mathews, *Log of the Easy Way*, 3–5, 268.

27. Lighty and Lighty, *Shantyboat*, 3, vi.

28. Speakman, *Mostly Mississippi*, 307.

29. Heat-Moon, intro. to Jonk, *River Journey*, ix–xiii, x–xi.

30. Eggleston, *Last of the Flatboats*, 23–24.

31. Cox, *Dreaming of Dixie*, 16.

32. Ward, "Music, Musical Theater, and the Imagined South," 41.

33. Carroll, Fields, and Macdonald, "On the Mississippi."

34. Gilbert and Muir, "Waiting for the Robert E. Lee."

35. Burton, "Honor Roll of Popular Songwriters, No. 31: Harry Carroll," 34.

36. Ward, "Music, Musical Theater, and the Imagined South," 46.

37. "Steam Displaces Men," 6.

38. "Dago Deckhands Now," 4.

39. Kenney, *Jazz on the River*, 1–2, 29, 11.

40. Nott, "Woman Plot Recalls River Packet Days."

41. Ferber, *Show Boat*, 25, 83, 150, 84, 111.

42. Barry, *Rising Tide*, 285–86.

43. "7 More Die in Flood along Mississippi," *New York Times*, April 17, 1927, 9.

44. Oliver et al., *Yonder Come the Blues*, 277.

45. Mizelle, *Backwater Blues*, 20, 28, 14–15.

46. Hughes, "Negro Speaks of Rivers," 71.

47. Kent, liner notes to *St. Louis Town*.

48. Spaulding, "Cairo Blues."

49. Taft, *Talkin' to Myself*, 556.

50. "John Hay Speaks for the Nation," 137–38.

51. Bikle, *George W. Cable,* 286–87.

52. Sutcliffe, "Fulton's Invention of the Steamboat," 819–20.

53. Bikle, *Cable,* 287–88.

54. Cable, *Gideon's Band,* 31, 41, 126, 463, 431–32.

55. Cable, *Gideon's Band,* 391, 255, 429, 201.

56. Cable, *Gideon's Band,* 439–40.

57. Payne, "George Washington Cable's John March and Gideon's Band," 243.

58. Dawson and Goodman, *William Dean Howells,* 371.

59. Howells, *Literature and Life,* 309, 322, 311, 313, 317.

60. Howells, *Literature and Life,* 309, 314, 322–24.

61. Howells, *Daughter of the Storage,* 67–70, 72–74, 76–77.

62. Howells, "Pearl," 409, 413.

63. Howells, "Tale Untold," 236–37, 240–42.

64. Sorrentino, "Mark Twain's 1902 Trip to Missouri," 13.

65. Sorrentino, "Mark Twain's 1902 Trip to Missouri," 29, 25.

66. "Mark Twain among Scenes of His Early Life," 28.

67. Scharnhorst, *Mark Twain,* 415–17.

68. Sorrentino, "Mark Twain's 1902 Trip to Missouri," 26–27, 35.

69. Twain, *Mark Twain's Speeches,* 369–70.

70. Twain, *Mark Twain's Speeches,* 423

71. Scharnhorst, *Mark Twain,* 461.

72. Sorrentino, "Mark Twain's 1902 Trip to Missouri," 38.

73. Scharnhorst, *Mark Twain,* 461.

74. Sorrentino, "Mark Twain's 1902 Trip to Missouri," 38–39.

75. Scharnhorst, *Mark Twain,* 461.

76. "Mark Twain on the River," 4.

77. Scharnhorst, *Mark Twain,* 466.

78. Sorrentino, "Mark Twain's 1902 Trip to Missouri," 32.

79. "Races on the Mississippi," 9.

80. Twain, *Autobiography,* 1:196.

81. Paine, *Mark Twain,* 3:1377–78.

82. Twain, *Autobiography,* 3:245, 136–37.

83. Paine, *Mark Twain,* 1368.

BIBLIOGRAPHY

Abbott, Lynn, and Doug Seroff. *Out of Sight: The Rise of African American Popular Music, 1889–1895.* Jackson: University Press of Mississippi, 2002.

"Afloat." *Indianapolis Sentinel,* August 26, 1874.

Agruss, David. "'Boys Gone Wild': Island Stranding, Cross-Racial Identification, and Metropolitan Masculinity in R. M. Ballantyne's *The Coral Island.*" *Victorian* 1, no. 1 (2013): 1–19.

Alcott, Louisa May. *An Old-Fashioned Girl.* Boston: Roberts Brothers, 1870.

Alden, William Livingston. *The Cruise of the Canoe Club.* New York: Harper & Brothers, 1883.

———. "The Perfect Canoe." *Harper's New Monthly Magazine,* April 1878.

Aldrich, Lilian Bailey. *Crowding Memories.* Boston: Houghton Mifflin, 1920.

Aldrich, Thomas Bailey. *The Story of a Bad Boy.* Boston: Fields, Osgood, & Co., 1870.

Allen, William Francis, Charles Pickard Ware, and Lucy McKim Garrison, eds. *Slave Songs of the United States.* New York: Peter Smith, 1950.

Ammen, Sharoin. *May Irwin: Singing, Shouting, and the Shadow of Minstrelsy.* Urbana: University of Illinois Press, 2017.

"Amusing the Children." *Washington Post,* July 13, 1886.

Anderson, David. "Down Memory Lane: Nostalgia for the Old South in Post–Civil War Plantation Reminiscences." *Journal of Southern History* 71, no. 1 (February 2005): 105–36.

Anthony, Irvin. *Paddle Wheels and Pistols.* Philadelphia: Macrae Smith Co., 1929.

Aron, Albert W. "Mark Twain and Germany." *Monatshefte für Deutsche Sprache und Pädagogik* (1925): 65–80.

Ashton, Warren T. [William T. Adams]. *Hatchie, the Guardian Slave; or, The Heiress of Bellevue.* Boston: B. B. Mussey and Co., 1853.

Aspiz, Harold. "Tom Sawyer's Games of Death." *Studies in the Novel* 27, no. 2 (Summer 1995): 141–53.

"At Home." *Indianapolis Sentinel,* June 8, 1876.

Aylward, William J. "Steamboating through Dixie." *Harper's Magazine,* September 1915.

Baetzhold, Howard G. *Mark Twain & John Bull: The British Connection.* Bloomington: Indiana University Press, 1970.

Baker, James H. *The Sources of the Mississippi: Their Discoverers, Real and Pretended.* Minnesota Historical Collections 6, no. 1. St. Paul: Brown, Treacy & Co., 1887.

Ballantyne, R. M. *The Coral Island: A Tale of the Pacific Ocean.* Boston: Phillips, Sampson & Co., 1859.

————. *Personal Reminiscences in Book-Making.* London: James Nisbet & Co., 1893.

Banham, Christopher. "'England and America against the World': Empire and the USA in Edwin J. Brett's *Boys of England,* 1866–99." *Victorian Periodicals Review* 40, no. 2 (Summer 2007): 151–71.

Banvard, John. *Description of Banvard's Panorama of the Mississippi River.* Boston: John Putnam, 1847.

Barry, John M. *Rising Tide: The Great Mississippi Flood of 1927 and How It Changed America.* New York: Touchstone, 1998.

Bassett. John E. "*The Gilded Age:* Performance, Power, and Authority." *Studies in the Novel* 17, no. 4 (Winter 1985): 395–405.

Bates, Allan. "Mark Twain and the Mississippi River." Ph.D. diss., University of Chicago, 1968.

Beckson, Karl. *London in the 1890s: A Cultural History.* New York: W. W. Norton, 1992.

Bell, Bernard W. "Twain's 'Nigger' Jim: The Tragic Face behind the Minstrel Mask." In *Satire or Evasion? Black Perspectives on Huckleberry Finn,* edited by James S. Leonard, Thomas A. Tenner, and Thadious M. Davis, 124–40. Durham, N.C.: Duke University Press, 1992.

Bell, Michael Davitt. *The Problem of American Realism: Studies in the Cultural History of a Literary Idea.* Chicago: University of Chicago Press, 1993.

Berkove, Lawrence I. "Dan De Quille and 'Old Times on the Mississippi.'" *Mark Twain Journal* 24, no. 2 (Fall 1986): 28–35.

Berret, Anthony J. "Huckleberry Finn and the Minstrel Show." *American Studies* 27, no. 2 (Fall 1986): 37–49.

Betts, John Rickards. "The Technological Revolution and the Rise of Sport, 1850–1900." *Mississippi Valley Historical Review* 40, no. 2 (September 1953): 231–56.

Bikle, Lucy Leffingwell (Cable). *George W. Cable: His Life and Letters.* New York: Charles Scribner's Sons, 1928.

Bird, John. *Mark Twain and Metaphor.* Columbia: University of Missouri Press, 2007.

Bishop, Nathaniel H. *Four Months in a Sneak-Box.* Boston: Lee & Shepard, 1879.

Bisland, Elizabeth. *The Life and Letters of Lafcadio Hearn.* 2 vols. London: Archibald Constable & Co., 1906.

Blair, Walter. *Mark Twain & Huck Finn.* Berkeley: University of California Press, 1960.

Blake, Peter. "George Augustus Sala and the English Middle-Class View of America."

19: Interdisciplinary Studies in the Long Nineteenth Century 9 (2009). http://doi.org/10.16995/ntn.509.

Blakeslee, George H. "The Results of the Panama Canal on World Trade: 1." *Outlook,* October 27, 1915.

Blanck, Jacob. *Harry Castlemon: Boys' Own Author.* New York: R. R. Bowker Co., 1941.

Bolton, Sarah K. *Famous American Authors.* New York: Thomas Y. Crowell & Co., 1887.

"Books of the Month." *Atlantic Monthly,* August 1890.

Boyton, Paul. *The Story of Paul Boyton.* London: George Routledge & Sons, 1893.

Bradshaw, George. *Bradshaw's Hand-Book for Belgium and the Rhine, and Portions of Rhenish Germany; With a Ten Days' Tour in Holland.* London: W. J. Adams & Sons, 1876.

Branch, Edgar M. "A Proposed Calendar of Samuel Clemens's Steamboats, 15 April 1857 to 8 May 1861, with Commentary." *Mark Twain Journal* 24, no. 2 (Fall 1986): 2–27.

Brandon, Gary. *A Lake to the South of Itasca: Willard Glazier and the Mississippi Fiasco, 1881–1891.* Waterloo, Ont.: Escart Press, 1990.

Bratton, J. S. *The Impact of Victorian Children's Fiction.* New York: Routledge, 2016.

Bristow, Joseph. *Empire Boys: Adventures in a Man's World.* London: HarperCollins, 1991.

"British Jack and Yankee Doodle." *Boys of England,* May 8, 1880.

"British Jack and Yankee Doodle." *Boys of England,* May 28, 1880.

"British Jack and Yankee Doodle." *Boys of England,* July 9, 1880.

"British Jack and Yankee Doodle." *Boys of England,* July 23, 1880.

"British Jack and Yankee Doodle." *Boys of England,* August 13, 1880.

"British Jack and Yankee Doodle." *Boys of England,* August 20, 1880.

"British Jack and Yankee Doodle." *Boys of England,* August 27, 1880.

"British Jack and Yankee Doodle." *Boys of England,* September 10, 1880.

"British Jack and Yankee Doodle." *Boys of England,* September 17, 1880.

"British Jack and Yankee Doodle." *Boys of England,* September 24, 1880.

Brodhead, Richard. *Cultures of Letters: Scenes of Reading and Writing in Nineteenth-Century America.* Chicago: University of Chicago Press, 1993.

Brown, Cecil. *Stagolee Shot Billy.* Cambridge: Harvard University Press, 2003.

Brown, William Wells. *Clotel; or, The President's Daughter.* London: Partridge & Oakey, 1853.

———. *A Description of William Wells Brown's Original Panoramic Views of the Scenes in the Life of an American Slave.* London: Charles Gilpin, 1849.

———. *My Southern Home: or; The South and Its People.* Boston: A. G. Brown & Co., 1882.

———. *Narrative of William W. Brown, a Fugitive Slave.* Boston: Published at the Anti-Slavery Office, 1847.

Bryant, William Cullen, ed. *Picturesque America; or, The Land We Live In.* 2 vols. New York: D. Appleton & Co., 1872–74.

Buchanan, Thomas C. *Black Life on the Mississippi: Slaves, Free Blacks, and the Western Steamboat World.* Chapel Hill: University of North Carolina Press, 2004.

Budd, Louis J. *Mark Twain: The Contemporary Reviews.* Cambridge: Cambridge University Press, 1999.

———. "The Southward Currents under Huck Finn's Raft." *Mississippi Valley Historical Review* 46, no. 2 (September 1959): 222–37.

Buehler, Richard E. "Stacker Lee: A Partial Investigation into the Historicity of a Negro Murder Ballad." *Keystone Folklore Quarterly* 12, no. 3 (Fall 1967): 187–91.

Bulwer-Lytton, Edward. *The Pilgrims of the Rhine.* London: Saunders & Otley, 1834.

Buntline, Ned. *Black Avenger of the Spanish Main; or, The Fiend of Blood: A Thrilling Tale of the Buccaneer Times.* Boston: F. Gleason, 1847.

Burde, Edgar J. "Mark Twain: The Writer as Pilot." *PMLA* 93, no. 5 (October 1978): 878–92.

Burnett, Frances Hodgson. *The One I Knew the Best of All: A Memory of the Mind of a Child.* New York: Charles Scribner's Sons, 1893.

Burton, Jack. "The Honor Roll of Popular Songwriters, No. 31: Harry Carroll." *Billboard,* August 6, 1949.

Bush, Harold K., Steve Courtney, and Peter Messent, eds. *The Letters of Mark Twain and Joseph Hopkins Twichell.* Athens: University of Georgia Press, 2017.

Byerly, Alison. *Are We There Yet? Virtual Travel and Victorian Realism.* Ann Arbor: University of Michigan Press, 2012.

Cable, George Washington. "Dr. Sevier." *Century Magazine,* August 1884.

———. "Dr. Sevier." *Century Magazine,* September 1884.

———. "The Freedman's Case in Equity." *Century Magazine,* January 1885.

———. *Gideon's Band: A Tale of the Mississippi.* New York: Charles Scribner's Sons, 1914.

———. *The Grandissimes.* New York: Charles Scribner's Sons, 1880.

———. "New Orleans." *St. Nicholas,* November 1893.

———. *Old Creole Days.* New York: Charles Scribner's Sons, 1879.

Cable, James Boardman. "Southern Silhouettes I: Mammy." *Current,* December 22, 1883.

———. "Southern Silhouettes VII: The Roustabout." *Current,* February 2, 1884.

"Cable's 'Grandissimes.'" *Scribner's Monthly,* November 1880.

Cady, Edwin. "Howells on the River." *American Literary Realism* 25, no. 3 (Spring 1993): 27–41.

Cardwell, Guy. "Mark Twain, James R. Osgood, and Those 'Suppressed' Passages." *New England Quarterly* 46, no. 2 (June 1973): 163–88.

Carr, Nicholas. "'I Have Not Abandoned Any Plan': The Rage in Francis Parkman." *Massachusetts Historical Review* 17 (2015): 1–34.

Carroll, Harry, Arthur Fields, and Ballard Macdonald. "On the Mississippi." Sheet music. New York: Shapiro Music Publishing Co., 1912.

Carter, John Henton. *The Log of Commodore Rollingpin.* New York: G. W. Carleton & Co., 1874.

Castlemon, Harry. *Frank before Vicksburg.* Cincinnati: R. W. Carroll & Co., 1866.

———. *Frank on a Gun-Boat.* Cincinnati: R. W. Carroll & Co., 1869.

———. *Frank on the Lower Mississippi.* Cincinnati: R. W. Carroll & Co., 1869.

———. *Frank, the Young Naturalist.* Cincinnati: R. W. Carroll & Co., 1866.

———. "How to Write Stories for Boys—III." *Writer,* January 1896.

Castlemon, Harry. *Snagged and Sunk: The Adventures of a Canvas Canoe.* Philadelphia: Porter & Coates, 1888.

Chambers, Julius. *The Mississippi River and Its Wonderful Valley.* New York: G. P. Putnam's Sons, 1910.

Chapin, A. B. "A Short Canoe Trip." *American Canoeist* 2, no. 2 (March 1883): 29–30.

Clark, George P. "Joseph Conrad and Mark Twain." *Mark Twain Journal* 19, no. 2 (Summer 1978): 12–15.

Clark, Speaker Champ. "A Perennial National Problem." *North American Review* (July 1914): 25–34.

Cochran, Miss F. A. "The Mississippi." *Ladies' Repository,* March 1873.

Cockrell, Dale. *Demons of Disorder: Early Blackface Minstrels and Their World.* Cambridge: Cambridge University Press, 1997.

Collins, K. K., ed. *George Eliot: Interviews and Recollections.* New York: Palgrave Macmillan, 2010.

Conway, H. J. "Uncle Tom; or, Life among the Lowly." MS promptbook. Boston, ca. 1876. Uncle Tom's Cabin & American Culture.utc.iath.virginia.edu/onstage/scripts/osplhcbIIt.html.

Cooley, Stoughton. "The Mississippi Roustabout." *New England Magazine,* November 1894.

"Correspondence." *Boys of England,* August 3, 1867.

Cott, Jonathan. *Wandering Ghost: The Odyssey of Lafcadio Hearn.* Tokyo: Kodansha International, 1992.

Courtney, Steve. *Joseph Hopkins Twichell: The Life and Times of Mark Twain's Closest Friend.* Athens: University of Georgia Press, 2008.

Covici, Pascal, Jr. "Dear Master Wattie: The Mark Twain–David Watt Bowser Letters." *Southwest Review* 45, no. 2 (Spring 1960): 105–21.

Cox, Karen. *Dreaming of Dixie: How the South Was Created in American Culture.* Chapel Hill: University of North Carolina Press, 2011.

Craddock, Charles Egbert [Mary Noailles Murfree]. *The Fair Mississippian.* Boston: Houghton Mifflin, 1908.

———. *The Story of Duciehurst: A Tale of the Mississippi.* New York: Pan Macmillan, 1914.

Curtis, David A. "The Mississippi River Problem." *Harper's New Monthly Magazine,* September 1882.

"Dago Deckhands Now." *Washington Post,* April 25, 1909.

Dahl, Curtis. "Mark Twain and the Moving Panoramas." *American Quarterly* 13, no. 1 (Spring 1961): 20–32.

Davis, John H. "Bridging the Gap: The Twin Kingdoms of *The Prince and the Pauper.*" In *Mark Twain's Geographical Imagination,* edited by Joseph A. Alvarez, 17–34. Newcastle: Cambridge Scholars Publishing, 2009.

Dawson, Carl, and Susan Goodman. *William Dean Howells: A Writer's Life.* Berkeley: University of California Press, 2005.

Deane, Bradley. "Imperial Boyhood: Piracy and the Play Ethic." *Victorian Studies* 53, no. 4 (Summer 2011): 689–714.

De Leon, Thomas Cooper. "A Western River-Race." *Appletons' Journal,* April 6, 1872.

Dempsey, Terrell. *Searching for Jim: Slavery in Sam Clemens's World.* Columbia: University of Missouri Press, 2003.

De Quille, Dan. "Pilot Wylie." *Hartford Daily Courant,* February 8, 1875.

Devol, George H. *Forty Years a Gambler on the Mississippi.* New York: Home Book Co., 1887.

DeVoto, Bernard. *Mark Twain's America.* 1932. Reprint, Lincoln: University of Nebraska Press and Bison Books, 1997.

Dickens, Charles. *American Notes.* 2 vols. London: Chapman & Hall, 1842.

———. "The American Panorama." *Littell's Living Age,* February 17, 1849.

———. *The Life and Adventures of Martin Chuzzlewit.* London: Chapman & Hall, 1844.

Disturnell, J. *Tourist's Guide to the Upper Mississippi River.* New York: American News Co., 1866.

Dix, Andrew. "Twain and the Mississippi." In *A Companion to Mark Twain,* edited by Peter Messent and Louis J. Budd, 293–308. Oxford: Wiley Blackwell, 2005.

Dormon, James H. "Shaping the Popular Image of Post-Reconstruction American Blacks: The 'Coon' Song Phenomenon of the Gilded Age." *American Quarterly* 40, no. 4 (December 1988): 450–71.

"Down the River." *Indianapolis Sentinel,* October 4, 1874.

Drake, Benjamin. *Tales and Sketches from the Queen City.* Cincinnati: E. Morgan and Co., 1838.

"Down to the Delta." *Indianapolis Sentinel,* December 15, 1874.

"Drifting." *American Canoeist,* February 1882.

Dunae, Patrick A. "Boys' Literature and the Idea of Empire, 1870–1914." *Victorian Studies* 24, no. 1 (Fall 1980): 105–21.

Dunkin, Jessica. "The Labours of Leisure: Work and Workers at the Annual Encampments of the American Canoe Association, 1880–1910." *Labour / Le Travail* 73 (Spring 2014): 127–50.

———. "Producing and Consuming Spaces of Sport and Leisure: The Encampments and Regattas of the American Canoe Association, 1880–1903." In *Moving Natures:*

Mobility and the Environment in Canadian History, edited by Ben Bradley, Jay Young, and Colin M. Coates, 229–50. Calgary: University of Calgary Press, 2016.

"A Duty of the South to Itself." *Century Magazine,* August 1912.

Eads, James B. "Battles and Leaders of the Civil War: Recollections of Foote and the Gun-Boats." *Century Magazine,* January 1885.

Eberhart, George M. "Stack Lee: The Man, the Music, and the Myth." In *A Question of Manhood: A Reader in U.S. Black Men's History and Masculinity,* edited by Earnestine Jenkins and Darlene Clark Hine, 2:387–440. Bloomington: Indiana University Press, 1999.

"Editor's Open Window." *Outing,* August 1886.

"Editor's Table." *Harper's New Monthly Magazine,* February 1863.

Egan, Michael. *Mark Twain's Huckleberry Finn: Race, Class and Society.* London: Chatto & Windus, 1977.

Eggleston, Edward. *The End of the World.* New York: Orange Judd & Co., 1872.

———. *The Hoosier Schoolmaster.* New York: Orange Judd & Co., 1871.

Eggleston, George Cary. *The Last of the Flatboats.* Boston: Lothrop Publishing Co., 1900.

———. *Recollections of a Varied Life.* New York: Henry Holt, 1910.

Eliot, T. S. Introduction to *Adventures of Huckleberry Finn,* by Mark Twain. London: Cresset Press, 1950.

Elliott, Kate. "Reclaiming the Land, Reclaiming the Indian: The *La Salle* Series of George Catlin." *American Nineteenth Century History* 15, no. 3 (2014): 237–61.

Emerson, Ken. *Doo-Dah! Stephen Foster and the Rise of American Popular Culture.* New York: Da Capo Press, 1998.

Ernest, John. "William Wells Brown Maps the South in *My Southern Home: or, The South and Its People.*" *Southern Quarterly* 45, no. 3 (April 2008): 88–107.

"Ernest Morris: Boy Traveler and Explorer." *Frank Leslie's Illustrated Newspaper,* August 18, 1877.

Eskew, Garnett Laidlaw. *The Pageant of the Packets.* New York: Henry Holt, 1929.

Fabian, Ann. *Card Sharps and Bucket Shops: Gambling in Nineteenth-Century America.* 1990. Reprint, New York: Routledge, 1999.

Fahs, Alice. *The Imagined Civil War: Popular Literature of the North & South, 1861–1865.* Chapel Hill: University of North Carolina Press, 2001.

Fatout, Paul, ed. *Mark Twain Speaking.* Iowa City: University of Iowa Press, 1976.

"Federal Control of the Mississippi River." *Week,* September 16, 1914.

Ferber, Edna. *Show Boat.* New York: Doubleday, 1926.

Ferriss, George T. "Mark Twain." *Appletons' Journal,* July 1874.

Fisher, Benjamin F. "The Other Mary Murfree." *Arkansas Review: A Journal of Delta Studies* 43, no 3 (2013): 131–40.

Fishkin, Shelley Fisher. *Was Huck Black? Mark Twain and African-American Voices.* New York: Oxford University Press, 1993.

Flint, Timothy. "Progress of the West." *Western Magazine and Review* 1, no. 1 (May 1827): 25–27.

Foster, Daniel H. *Wagner's "Ring" Cycle and the Greeks.* Cambridge: Cambridge University Press, 2010.

"Fun on the Stage." *Brooklyn Daily Eagle,* November 23, 1884. Mark Twain in His Times. http://twain.lib.virginia.edu/onstage/maps/84rev05.html.

Galloway, Patricia Kay. *La Salle and His Legacy: Frenchman and Indians in the Lower Mississippi Valley.* Jackson: University Press of Mississippi, 1982.

"General City News." *Indianapolis Sentinel,* July 17, 1875.

"A German Traveler on the Mississippi." *New York Times,* January 30, 1882.

Gerteis, Louis S. "Blackface Minstrelsy and the Construction of Race in Nineteenth-Century America." In *Union & Emancipation: Essays on Politics and Race in the Civil War Era,* edited by David W. Blight and Brooks D. Simpson, 79–104. Kent, Ohio: Kent State University Press, 1997.

Gibson, Willis. "The Old Route to Orleans." *Scribner's Magazine,* January 1903.

Gilbert, L. Wolfe, and Lewis F. Muir. "Waiting for the Robert E. Lee." New York: F. A. Mills, 1912.

"The Gilded Age." *Old and New,* March 1874.

"The Gilded Age." *Saturday Review,* February 14, 1874.

Gilmore, Paul. "'De Genewine Artekil': William Wells Brown, Blackface Minstrelsy, and Abolitionism." *American Literature* 69, no. 4 (December 1997): 743–80.

Glazier, Willard [John Algernon Owens]. "Discovery of the True Source of the Mississippi." *Proceedings of the Royal Geographical Society and Monthly Record of Geography* 7, no. 1 (January 1885): 23–25.

——. *Down the Great River.* Philadelphia: Hubbard Brothers, 1887.

——. *Headwaters of the Mississippi.* Chicago: Rand, McNally & Co., 1893.

——. *Ocean to Ocean on Horseback.* Philadelphia: P. W. Ziegler Co., 1895.

——. *Peculiarities of American Cities.* Philadelphia: Hubbard Brothers, 1884.

——. *Sword and Pen; Ventures and Adventures of Willard Glazier, (The Soldier-Author,) in War and Literature.* Philadelphia: P. W. Ziegler & Co., 1883.

Gould, Emerson. *Fifty Years on the Mississippi.* St. Louis: Nixon-Jones Printing Co., 1889.

"The Great Race." *New Orleans Daily Picayune,* July 1, 1870.

"The Great Race." *New Orleans Daily Picayune,* July 2, 1870.

Greenslet, Ferris. *The Life of Thomas Bailey Aldrich.* Cambridge: Riverside Press, 1908.

Greenspan, Ezra. *William Wells Brown: An African American Life.* New York: W. W. Norton, 2014.

Greeson, Jennifer Rae. *Our South: Geographic Fantasy and the Rise of National Literature.* Cambridge: Harvard University Press, 2010.

Gribben, Alan. "Manipulating a Genre: *Huckleberry Finn* as Boy Book." *South Central Review* 5, no. 4 (Winter 1988): 15–21.

———. *Mark Twain's Library: A Reconstruction.* 2 vols. Boston: G. K. Hall, 1980.

———. "Mark Twain's Lifelong Reading." In *Mark Twain and Youth: Studies in His Life and Writings,* edited by Kevin MacDonnell and R. Kent Rasmussen, 30–46. New York: Bloomsbury, 2016.

Griffen, Benjamin, ed. *A Family Sketch and Other Private Writings.* Berkeley: University of California Press, 2014.

Habermehl, John. *Life on the Western Rivers.* Pittsburgh: McNary & Simpson, 1901.

Hale, Sarah Josepha. "The Mississippi River." In *Poems of Places: America: Western States,* edited by Henry Wadsworth Longfellow, 114–15. Boston: Houghton, Osgood & Co., 1879.

Handy, W. C. *Father of the Blues: An Autobiography.* New York: Macmillan, 1947.

Harris, Joel Chandler. "To the Editors of the Critic." *Critic,* November 28, 1885.

Harrison, Jonathan Baxter. "Studies in the South." *Atlantic Monthly,* June 1882.

Hatch, James V. Introduction to *Lost Plays of the Harlem Renaissance, 1920–1940,* edited by James V. Hatch and Leo Hamalian, 9–20. Detroit: Wayne State University Press, 1996.

Hauk, Minnie. *Memories of a Singer.* London: A. M. Philpot, Ltd., 1925.

Hawkins, Hunt. "Mark Twain's Involvement with the Congo Reform Movement: 'A Fury of Generous Indignation.'" *New England Quarterly* 51, no. 2 (June 1978): 147–75.

Hay, John. "The Foster-Brothers." *Harper's New Monthly Magazine,* September 1869.

"Jim Bludso (of the Prairie Belle)." *New York Tribune,* January 5, 1871.

Hearn, Lafcadio. *Children of the Levee.* Edited by O. W. Frost. Lexington: University of Kentucky Press, 1957.

———. *Fantastics and Other Fancies.* Boston: Houghton Mifflin, 1914. "The Heart of Africa." *Scribner's Monthly,* August 1874.

Heat-Moon, William Least. Introduction to *River Journey,* by Clarence Jonk, ix–xiii. St. Paul: Borealis Books / Minnesota Historical Society Press, 2003.

Hellwig, Harold H. *Mark Twain's Travel Literature: The Odyssey of a Mind.* Jefferson, N.C.: McFarland & Co., 2008.

Henson, Josiah, Rev. *"Uncle Tom's Story of His Life": An Autobiography of the Rev. Josiah Henson.* Edited by John Lobb. London: "Christian Age" Office, 1877.

Herndon, William Lewis, and Lardner Gibbon. *Exploration of the Valley of the Amazon, Made under Direction of the Navy Department.* 2 vols. Washington, D.C.: Robert Armstrong, 1854.

Hesse-Wartegg, Ernst von. *Travels on the Lower Mississippi, 1879–1880.* Edited and translated by Frederic Trautmann. Columbia: University of Missouri Press, 1990.

Hochschild, Adam. *King Leopold's Ghost: A Story of Greed, Terror, and Heroism in Colonial Africa*. Boston: Mariner Books, 1999.

Hofer, Matthew, and Gary Scharnhorst, eds. *Oscar Wilde in America: The Complete Interviews*. Urbana: University of Illinois Press, 2010.

Hoffman, Andrew. *Inventing Mark Twain: The Lives of Samuel Langhorne Clemens*. London: Orion Books, 1998.

Honaker, Lisa. "'One Man to Rely On': Long John Silver and the Shifting Character of Victorian Boys' Fiction." *Journal of Narrative Theory* 34, no. 1 (Winter 2004): 27–53.

Hood, Thomas. *Up the Rhine*. London: A. H. Baily & Co., 1840.

Horwitz, Howard. "'Ours by the Law of Nature': Romance and Independents on Mark Twain's River." *boundary 2* 17, no. 1 (Spring 1990): 243–71.

Howe, Lawrence. *Mark Twain and the Novel: The Double-Cross of Authority*. Cambridge: Cambridge University Press, 1998.

———. "Transcending the Limits of Experience: Mark Twain's *Life on the Mississippi*." *American Literature* 63, no. 3 (September 1991): 420–39.

Howells, William Dean. *A Boy's Town*. New York: Harper & Brothers, 1890.

———. *The Daughter of the Storage*. New York: Harper & Brothers, 1916.

———. "Editor's Study." *Harper's New Monthly Magazine*, January 1888.

———. *Literature and Life*. New York: Harper & Brothers, 1902.

———. *My Mark Twain*. New York: Harper & Brothers, 1910.

———. "The Pearl." *Harper's New Monthly Magazine*, August 1916.

———. "The Pilot's Story." *Atlantic Monthly*, September 1860.

———. "Recent Literature." *Atlantic Monthly*, May 1876.

———. "A Tale Untold." *Atlantic Monthly*, August 1917.

———. *Their Wedding Journey*. Boston: James R. Osgood & Co., 1872.

Hoyt, J. K. *The Romance of the Table*. New Brunswick, N.J.: Times Publishing Co., 1872.

Hughes, Langston. "The Negro Speaks of Rivers." *Crisis*, June 1921.

Hughes, Thomas. *Tom Brown's Schooldays*. Cambridge: Macmillan, 1862.

———. *Tom Brown's School Days*. New York: Harper & Brothers, 1911.

———. *Tom Brown's School Days, by an Old Boy*. Cambridge: Macmillan, 1857.

Hunter, Louis C. *Steamboats on the Western Rivers*. 1949. Reprint, New York: Dover Publications, 1993.

"An Indiana Boy's Romantic Adventures in Brazil." *Crawford County Bulletin* (Denison, Iowa), May 4, 1876.

Ingraham, Colonel Prentiss. *Darkie Dan, the Colored Detective; or, The Mississippi Mystery*. New York: M. J. Ivers & Co., 1902.

"Interviews with William Dean Howells." *American Literary Realism, 1870–1910* 6, no. 4 (Fall 1973): 274–416.

James, Henry. "London." *Century Magazine*, December 1888.

James, Louis. "Tom Brown's Imperialist Sons." *Victorian Studies* 17, no. 1 (September 1973): 89–99.

James, William. *The Principles of Psychology.* New York: Henry Holt, 1890.

Jeal, Tim. *Stanley: The Impossible Life of Africa's Greatest Explorer.* London: Faber & Faber, 2007.

Jerome, Jerome K. *Three Men in a Boat (To Say Nothing of the Dog).* Bristol: J. W. Arrowsmith, 1889.

"John Hay Speaks for the Nation." *National Magazine,* November 1904.

Johnson, Clifton. *Highways and Byways of the Mississippi Valley.* New York: Macmillan, 1906.

Johnson, James Weldon. *The Autobiography of an Ex-Colored Man.* Boston: Sherman, French & Co., 1912.

———. *The Book of American Negro Poetry.* New York: Harcourt, Brace & Co., 1922.

Johnson, Robert Underwood. *Remembered Yesterdays.* Boston: Little, Brown, 1923.

Johnson, Walter. *River of Dark Dreams: Slavery and Empire in the Cotton Kingdom.* Cambridge: Harvard University Press, 2013.

Jones, Betty H. "Huck and Jim: A Reconsideration." In *Satire or Evasion? Black Perspectives on* Huckleberry Finn, edited by James S. Leonard, Thomas A. Tenney, and Thadious M. Davis, 154–72. Durham, N.C.: Duke University Press, 1992.

Jones, Charles H. *Appletons' Hand-Book of American Travel: Southern Tour.* 1871. Reprint, New York: D. Appleton and Co., 1874.

"Juvenile Reading." *Oliver Optic's Magazine,* June 1875.

Keeler, Ralph. "On the Mississippi." *Every Saturday,* May 20, 1871.

———. "On the Mississippi." *Every Saturday,* September 2, 1871.

———. "On the Mississippi." *Every Saturday,* September 30, 1871.

———. *Vagabond Adventures.* Boston: Fields, Osgood, & Co., 1870.

Keller, Helen. *Midstream: My Later Life.* New York: Doubleday, Doran & Co., 1929.

Kenney, William Howland. *Jazz on the River.* Chicago: University of Chicago Press, 2005.

Kent, Don. Liner notes to *St. Louis Town, 1929–1933.* Yazoo Records L-1003, 1968.

King, Edward. "An Expedition with Stanley." *Scribner's Monthly,* November 1872.

———. "The Great South." *Scribner's Monthly,* October 1874.

———. *The Great South.* Hartford, Conn.: American Publishing Co., 1875.

King, Grace. *Grace King of New Orleans: A Selection of Her Writings,* edited by Robert Bush. Baton Rouge: Louisiana State University Press, 1973.

———. "The Little Convent Girl." *Century Magazine,* August 1893.

———. *Memories of a Southern Woman of Letters.* New York: Macmillan, 1932.

Klein, Christine A., and Sandra B. Zellmer. *Mississippi River Tragedies: A Century of Unnatural Disaster.* New York: New York University Press, 2014.

Krauth, Leland. *Mark Twain & Company: Six Literary Relations*. Athens: University of Georgia Press, 2003.

Kruse, Horst H. *Mark Twain and "Life on the Mississippi."* Amherst: University of Massachusetts Press, 1981.

———. "Mark Twain's 'Nom de Plume': Some Mysteries Resolved." *Mark Twain Journal* 30, no. 1 (Spring, 1992): 1–32.

Kuntz, Jerry. *A Boy Naturalist in the Amazon: The Travels of Ernest T. Morris*. New York: Jerry Kuntz, 2017.

Lang, Andrew. "For Mark Twain." *Longman's Magazine*, February 1886.

Lawson, R. A. *Jim Crow's Counterculture: The Blues and Black Southerners, 1890–1945*. Baton Rouge: Louisiana State University Press 2010.

"Letter from 'Mark Twain.'" *Daily Alta California*, May 19, 1867.

The Life and Adventures of John A. Murrell, the Great Western Land Pirate. New York: H. Long & Brother, 1848.

Lighty, Kent, and Margaret Lighty. *Shantyboat*. New York: Century Co., 1930.

Lillard, J.F.B. *Poker Stories*. London: Gibbings & Co., 1896.

Lloyd, James T. *Lloyd's Steamboat Directory, and Disasters on the Western Waters*. Cincinnati: James T. Lloyds & Co., 1856.

Lomax, Alan. *American Ballads and Folk Songs*. 1934. Reprint, New York: Dover, 1994.

Longfellow, Henry Wadsworth. *Evangeline: A Tale of Acadie*. Boston: William D. Ticknor & Co., 1847.

———. *Evangeline: A Tale of Acadie*. Boston: Houghton, Mifflin, 1900.

———, ed. *Poems of Places*, vol. 2: *Germany*. Boston: Houghton, Osgood & Co., 1877.

———, ed. *Poems of Places*, vol. 3: *England*. Boston: Houghton, Osgood & Co., 1876.

Lorch, Fred W. "A Source for Mark Twain's 'The Dandy Frightening the Squatter.'" *American Literature* 3, no. 3 (November 1931): 309–13.

Ludlow, Noah. *Dramatic Life as I Found It*. St. Louis: G. I. Jones & Co., 1880.

MacDonnell, Kevin. "How Samuel Clemens Found 'Mark Twain' in Carson City." *Mark Twain Journal* 50, nos. 1–2 (Spring–Fall 2012): 8–47.

MacGregor, John. *A Thousand Miles in the Rob Roy Canoe on Rivers and Lakes of Europe*. London: Sampson, Low, Son, & Marston, 1866.

MacKethan, Lucinda H. "Huck Finn and the Slave Narratives: Lighting Out as Design." *Southern Review* 20 (Spring 1984): 247–64.

"Mad Freaks of the Mississippi." *Memphis Old Folks' Record*, May 1875.

"The Magazines for January." *Critic*, December 27, 1884.

Mahar, J. William J. *Behind the Burnt Cork Mask: Early Blackface Minstrelsy and Antebellum American Popular Culture*. Urbana: University of Illinois Press, 1999.

Maher, Susan Naramore. "Recasting Crusoe: Frederick Marryat, R. M. Ballantyne and the Nineteenth-Century Robinsonade." *Children's Literature Association Quarterly* 13, no. 4 (Winter 1988): 169–75.

"Mark Twain." *Bookman*, June 1910.

"Mark Twain among Scenes of His Early Life." *New York Times*, June 8, 1902.

"Mark Twain at the Shrine of St. Wagner." *New York Sun*, December 6, 1891.

"Mark Twain on the River." *St. Louis Republic*, June 16, 1902.

"Mark Twain Says." *Boys of England*, January 21, 1876.

"Mark Twain's Latest Book." *New York Times*, July 9, 1883.

Marleau, Michael H. "'The Crash of Timbers Continued—the Deck Swayed under Me': Samuel L. Clemens, Eyewitness to the Race and Collision between the *Pennsylvania* and *Vicksburg*." *Mark Twain Journal* 28, no. 1 (Spring 1990): 1–36.

Marryat, Captain C. B. [Frederick]. *A Diary in America with Remarks on Its Institutions.* 2 vols. Philadelphia: Carey & Hart, 1839.

Marx, Leo. *The Machine in the Garden: Technology and the Pastoral Ideal in America.* 1964. Reprint, New York: Oxford University Press, 2000.

———. "Mr. Eliot, Mr. Trilling, and Huckleberry Finn." *American Scholar* 22, no. 4 (Fall 1953): 423–40.

Mathews, John Lathrop. *The Log of the Easy Way.* Boston: Small, Maynard & Co., 1911.

Matthews, Brander. *Inquiries and Opinions.* New York: Charles Scribner's Sons, 1907.

McCoy, Sharon D. "'The Trouble Begins at Eight': Mark Twain, the San Francisco Minstrels, and the Unsettling Legacy of Blackface Minstrelsy." *American Literary Realism* 41, no. 3 (Spring 2009): 232–48.

McDermott, John Francis, ed. *Before Mark Twain: A Sampler of Old, Old Times on the Mississippi.* Carbondale: Southern Illinois University Press, 1968.

McIntire-Strasburg, Janice. "Mark Twain, Huck Finn, and the Geographical 'Memory' of a Nation." In *Mark Twain's Geographical Imagination*, edited by Joseph A. Alvarez, 83–101. Newcastle: Cambridge Scholars Publishing, 2009.

McMillin, T. S. *The Meaning of Rivers: Flow and Reflection in American Literature.* Iowa City: Iowa City Press, 2011.

Meer, Sarah. *Uncle Tom Mania: Slavery, Minstrelsy, and Transatlantic Culture in the 1850s.* Athens: University of Georgia Press, 2005.

Melton, Jeffrey Alan. *Mark Twain, Travel Books, and Tourism: The Tide of a Great Popular Movement.* Tuscaloosa: University of Alabama Press, 2002.

Merrick, George Byron. *Old Times on the Upper Mississippi: The Recollections of a Steamboat Pilot from 1854 to 1863.* Cleveland, Ohio: Arthur H. Clark Co., 1909.

Messent, Peter. "Tramps and Tourists: Europe in Mark Twain's *A Tramp Abroad*." *Yearbook of English Studies* (2004): 138–54.

"Mississippi River Steamboats." *New York Tribune*, September 22, 1895.

"The Mississippi Steamboat Outrage." *New York Tribune*, August 4, 1869.

Mizelle, Richard M., Jr. *Backwater Blues: The Mississippi Flood of 1927 in the African American Imagination.* Minneapolis: University of Minnesota Press, 2014.

Monod, David. *The Soul of Pleasure: Sentiment and Sensation in Nineteenth-Century American Mass Entertainment.* Ithaca: Cornell University Press, 2016.

Morris, Christopher. "Only a River." *Iowa Review* 39, no. 2 (Fall 2009): 149–65.

Morris, John [John O'Connor]. *Wanderings of a Vagabond.* New York: Published by the author, 1873.

"Mrs. Walworth's 'Southern Silhouettes.'" *Critic,* December 17, 1887.

Munroe, Kirk. "Modern Canoeing." *Outing* 3 no. 3 (December 1883): 217–24.

Murfree, William L., Sr. "The Levees of the Mississippi." *Scribner's Monthly,* July 1881.

Najder, Zdzisław. *Joseph Conrad: A Life.* Rochester, N.Y.: Camden House, 2007.

Neidé, Charles A. *The Canoe Aurora: A Cruise from the Adirondacks to the Gulf.* New York: Forest & Stream Publishing Co., 1885.

Nevin, Robert P. "Stephen C. Foster and Negro Minstrelsy." *Atlantic Monthly,* November 1867.

"New Story." *Boys of England,* May 21, 1880.

Nichols, George Ward. "Down the Mississippi." *Harper's New Monthly Magazine,* November 1870.

Nott, G. William. "Woman Plot Recalls River Packet Days: Romance of Mississippi River Is Told by Blanche Leathers, Pilot of Famous Packett [sic] Natchez." *New Orleans Item-Tribune,* February 13, 1927. State Library of Louisiana. http://louisiana digitallibrary.org/islandora/object/state-lwp%3A8276.

"Novels of the Week." *Athenaeum,* January 10, 1874.

Nowatzki, Robert C. "'Our Only Truly National Poets': Blackface Minstrelsy and Cultural Nationalism." *American Transcendental Quarterly* 20, no. 1 (March 2006): 361–78.

Oakley, Thornton. "Mississippi Sketches." *Harper's New Monthly Magazine,* August 1905.

Oliver, Paul. "Lookin' for 'The Bully': An Enquiry into a Song and Its Story." In *Nobody Knows Where the Blues Come From: Lyrics and History,* edited by Robert Springer, 108–25. Jackson: University Press of Mississippi, 2006.

Oliver, Paul, et al. *Yonder Come the Blues: The Evolution of a Genre.* Cambridge: Cambridge University Press, 2001.

Optic, Oliver [William T. Adams]. *Down the River; or, Buck Bradford and His Tyrants.* Boston: Lee & Shepard, 1869.

"Our 'Forty Immortals.'" *Critic,* April 12, 1884.

Paine, Albert Bigelow. *Mark Twain: A Biography.* 3 vols. New York: Harper & Brothers, 1912.

Parkman, Francis. *The Discovery of the Great West.* Boston: Little, Brown, 1869.

Patrick, G.T.W. *The Fragments of the Work of Heraclitus of Ephesus on Nature.* Baltimore: N. Murray, 1889.

Paul, Howard. "Recollections of Edgar Allen [sic] Poe." *Munsey's Magazine,* August 1892.

Payne, James Robert. "George Washington Cable's John March and Gideon's Band: A (White) Boy Is Being Beaten." *American Literary Realism* 38, no. 3 (2006): 239–48.

Pennell, Elizabeth Robins. *The Life and Letters of Joseph Pennell*, vol. 1. Boston: Little, Brown, 1929.

Pennell, Elizabeth Robins, and Joseph Pennell. *The Life of James McNeill Whistler*. London: William Heinemann, 1911.

———. *The Stream of Pleasure: A Narrative of a Journey on the Thames from Oxford to London*. London: T. Fisher Unwin, 1891.

Pennell, Joseph. *The Adventures of an Illustrator, Mostly in Following His Authors in America & Europe*. Boston: Little, Brown, 1925.

———. "The Trip of the 'Mark Twain.'" *Century Magazine*, January 1883.

Pisani, Donald J. "Water Planning in the Progressive Era: The Inland Waterways Commission Reconsidered." *Journal of Policy History* 18, no. 4 (2006): 389–418.

Pond, James B. *Eccentricities of Genius: Memories of Famous Men and Women of the Platform and Stage*. New York: G. W. Dillingham Co., 1900.

"A Postbellum Sketch of Mississippi River Life." *Literary Digest*, April 15, 1905.

Prchal, Tim. "The Bad Boys and the New Man: The Role of Tom Sawyer and Similar Characters in the Reconstruction of Masculinity." *American Literary Realism* 36, no. 3 (Spring 2004): 187–205.

"Publishers' Announcements." *Every Saturday*, May 6, 1871.

Quick, Herbert, and Edward Quick. *Mississippi Steamboatin'*. New York: Henry Holt, 1926.

Quirk, Tom. *Coming to Grips with Huckleberry Finn: Essays on a Book, a Boy, and a Man*. Columbia: University of Missouri Press, 1993.

"Races on the Mississippi." *New York Times*, March 31, 1903.

"Racing on the Mississippi." *New York Times*, July 4, 1870.

Railton, Stephen. "The Twain-Cable Combination." In *A Companion to Mark Twain*, edited by Peter Messent and Louis J. Budd, 172–86. Chichester: Wiley Blackwell, 2015.

Rainey, Sue. *Creating Picturesque America: Monument to the Natural and Cultural Landscape*. Nashville: Vanderbilt University Press, 1994.

Ralph, Julian. "The Old Way to Dixie." *Harper's New Monthly Magazine*, January 1893.

Rampersad, Arnold. "*Adventures of Huckleberry Finn* and Afro-American Literature." *Mark Twain Journal* 22, no. 2 (Fall 1984): 47–52.

Raven-Hart, Major Rowland. *Canoe Errant on the Mississippi*. London: Methuen & Co., 1938.

Read, Opie. *Mark Twain and I*. Chicago: Reilly & Lee, 1940.

"Recent Literature." *Atlantic Monthly*, December 1872.

Reid, Captain Mayne. *The Boy Hunters; or, Adventures in Search of a White Buffalo*. London: David Bogue, 1853.

——. *The Desert Home; or, The Adventures of a Lost Family in the Wilderness.* London: David Bogue, 1852.

——. "The Fatal Cord: A Tale of Backwoods Retribution." *Boys of England,* December 28, 1867.

——. *The Forest Exiles; or, The Perils of a Peruvian Family amid the Wilds of the Amazon.* Boston: Ticknor & Fields, 1855.

——. *The Island Pirate: A Tale of the Mississippi.* New York: Beadle & Adams, 1874.

——. *The Quadroon; or, A Lover's Adventures in Louisiana.* New York: Robert M. De Witt, 1856.

Reid, Elizabeth Hyde. *Captain Mayne Reid: His Life and Adventures.* London: Greening & Co., 1900.

Reid, Whitelaw. *After the War: A Southern Tour.* Cincinnati: Moore, Wilstach & Baldwin, 1866.

Representatives of the Mercantile and Commercial Interests of the City of New Orleans. Grand Banquet to Capt. Jas. B. Eads. New Orleans: W. B. Stansbury & Co., 1882.

Review of *Huckleberry Finn. Hartford (Conn.) Courant,* February 20, 1885. Mark Twain in His Times. http://twain.lib.virginia.edu/huckfinn/harcour2.html.

Review of "Mark Twain and George W. Cable." *St. Louis Daily Globe Democrat,* January 10, 1885. Mark Twain in His Times. http://twain.lib.virginia.edu/onstage/maps /84rev17.html.

Reynolds, David S. *Beneath the American Renaissance.* New York: Oxford University Press, 2011.

Rice, T. D. *Jim Crow, American: Selected Songs and Plays.* Edited by W. T. Lhamon Jr. Cambridge: Belknap Press of Harvard University Press, 2009.

"River Intelligence." *Cincinnati Daily Enquirer,* January 1, 1870.

"River Life: The Roustabouts of the Mississippi." *New York Times,* July 25, 1874.

"River News." *Cincinnati Daily Gazette,* July 8, 1870.

"River News." *Cincinnati Daily Gazette,* November 16, 1868.

Rogers, Franklin R. *Mark Twain's Burlesque Patterns as Seen in the Novels and Narratives, 1855–1885.* Dallas: Southern Methodist University Press, 1960.

Rohman, Chad. "A River 'Ready for Business': Life down the Mississippi as a Main Undercurrent in Mark Twain's *Pudd'nhead Wilson.*" *American Literary Realism* 39, no. 3 (Spring 2007): 241–51.

Roosevelt, Theodore. *Theodore Roosevelt: An Autobiography.* New York: Macmillan, 1913.

Rose, Kenneth D. *Unspeakable Awfulness: America through the Eyes of European Travelers, 1865–1900.* New York: Routledge, 2013.

"The Roustabouts' Farewell." *New York Tribune,* August 8, 1886.

Sala, George Augustus. *America Revisited.* 2 vols. London: Vizetelly & Co., 1882.

———. *My Diary in America in the Midst of War.* 2 vols. London: Tinsley Brothers, 1865.

Sandweiss, Lee Ann. *Seeking St. Louis: Voices from a River City, 1670–2000.* St. Louis: Missouri Historical Society Press, 2000.

Saxton, Alexander. "Blackface Minstrelsy." In *Inside the Minstrel Mask: Readings in Nineteenth-Century Blackface Minstrelsy,* edited by Annemarie Bean, James V. Hatch, and Brooks McNamara, 67–85. Middletown, Conn.: Wesleyan University Press, 1996.

Scharnhorst, Gary, ed. *Critical Essays on* The Adventures of Tom Sawyer. New York: G. K. Hall & Co., 1993.

———. *The Life of Mark Twain: The Early Years, 1835–1871.* Columbia: University of Missouri Press, 2018.

———, ed. *Mark Twain: The Complete Interviews.* Tuscaloosa: University of Alabama Press, 2006.

Scheick, William J. "Going to Find Stanley: Imperial Narratives, Shilling Shockers, and *Three Men in a Boat.*" *English Literature in Transition, 1880–1920* 50, no. 4 (2007): 403–14.

Schmitt, Peter J. *Back to Nature: The Arcadian Myth in Urban America.* Baltimore: Johns Hopkins University Press, 1990.

Schoolcraft, Henry Rowe. *Algic Researches, Comprising Inquiries Respecting the Mental Characteristics of the North American Indians.* 2 vols. New York: Harper & Brothers, 1832.

Schulz-Forberg, Hagen. "The Sorcerer's Apprentice: English Travellers and the Rhine in the Long Nineteenth Century." *Journeys* 3, no. 2 (2002): 86–110.

Scott, Arthur L. "*The Innocents Adrift* Edited by Mark Twain's Official Biographer." *PMLA* 78, no. 3 (June 1963): 230–37.

Seelye, John. "What's in a Name: Sounding the Depths of *Tom Sawyer.*" *Sewanee Review* 90, no. 3 (Summer 1982): 408–29.

"7 More Die in Flood along Mississippi." *New York Times,* April 17, 1927.

Shaler, N. S. "The Floods of the Mississippi Valley." *Atlantic Monthly,* May 1883.

Siegfried, A. H. "Canoeing on the High Mississippi." *Lippincott's Monthly,* August 1880.

Silber, Nina. *The Romance of Reunion: Northerners and the South, 1865–1900.* Chapel Hill: University of North Carolina Press, 1993.

Slout, William L. *Burnt Cork and Tambourines: A Source Book of Negro Minstrelsy.* Rockville, Md.: Borgo Press, 2007.

Smith, Henry Nash. *Mark Twain: The Development of a Writer.* New York: Atheneum, 1967.

Smith, Thomas Ruys. *Blacklegs, Card Sharps, and Confidence Men.* Baton Rouge: Louisiana State University Press, 2010.

———. "'Dead Men Tell No Tales': Outlaw John A. Murrell on the Antebellum Stage." *European Journal of American Culture* 28, no. 3 (October 2009): 263–76.

———. "Independence Day, 1835: The John A. Murrell Conspiracy and the Lynching of the Vicksburg Gamblers in Literature." *Mississippi Quarterly* 59, nos. 1–2 (Winter–Spring 2006): 129–60.

———. *River of Dreams: Imagining the Mississippi before Mark Twain.* Baton Rouge: Louisiana State University Press, 2007.

Sorrentino, Paul. "Mark Twain's 1902 Trip to Missouri: A Reexamination, a Chronology, and an Annotated Bibliography." *Mark Twain Journal* 38, no. 1 (Spring 2000): 13–44.

"The Source of the Mississippi." *American Canoeist,* November 1886.

Spaulding, Henry. "Cairo Blues." *St. Louis Town, 1929–1933.* Yazoo Records L-1003, 1968.

Speakman, Harold. *Mostly Mississippi.* Minneapolis: University of Minnesota Press, 2004.

Spears, Raymond S. "The Moods of the Mississippi." *Atlantic Monthly,* September 1908.

Springhall, John. "'A Life Story for the People?' Edwin J. Brett and the London 'Low-Life' Penny Dreadfuls of the 1860s." *Victorian Studies* 33, no. 2 (Winter 1990): 223–46.

Stanley, Henry Morton. *The Autobiography of Sir Henry Morton Stanley.* Boston: Houghton Mifflin, 1909.

———. *The Congo and the Founding of Its Free State.* 2 vols. New York: Harper & Brothers, 1885.

———. *How I Found Livingstone.* London: Sampson Low, Marston, Low, & Searle, 1872.

———. *Through the Dark Continent.* 2 vols. New York: Harper & Brothers, 1878.

"A Steamboat Race." *New York Times,* July 2, 1870.

"Steam Displaces Men." *Washington Post,* December 19, 1910.

Stevens, Walter B. *The Log of the Alton.* St Louis: Printed by the Voyagers for Private Distribution, 1909.

"The St. Louis Bridge." *New York Times,* May 17, 1873.

Stoll, Mark. *Inherit the Holy Mountain: Religion and the Rise of American Environmentalism.* New York: Oxford University Press, 2015.

Storey, Mark. *Rural Fictions, Urban Realities: A Geography of Gilded Age American Literature.* New York: Oxford University Press, 2013.

Stowe, Harriet Beecher. *Uncle Tom's Cabin.* London: C. H. Clarke & Co., 1852.

Stuart, Ruth McEnery. *The River's Children: An Idyl of the Mississippi.* New York: Century Co., 1904.

Sutcliffe, Alice Crary. "Fulton's Invention of the Steamboat." *Century Magazine,* October 1909.

"Swimming down the Mississippi." *New York Times,* June 20, 1881.

Taft, Michael. *Talkin' to Myself: Blues Lyrics, 1921–1942.* New York: Routledge, 2005.

Taylor, Robert S. "The Subjugation of the Mississippi." *North American Review,* March 1883.

Thackeray, William Makepeace. "A Legend of the Rhine." In *George Cruikshank's Table Book*. Edited by Gilbert Abbott À Beckett. Illustrated by George Cruikshank. London: Published at the Punch Office, 1845.

Thompson, Charles Miner. "Mark Twain as an Interpreter of American Character." *Atlantic Monthly*, April 1897.

Ticknor, Caroline. "'Mark Twain's' Missing Chapter." *Bookman*, May 1914.

Tindol, Robert. "Tom Sawyer and Becky Thatcher in the Cave: An Anti-Captivity Narrative?" *Mark Twain Annual* 7 (2009): 118–26.

Tousley, Albert S. *Where Goes the River*. Iowa City: Tepee Press, 1928.

Trevathan, Charles E. *May Irwin's Bully Song*. New York: New York Journal, 1896.

Trilling, Lionel. "Huckleberry Finn." *The Liberal Imagination: Essays on Literature and Society*, 104–17. New York: New York Review Books, 2008.

Trollope, Frances. *Domestic Manners of the Americans*. 2 vols. London: Whittaker, Treacher, & Co., 1832.

"The Trouble with Our Waterways." *Literary Digest*, October 20, 1917.

Trowbridge, John. *The South: A Tour of Its Battlefields and Ruined Cities*. Hartford, Conn.: L. Stebbins, 1866.

Turner, Arlin. *George W. Cable: A Biography*. Baton Rouge: Louisiana State University Press, 1966.

Twain, Mark. *Adventures of Huckleberry Finn*. New York: Charles L. Webster and Co., 1884.

———. *The Adventures of Tom Sawyer*. Hartford, Conn.: American Publishing Co., 1876.

———. *The Adventures of Tom Sawyer*. New York: Penguin, 1986.

———. *Autobiography of Mark Twain*. 3 vols. Vol. 1 edited by Harriet Elinor Smith; vols. 2–3 edited by Benjamin Griffin and Harriet Elinor Smith. Berkeley: University of California Press, 2010–15.

———. *A Connecticut Yankee in King Arthur's Court*. New York: Charles L. Webster & Co., 1889.

———. *Early Tales & Sketches: 1851–1864*. Vol. 1. Edited by Edgar Marquess Branch and Robert H. Hirst. Berkeley: University of California Press, 1979.

———. *Europe and Elsewhere*. New York: Harper & Brothers, 1923.

———. *Fables of Man*. Edited by John S. Tuckey. Berkeley: University of California Press, 1972.

———. *Huck Finn and Tom Sawyer among the Indians: And Other Unfinished Stories*. Edited by Walter Blair. Berkeley: University of California Press, 2011.

———. *The Innocents Abroad; or, The New Pilgrims' Progress*. Hartford, Conn.: American Publishing Co., 1869.

———. "Jim's Investments, and King Sollermun." *Century Magazine*, January 1885.

———. Letter to Andrew Chatto, August 19, 1879. Mark Twain Project. http://www.marktwainproject.org/xtf/view?docId=letters/UCCL02533.xml;style=letter;brand=mtp.

——. Letter to Orion Clemens, February 26, 1880. Mark Twain Project. http://www
.marktwainproject.org/xtf/view?docId=letters/UCCL01763.xml;style=letter;brand
=mtp.

——. Letter to "Unidentified," October 25, 1876. Mark Twain Project. http://www.mark
twainproject.org/xtf/view?docId=letters/UCCL01379.xml;style=letter;brand=mtp.

——. *Life on the Mississippi.* Boston: James R. Osgood & Co., 1883.

——. *Life on the Mississippi.* Edited by James M. Cox. New York: Penguin, 1986.

——. *The Love Letters of Mark Twain.* Edited by Dixon Wecter. New York: Harper &
Brothers, 1949.

——. *Mark Twain's Correspondence with Henry Huttleston Rogers, 1893–1909.* Edited by
Lewis Leary. Berkeley: University of California Press, 1969.

——. *Mark Twain's Letters.* 2 vols. Edited by Albert Bigelow Paine. New York: Harper
& Brothers, 1917.

——. *Mark Twain's Letters,* vol. 1: *1853–1866.* Edited by Edgar Marquess Branch, Michael B. Frank, and Kenneth M. Sanderson. Berkeley: University of California
Press, 1988.

——. *Mark Twain's Letters,* vol. 3: *1869.* Edited by Victor Fischer and Michael B.
Frank. Berkeley: University of California Press, 1992.

——. *Mark Twain's Letters,* vol. 4: *1870–1871.* Edited by Victor Fischer and Michael B.
Frank. Berkeley: University of California Press, 1995.

——. *Mark Twain's Letters,* vol. 5: *1872–1873.* Edited by Lin Salamo and Harriet Elinor
Smith. Berkeley: University of California Press, 1997.

——. *Mark Twain's Letters,* vol. 6: *1874–1875.* Edited by Michael B. Frank and Harriet
Elinor Smith. Berkeley: University of California Press, 2002.

——. *Mark Twain's Letters to His Publishers, 1867–1894.* Edited by Hamlin Hill. Berkeley: University of California Press, 1967.

——. *Mark Twain's Notebooks & Journals,* vol. 1: *1855–1873.* Edited by Frederick Anderson, Michael Barry Frank, and Kenneth M. Sanderson. Berkeley: University of
California Press, 1976.

——. *Mark Twain's Notebooks & Journals,* vol. 2: *1877–1883.* Edited by Frederick Anderson, Lin Salamo, and Bernard L. Stein. Berkeley: University of California Press,
1975.

——. *Mark Twain's Notebooks & Journals,* vol. 3: *1883–1891.* Edited by Robert Pack
Browning, Michael B. Frank, and Lin Salamo. Berkeley: University of California
Press, 1979.

——. *Mark Twain's Satires & Burlesques.* Edited by Franklin R. Rogers. Berkeley: University of California Press, 1967.

——. *Mark Twain's Speeches.* Edited by William Dean Howells. New York: Harper &
Brothers, 1910.

——. "Old Times on the Mississippi: I." *Atlantic Monthly,* January 1875.

———. "Old Times on the Mississippi: II." *Atlantic Monthly*, February 1875.

———. "Old Times on the Mississippi: III." *Atlantic Monthly*, March 1875.

———. "Old Times on the Mississippi: IV." *Atlantic Monthly*, April 1875.

———. "Old Times on the Mississippi: V." *Atlantic Monthly*, May 1875.

———. "Old Times on the Mississippi: VI." *Atlantic Monthly*, June 1875.

———. "Old Times on the Mississippi: VII." *Atlantic Monthly*, August 1875.

———. *The Prince and the Pauper*. Boston: James R. Osgood & Co., 1882.

———. *Pudd'nhead Wilson*. Hartford, Conn.: American Publishing Co., 1894.

———. *Roughing It*. Hartford, Conn.: American Publishing Co., 1872.

———. *Tom Sawyer Abroad*. New York: Charles L. Webster & Co., 1894.

———. *Tom Sawyer Abroad, Tom Sawyer, Detective and Other Stories*. New York: Harper & Brothers, 1896.

———. *A Tramp Abroad*. Hartford, Conn.: American Publishing Co., 1880.

Twain, Mark, and William Dean Howells. *Mark Twain–Howells Letters: The Correspondence of Samuel L. Clemens and William D. Howells, 1872–1910*. 2 vols. Edited by Henry Nash Smith, William Gibson, and Frederick Anderson. Cambridge: Belknap Press of Harvard University Press, 1960.

Twain, Mark, and Charles Dudley Warner. *The Gilded Age: A Tale of Today*. Hartford, Conn.: American Publishing Co., 1874.

"Twain's Friend Held." *Washington Post*, September 8, 1912.

Twombly, A. S. "The Illinois and St. Louis Bridge." *Scribner's Monthly*, June 1871.

"The Two Racers." *Cincinnati Daily Gazette*, July 6, 1870.

Vlach, John Michael. *The Planter's Prospect: Privilege and Slavery in Plantation Paintings*. Chapel Hill: University of North Carolina Press, 2002.

Wadsworth, Sarah. "Louisa May Alcott, William T. Adams, and the Rise of Gender-Specific Series Books." *Lion and the Unicorn* 25, no. 1 (January 2001): 17–46.

Walworth, Jeannette H. *Southern Silhouettes*. New York: Henry Holt, 1887.

Ward, Brian. "Music, Musical Theater, and the Imagined South in Interwar Britain." *Journal of Southern History* 80, no. 1 (2014): 39–72.

Warner, Charles Dudley. *In the Wilderness*. Boston: Houghton, Osgood & Co., 1878.

———. *My Winter on the Nile*. Boston: Houghton Mifflin, 1881.

Waugh, William F. *The Houseboat Book*. Chicago: Clinic Publishing Co., 1904.

Webster, Samuel Charles. *Mark Twain, Business Man*. Boston: Little, Brown, 1946.

Wheeler, Mary. *Steamboatin' Days: Folk Songs of the River Packet Era*. Freeport, N.Y.: Books for Libraries Press, 1969.

White, Richard White. *Railroaded: The Transcontinentals and the Making of Modern America*. New York: W. W. Norton, 2011.

Whitman, Walt. *Specimen Days & Collect*. Philadelphia: David McKay, 1882–83.

Wilkins, Ben C. *Cruise of the "Little Nan," Five Hundred Miles down the Mississippi River*. 1881. Reprint, Huron, S.D.: Huronite Publishing House, 1886.

Willett, Edward. *Flush Fred's Full Hand*. New York: Beadle & Adams, 1884.

Wilson, Anthony. *Shadow and Shelter: The Swamp in Southern Culture*. Jackson: University Press of Mississippi, 2006.

Windholz, Anne M. "An Emigrant and a Gentleman: Imperial Masculinity, British Magazines, and the Colony That Got Away." *Victorian Studies* 42, no. 4 (Summer 1999–2000): 631–58.

Winks, Robin W. "The Making of a Fugitive Slave Narrative: Josiah Henson and Uncle Tom—A Case Study." In *The Slave's Narrative*, edited by Charles T. Davis and Henry Louis Gates Jr., 112–47. New York: Oxford University Press, 1985.

Wondrich, David. *Stomp and Swerve: American Music Gets Hot, 1843–1924*. Chicago: A Capella Books / Chicago Review Press, 2003.

Wonham, Henry B. "'I Want a Real Coon': Mark Twain and Late-Nineteenth-Century Ethnic Caricature." *American Literature* 72, no. 1 (March 2000): 117–52.

———. "The Minstrel and the Detective: The Functions of Ethnic Caricature in Mark Twain's Writings of the 1890s." In *Constructing Mark Twain: New Directions in Scholarship*, edited by Laura E. Skandera Trombley and Michael J. Kiskis, 122–38. Columbia: University of Missouri Press, 2001.

Woodard, Frederick, and Donnarae MacCann. "Minstrel Shackles and Nineteenth-Century 'Liberality' in *Huckleberry Finn*." In *Satire or Evasion? Black Perspectives on* Huckleberry Finn, edited by James S. Leonard, Thomas A. Tenney, and Thadious M. Davis, 141–53. Durham, N.C.: Duke University Press, 1992.

Wortham, Thomas, ed. *The Early Prose Writings of William Dean Howells*. Athens: Ohio University Press, 1990.

Young, John Russell. "Through the Dark Continent." *Harper's New Monthly Magazine*, October 1878.

INDEX